Spirited Lives

Spirited Lives

How Nuns Shaped Catholic Culture

and American Life, 1836–1920

Carol K. Coburn and Martha Smith

The

University

of North

Carolina

Press

Chapel Hill

and London

Designed by April Leidig-Higgins

Typeset in Monotype Garamond

by Running Feet Books

Manufactured in the United States of America

The paper in this book meets the guidelines for
permanence and durability of the Committee on
Production Guidelines for Book Longevity of the
Council on Library Resources.

Library of Congress Cataloging-in-Publication Data
Coburn, Carol K. Spirited lives: how nuns shaped
Catholic culture and American life, 1836–1920 /
by Carol K. Coburn and Martha Smith.
p. cm. Includes bibliographical references and index.
ISBN 0-8078-2473-9 (cloth : alk. paper)
ISBN 0-8078-4774-7 (pbk. : alk. paper)
1. Nuns—United States—History. 2. Monasticism and
religious orders for women—United States—History.
3. Monastic and religious life of women—United
States—History. 4. Catholic Church—United States—
History. I. Smith, Martha, 1928 Sept. 7– II. Title.
BX4220.U6C63 1999 271'.90073—dc21 98-30828 CIP

03 02 01 00 99 5 4 3 2 1

Contents

Illustrations

Preface

In many ways ours has been an unlikely collaboration. Separated by religion, ethnicity, professional background, life experience, and age, a fifth-generation German Lutheran, American historian began a professional collaboration with a fourth-generation Irish Catholic, European historian, who has spent her entire adult life in a religious community. In May 1990, we began researching, discussing, debating, and teaching each other as we interacted with the rich primary sources. Exchanging ideas on scholarship, methodology, and religious and life experiences became a way of life as the project unfolded. We spent years immersed in research and thousands of hours in conversation, one of us learning to think and talk like a "Catholic" and the other learning to think and talk like a "feminist," both of us expanding our worldview and realizing that much was to be gained from listening to the other. We challenged each others' perceptions on the historical context of gender, religion, and power, modifying each others' assumptions (if not stereotypes), even as we challenged ourselves and each other to be bold in our writing and analysis. This collaboration allowed us to use our insider-outsider viewpoints that we believe bring a balanced and unique perspective to the work. In the jargon of late-twentieth-century discourse this could be called "feminist collaboration" or, using the language of the nineteenth-century convent, our joint project could be described as avoiding "singularity." In reality, it is probably a little of both.

From the beginning, however, our goals were shared. We intended to place Catholic sisters within the mainstream of American history and women's history, and show the sisters' lives and activities to be as complex, varied, and interesting as the lives of their Protestant and secular peers. We intended for our research not only to explore commonalities and differences between these women's groups but to examine further the intersection of gender, religion, and power in nineteenth- and early-twentieth-century America. Catholic nuns struggled with the barriers inherent in gender, religion, class, race, and ethnicity in both the American Catholic culture and the larger American public culture. We believe this book makes an important beginning toward understanding their lives and experiences within the context of their time.

Carol Coburn and Martha Smith
Kansas City, Missouri
May 1998

Acknowledgments

As with most large historical projects, collaboration extends far beyond the authors, and this research is certainly no exception. We would like to thank all the archivists at the four csj provincial archives and the generalate, particularly Sisters Charline Sullivan, Mary Kraft, Mary Ellen Sprouffske, Anne Xavier Boyle, Elizabeth Deutsch, and Patricia Kelly. The list of csjs who have talked with us, supported us, and provided meals and accommodations is endless, and we thank you for your support when we were guests in your cities, convents, and institutions. A special thanks to Sisters Margery Smith, Mary Ann Lavin, Marie Damien Adams, Alberta Cammack, Catherine McCaffrey, and Mary Margaret Lazio, and Denver archivist Sister Ann Walter, osb. Sister Germaine Matter and Virginia May Palmer provided translations for important csj documents, and Anita Pileggi spent hours transcribing taped interviews. The analysis of the csj Profession Book could not have been completed without the computer expertise of Cathy Bogart, who created a database for the demographic information, and Molly McNamara, who provided data entry.

A heartfelt thanks to Avila College and our colleagues and friends, particularly to the Humanities Department whose patience and support during Carol's sabbatical allowed the writing to happen. A special thanks to Sister Marie Joan Harris, vice president and academic dean, for her personal interest and for supporting sabbatical leaves and faculty grants for both of us throughout the project. We would also like to thank the staff of the Hooley-Bundschu Library at Avila College, particularly Mary Woods and Kathleen Finegan, who always fit our requests into their busy schedules and provided continuous and helpful support.

We would like to thank our readers, Kathryn Kish Sklar and Mary J. Oates, who provided careful analysis, helpful suggestions, and encouraging words for our manuscript. Also, our heartfelt thanks to Elaine Maisner and the staff at the University of North Carolina Press for their professional expertise and support.

Finally, Carol would like to thank Kathryn Kish Sklar, Thomas Dublin, and her fellow participants in the National Endowment for the Humanities Seminar at SUNY-Binghamton during the summer of 1996. The financial and intellectual support was most helpful and stimulating and came at a very opportune time in this research.

Spirited Lives

The story begins when women are there. Where women are present, religion flourishes, where they are absent, it does not.

—"Women's History *Is* American Religious History"

Introduction

After forty-nine days of rough seas and a near-disastrous storm in the Gulf of Mexico, the sailing vessel *Natchez* arrived safely in port at New Orleans on March 5, 1836. Six young French women, ages twenty-one to thirty-one, disembarked into a world whose people, language, and customs were foreign to them in every way. For ten days Ursuline nuns boarded the women and provided them with a "disguise" as they traveled throughout the city. On March 15, dressed in their widow's garb of caps and heavy veils, they booked passage on the steamer *George Collier*, traveling up the Mississippi River to their final destination in St. Louis. Particularly curious to see the African American slaves and American Indians they had read about in France, the women spent most of their ten-day journey on deck absorbing the sights and sounds of the river ports and the people en route.[1]

Neither tourists nor spies or saboteurs, these young French nuns, Sisters of St. Joseph, came to St. Louis to begin a school for deaf children. The disguise was necessary in an often hostile Protestant milieu, where less than two years before their arrival the Ursuline convent of Charlestown, Massachusetts, had been plundered and burned. Much to their astonishment, the young nuns learned that in early-nineteenth-century America, Catholic women religious traveled in disguise to avoid insults and the possibility of being labeled "escaped nuns."[2]

This inauspicious beginning is representative of the initial foundings of many religious communities of women in the United States. Most began with a small band of women—European-, Canadian-, or American-born —who began living and working together in spiritual, emotional, physical, and economic support networks that eventually spanned every region of the country. After the initial Ursuline foundation in New Orleans in 1727, Catholic women religious[3] expanded their numbers to 46,000 by 1900. By 1920, approximately 90,000 women, representing over 300 separate religious communities, were working in American education, health care, or social service institutions.[4]

The expansion of American Catholic culture and identity and its subsequent influence in American society could not have occurred without the activities and labor of these women. The proliferation of schools, hospitals, and orphanages boggles the contemporary mind. By 1920, Catholic sisters had created and/or maintained approximately 500 hospitals, 50 women's colleges, and over 6,000 parochial schools, serving 1.7 million schoolchildren in every region of the country, both urban and rural.[5] These figures do not include the vast number of orphanages, private academies, schools for the handicapped, homes for unwed mothers, homes for working girls, and homes for the elderly also conducted by the nuns. Bishops vied for opportunities to lure sisters to their dioceses and boasted about the numbers and types of institutions under their jurisdiction, most of which were staffed, if not owned, by women religious. American Catholics, whose numbers exploded in the late nineteenth and early twentieth centuries, maintained a network of support and services that insured the transmission of Catholic values, culture, and education from generation to generation. What made this possible, and how did American sisters help create such a legacy that has lasted to the end of the twentieth century?

To understand the role that women religious played in the shaping of Catholic culture and American life, it is necessary to examine gender, religion, and power within the convent culture and how nuns functioned within the church and within American society. The religious community is one of the oldest and least analyzed of women's groups in the United States. As a woman-defined space and culture within the highly structured American Catholic Church, it provides an intriguing challenge to historians of women to expand our understanding of nineteenth-century women's culture within a patriarchal setting that had the potential to exploit or co-opt women's work and contributions. Common myths and stereotypes of Catholic nuns conceal complex realities in the lives of these women who struggled to achieve ambitious goals in an environment—secular and religious—that offered many obstacles.

Historically seen as docile handmaidens and submissive subordinates in the expansion and growth of the Catholic Church, nuns have only recently become subjects of serious scholarship. Caught in a double bind of gender and religious marginality, American sisters have consistently been ignored by scholars of Catholic history and women's history.[6] This is a remarkable omission since the majority of Catholic schools, hospitals, and charitable agencies available in the nineteenth- and early-twentieth-century United States were created and/or maintained by American nuns. Although historically almost invisible, American sisters were some of the best educated and most publicly active women of their time. Talented and ambitious women from working-class and middle-class backgrounds, regardless of ethnicity, advanced to teaching, nursing, administration, and other leadership positions in Catholic religious communities. The reverend mothers or superiors general of these religious congregations functioned as some of the first female CEOs, administering institutions, personnel, and financial resources throughout the country.[7]

Although women religious had freedoms unknown to most other nineteenth-century women, this fact easily escapes notice because of the powerful and pervasive stereotype of nuns as otherworldly creatures, naive and unassuming, sheltered from the secular world. Nineteenth-century gender ideology and convent education helped maintain and reinforce this stereotype. Like Protestants, Catholic clergy and laity accepted gender ideology very similar to the pervasive model of Victorian womanhood that encouraged piety, purity, submissiveness, and domesticity. One scholar argues that "domestic ideology never was limited to advocates of a single theological persuasion. . . . American Catholics adopted all the accoutrements of domesticity without notable theological change."[8] The public image of Catholic nuns supported and reinforced this gender ideology. Women religious also learned to adopt "convent manners," which meant they were encouraged to avoid "singularity," or attempts to stand out in any way.[9] However, the daily reality of many sisters' lives demonstrates how their behavior and activities expanded far beyond expectations based on ideology and training. Like other nineteenth- and early-twentieth-century churchwomen, they learned to work within the confines of traditional ideology while expanding and reinterpreting their gender and religious activities. In developing and sustaining multiple institutions, the sisters interacted with laity of all ethnic and socioeconomic classes, from clerics, attorneys, doctors, and bankers to soldiers, miners, orphans, and schoolchildren. Some members of the religious community traveled extensively to secure monetary and material gifts for their institutions. Catholic nuns were free of the responsibilities of marriage and motherhood and had opportunities to live in female settings where egalitarian friendships flourished.[10]

In this study, we analyze this convent culture and demonstrate how religious communities of women shaped the creation, development, and extent of American Catholic culture and its subsequent impact on American life. Vastly outnumbering male religious and clergy, the sisters directly impacted the lives of immigrant and native-born Americans, Catholic and Protestant, through their teaching, nursing, and other service activities.[11] The sisters' convent communities and female-defined networks provided physical, emotional, economic, and spiritual sustenance for themselves and the people they served. Far from functioning as passive handmaidens for Catholic clergy and parishes, the nuns created, financed, and administered institutions, struggling with, and at times challenging and resisting, male secular and clerical authority. Furthermore, their ability to adapt to the frequently hostile American milieu and the rugged and often primitive conditions they encountered was firmly grounded in their view of themselves as vowed religious women. For them religion and gender were tightly bound into a single identity.

Using the Sisters of St. Joseph of Carondelet (csjs) as a case study, we will ask the following questions: How did the religious community shape and form the sisters' individual and collective identity in Protestant America? How did the nuns utilize religious and gender ideology to define, justify, and expand their behavior and activities? How did the sisters deal with patriarchal power (secular and clerical) and with governance in their all-female setting? And finally, in what activities were the sisters involved, and how did these activities shape Catholic culture and American life in the nineteenth and early twentieth centuries?

We recognize that no one congregation can be seen as "typical" of the more than 300 American sisterhoods, which included large and small, rural and urban, localized and extended, ethnically diverse and homogeneous groups, some focused on one particular activity while others engaged in multiple occupations. However, we believe that the CSJS are quite representative of American sisterhoods because their characteristics encompassed much of the rich diversity and variety of experience of other congregations. The CSJS were geographically diverse, having worked in nineteen states in every region of the United States, in large urban centers as well as small towns, mining communities, and Indian reservations. One of the largest American sisterhoods, they had a heterogeneous mix of ethnic and class membership that mirrored the larger American Catholic population. They also engaged in all three of the main activities characteristic of American nuns: education, health care, and social service. Some Catholic women's communities worked in only one of these areas, some in two, but the CSJS from the earliest years worked in all three areas.[12]

Like many European communities of women religious, the French CSJS came to the United States at the request of American clergy. In 1836, Bishop Joseph Rosati invited them to St. Louis to open a school for deaf children. By 1860, their revised "American" constitution had established a central government and effectively severed the American community's ties with the motherhouse[13] in France, establishing their own American power base. Significantly, in 1872 they elected their first American-born superior general who effectively mobilized and expanded a community of ethnically diverse women, native-born American, Irish, German, French, and Canadian-born sisters, into a large religious workforce. By 1920, 2,300 CSJS were supporting approximately 200 institutions including 175 elementary and secondary parish schools and private academies, two schools for the deaf, three women's colleges, ten hospitals, and nine orphanages. This massive expansion and institution building brought the CSJS directly into the lives of thousands of American Catholics and into American public life.[14]

Religion and Gender in Women's Lives

It is impossible to analyze the activities of women religious without expanding our understanding of the importance religion played in the lives of nineteenth- and early-twentieth-century American women. The overwhelming presence of women in American religious history in no way equates to female dominance. Likewise, women have not been passive victims within the male-defined traditions that are embedded in religious ideologies. Discussing the Judeo-Christian heritage and its importance to women, Ann Braude writes,

There could be no lone man in the pulpit without the mass of women who fill the pews. There would be no clergy, no seminaries to train them, no theology to teach them and no hierarchies to ordain them, unless women supported all of these institutions from which they historically have been and still are excluded by Catholics, conservative Protestants, and Orthodox Jews. To understand the history of religion in America, one must ask what made each group's teachings and practices meaningful to its female members.[15]

Discovering the ways that women have negotiated their roles within the gendered power dynamics of these religious traditions provides the key to understanding and analyzing women's contributions in the church and in the larger society.

Scholars in women's history have consistently demonstrated that large numbers of Euro-American and African American women within Judeo-Christian traditions used religion and the church to justify, define, and expand their role in American society. Religious beliefs and ideology have been the prime movers in many women's lives, encouraging them to enter the public realm, inviting them to behave in ways that have brought them into conflict with clerical and lay males, and allowing them to broaden Victorian ideologies defining race, class, and gender.[16]

With few exceptions, when religion has been researched and integrated into women's history, the studies have focused on middle- and upper-class, white Protestant women. Discussing the historiography of women and religion, Leslie Woodcock Tentler chides historians of women for their lack of interest in the study of women religious. In light of the sheer quantity of educational, charitable, health care, and social service institutions created by American nuns in the nineteenth and twentieth centuries, she states, "Had women under secular or Protestant auspices compiled this record of achievement, they would be today a thoroughly researched population. . . . Remedy is surely needed."[17] As a remedy, this study will attempt to place nuns within the mainstream of American history between 1836 and 1920.

The rich array of scholarship demonstrating how Protestant and secular women used gender, religion, and power in the formation of women's organizations and associations in nineteenth- and early-twentieth-century America provides critical insights into what these women accomplished and how they felt about their work.[18] Much of this information is relevant to the experiences of American sisters, and although the comparison is rarely made, commonalities are many. First, Protestant and secular women's groups and Catholic sisterhoods created opportunities for lifelong friendships and physical and emotional support networks, providing opportunities for shared experience and collective gender consciousness in school and work settings. Second, Catholic sisterhoods and Protestant and secular women's groups created public space for women, justifying their presence through gender-appropriate activity in charitable endeavors, hospitals, settlement houses, and schools. Third, these "public" activities helped churchwomen develop a variety of skills, such as leadership and financial and business acumen, outside the family or home setting. Fourth, through their activities, Catholic sisterhoods and Protestant and secular women provided needed caregiving functions to society through teaching, nursing, offering support services for women, and nurturing children and the poor. American nuns were often the first organized group of white women in remote settings in the trans-Mississippi West. Finally, Catholic women religious and Protestant and secular women's organizations expanded women's public culture, allowing single women to work and live in a meaningful way in society outside of marriage and motherhood.

In spite of these positive attributes of women's associations, nuns, like their Protestant and secular counterparts, suffered the negative effects of gender in a patriarchal society. Resources and activities could be limited or taken away by uncooperative males. All-female settings were often marginalized or ghettoized in patriarchal society or church. Women's organizations, activities, and finances were sometimes co-opted or dissolved because of male interference.

Unique Characteristics of Communities of Women Religious

Communities of women religious fit nicely into this paradigm of women's associational and organizational characteristics used to analyze the lives of Protestant and secular women. However, the Catholic sisterhoods that flourished in the United States had four unique qualities or characteristics that made them distinctly different from Protestant women's organizations. These unique qualities—ethnic and class diversity, lifelong education and work, perpetual vows, and a distinctive environment and tradition—insured the effectiveness, longevity, and growth of American Catholic sisterhoods well into the twentieth century. For some religious communities, these qualities created an unprecedented female power base that enabled independent activity, limited patriarchal interference and control, and significantly shaped American Catholic culture and public life.

The first distinguishing quality of religious communities was that they integrated more ethnic and class diversity than most Protestant women's organizations. In the nineteenth century, European-based communities, like the CSJs, were initially ethnically homogeneous, most often French or German. Many, like the CSJs, had to "Americanize" quickly to ensure survival in the United States and in so doing became ethnically diverse, reflecting the American Catholic population that provided their membership. Young German, French, and Irish immigrants and daughters of immigrants who entered the CSJ community in the nineteenth and early twentieth centuries had to set aside their own ethnic and class prejudices and focus on their identity as religious women in an American milieu. In turn, as they worked among their ethnically diverse clientele, the nuns achieved rapport and acceptance by focusing on their parishioners' Catholic *and* American identities.[19]

Elitist and class privileges prevalent in European convents had to be downplayed, if not discarded, in the more egalitarian atmosphere of the United States. Similar to many other transplanted European communities, the CSJs eventually abolished the class distinction between "choir" and "lay" sisters in 1908. Working-class, middle-class, and upper-class women came together to share community identity and goals.[20]

Another reason for minimizing ethnic and class diversity in American religious communities was the need to overcome anti-Catholic prejudice, which was especially strong regarding cloistered religious who remained mysteriously secluded behind convent walls with no apparent purpose in society. However, cloister, in the sense of strict enclosure, was not a feature of most communities who came to America. Since the great majority of nuns came to America at the request of bishops seeking teachers, nurses, and social workers, most transplanted European communities were already engaged in these active works in their native countries. Their visible and useful contributions that served community needs helped alleviate Protestant suspicion and prejudice. The more homogeneous Protestant women's organizations rarely had to prove their Americanism or their patriotism.[21]

A second distinguishing characteristic was the sisters' approach to life-long education and work. In every stage of a nun's community life, as postulant, novice, and professed sister, education played a significant role. Postulants and novices had a rigorous schedule that included studies in spirituality, religious exercises, church history, CSJ community history, music, vocational training, theology, study of the vows (poverty, chastity, obedience), and by the early twentieth century, formal classes in teacher training and nursing.[22]

Professed sisters continued their spiritual exercises and began on-the-job training for teaching, nursing, or child care. Each young sister had mentors who guided her in her work setting. The wide variety of schools, hospitals, and other social institutions provided ongoing, oftentimes intense educational experiences. Sisters were frequently moved from one setting to another as the need arose, and they typically encountered many diverse travel, work, and learning experiences in a variety of situations.[23] Although many Protestant women spent decades of their lives involved in various religious and secular organizations, most of these women were married and had to balance organizational activities with childbirth, child rearing, and other family duties. For women religious, the community functioned as family and work, an inseparable and lifelong educational experience and commitment.

A third unique quality of Catholic sisterhoods includes the taking of perpetual vows. Women religious, including the CSJs, learned to utilize their three vows (poverty, obedience, chastity) to justify, create, and control space for their public endeavors. The vow of poverty provided the justification for their own hardship and deprivation and also helped them understand the daily trials and needs of many Catholic and non-Catholic working-class immigrants. Although sisters were elevated spiritually in the eyes of their parishioners, their lack of financial security enabled them to empathize with the people they served. Their own poverty helped the CSJs avoid a tendency to patronize the needy, a tendency prevalent in many middle- or upper-class, Protestant women's organizations.[24]

The sisters' vow of "holy obedience" to their female superior provided a buffer to patriarchal authority, permitting them to resist pressure from male clerics, who utilized gender and hierarchical privileges to manipulate the sisters. This was an effective method even when the demands were inconsequential or for domestic services. In 1911, the parish priest in Georgetown, Colorado, wrote to Reverend Mother Agnes Gonzaga Ryan that the CSJs refused to clean his house and that all the parish was "upset" about this lack of subservience. Ryan wrote back, stating emphatically that "The Rule" (constitution) forbade CSJs to provide housekeeping for priests and that he would have to find his own housekeeper.[25]

The sisters' religious vow of chastity, of which most Protestants and Catholics alike were aware, afforded the nuns "asexual" status that proved useful when they were interacting in the public domain. Traveling across the country and creating, administering, and working in numerous institutions kept CSJs in close contact and in frequent interaction with all manner of secular men. Seemingly, the sisters had the best of both worlds: gender afforded them the special courtesy given to most nineteenth-century white women, even as their vow of chastity effectively shielded them from most male sexual advances or unwanted attention.

Finally, the religious community was a highly distinctive and inclusive environment that permitted multiple generations to live and work together within woman-only space and tradition. In this communal setting, meals, lodging, celebration, deaths, privileges, and deprivations were shared by all. Some sisters spent fifty or sixty years in a religious community that provided a familial atmosphere in which nuns functioned as mothers, teachers, mentors, friends, confidants, and role models of religious life. Additionally, since many secondary academies and colleges included both boarders and day students, many adolescent girls and young women followed a daily schedule that paralleled or mirrored much of convent life, and thus they interacted daily with sisters in all religious and social activities of the schools.

In addition to the familial setting, centuries of tradition, sacred symbols, and "sheltered space" have confirmed and enhanced the nun's status in what has been mostly male-defined and -controlled "sacred space." In her two-volume history of women, Gerda Lerner has written extensively about the importance of "free space," sacred symbols, and feminine and divine role models (female saints, mystics, teachers, writers) to women. Catholic nuns have had a long, rich history of religious foremothers and role models who for sixteen centuries have used the convent setting to write, learn, think, and experience the divine through their "women-focused" lives in one of the few spaces available to them outside of marriage and motherhood—a setting that had the power to teach, nurture, and build a female power base.[26] This history and tradition added significance and validation to the lives of nineteenth- and early-twentieth-century women who chose to emulate these women and recreate this "sacred space." Although small numbers of non-Catholic sisterhoods existed in the United States, there was no comparable heritage or tradition for women in Protestantism.[27]

If one analyzes the development of a large, active religious community like the CSJs, a multifaceted story unfolds—a truly American narrative. It is a story of immigrants and native-born and the intersection of cultures:

Anglo, African American, European, Hispanic, and Native American. It is a story of a religious minority and its growth and survival in a sometimes unfriendly Protestant setting. It is a story of a community of women whose massive institution building of schools, hospitals, and social services, combined with their faith and labor-intensive work, helped build and shape Catholic culture and American life. And finally, it is a story of change and adaptation and how centuries of European religious, class, and gender traditions clashed with democratic ideals and eventually realigned within nineteenth- and early-twentieth-century American society.

This study ends in 1920 even though the history of women religious, including the CSJs, continues to the present day. For many historians of women, 1920 was a seminal year. With suffrage and other social, educational, economic, and political changes, American women's lives began to encompass new sets of challenges and opportunities very different from those of their mothers or grandmothers. Besides changes in women's roles, the American Catholic Church also began to "come of age" in modern America. By 1920, the United States, no longer considered a mission territory by the Vatican, came more directly under traditional papal control. American bishops began to consolidate their power, and lay Catholics began to lose some of their immigrant stigma, moving into the American middle class and mainstream society. The 1917 change in canon law (church law) mandated new restrictions and uniformity for Catholic nuns that, in essence, limited community autonomy and insured more hierarchical control and management. This occurred even as American religious communities began to grow in unprecedented numbers. The years after 1920, including pre– and post–Vatican II changes for American sisters, begin another story that deserves analysis in its own right.

I

The French Connection

Founders, Origins, and Early Activities

In spite of a storm of opposition from church authorities and social elites, legions of Catholic women responded to the social and religious exigencies of seventeenth-century Europe by becoming religious activists. Although the Council of Trent had renewed an earlier papal order mandating strict enclosure for all women religious, and five papal decrees after Trent reinforced this ruling, these edicts were soon followed by the creation of dozens of new uncloistered communities of nuns.[1] They were especially numerous in France, where more than ninety congregations founded between 1600 and 1720 became active in teaching, nursing, and other charitable work.[2] Among them were the Sisters of St. Joseph, established at Le Puy around 1650. Like their sister communities, they appeared at a time when prevailing norms precluded almost any type of female leadership in the public sphere. A brief look at the context in which the CSJs emerged is helpful for understanding this community and others like it that pioneered new roles for women in society and the church and provided the foundation for the American CSJs almost two centuries later.

When first established, the new service-oriented religious congregations were suspect in the eyes of both civil and ecclesiastical authorities. Unlike officially sanctioned female monasticism with enclosure, solemn vows, and daily chanting of the Divine Office, the new communities engaged in work outside their convents, took simple vows, and were in constant contact with lay people.[3] The Council of Trent had forbidden nuns to mix with the world, and respectable society saw an uncloistered religious lifestyle as improper and undignified. Members of the new women's communities were labeled "Jesuitesses" and "galloping girls" and criticized for trying to do men's work.[4] French *parlements* condemned women religious "seen in the streets of the town and *faubourg* though forbidden to be out" and ordered that they be returned to their convents immediately "under good and secure guard" at the convent's expense.[5]

Actually, uncloistered women religious had been numerous in earlier European society. Even after official papal prohibition, many medieval women continued to live like religious, though not in traditional monasteries. Such groups as tertiaries, beguines, and Sisters of the Common Life lived in communal houses or with their families, devoting themselves to prayer and helping others. Some were mystics, like Catherine of Siena; others, like the Grey Sisters, nursed the sick in hospitals or in their homes.[6] They continued this unorthodox lifestyle as long as rules on enclosure were not consistently enforced, but the Reformation's focus on abuses in the church prompted religious authorities to take a harder line on violations of canon law. Like earlier Catholic reformers, church leaders emphasized stricter control of females, and papal decrees after Trent signaled a renewed and serious intent to suppress all organizations of activist women.[7]

In seeking to restrict female endeavors, the Catholic Church followed long-established doctrine and practice. From earliest times Christian theology had taught the inferiority of women. St. Paul said: "Wives be subject to your husbands as to the Lord" and "I permit no woman to teach or to have authority over men; she is to keep silent."[8] Aquinas argued that "woman is by nature subject to man, because the power of rational discernment is by nature stronger in man."[9] Canon law, like many civil law codes, entitled men to beat their wives. In the post-Reformation church the drive to enforce clerical celibacy produced a more intense hostility toward the "guilty" sex. Attempting to eliminate priests' wives and concubines, preachers and confessors frequently described women as threats to male virtue and instruments of the devil.[10]

Prevailing social trends also limited women's roles in early modern Europe. The economy's emphasis on large-scale production gave females fewer opportunities as independent artisans and entrepreneurs, and increasing political centralization encouraged greater legal subjugation of wives to husbands. New laws gave male heads of families more control of property, curtailing the ability of married women to control their wealth. They could be punished and imprisoned at their husband's wish. Both civil and religious authorities became more hostile toward unmarried women.[11] Symptomatic of the mentality of the times was the persecution of witches, which reached its height between 1600 and 1650. Although estimates have varied, recent figures indicate that more than 100,000 people were prosecuted throughout Europe on charges of witchcraft—80 percent of them women. The Papacy legitimized the persecution in Catholic areas by defining witchcraft as a heresy to be eradicated.[12]

In view of prevailing opinion and custom, the mass movement of Catholic women into active religious communities at this particular time was profoundly countercultural. The impetus for what Elizabeth Rapley called a "fantastic conventual invasion" came from the wars, natural disasters, and grim socioeconomic conditions of the time and the intense spiritual fervor generated within Catholicism by the Catholic Reformation. Initiative, however, came from the women themselves. Far from being "called forth" by the church, they struggled to win acceptance, often against great odds, from ecclesiastical leaders. Eventually they met less opposition as the value of their services was recognized. Their existence was still contrary to papal decrees, but in France, religious and civil officials who supported them had precedents for ignoring unwelcome mandates from Rome. The patronage of influential elites also helped them survive.[13]

Life in Seventeenth-Century France

Ravaged by bloody civil and foreign wars, devastating plagues, famines, and epidemics, and torn by religious fanaticism and peasant unrest, France in the seventeenth century was a nation of extreme contrasts. The magnificence of classical literature and baroque architecture, the grandeur of Versailles, and the wealth of great aristocrats led earlier historians to write of the "splendid" century. More recently the research of economic and social historians has suggested that this was a tragic century during which most of the population suffered grinding poverty, misery, and often untimely death. Like other European states of the time, France was predominantly an agrarian society where approximately 90 percent of its eighteen to twenty million people lived in small towns and villages or were dispersed throughout the rural countryside. By the early 1600s the traditional agricultural economy was becoming increasingly inadequate to support the population as concentration of land in the hands of privileged elites expanded. Since most peasants, wage earners, and day laborers made a precarious living in the best of times, they were extremely vulnerable to adverse developments whether of natural or human origin.

Unfortunately, early modern France had no shortage of adversity. In the late sixteenth century, Europe had entered into a "little ice age" when average temperatures fell, shortening the growing season, reducing harvests, and causing famines. Malnutrition and starvation brought heavy mortality and a deeper and more widespread poverty. France had four deadly famines between 1630 and 1694 and several others almost as severe. The people also endured almost continuous warfare—international wars, civil wars, and a number of peasant and lower-class uprisings. These brought widespread devastation and destitution and inflicted the dreaded passage and/or billeting of soldiers upon peasants and townspeople. Periodic outbreaks of the plague increased the general misery.[14]

Contemporary observers painted a grim picture of appalling conditions. A physician in Blois wrote in 1662:

> I have been practicing medicine in this part of the country for thirty-two years. I have never seen such desolation, not only in Blois[,] where there are about four thousand poor, including migrants from neighboring parishes in addition to the local indigent, but in the whole country. The famine is so great that peasants have no bread and consume decaying carcasses. As soon as a horse or any other animal dies they eat it. . . . Malignant fevers are beginning to spread, and with the heat, and so much humidity and rot, all these miserable people who are already weak will die very quickly. If God does not give us extraordinary assistance we can expect an enormous death toll.[15]

Children were particularly at risk under such circumstances. Some of those placed in the *Couche* of Paris, a home for the orphaned or abandoned, "were sold at eight *sols* apiece to beggars who broke their arms and legs so that people would be inclined to give them alms, and then let them die of hunger."[16]

These tragedies coincided with the vast outpouring of religious energy produced in France by the Catholic Reformation. In part a reaction against Protestantism, the spiritual renewal within Catholicism found official expression in the Council of Trent, which met in several sessions between 1545 and 1563. Insisting, in opposition to Luther, that salvation requires the performance of good works in addition to divine grace, the council set the tone for Catholic post-Reformation spirituality. It was to be active and apostolic, directed outward toward the world and the salvation of souls. The individual search for holiness, including prayer and meditation, was to be combined with service of God in society.[17]

In France, the Catholic Reformation began with the close of the Wars of Religion at the end of the sixteenth century. By that time, decades of military combat between Catholics and Protestants and the partial toleration granted to Protestants in the Edict of Nantes had created religious zeal of exceptional intensity, in some cases fanaticism, among many adherents of both faiths. By recognizing two hostile churches in a society where Catholicism had been entrenched for centuries, the French government set the stage for an impassioned contest for souls. Besides trying to transform ignorant and nonobservant Christians into informed and devout believers, Catholic reformers struggled to win back Protestants to the "true faith." The large scale of the institutional church, its network of parishes and personnel throughout the country, and its intimate connections with the upper levels of French society made its influence powerful and pervasive.[18] As religious zeal became fashionable among French elites, prominent aristocrats and royal officials joined religious leaders in a crusade to implement the reforms of Trent and address the social problems of the age.[19] Seeing monasticism as essential for the vitality of the church, they placed the reform of existing monasteries and creation of new ones among their first priorities.[20]

The interest of early French reformers in monasticism, especially for women, was partly inspired by the printing press. In the late sixteenth century many important religious works were published in the vernacular and disseminated in France, including those of Teresa of Avila. Her humility, humor, and forthright common sense captivated her readers, mostly upper-class French women, who adopted the "devout" life and became active reformers. One of them, Madame Acarie, made her home a center for frequent meetings of the French *dévots*, including government officials, leaders of the clergy, and prominent aristocrats.[21] Madame Acarie sponsored a foundation of Carmelites in Paris in 1605 and later entered the order herself. Carmelite foundations increased to fifty-six in the next forty years, and Teresian spirituality came to permeate the community of French *dévots*, promoting the revitalization of existing groups of cloistered nuns and the creation of many new congregations of religious women.

Active Communities of Women

Among forerunners of the CSJs in France as active women religious were the Ursulines, Visitandines, and Daughters of Charity. In 1607 Madame de Sainte-Beuve, a Parisian *dévote*, founded an Ursuline convent in Paris.[22] The order had been introduced into France some years before in Avignon, and by 1630 over eighty houses of French Ursulines had been established, some by bishops but many by groups of local women who set up their own individual convents and later were officially absorbed into the Ursuline order.[23] In 1610 the Visitation order was founded by Jane Frances de Chantal and Francis de Sales. De Chantal, a noblewoman and widowed mother of four children, had taken a vow of chastity after her husband's death and devoted herself to charity, nursing the sick, and assisting the poor in her neighborhood. Seeking a more complete religious life, she placed herself under de Sales for spiritual direction. The community they founded was designed for women like herself who desired a life of prayer and meditation but whose health, age, or family circumstances disqualified them for the austerities of traditional monasticism. While emphasizing prayer and contemplation, the sisters also undertook charitable work among the sick and poor because the founders thought a life combining prayer and good works was most pleasing to God. The order soon became extremely popular and had seventy-two foundations when de Chantal died in 1641.[24]

The experience of the Ursuline and Visitation nuns illustrates the formidable obstacles faced by the first generation of active women religious. In spite of their intention to be active "in the world," both eventually had to accept solemn vows and cloister. In the case of the Visitation, Francis de Sales acceded to the objections of a fellow bishop who argued that exceptions to the rule of cloister would cause "scandal" and permit nuns without solemn vows to leave their convents and legally claim succession rights to family properties if they so desired. Upper-class families, from whom most candidates for the convent came at this time, saw this possibility as highly objectionable. De Sales accepted defeat when he saw that both secular and ecclesiastical elites were prepared to oppose him. For the Ursulines the decision to adopt cloister occurred gradually as one convent after another yielded to pressure from the hierarchy, local notables, or from some of the nuns themselves. Both Ursulines and Visitandines, however, deviated from traditional monastic discipline by continuing to educate girls and young women within their convents. They expanded the options for women religious by becoming "active contemplatives."[25]

Many pious women unable or unwilling to follow their peers into convents found an alternative in personal prayer and charity, motivated by the suffering they saw around them: "What misery we saw before our eyes and what importunings assaulted our ears from the innumerable poor vagabonds who filled the streets and churches, never giving our spirits repose; our sacrifices brought no silence nor our prayers response."[26] Besides visiting hospitals, prisons, and the homes of the sick, they gave religious instruction and alms to the poor in Paris and in rural areas. Their efforts in the countryside were inspired and guided by Vincent de Paul, one of the most effective friends of the poor in the history of the Catholic Church. Of peasant origin, de Paul rose rapidly to a position of influence in both religious and secular society. A friend of most of the devout reformers of Paris, he also had close connections to the powerful at court, and for a time he belonged to one of the royal councils. He began working in a small rural parish near Lyons in the 1620s and created a confraternity (lay organization) of well-to-do women to provide food, medicine, and spiritual counsel for those in need. Similar confraternities soon appeared in many other villages, most often under the patronage of the lord or lady of the locale, usually a Parisian *dévot*.[27] Local women volunteers, assisted by some from Paris, did the actual work. One of de Paul's helpers, Louise de Marillac, was the cofounder with him of the Daughters of Charity, a major prototype of the CSJS.

The Daughters of Charity, the largest and best known of the early post-Reformation women's communities to survive without cloister and solemn vows, evolved from a confraternity established to aid the poor in Paris. The organization soon had problems because upper-class Parisian ladies, often reluctant to perform personally the menial services required, sent servants, who sometimes neglected or abused the poor whom they were supposed to help. Some young peasant women whom de Paul had met on one of his rural missions offered to do the work that was repugnant to the Parisian *dévotes*, and Louise de Marillac took them into her home to provide some preliminary training for their work in the city. At first simply secular women, free to go and come as they wished, they soon began to adopt the customs and lifestyle of religious. To prevent an outcry from ecclesiastical authorities, de Paul forbade them to take public vows and required them to continue to wear secular dress and to call themselves a confraternity rather than a congregation. He advised that if a bishop should inquire whether they were religious they were to "tell him no, by the grace of God. . . . Tell him that you are poor Daughters of Charity, and that you are given to God for the service of the poor."[28] The strategy was successful. Although a few difficulties occurred and the sisters were occasionally harassed in public, the need for their services made them generally welcome. In less than thirty years the small group of village girls working in Paris confraternities had grown to over 800 women spread throughout the country.[29]

Although the Daughters of Charity were among the first post-Reformation women's communities working in the lay world, a number of similar groups preceded and followed them. According to scholar Judith Taylor, six active French congregations were founded in the 1620s, and nine more, in addition to the Daughters, between 1630 and 1640.[30] Usually small, sometimes consisting of only two or three women, they were most often created to staff and/or administer a charitable institution—orphanage, hospital, refuge, workshop, or school. Foundations were frequently established by a local person of means who gave the women a *règlement* (religious rule or constitution) to foster appropriate behavior and spirituality.[31]

The most disastrous period in seventeenth-century France came at mid-century, when poor harvests combined with civil war caused mass migrations of desperate peasants to the cities and threatened a breakdown of public order.[32] These years also saw the most rapid growth of new active congregations of women religious. Judith Taylor lists seventy created in France between 1650 and 1720, which together maintained more than 1,100 separate foundations by 1789. One of them was the Sisters of St. Joseph, founded, according to long-standing tradition, at Le Puy around 1650.[33] Surviving documents give considerable information about the early Sisters of St. Joseph, but tantalizing gaps in the record remain.[34]

CSJ Origins and Activities before the Revolution

In 1644 Henry de Maupas, bishop of Le Puy, authorized a group of religious women "to raise and instruct the poor girls of Le Puy, with neither mother nor father, who have been sent to Montferrand [a hospital in the city]." By 1648 the hospital had a chapel and was known as "the St. Joseph home for orphan girls on Montferrand street in Le Puy." In 1651 the bishop approved the presence of a congregation of women at the Montferrand hospital, "under the name and title of the *Filhes de Sainct-Joseph*," and later that year six Daughters of St. Joseph formed a legal contract of association. The name of one of them, Françoise Eyraud, had appeared in hospital documents in 1647, indicating a connection between the Daughters of St. Joseph and the first group of religious women at Montferrand. Because of its formal approbation by the bishop, the Le Puy foundation has customarily been considered the official beginning of the congregation.[35]

Surviving records indicate a relationship between the Montferrand CSJs and Jean-Pierre Médaille, a Jesuit priest active in Le Puy and neighboring dioceses. Sources show that Médaille helped create six early communities of St. Joseph, at Dunières, Marlhes, Saint Romain-Lachalm, Arlanc, Sauxillanges, and an unidentified location. The documents establishing the existence of the unnamed community are two letters written by the Jesuit father general in March of 1647 criticizing Médaille for having "prescribed rules for a grouping of women without the approval of the Provincial." By the time of Médaille's death in 1669, thirty-four communities of St. Joseph had been founded, a good number probably with his assistance.[36]

Like his contemporary Vincent de Paul, Jean-Pierre Médaille worked as a missionary in the rural areas of seventeenth-century France. Assigned to various Jesuit colleges in the Massif Central, he combined administrative responsibilities with apostolic activity.[37] Correspondence in the archives of the Society of Jesus in Rome indicates that Médaille's involvement with the sisters was not welcomed by his superiors. The Jesuit father general, Francis Piccolomini, wrote in 1651: "They say at Le Puy that Father Pierre Médaille is launching an extraordinary undertaking, for the institution of I know not what sort of a group of women. I want to know the nature of his plan and from whom he obtained permission to busy himself with such matters which are hardly in accordance with our institute." Médaille was aware of these suspicions because his superiors warned him about the irregularity of his work with the sisters. No doubt he also knew that the Jesuit rule did not allow its members to be spiritual directors or regular confessors of religious women.[38] However, he maintained contact with the Sisters of St. Joseph, helping in the establishment of at least two communities in the 1660s, the last in 1665, four years before his death. In these endeavors he was unusual among his fellow Jesuits, most of whom seem to have shared contemporary gender biases. In rejecting these biases and ignoring the disapproval of his superiors, Médaille not only challenged prevailing opinion but risked his own reputation and official standing in the Jesuit community. After his death, the Jesuit necrology described him as a man of zeal and holiness, respected by the people and especially by the bishops under whom he served. No mention was made of his work with the CSJs, perhaps because his colleagues saw it as insignificant, or possibly from a desire not to speak ill of the dead.[39]

In official histories of female religious communities the role of males as "founders" has often attracted far more attention than the contributions of the women themselves. Recent research on the origins of women's congregations has shown, however, that women were often the actual architects of the new socially active female congregations.[40] Archival records of two early CSJ foundations mention female initiative, identifying Anne Deschaux at Dunières and Catherine Frappa at Marlhes as Médaille's collaborators. At Le Puy records show Françoise Eyraud functioning as administrator in 1647, suggesting that she had probably already been there for some time, possibly as leader of the group of "religious women" introduced by Bishop de Maupas in 1644.[41] Clearly the religious energy of the women who offered to work for the service of God and neighbor was the creative force that made the community of the Sisters of St. Joseph possible.

Marguerite de Saint-Laurans, described by a contemporary as a saint and a cofounder with Father Médaille of the CSJ convent in Le Puy, also had a key role in its early history. A merchant of Le Puy and benefactor of the sisters recorded most of what is known about her in a memoir written after 1664. Marguerite came from the diocese of Saint-Flour, where Médaille was stationed between 1642 and 1650, and she may have known him there. He became her spiritual director, and she followed him in his missions. In 1648 she came to the hospital at Montferrand to assist Françoise Eyraud, who, being illiterate, had asked the administrators for someone to help educate the girls and keep financial records. Several sources suggest that Marguerite functioned as novice mistress for a time. However, she did not remain permanently with the CSJs, did not sign the contract of association with the other six sisters in 1651, and left Le Puy after 1654 to become a hermit. Her biographer wrote that she had problems with the bishop of Saint-Flour, who "persecuted her strangely," and that she lived in a cave on bread and water, slept on straw, and "wrote incessantly . . . on the duty of ecclesiastics." Educated, charismatic, and devout, Marguerite probably helped to shape the spirituality of the early csj community through her interactions with Médaille and the sisters. The mystical emphasis on inner union with God found in early csj documents may reflect her influence as well as Médaille's, since she was clearly attracted to contemplation and later pursued it in her hermitage.[42]

Although the extent of Marguerite's spiritual influence on the csjs is speculative, Jean-Pierre Médaille left written evidence of his contributions in four documents that served to unify and stabilize the early community.[43] His writings reveal a gifted spiritual director, sensitive to the aspirations and capabilities of the women he counseled and aware of contemporary social realities. He also had multiple inspirations and models in seventeenth-century French spirituality from which to choose in devising constitutions for a religious community.[44] Influenced by devout women seeking to serve God in the world, and conscious of desperate social and religious needs, Médaille formulated a rule for the early sisters that combined intense spirituality with practical responsiveness to contemporary demands.

Fundamentally the directives proposed for the csjs were based on the Gospels, specifically the two great commandments, love of God and love of neighbor.[45] Early csj documents stress these repeatedly: "They should so live that their Congregation may bear the name of the Congregation of the great love of God. . . . They will also show great charity towards all classes of neighbors, particularly toward the poor. . . . Let all dread the slightest disunion as they would a monster. They should be formed with extraordinary care in this spirit of love and charity."[46] Also fundamental was an emphasis on active effort to assist in Christ's redemptive work for the salvation of souls. "Their very little institute has been founded to bring many souls to a great and true love of God. . . . [T]o achieve this purpose more fully, they will undertake all the spiritual and corporal works of mercy of which women are capable."[47] The documents encouraged the sisters to imitate Christ's virtues, especially humility, mentioning it more than twenty-five times in the collection of one hundred recommended rules of behavior, titled *Maxims of the Little Institute*. They also advocated selfless striving "toward the greater glory of God," the motto of the Jesuits.[48]

Understandably, Médaille's suggestions for the sisters reflect his Jesuit training, but elements from other sources are present also. Like Francis de Sales, he frequently recommended gentleness, moderation, peace, and trust.[49] At times his advice used gendered language that recalled the writings of medieval mystics like Julian of Norwich and anticipated insights of some post–Vatican II theologians, as in a passage from *The Eucharistic Letter*: "In imitation of this dear Savior, let us obey as a child, without questioning, without worrying about anything except allowing Divine Providence to guide us as a gentle mother who truly knows our needs and who by her very nature rears children lovingly nestled at her breast."[50] Foundational texts of the CSJs indicate that the desire to achieve holiness for both members and "the dear neighbor" was the primary impetus for the congregation, and that charitable works were the preferred means to achieve this goal. While usually compatible with the teachings of Trent, the documents also depart from them in significant ways, especially in proposing an active role for women religious and attributing feminine qualities to God.

Although their constitutions plainly said that they intended to live "in the manner of religious" and without cloister, the Sisters of St. Joseph did not encounter the same degree of opposition met by earlier active female congregations. By the time of their foundation at midcentury, similar communities already existed and were multiplying rapidly, mainly because of the immense social needs they were addressing. Acceptance came more readily because their members, unlike upper-class women, could work for a living without censure and were unlikely to be potential claimants to a family inheritance—the issue that had caused trouble for early Visitation and Ursuline nuns. Also, although of humble background themselves, the sisters often had influential sponsors who helped them obtain official recognition and sometimes financial support. According to Judith Taylor, "The secular congregation might have withered in France as quickly and quietly as it already had in late Renaissance Italy. That it did not is attributable to the *dévots*, their influence and rank, their cohesion and persistence. . . . [C]onfirmation [was] secured as often as not by an old family friend of a founder or by an influential Lady of Charity in a position to exchange favors. . . . By 1650 the female secular congregation had been irrevocably established in France."[51]

The early Sisters of St. Joseph fit the social profile that enabled many similar congregations to survive in France at midcentury. Four of the seven original sisters at Le Puy were from middle-class families, two of more humble origins, while Marguerite de Saint-Laurans probably had connections with the nobility. All were from small towns, and of the six who made the contract of association in 1651, only one could sign her name. Only two brought dowries.[52] Like many of the other new active communities, the CSJs needed the influential supporters, male and female, who helped them survive, most importantly Henry de Maupas du Tour, the bishop of Le Puy and count of Velay. An aristocrat whose father had been a counselor of King Henry IV, de Maupas had wealth and patronage as well as religious authority to enhance his power. He was a disciple and friend of Vincent de Paul, an admirer and biographer of Francis de Sales, and a close associate of many leaders of the *dévot* group in Paris. His support and formal approbation of the CSJ foundation were vital for its continuance and success.[53] Another early benefactor of the sisters was Lucrèce de la Planche, an aristocratic and "very virtuous woman" who made them welcome in her home for several months after their arrival in Le Puy. "She not only did everything in her power for the establishment of these sisters, but continued until her death to work with extraordinary zeal and charity for the advancement of their congregation."[54]

The first CSJs did experience hostility from local secular authorities, a type of opposition commonly encountered by religious of the period and one that could have put an end to their efforts in Le Puy. The rapid proliferation of convents at this time was making French municipal authorities increasingly nervous about the loss of precious urban space to women religious. The fear was that, as women, they might incur financial losses and become a public charge. In 1631 irate citizens of Troyes had "dragged a coachload of Visitandine nuns backwards away from the city gates."[55] The CSJs' experience was less dramatic, but in 1654 when, after a worried discussion of the numerous convents in the city, Le Puy officials learned that a new foundation had been made without municipal approval, they sent six members of the city assembly to expel the sisters from the town. According to one eyewitness, when the angry male delegation reached the Montferrand hospital they encountered Françoise Eyraud and Marguerite de Saint-Laurans, who brought them into a room where the sisters made ribbon. Soon their hostility vanished and the meeting became a "courteous and very civil visit." Understanding the gender politics of the situation, Françoise and Marguerite had seen the need to justify their existence as women independent of male supervision. They knew the ribbon room would reassure their visitors that the sisters could not only earn money to support themselves but also teach the orphan girls a trade that might be of future benefit to the city.[56]

The community of the Sisters of St. Joseph grew rapidly. In just ten years there were twenty houses in three dioceses and by 1790 approximately 153 foundations in fourteen dioceses.[57] Such expansion indicates that the congregation meshed well with the social and religious needs of its environment. Open to women of all classes, it did not limit its mission to any particular type of activity and did not require a large dowry, lengthy preparation for entrance, or education.[58] Each community was autonomous and needed only the approval of the local bishop or his representative to exist and begin its work. Acting within accepted gender parameters, the sisters were willing to work for minimal salaries, sometimes for nothing, and adapt to a variety of institutional settings, types of housing, and educational and relief activities. Besides caring for orphans as they did in Le Puy, they administered and staffed hospitals, boarding schools, homes for fallen women, schools for "converted" Protestants, workshops for making lace and ribbon, and dispensaries of medications for the sick. They also taught poor children and assumed total responsibility for charitable relief in many rural parishes.[59]

In Le Puy, the CSJs became responsible for the care of about forty orphans and soon assumed additional duties.[60] Empowered by their constitution to undertake all the works of charity "of which women are capable," they opened a free school for poor children and a boarding school for girls of higher social status, which provided a regular income to help subsidize their nonpaying activities. Françoise Eyraud's competent management during her thirty years as superior secured additional income with the acquisition of eight houses and two gardens in the Montferrand area. Approximately 100 years later, when required to disclose their financial status to the revolutionary government, the Le Puy community declared investments valued at 73,000 livres, which yielded an annual income of 4,000 to 5,000 livres. This was enough to maintain sixteen sisters, two lay sisters, and twelve destitute orphans funded by benefactors, to educate virtually free of charge sixty poor girls, and to help local families who were unable to support their children. In comparison with other religious communities in Le Puy at the time, the CSJs were among the less affluent, with annual expenses far greater than their income from operations.[61] Testimony from the head of the city council of Le Puy indicates that their efforts were appreciated:

> One of the most useful establishments for this city [is] that of the Sisters of the Congregation of St. Joseph, who live with great edification, and who, not satisfied to retire within their own house, and to raise the poor orphan girls according to the object of their foundation, take in many other children besides, whose poverty-stricken parents are not able to provide them a livelihood, still less an education; that moreover

they instruct and raise the boarders whom they have with a care and regard which is rarely seen elsewhere.[62]

The Le Puy community became a model for other CSJ communities, which sometimes sent novices there for initial formation (training).

Hospitals staffed by the CSJs included both general and traditional hospitals and *hôtels-Dieu*. At Mende they directed a general hospital, one of those originally intended to discipline vagrants and able-bodied beggars by forcing them to work. Over time the policy of confinement was gradually abandoned because of its obvious failure, and general hospitals came to be homes for the "deserving poor"—the aged, disabled, and children. The size and staffing of sisters' institutions varied widely. By 1790 the Mende hospital had 152 residents, including 95 old and infirm, 29 children, 4 sisters of St. Joseph, and a number of employees involved in running the house. The CSJs in Mende were more fortunate than four sister-nurses at a hospital in Rodez who cared for 472 poor, of whom almost half were totally incapacitated, many bedridden. The sisters had to enlist a number of the able-bodied but frail and elderly residents to help in tending the sick and the orphaned children.[63]

An important CSJ hospital foundation was made in 1668 when Sister Jeanne Burdier, one of the six foundresses of the Le Puy community, and two companions took charge of the *hôtel-Dieu* in Vienne. The support of the archbishop and Burdier's leadership as superior led to a remarkable expansion of the CSJ presence in Vienne and neighboring areas. The first new mission was at Gap in the French Alps, where Burdier witnessed the misery of the poor in the small local hospital and offered to send three sisters to help. The bishop and town consuls responded positively, even after Burdier told them that renovations were needed before the sisters would come, "to give it [the hospital] a form other than it has at present in order to avoid the mixture of those who are healthy with the sick, and to separate the men from the women, in order to prevent many evil consequences."[64] Some years later the sisters at Gap faced a severe test of their dedication to health care. In 1691, when the armies of Louis XIV passed through the town en route from Italy, an epidemic among the troops left their tiny hospital swamped with patients, and all the hospital nuns died as a result of caring for them. Mother Burdier later sent other sisters to replace them.

Superior at Vienne until her death in 1700, Burdier began some ten new CSJ foundations in hospitals or houses of refuge in neighboring areas.

Their sisters remained in touch with the Vienne community and depended on it in various ways. Novices came to Vienne for training and then were sent to serve in other missions, sometimes to be transferred later as the need arose. Mutual assistance between communities included everything from financial aid and religious habits to spiritual books. Vienne began to function like a motherhouse, and under Burdier as superior it exerted a powerful influence over its "daughter" houses, always with the approval of the respective bishops. The rapid expansion of the community presented some logistical problems, however, because transmission of the CSJ constitutions in handwritten copies to new houses led to numerous textual variations and discrepancies. Mother Burdier took the lead in convoking a group of sisters to compare different versions of the constitutions, formulate an acceptable text, and obtain permission from the archbishop to have an official copy printed in Vienne. The bishop gave his approval in November of 1693, and the first printed version of the CSJ constitutions appeared in 1694.

Burdier was a practical, compassionate, and determined superior. She monitored the well-being of the sisters and the sick, making sure that sister-nurses were not overwhelmed with work and patients were well cared for, and used the sisters' religious identity to create space for them in the secular world. In dealings with lay administrators, she maintained a clear distinction between the sisters' accountability to them for hospital management and their religious obedience to the archbishop, not hesitating to remind officials on occasion that the CSJs, as women religious, obeyed the bishop, rather than laymen, in spiritual matters. When important requests were not honored by the hospital board she found other options. For example, after several fruitless attempts to obtain a separate area in the hospital where the sisters could pray and meditate without distraction, she finally purchased a house to serve as their convent as well as a refuge for penitent women. She modeled effective leadership and dedication for many young sisters who made their novitiate at Vienne before leaving to work elsewhere in the region.

Unfortunately, Burdier's legacy was considerably weakened after class pressures made themselves felt within the Vienne community. The influence of a wealthy aristocratic benefactor had caused a number of young upper-class women to be admitted as novices to the convent, and in time the tenor of the community began to change. Administrators began to complain that the sisters relegated hospital tasks to domestic help instead of caring for patients themselves, gave patients food inferior to their own, turned revenues of the *hôtel-Dieu* to their own profit, and lived like ladies of "a certain social condition." Whether the assertions were all true cannot be determined, but it is clear that the sisters at this time began to take on more of the upper-class characteristics of cloistered religious. After a long conflict and several failed attempts at reconciliation, the administrators dismissed the sisters from the *hôtel-Dieu* in 1755. In 1777, with the permission of the archbishop's vicar general, the CSJs at Vienne became officially cloistered.[65]

A different but in some ways similar story unfolded at the *hôtel-Dieu* in Sauxillanges, where the CSJs were also eventually dismissed. Although the sisters had accepted a contract to care for the sick poor of the town, they admitted only orphans to the hospital and visited the sick in their homes. Eventually, and not without difficulty, the well-to-do merchant who had established the hospital succeeded in having patients admitted to it. However, when he demanded that a man suffering from a "repugnant disease" be admitted, the sisters "with violence extraordinary to their sex and scandalous for their profession" punched the elderly gentleman in the nose and pushed him into the street, "practically knocking him to the ground." They said "they would rather die than have this illness in their house." Both sides sued in court, and the sisters refused to accept a court-ordered compromise. Finally, after the superior had died, the citizens of Sauxillanges forced the two remaining sisters to leave the town. They did so, leaving behind their home and most of their meager possessions.[66]

As both incidents demonstrate, religious ideals did not always prevail over more self-serving considerations among the early CSJs. Although of modest social status, the sisters at Sauxillanges showed no greater zeal for the humble tasks involved in serving the poor than some of the "ladies of condition" in Vienne. A major difference in the two cases is that the community in Vienne survived, thanks to the patronage of powerful protectors. When the Vienne nuns left the *hôtel-Dieu*, they joined another CSJ community in the city that managed the Providence, a refuge for penitent women located in a building donated by the archbishop of Vienne. The sisters at the Providence had earlier received letters patent from King Louis XV that freed them from oversight by the hospital administrators and placed them under the archbishop's jurisdiction.[67] Their land, house, oratory, and garden were declared inalienable as things of God used in the service of the poor. Such guarantees, obtained through the intervention of Archbishop Henry Oswald de la Tour d'Auvergne, a cousin of the king, had not been granted to the less well connected community at Sauxillanges. Social class played a part in events in Vienne and Sauxillanges as did the powerful influence of what has been called the "monastic temptation."[68] In contrast to the women with solemn vows and cloister who enjoyed status as "true" religious with special privileges and exemptions, those with simple vows were seen as lesser beings with no claim to society's special consideration or respect. Throughout this period the cloister continued to elicit a strong fascination, representing the more perfect life choice, the "true" religious vocation, for all women and especially for the upper classes.

The first constitution of the Sisters of St. Joseph indicated that the sisters would engage in "hospital work, the direction of orphanages [and] the visitation of the sick poor" and mentioned somewhat tentatively that they might undertake "even the instruction of girls in places where the religious communities already established are not doing this."[69] The kind of teaching originally intended was religious instruction and training in practical skills, but the CSJs soon responded to growing demands for a broader feminine education. Early in the seventeenth century the Catholic Church had been adamantly opposed to women teaching, later reluctantly allowing it only within the cloister. A highly placed Vatican official spoke for many when he said, "It matters little what the times demand . . . all [female] congregations that refuse the enclosure must be suppressed."[70] However, by midcentury the realization had dawned that while the Council of Trent had mandated cloister for nuns, it had also stressed the duty to instruct the faithful, and since knowledge of the faith was believed essential for salvation, religious instruction should have priority over other considerations. The key that finally opened school doors to the female congregations was the growing awareness of the importance of education for girls. Little girls were potential future mothers and future teachers of their children, capable of sharing the faith in which they had been instructed. However, if they were to be instructed, women must teach them, because both religious and secular authorities objected to coeducation and to male instructors for female students.[71]

From the start, the first Sisters of St. Joseph to come to Le Puy taught a variety of subjects and students: religious education for young girls and women, ribbon making and probably other practical skills for the orphans, and a broader curriculum of study in the boarding school for girls from middle- and upper-class families. As the CSJs expanded into small rural villages and began work in hospitals or refuges in larger towns and cities, almost all communities were involved in some kind of teaching.[72] At

Vienne, in addition to the hospital, the sisters ran a house of refuge and a day school; at Clermont and Avignon they offered free classes for poor girls; at Aubenas they taught young girls of the town reading, writing, and religion; and at Tence, Satillieu, Cheylard, and Gap they taught young "converts" from Protestantism and educated other girls and women in religion, reading, writing, and other subjects.[73] Many of the hospitals they served were small parish institutions of twenty to thirty beds that in addition to caring for the sick offered basic instruction for poor girls.

Although surviving documents do not describe curricula offered in their schools, it is reasonable to assume that the Sisters of St. Joseph provided instruction comparable to that given by other religious communities in French schools of the period. The largest number of CSJ students were at the elementary level in both urban and rural areas, and the typical curriculum of such French *petites écoles* consisted mainly of religion, with a strong emphasis on morality, the three R's, and needlework. Religious instruction focused on learning prayers, studying the catechism, preparation for confirmation and first communion, and behavior training in "Christian duties, hatred of sin, love of virtue, and *civilité* and good manners."[74] Of the other subjects taught, reading was the most important since it gave children access to the word of God, and all elementary schools claimed to teach it. Although writing was usually considered part of the curriculum, it was less likely to be taught to all students. One reason was lack of preparation on the part of some teachers; another was that writing was not taught until after reading had been mastered, and some pupils did not progress that far. Writing also required additional tools and facilities— knife, paper, inkwell, powder, and tables in addition to the standard school benches. Sometimes writing students had to pay an extra fee. Arithmetic did not receive much emphasis, its minor importance indicated by the hour per week usually allotted to it.

Reflecting the gendered nature of the curriculum, handwork came next in importance after religion and reading. It was considered essential for all girls, rich and poor, "to avoid the evils of idleness." In elite schools girls learned tapestry, embroidery, French and English sewing, and other "accomplishments" valued by the upper class, while in the many free schools and workshops they learned ribbon and lace making, stocking knitting, and other practical skills that would help them earn a respectable living. The number of free charity day schools expanded rapidly with the post-Reformation Catholic missionary effort, and classes were typically large, ranging from 40 to 100 pupils. Some schools financed themselves in part with proceeds from the sale of students' handwork. In rural areas girls had more difficulty attending school, since villages often hired schoolmasters to teach boys but seldom provided schoolmistresses for the girls. Nearly all rural girls' schools were conducted by religious communities, and the disparities among peasant girls' educational opportunities in different regions reflected the presence or absence of the sisters: "The Vatelotes, for example . . . staffed 124 schools in Lorraine in 1789. . . . The Filles de la Sagesse . . . operated 66 schools in lower Normandy and Saintonge. . . . The Auvergne and Velay regions were served by the Béates, the Demoi-selles de l'Instruction, and the Soeurs de Saint-Joseph."[75] Social class affected both curriculum and tuition in educational institutions. Boarding schools for upper-class girls not only gave instruction in the basics—cat-echism, reading, writing, arithmetic, spelling, and handwork—but usually added other options such as history, geography, music, drawing, and dancing. The most elite and expensive Parisian boarding schools charged tuition of 400 to 500 livres per year and employed private tutors to give special lessons. Tuition at Ursuline schools was somewhat less, ranging from 240 livres in Paris to 100 in small towns. At their boarding school in Clermont the csjs charged tuition of about 200 livres, suggesting that they must have offered an education comparable to that provided by the other religious congregations in the city—Ursulines, Bernardines, and Benedictines.[76]

In post-Reformation Europe, the preoccupation of religious and sec-ular authorities with control of women was demonstrated not only through emphasis on male authority in the family and cloister for religious women but also in the creation of "refuges" for sexually vulnerable and wayward women. Prostitution, legal in medieval times, was gradually criminalized in most European cities at this time, and even before municipal bordellos were closed, officials tried to control women who worked outside the authorized houses. In France in 1644 the city council of Nîmes decided to imprison all native prostitutes in a tower, where they would be fed bread and water, and drive the "foreign" offenders out after shaving their heads. Beginning in 1684 national laws established severe penalties for prostitu-tion, including incarceration in a special hospital. In addition to punishing immoral women, authorities also attempted to confine unwed mothers, females who had been raped or seduced, and those thought to be in danger of becoming prostitutes. Sometimes such women were confined in the same institution with prostitutes, but the two groups were usually separated, the incorrigible receiving harsher treatment.[77]

The early constitution of the Sisters of St. Joseph showed an awareness of the difficulties of sexually vulnerable women and addressed the ways of protecting them, while also expressing some of the more punitive gendered sentiments of the time toward "fallen women." It advised the sisters to "be watchful in providing for young girls who are in danger of losing their virtue because they have no one to help or direct them, or because they are in need of money . . . and [to] try to find a home and work for such girls. . . . [But] if they should come in contact with prostitutes, let them consider whether they should, after having punished them, have them driven out or place them in a house of confinement."[78] As caregivers in a network of institutions in early modern France where the line between charity and control was not too clear, the CSJs themselves staffed several houses for the confinement of women. The Providence in Vienne was one of the first; others included a prison for prostitutes in Lyons and establishments known as Bon Pasteur (Good Shepherd) in Clermont and Avignon. The Lyons prison was part of a larger complex that also included a refuge for penitent women run by the Sisters of the Visitation. In time the number of women in the prison increased to eighty, and shortly before the Revolution the administrators were planning to enlarge the building. Meanwhile, the CSJ community there had expanded from the original three sisters to twelve. In a document dating from 1790 a revolutionary official made derogatory and obscene comments about the House of Penitents and the Visitation nuns but also praised the organization of the prison and the way the women were treated and taught to work. The CSJs were not mentioned, but they were the ones responsible for the humane atmosphere in the prison and for helping the women learn a useful trade.[79]

The Bon Pasteur in Clermont included both penitent women and prostitutes interned by the police, but the prostitutes were kept in cells apart from the rest of the house and were supervised by the administrators rather than the sisters. As in Lyons, the growing number of residents caused an increase in the size of the sisters' community, and a novitiate was established. Eventually the administrators authorized construction of a larger facility, but loss of funding threatened its completion until the CSJ superior, Mother Saint-Agnes Labas, decided that the sisters could help financially by opening a boarding school for young ladies, a strategy often used by European nuns at this time and later in the United States. Within three years the new school had twenty-seven students, providing sufficient revenue to complete the construction and help maintain the penitents. Besides their work with penitents and students in the boarding school, the sisters housed and educated about twelve children from poor families and cared for two elderly and eight insane women. With twelve sisters, two novices, and five servants, the house had close to 100 residents in 1772, not counting the prostitutes.

As in other contemporary institutions of this type, the daily routine of the penitents at the Bon Pasteur consisted of work and prayer. The women followed the convent schedule, which included morning and evening prayer, Mass, Office of the Holy Spirit, Office of the Blessed Virgin, examination of conscience, spiritual reading, and other prayers at specified times during the day. The sisters also provided spiritual formation for the residents by giving instructions based on passages from the Gospel or chapters of the catechism. When not engaged in religious exercises the women worked, mainly at sewing and embroidery. The women ate their meals in silence while they listened to spiritual reading, and one of the sisters was present to monitor the hour of recreation permitted in the evening. Not all of the penitents were amenable to this routine, and occasional escapes occurred, sometimes facilitated by the sisters if the escapee had been particularly disruptive and unmanageable.

In addition to the semimonastic schedule of religious duties and work, most institutions for the poor and "deviant" used corporal punishment as an incentive to good behavior. The General Hospital in Paris had whipping posts and dungeons, and the Refuge of Riom run by the apparently draconian Ladies of Mercy used leg and hand irons and other more esoteric equipment. At the Bon Pasteur in Clermont penitents were usually kept in cells when first admitted and urged to make their confession in order to be transferred into more comfortable quarters. However, the sisters' financial accounts do not mention chains, handcuffs, and other items listed in the invoices of the administrators. These were probably reserved for the women held in the cells, but it is difficult to be sure. The CSJs may have used corporal punishment, since it was taken for granted at the time, but they also tried more positive means of behavior modification. Mother Saint-Agnes developed a rating system by which the penitents' progress in good conduct was noted by the sisters and rewarded.[80]

Besides their work in hospitals, refuges, schools, and other institutions in larger towns and cities, the CSJs were also present in large numbers in the rural countryside. Their first known community was in the small village of Dunières, and until the Revolution the majority of CSJ houses were rural. Village communities were typically small, consisting of three to six sisters, and accommodations were very simple, sometimes a rented room, although in most cases sisters eventually managed to obtain a small house. In a village the nuns were likely to be daughters of local families and typically expected to spend their entire lives in the area. The family ties, patterns of speech and custom, and modest social and economic status that they shared with the villagers made the sisters an integral part of the local community and facilitated their mission, which usually involved provision of most of the educational and charitable services in the locality.

The CSJs always staffed the local elementary school, teaching catechism, reading, writing, and practical skills, including lace making, which was centered in the Le Puy area. In some cases they were entirely responsible for the religious education of parish women and held weekly catechism classes for them. They also served as sacristans for the church. Since separation of church and state did not exist in France prior to the Revolution, the parish was responsible for public assistance, which usually meant that the sisters did whatever needed to be done. They maintained small dispensaries where the sick and poor could obtain medicines, bedding, and other necessities, visited and cared for the sick in their homes, and distributed alms to the poor, often from the small local hospital or schoolhouse. Their importance to village communities is indicated in a testimonial from the parish of Job:

> They continually attend to the instruction of the young girls both of the parish of Job and of the places nearby. They take into their house—and particularly during the winter when farm work comes to a halt—as many little peasants as they have space for, and give them room and board at a low price. In general, they instruct them thoroughly in the principles of religion and piety; they teach them to read, to write, and to work, in order to train them one day to be mothers who are equally hard-working and Christian. . . . [They] comfort the sick poor.[81]

The French Revolution and After

The Revolution in 1789 brought radical change to religious institutions in France. The Catholic Church came under attack as an important pillar of the old order and was used as a means of alleviating governmental bankruptcy. It was secularized and most of its lands confiscated, and a new Civil Constitution of the Clergy provided that bishops and priests would be paid by the state. Clergy were required to swear an oath of allegiance to the Civil Constitution, but since the pope forbade it, only 54 percent of the parish clergy complied and only 7 of the 160 bishops did so. The new religious policies caused deep divisions among the people and made the Catholic Church, which continued to be very influential, an enemy of the Revolution. In 1789 religious communities staffed 2,200 hospitals and the great majority of schools in France. Lacking a lay nursing service and a substitute for the teaching congregations, the government, although suppressing monastic orders and seizing their property, allowed active religious communities like the CSJs to continue for a time.[82]

In the Massif Central, where most of the Sisters of St. Joseph were located, popular resistance to the Civil Constitution was widespread and many priests refused the oath. Most sisters actively resisted secular authority by supporting these "refractory" priests, since they shared their opinions, and invited them to say Mass in their convents when they were excluded from the churches. CSJs also expressed subversive views to parishioners and students by encouraging them to hear Mass at the convent rather than attend services of the "constitutional" clergy. In Craponne one of the Sisters of St. Joseph was denounced to the authorities for "having accused the new constitutional curé of being an intruder, a fanatic, and a schismatic, saying that it was better to sit by her fire than go to [his] Mass."[83] Revolutionary leaders, soon forced to cope with foreign and civil war and severe economic distress while trying to transform the government, became increasingly radicalized and intolerant of opposition, including that of religious congregations. In a 1792 Assembly debate on whether to exempt hospitallers from suppression, the Sisters of St. Joseph were singled out for criticism: "Those of these *filles* [CSJs] who know how to read and write have managed to turn themselves into charlatans: some are lawyers, the others doctors, pharmacists, and even surgeons. You would therefore, under these exceptions, allow to exist in the countryside this vermin which lays them waste, and you would preserve establishments which have become the haunt and foul refuge of all the refractory priests."[84] In August 1792 the Assembly suppressed all religious congregations, declared their belongings national property, and ordered them to evacuate "the national houses which they occupy." However, since many local officials tended to be lenient with the sisters, especially in the Haute Loire, the CSJs' treatment varied according to local circumstances.

Most Sisters of St. Joseph did leave their houses after August 1792, but timing varied and a few hospital communities apparently remained undisturbed throughout the entire Revolution. The greatest danger came during the Terror in 1793–94. The Law of Suspects of September 1793, so vague that almost anyone could be arrested under suspicion of disloyalty, and the Oath of Liberty-Equality imposed on former religious in October 1793, which most refused as equivalent to renouncing the faith, accounted for the imprisonment of many. Some of the sisters were incarcerated in their former convents, which as properties of the state had been turned into prisons for women. Four, possibly five, CSJs were guillotined during the Terror, all for the crime of helping to conceal refractory priests.[85]

In the aftermath of the Terror many sisters were asked to return to hospitals they had been forced to leave. At Gap all the former hospitallers returned to help when Austrian soldiers taken prisoner by Napoleon and suffering from typhus were brought to the hospital. Religious education also revived, and private girls' schools reappeared in former CSJ locations such as Le Puy, Craponne, Saint-Georges-l'Agricol, Beaune, Chomélix, and Saint-Paulien. With the end of the Revolution, many St. Joseph communities began to reorganize, some picking up where they left off, others combining members from several earlier CSJ houses. Initially all were self-contained convents under their local superior, as had been true before the Revolution, but the reconstituted communities were operating in a new environment. Many suffered from the permanent loss of their former property, and all had to live under the conditions imposed in Napoleon's Concordat of 1801, which made peace with the church but permitted considerable government regulation of its affairs.

Napoleon's religious policy, including toleration of active religious, was based on purely pragmatic considerations—the need to stabilize his regime and remedy the chaotic postrevolutionary state of French charitable and educational institutions. He also understood the need for women's labor and that it could easily be exploited. Local officials took the lead in recruiting the sisters, recognizing their value, as hospital administrators at Béziers indicated: "With them [the sisters] no need whatever for seamstresses, for a cook, for an apothecary, for serving-boys, or for almost any domestics at all; there are virtually no wages to outside help. What appears as an expense for them is recovered on the other hand with interest by means of their industrious charity." Describing his plan for running local primary schools efficiently, a rector at Lyons wrote to Napoleon: "These *filles* . . . are satisfied with a very modest salary. Moreover, they live more cheaply than a schoolmaster; they have no family to support and they thus devise a way to survive where a male teacher would die of hunger. They are furthermore, pious, respectful, and submissive toward their pastors, who for this reason prefer them to a male teacher, from whom it cannot be hoped to have good work, because there is nothing to offer him in order to attract or keep him."[86] Under Napoleon only "useful" and "compliant" religious communities were allowed to exist and all had to submit their statutes and rules for governmental approval and formal authorization. Napoleon had dreamed of uniting all women's congregations in one single group, but when advisers convinced him this would never succeed, he subjected them to secular authorities in civil and police matters and to the local bishop in ecclesiastical affairs.

Encouraged by the government, most French bishops promoted centralization of communities within their jurisdiction, and in the following years many diocesan congregations appeared. Some sisters, such as the Ursulines, remained in autonomous houses, but the Sisters of St. Joseph gradually became diocesan communities with local houses grouped under a motherhouse and a superior general subject to the local bishop. The largest of the new diocesan communities, centered in Lyons under its superior general Mother St. John Fontbonne, generated the first CSJ missionary foundation in North America.[87] In 1836 Mother St. John sent six sisters from the Lyons motherhouse to the United States to establish the Sisters of St. Joseph in the recently created diocese of St. Louis.

The main initiative for this project came from a laywoman who exemplified the intense religious fervor of many Catholics in postrevolutionary France. Félicité de Duras, countess de la Rochejaquelin, had read the appeals for missionaries and financial aid from Joseph Rosati, bishop of St. Louis, in the *Annales* of the Society for the Propagation of the Faith, an organization centered in Lyons. She knew the Sisters of St. Joseph, having already assisted them in establishing houses in France, and decided to offer financial support to send a group of sisters to America. After obtaining a promise from Mother St. John Fontbonne that she would provide sisters for St. Louis if the bishop requested them, she wrote to Rosati in June 1835 to explain her plan and her reasons for choosing the CSJs:

> I promised God, insofar as he would deign to bless this design, to send six Sisters of Saint Joseph to North America to convert the savages, to teach their children and those of Protestant families, and to convert also those to whom the missionaries, too busy or too few, are able to make but passing visits. . . . [The sisters'] rule obliges them to all the virtues of the cloister, joined to those which exact an ardent charity for their fellow beings. . . . [T]heir spirit of poverty and humility . . . is evangelical. . . . I know a foundation which began in a stable and with only six

cents. . . . [T]his establishment prospered, as well as others begun in a like manner.

The countess indicated the qualifications of the CSJS for the new enterprise by mentioning their multiple activities in "free schools and boarding schools of paying students, large hospitals and homes for the aged or for abandoned children, prisons, help for the poor and the sick in their homes, the care of those afflicted with scurvy and other skin diseases . . . the upkeep of small dispensaries in some of their houses, manual labor, sewing or even the trades. In Lyon they make ribbons."[88] Bishop Rosati accepted the offer and asked that two additional sisters be sent to teach deaf children.

By the time she agreed to the foreign mission in America, Mother St. John Fontbonne, age seventy-six, was a seasoned leader and decision maker. Appointed superior at Monistrol in 1785, she had led her community through the turbulent revolutionary period, enduring nine months of imprisonment and reportedly the threat of execution. After the Revolution she reestablished the CSJ community in St. Etienne and later became superior general of all CSJ houses in the Lyons diocese. Under her direction the congregation attracted large numbers of novices and expanded rapidly to number some 200 foundations when she finally retired in 1839.[89] The mission to America followed an established pattern of generous response to human need. Mother St. John readily agreed to send two sisters for the necessary training in deaf education and began the process of selecting the first six sisters for St. Louis. From the large group who volunteered, the chosen missionaries included Febronie and Delphine Fontbonne, nieces of Mother St. John, Marguerite-Félicité Bouté, Febronie Chapellon, Saint Protais Deboille, and Philomene Vilaine. The two who would follow later were Celestine Pommerel and Julie Fournier, a postulant. The six sisters left Lyons by stagecoach on January 4, 1836, and after brief stays in Paris and Havre, boarded the *Natchez* for the journey to America and their new life.

Although the young French-speaking Catholic nuns who set out for St. Louis in 1836 faced many daunting challenges in a foreign and largely Protestant setting, their heritage gave them certain advantages. Probably most important was the flexibility of their constitution, which allowed them to respond to virtually every need they encountered within the gendered parameters of nineteenth-century American society, whether in educational, health-related, or social service areas. Almost equally significant were the resourcefulness and adaptability learned "on the job" in the varied and sometimes difficult circumstances of CSJ houses in France. The foundation "begun in a stable and with only six cents" would have its parallels in the United States, where the sisters would many times subsist on their own earnings and offer services gratis. Also useful was their experience in dealing with patriarchal authority and the sometimes not so benevolent despotism of French ecclesiastics, for they would encounter similar obstacles in America, where bishops reigned supreme in their dioceses and sisters were perceived as a readily exploitable labor source. Even the hostility of American Protestants was not totally foreign to the French sisters after the experiences of the Revolution and the climate of anticlericalism that reappeared in France with the July Revolution of 1830. In America CSJs would also enjoy the friendship and assistance of laywomen, benefactors like those who had appeared at key points in their previous history. Finally, the vast expansion of the role of women in church and society that began in response to the exigencies of Counter Reformation Europe would continue in the United States in the context of a rapidly expanding Catholic population seeking to meet its educational and charitable needs. As so often in the past, social and religious crisis gave women opportunities to realize their potential and expand gender parameters in both secular and religious settings.

They venerated the sisters as saint[s] and charitable country women coming from the same Mother as them, the Catholic France to have care of their sick, their poor, their children. . . . [T]hey think of them as their Mother. —Sister St. Protais Deboille

2

Creating an American Identity

Survival and Expansion in the American Milieu

For Sister St. Protais, a twenty-one-year-old, French-born novice, the reception at Cahokia, Illinois, was most welcome after the difficult sea voyage and riverboat journey that she and her five CSJ companions experienced on their way to the United States.[1] After the perils of the trip and the culture shock of needing to disguise themselves in Protestant America, the sisters found excited and enthusiastic French Canadians at Cahokia who welcomed and appreciated the CSJs' ethnic and religious backgrounds.

Although Sister St. Protais would live to see many changes, she probably never dreamed in 1836 that the CSJs would need to Americanize so quickly in order to avoid anti-Catholic hostilities, to insure financial and physical survival, to recruit American novices, and to create and maintain institutions and Catholic culture throughout the United States. This was the reality for most European women's communities that immigrated to the United States and successfully established American foundations. In her study on American sisters in the nineteenth century, Mary Ewens states, "Since Canon Law definitions of the role of nuns in the nineteenth century were based on medieval European attitudes toward women, one would expect that role conflict would occur when American women of the nineteenth century tried to live according to them and that various adjustments would have to be made to reduce the conflict. This is exactly what happened."[2]

In the early nineteenth century, Catholic sisters coming from European convents rarely received the warm reception described by Sister St. Protais, or if they did it was often short-lived. For many nativists, "American" meant not only white and Anglo-Saxon but also Protestant. Except in a few eastern cities, American Catholics were a small minority in the United States until the late nineteenth century.[3] However, during the three decades prior to the Civil War, with burgeoning numbers of Irish and German Catholics emigrating to America, many priests and male and female religious found themselves in settings where their patriotism was often questioned and where violence against clergy, churches, and religious was a reality of life. In 1830 *The Protestant*, an anti-Catholic weekly, began publication with the objective "to inculcate Gospel doctrines against Romish corruptions . . . to maintain the purity and sufficiency of the Holy Scriptures against Monkish Traditions," asserting that no article would be printed unless it promoted this goal.[4] Although prior to the 1830s relationships between Protestants and Catholics had been good in St. Louis, *The Protestant* and Eli P. Lovejoy's *St. Louis Observer* denounced the Catholic Church and inflamed passions that produced mobs and threats against the CSJS and other Catholic institutions up until the Civil War.[5] Beginning in antebellum America and continuing throughout the nineteenth century, groups such as the American Protestant Association, the Know-Nothing Party, the Ku Klux Klan, and the American Protective Association had many willing members anxious to stamp out "popery."[6]

Communities of women religious often took the brunt of anti-Catholic prejudice. As women who lived and worked in all-female environments, created and maintained schools and institutions in the public domain, wore "mysterious," distinctive clothing, and took vows of chastity and obedience while rejecting heterosexual marriage, nuns elicited a gamut of Protestant fantasies. Alternatively seen either as captive, docile minions and concubines for male clergy or as uptight "abnormal" women, rejected by males as unfit for marriage and motherhood and allowed to run amuck as "independent" women with masculine tendencies, American sisters had to cope with gender, religious, and ethnic bigotry in a patriarchal society that limited the power and aspirations of many people according to their sex, race, church affiliation, and native birthright. Before the Civil War the CSJs and most women religious traveled in secular clothing to avoid potential insults and harassment that included death threats, convent burnings, and bodily assaults. Sister St. Protais recalled that upon arrival at the Ursuline convent in New Orleans, the sisters insisted that the CSJs change into secular clothing before going out in public because "people would think that some nuns had escape[d] from the convent."[7]

In popular literature, stories of "captive" or "escaped" nuns promised lucrative rewards for authors and publishers. Akin to the contemporary tell-all exposé, sensationalized books about convent life provided lurid and fascinating reading for a Protestant population that found nuns and their presence on American soil frightening, if not dangerous. The looting and burning of the Ursuline convent in Charlestown, Massachusetts, in 1834 proved that such books could and did provoke Protestant ire of the most virulent forms.[8]

Another factor that seemed to place nuns at the flash point of anti-Catholic bigotry was related to Protestant perspectives on what was perceived to be the "feminization" of the Catholic Church. Ann Braude states that Protestant scorn of the "rich sensual environment . . . the cult of saints and especially the veneration of the Virgin . . . retains the anti-Catholic as well as the anti-woman bias of the standard narratives of American religion."[9] Viewed through a Protestant lens, religious statues, holy cards, incense, rosaries, priests in "skirts," and nuns in religious habit symbolized this "feminization."

The CSJs, who arrived in 1836, were not the first community of nuns to bring such visible symbols of Catholicism to the St. Louis area. The Society of the Sacred Heart, the Sisters of Loretto, the Sisters of Charity, and the Visitandines preceded the CSJs, settling in and around St. Louis and across the Mississippi River in Illinois in 1818, 1823, 1828, and 1833, respectively.[10] Soon after disembarking in St. Louis, the six CSJs separated: three sisters headed for Cahokia, Illinois, a French Canadian parish, while three stayed in St. Louis, lodging with the Sisters of Charity and taking English lessons at the Sacred Heart Academy until they could move into their log cabin convent in Carondelet, a village six miles south of the city.[11]

The sisters sent to Cahokia found there a prosperous village and a Catholic population of several hundred highly devout parishioners, who with their priest, Father Peter Doutreluingne, had provided a set of buildings in the center of the village that the sisters could use for a convent and school. Affectionately, and to add dignity to the setting, the villagers dubbed the site "The Abbey," and the townspeople provided for all the sisters' needs both large and small. Sister St. Protais described one "rich lady" who built the CSJs a small chapel so they could "decorate it with ornaments that they brought from France." Likewise, a well-intentioned woman of simpler means brought the sisters "a bowl of pottage of rice gumbeau [*sic*] and chicken." When she proudly put it on the table the nuns were horrified because it was Friday and they could not eat meat. The woman told them it was all right because she had only boiled the chicken in it! Although they thanked her for her kindness, after she left, the sisters "had a grand laugh at her simplicity."

By contrast, the three sisters who opened the convent in Carondelet, Missouri (outside St. Louis), rarely experienced such devotion and prosperity. Carondelet was originally named *Vide Poche* ("Empty Pocket"). The sisters understood immediately the significance of the name. Their log cabin convent, set high on a bluff overlooking the Mississippi River, had a beautiful view, but with the exception of a cot, a table, and two chairs, the two rooms and attic were destitute of furniture. Their first meal was meager bread and cheese that they shared with the parish priest, Father Edmund Saulnier, in the rectory. When the sisters returned the next morning for breakfast, Father Saulnier informed them that he barely had enough to feed himself and they would have to fend for themselves and "beg" the parishioners for food. And, unlike their Cahokia counterparts, the Creole parishioners at Carondelet were not only poor but "had neither taste for religion or instruction."

Although separated by the Mississippi River, the sisters in the two CSJ mission sites continued to see themselves as one community. At first it seemed that Cahokia, Illinois, would provide the financial and social advantages for success, but it was the poverty-stricken mission in Carondelet, Missouri, that became the "cradle of the institution" and birthplace of the American foundation.

Sisters on both sides of the river experienced deprivations and trials both physical and emotional that threatened their survival. The Cahokia sisters had material and social support, but the unhealthy, swampy climate and the unpredictable Mississippi River produced major setbacks for them. The three sisters were chronically ill with "fevers," and all three spent time in Carondelet recuperating. These French women, most of whom came from comfortable, middle-class homes in France, battled illness and something even more powerful—the floods of the Mississippi. The village of Cahokia was nestled perilously close to the river, and the sisters' "Abbey" was its victim on numerous occasions.[12]

Carondelet, located on a hill on the Missouri side of the river, provided a healthier climate for the sisters but offered deprivations of a different sort. In contrast to their experiences in France, where church and state were ordinarily closely associated, the American CSJs could not depend on subsidies or contracts from local officials to help finance their institutions.[13] Financial problems were constant for transplanted European communities that had to learn to survive without wealthy benefactors or royal grants. Spinning, sewing, raising food, and farm work were necessary to earn a livelihood in nineteenth-century America.[14] The Carondelet sisters tried to "grub their field" for food, "but they were not strong enough," so they employed a hired man for the field and created their own industry by making "sacs for powder," selling them for a penny apiece. The school enrollment was small, and the meager accommodations, primitive conditions, and knee-deep mud after a rain limited the numbers of children who could attend. Boarders brushed snow from their bedding, and an umbrella protected the cook stove from rain and snow during the first winter. Students were encouraged to bring their own supplies or bring firewood in lieu of tuition.[15]

In the spring of 1837 the early CSJs were reminded of the perilous environment of their new country. Mother Febronie Fontbonne,[16] who was superior of the Cahokia community, was returning to Cahokia after spending some time with her biological sister, Sister Delphine, at Carondelet. After disembarking on the Illinois side of the river, Mother Febronie missed the path through the woods to the convent. When she did not return, the sisters alerted the villagers of Cahokia. Groups of men gathered with torches and hunting horns in the center of the village:

The chief of the village said, "My friends our sisters are in great affliction, their superior is lost in [the] large forest and we must find her whatever it may cost us. . . . [Y]ou will shout out time to time, have not fear Mother of Cahokia[,] your children are looking for you." [Mother Febronie,] exhausted with hunger and fatigue[,] took shelter in the hole of an old tree recommending herself to God . . . prepar[ing] herself to die. . . . Happily her groans were heard by one of the good and brave Canadians.[17]

A drawing of the first CSJ convent in Carondelet, Missouri, 1836 (Courtesy of Sisters of St. Joseph of Carondelet Archives, St. Louis province)

As middle-class, educated French women, thousands of miles from home, the sisters and their religious community were challenged daily by harsh conditions, an unfamiliar climate, poverty, and isolation. It was a welcome relief when, in 1837, they received two long-awaited reinforcements from Lyons. The new arrivals, Sisters Celestine Pommerel and St. John Fournier, had been chosen to be members of the original group to come to the United States but had remained in France an extra year to learn sign language.[18] With two trained teachers, the community could now open its school for the deaf, which would provide the Carondelet sisters with additional income. Their numbers were bolstered even more with the entry of the first American-born postulant, Anne Eliza Dillon. In spite of the growing numbers and newfound financial resources, however, the CSJs' fragile successes were threatened by other foes: interfering male clerics, nepotism, sibling rivalry, and French autocratic tendencies.

The first such threat came from a rivalry between two parish priests. Assigned as the America-bound CSJs' "spiritual father" before they left France, Father Jacques Fontbonne had accompanied his two biological sisters (Sister Febronie and Sister Delphine) and the CSJ contingent to St. Louis. As a Cathedral parish priest, he visited the CSJs often, particularly at

Carondelet, where his sister Delphine was superior. This upset the local parish priest, Edmund Saulnier, who felt Father Fontbonne was infringing on his own rights as the "spiritual director" of the Carondelet community. Although Saulnier had a reputation for being "eccentric" and prone to alcohol problems, he probably faced a genuine rival in the younger Fontbonne.[19] Frustrated with what he perceived as Fontbonne's usurping of his duties, Saulnier wrote a series of letters to Bishop Joseph Rosati in 1837 and 1838, commenting on the csjs' internal affairs and his dislike of Father Fontbonne. In October 1837 he wrote that "[Fontbonne] comes almost continuously to Carondelet; he is certainly above reproach, but this offends the Sisters at [Cahokia] that he is fonder of his sister Delphine."[20]

Father Saulnier also expressed concerns about what he perceived as the nuns' lack of respect for his authority. Apparently rebuffed by the csjs when he requested that they sing at mass, he wrote the bishop that he only wanted "to express my opinion" to help the sisters reinterpret their constitution, which would have allowed them to sing at mass. When the sisters continued to refuse him, Saulnier wanted the bishop to intervene and require the sisters to "sing for parish mass when I need them." He also mentioned that other communities of sisters had "never complained about my management." Frustrated with the csjs' lack of submission, in one scathing letter to Bishop Rosati he threatened to refuse to have any dealings with the sisters in Carondelet.[21] Although no written documents remain to explain the situation from the csj perspective, the priest's letters suggest that the sisters had power struggles with Father Saulnier over his persistent demands and interference in their internal affairs, especially his insistence on interpreting their constitution in a way that would force them to acquiesce to his wishes.

Father Fontbonne had his own power struggles with the sisters, particularly in Cahokia, where his sister Febronie and her two companions were missioned. Whether Febronie was indeed offended by his attention to the younger Delphine at Carondelet is impossible to determine, but Febronie's companions at Cahokia refused to obey Father Fontbonne, ignoring his orders and going over his head to the bishop's assistant. Furious and utterly frustrated, Father Fontbonne wrote to Bishop Rosati that the sisters at Cahokia "refused to obey my younger sister Delphine [whom he had temporarily made superior in Cahokia]. . . . I must not have anything further to do with the Sisters of Cahokia, and I leave everything in the hands of your Greatness."[22] The sisters clearly understood how and who to resist. The gendered and hierarchical nature of the power dynamics and the sisters' French constitution made Bishop Rosati the ultimate authority to resolve any disputes, giving the nuns some leeway to resist unwanted demands from lesser male clerics.

The CSJS also had power struggles among themselves amid the strains of poverty, physical deprivations, and Americanization. Before the sisters left France their superior in Lyons, Mother St. John Fontbonne, had appointed one of her nieces, Febronie Fontbonne, to the position of superior. When the group divided to staff two mission sites, Febronie was located in Cahokia, and Bishop Rosati appointed the other niece, Delphine, as superior of the Carondelet group.[23] Young and full of fervor, Mother Delphine gained a reputation as an autocrat and rigid taskmaster, zealous to follow the French Rule exactly even in the primitive conditions of the early community and in a setting that demanded greater flexibility.

Sister Mary Joseph Dillon, the young American novice, distressed over what she saw as the tyrannical attitude of her superior, responded in a very assertive way to the situation, petitioning Bishop Rosati for relief. Only seventeen years old, Dillon was well educated, spoke fluent French and English, and came from a wealthy family in St. Louis. Her presence as the first American-born postulant and as the only fluent speaker of English made her a valuable resource for the struggling community, particularly in Carondelet, where the ability to speak and teach English was necessary for survival. Chafing under the rigid French regime of Mother Delphine, she wrote Bishop Rosati in March of 1838, "The Superior requires me to do work, for which I have not strength sufficient. My health is not very good and at times I have severe pains in my breast and side. Mother is forever scolding me, she says as a novice I ought to be employed in the kitchen and that it is an honor for me to teach."[24] In France, a young novice would probably not be teaching and would be expected to perform most of the domestic and manual labor in the community.

Sister Mary Joseph Dillon was not the only novice to resist Mother Delphine's regime. Sister St. John Fournier, who had arrived in 1837 from Lyons to teach the deaf with Sister Celestine Pommerel, wrote to Rosati describing the continuing conflict. She told the bishop that Mother Delphine was upset because "it is the sentiment of all the sisters" that they do not "trust" her but trust Sister Celestine instead. Fournier appealed for the removal of Mother Delphine and warned that if the bishop did not act "very soon[,] all religious spirit will be gone from this house." In a later letter she lamented, "I am so often threatened with being thrown out of the door that at any time I expect it."[25]

This type of assertiveness by the sisters, especially young novices, was unusual, but it proved to be critical to the community's survival.[26] Even Father Saulnier agreed that Mother Delphine needed to be removed, stating in a letter to Bishop Rosati that Mother Delphine's methods were excessive. He wrote that she treated the sisters "like slaves or Negro women" and "though she is a good nun and strictly observant, requires from the sisters more than God himself requires from his creatures."[27] By 1839 Bishop Rosati had heard enough from both mission sites. He limited unwanted clerical interference by reassigning Fathers Saulnier and Fontbonne and appointed Celestine Pommerel as superior at Carondelet, sending Sister Delphine to Cahokia.[28] Novices Dillon and Fournier and the other sisters had successfully challenged gender and hierarchical privilege to force the bishop's hand, first in active resistance to interfering clerics and second in demanding a more moderate, less autocratic superior. After a tumultuous three years the appointment of Mother Celestine Pommerel stabilized the faltering American foundation, and for almost two decades she led the CSJs toward stability, expansion, and autonomy in their new home.

Celestine Pommerel was twenty-six years old when she assumed the leadership of the CSJ foundation at Carondelet. Born in 1813 in Feillan, France, Pommerel was the oldest of four children of a wealthy and highly devout family who provided her with cultural and educational opportunities. She received the habit of the Sisters of St. Joseph in Lyons at eighteen, and four years later she volunteered to receive special training in sign language and to join the mission to the United States. As superior of the American CSJs, she inherited a small and struggling community of eight professed sisters and three novices who were attempting to staff schools at two mission sites in Cahokia and Carondelet.[29] Respected if not idolized by her peers and students, she possessed shrewdness and foresight that not only calmed the strife within the community but also created financial stability and fostered growth in personnel, institutions, and influence.

Early in 1839 the CSJs received monies from two unexpected sources—local and state government. St. Joseph's Institute for the Deaf, created by Mother Celestine Pommerel and Sister St. John Fournier, was gaining students and a statewide reputation. Leaders in Missouri wanted to establish a school for the deaf, but legislators could not agree on funding and location. Using his political connections, Bishop Rosati suggested that the sisters contract for state monies for deaf education until the legislature could build and fund a state institution. In February of 1839 the state legislature

agreed and later that year began sending the sisters annual stipends to board and teach Missouri children at the school for the deaf.[30] In April, the local village of Carondelet, which had no public school, agreed to pay the csjs "to educate in the ordinary branches of English and French languages the female children of the town of Carondelet, from six to eighteen years old." To alleviate hostility and out of kindness, the csjs had wisely never turned away children from the school for lack of tuition and thus made friends, both Protestant and Catholic, in local government.[31] With some financial stability assured, Mother Celestine then began her own projects to add further financial security to the American foundation.

A large contribution from a female benefactor, Mrs. John Mullanphy, allowed Mother Celestine to begin renovation of the convent/school to provide additional space for boarders and for a "select" school or academy.[32] Wisely promoting a "French" education to aspiring American parents, St. Joseph's Academy, or "Madame Celestine's School," as it was popularly called, attracted wealthy local girls and "daughters of Southern planters." Eliza McKenney Brouillet, the daughter of a Virginian, recalled that her mother sent her to St. Joseph's Academy to acquire "a French education in all the purity of the language."[33] By spring 1841 a new three-story brick building welcomed seven boarders, and by the mid-1840s, two additional wings had been added.

Boarding students, day students, deaf students, and orphans all interacted closely with the sisters in the 1840s, and their activities and experiences often intertwined in the multipurpose convent setting that housed an academy, orphanage, school for the deaf, parish school, and living accommodations for the sisters themselves. In 1840 the sisters taught and cared for twelve boarders, seventy day pupils, four orphans, and nine deaf children. By the end of the decade, fifty boarders, eighty day pupils and twenty-eight orphans and deaf students filled the premises.[34] As one of the first students at St. Joseph's Academy, Eliza McKenney (Brouillet), spent six years with the sisters, and her memoirs provide interesting insights about everyday life in the convent and the physical and emotional strains of the early years of the CSJ foundation.[35]

Coming to the academy at age nine, Eliza was boarded in Mother Celestine's room until dormitory space became available. This allowed her to observe the strains of leadership and responsibility experienced by the young superior. Brouillet wrote, "In many of [my] informal visits [to Mother Celestine] I found her in tears." Carrying the survival and future of the American community on her shoulders, Celestine Pommerel must have been burdened immensely indeed.

Brouillet also wrote of the harsh physical conditions the sisters and children endured. In winter, the "cold winds had a high carnival in our dormitory, particularly during snow storms," when the nuns would have to come in the middle of the night to wake the children and shake the snow from their beds. And on winter mornings "sometimes we would have to wait until we got downstairs to bathe our faces as the water in the pails would be one solid cake of ice."

According to Brouillet, the nuns were affectionate with the children and provided encouragement, hugs and kisses, and doting attention, particularly if the youngsters became ill. Because of the lack of space, and probably as a result of homesickness on the part of both sisters and children, during the early years the boarders often took recreation with the sisters, worked alongside them making "sacs for powder" to provide extra income, and visited the poor and infirm with the sisters.

This "relaxed" convent atmosphere was probably unique to the early years as the small CSJ community struggled to survive physically, emotionally, and financially. Tragedy and death were never far away. Young Eliza witnessed the death and funeral of Sister Mary Joseph Dillon and of one of the children, the five-year-old daughter of the "hired man" who had become the "pet" of the sisters and older students. The little girl was so taken with the sisters that she begged to wear a habit so she could be "a little Sister of St. Joseph." The csjs acquiesced, and a miniature habit was sewn to fit the child. At her untimely death two years later, her grieving father begged that his daughter be buried in her "habit"; the nuns agreed, placing her coffin in the sisters' chapel and burying the child in her "religious garb."

The early academy provided emotional sustenance and purpose for the csjs, but it also provided much needed financial support, particularly through the academy tuition. This select school supplied a moderate but steady income that helped pay the bills for the religious community and eventually helped finance other institutional work that was less lucrative. Although the csjs and other women's communities staffed parish schools and boarded orphans, rarely were the sisters paid regularly or more than subsistence wages. The degree of success of early academies often determined whether American sisters and their communities could survive financially.[36]

Even with some financial stability provided by academy tuition, recruiting new American novices was critical to the csjs' success. No European-based religious community could survive in the United States unless it recruited American women. Religious foundations of purely American origin were typically more successful in attracting American postulants because they were more willing to ignore or modify some European customs, particularly those pertaining to class differentiation.[37] By the mid-1840s and after the death of Mother St. John Fontbonne in France, the new French superior decided that no more sisters would be sent from the Lyons motherhouse to the United States. The French sisters were needed in their own country, and it was decided that "young American girls [were] better adapted physically to the severe climate, and better prepared by their knowledge of the language and customs of the country to take up the work of education."[38] Understanding that there would be no more recruits from France in the near future or possibly ever, Mother Celestine and the csjs made great strides in increasing their total numbers and recruiting American women. In response to new American recruits and to encourage more English-speaking novices, Mother Celestine had the csj French constitution translated into English in 1847. By 1850 the community had forty-four members, 36 percent of whom were American-born.

In the 1850s the community continued to grow; twelve more American-born women joined the community, as did ninety-two of European origin, primarily German and Irish. Additionally, to help meet demands for their services, the CSJs requested and received a large influx of sisters from the CSJ convent in Moutiers, France. The American-born contingent was still a minority, but it is important to note that most of the foreign-born recruits (80 percent of those who entered in the 1850s) resided in the United States before entering the CSJ community. Already the CSJs' ethnic diversity reflected the midcentury profile of the larger American Catholic population. This "French" religious community now included a sizable contingent born in America in addition to a large number from Ireland and Germany who immigrated prior to the Civil War, probably as children or adolescents, and who, technically, were first-generation Americans.[39] Mother Celestine's wise decision, made a decade earlier, to translate the constitution into English helped solidify the ethnically diverse community of the 1850s. By encouraging English as the language shared by all, regardless of birthplace, the Sisters of St. Joseph made their community more attractive to American girls and provided a common linguistic identity for training future sisters, particularly for teaching positions.

As the CSJ numbers grew in the 1840s and 1850s so did their outreach in St. Louis. The Carondelet convent and school housed a combination of boarders, day students, and orphans, and in 1845 the CSJs began teaching in an ethnically diverse parish school, St. Vincent de Paul, composed of German immigrants, English-speaking students, and, later, Irish-immigrant children. In 1845 the CSJs opened a school for "colored" children in downtown St. Louis, an outreach project that caused a flare-up of anti-Catholic and racist sentiment. Children of free blacks were taught a general elementary curriculum, along with French and ornamental needlework. After school hours and on Sundays, the children of slaves were prepared to receive the sacraments.[40] The school appeared to be welcomed by the black population as 100 children (mostly girls) attended. One of the pupils wrote, "We felt at home and were happy, because the time and attention of the Sisters was all our own, and there was no one to tease us."[41] This cross-cultural experience was short-lived, however. Within a year the sisters began to receive almost daily threatening demands to close the school. The director of the school, Sister St. John Fournier, wrote,

Finally, one morning as I was leaving the [school], several people called out to me and told me that they were coming that night to put us out of the house. . . . At eleven o'clock [that night] the sisters awoke with a start when they heard a loud noise. Out in the street was a crowd of people crying out and cursing. . . . Suddenly the police patrol came and scattered those villains who were trying to break open the door. They returned three times that same night, but our good Mother protected us and they were not able to open the door from the outside nor to break it down.

After the incident the mayor of St. Louis intervened, and upon his and Bishop Kenrick's advice the school was closed, although religious instruction was continued.[42] The CSJs had come to the United States to teach in antebellum St. Louis, but their "colored school" had to be abandoned if they were to survive in their new American home.

In 1846 the CSJs opened their first freestanding orphan home when they took over St. Joseph's Home for Boys. This was a significant decision on the part of Mother Celestine because it moved the American community beyond teaching into a second arena of service so vital to nineteenth-century American Catholic culture: the care of male and female orphans. Teaching boys and caring for male orphans made the CSJs especially popular with American bishops and local secular authorities because the need was great and some religious orders of women were forbidden by their European constitutions to work with male children.[43]

Buoyed by the growth and success of the CSJ community, Mother Celestine made a bold move to expand the CSJ sphere of influence beyond the diocese of St. Louis by accepting the invitation to send CSJs to Philadelphia to administer an orphan home for boys. This expansion to Philadelphia in 1847 was also significant because two years later the CSJs opened their first American hospital there.[44] Unlike some Catholic sisterhoods who concentrated on only one type of activity, the American CSJs, like their French counterparts, were willing to diversify; by 1849 they were involved in three main areas of service—teaching, nursing, and social welfare. With the increase in membership during the 1850s, the CSJs continued to move into other parts of the country, opening academies, teaching in parish schools, and administering and staffing hospitals and orphanages. Expansion continued north to Minnesota and Canada (1851), east to (West) Virginia (1853), northeast to upstate New York (1854), and south to Mississippi (1855).

By the late 1850s, the CSJ community had planted strong roots in most regions of the United States as the community grew in membership, ethnic diversity, and services provided. Mother Celestine Pommerel had fostered successful adaptation to America by creating new financial opportunities, encouraging ethnically diverse as well as English-speaking novices, and satisfying local and state secular authorities by providing needed services for poor or handicapped children, orphans, and the sick, regardless of religious affiliation. Because of the limited opportunities for communication and travel between the American nuns and their French motherhouse, Mother Celestine also began making plans for a central governance structure for the American community, separate from France, with regional provinces that would function independently but with some direction from the motherhouse in Carondelet (St. Louis). She died in 1857 before she could make this plan a reality, but her leadership had laid the necessary foundation. The eighteen years of her administration had transformed the CSJs from a small, struggling group of eleven sisters to a community of approximately 150 nuns working throughout the United States and Canada in numerous schools, hospitals, and social welfare institutions.[45]

Mother Celestine's death was a tremendous blow to the young CSJ community, particularly at a time when restructuring was necessary and a separate American foundation was being established. Her charismatic personality and sound judgment had pulled the community through rough times for almost two decades, unifying an ethnically diverse group of women around common goals. When representatives of the CSJ community assembled in St. Louis to elect her successor they chose American-born Seraphine Coughlin, a highly respected member of the community for eleven years who was currently the superior in St. Paul, Minnesota. Feeling ill and overwhelmed by the thought of the new task, Coughlin declined the position. Archbishop Peter Richard Kenrick called the sisters together in St. Louis to announce her refusal, deciding to make the appointment himself, which was his right under their existing French constitution.[46] He chose Sister St. John Facemaz, who had come to America only three years earlier from Moutiers, France. She had served as a counselor to Mother Celestine and also as mistress of novices at the motherhouse. When Archbishop Kenrick announced his unilateral decision in the chapel at Carondelet he received a stunning and totally unexpected reaction. Sister Febronie Boyer, who was present at the scene, described the sisters' response: "This announcement caused great excitement. The sisters screamed—threw themselves on the floor, etc. The Archbishop left immediately, even ran from the chapel and would not hear or see anyone."[47] What would cause a well-disciplined group of nuns to react with such an uncharacteristically emotional display that frightened even the archbishop? Unfortunately the sisters did not record the specific reasons for their displeasure, but the known facts provide some plausible theories.

Whoever was chosen to succeed the admired Mother Celestine would have had a difficult task, but St. John Facemaz was probably in a more tenuous situation than most. She had been in the United States for only three years and had not had an opportunity to build friendships with sisters who had spent years of their life developing the American community and personal associations with each other. More importantly, however, Facemaz personified, figuratively if not literally, the more rigid, French regime that Mother Celestine had been able to moderate. The 1857 CSJ community was not the 1836 "French" congregation of its origin. It had become an eclectic band of German, French, Irish, and American-born sisters, many of whom had resided in the United States and spoken English before entering the community. When given the opportunity, they had elected an American-born sister to lead them. When she unexpectedly declined, Archbishop Kenrick had taken matters into his own hands, unaware of the ethnic politics inherent in his decision. Sister Febronie Boyer wrote that "many of the sisters were so dissatisfied that they went to other houses and some gave up their [work]. . . . [O]thers who were not in favor of Mother St. John stayed."[48] Kenrick's decision and its aftermath created internal strife in the community that took years to resolve.

Mother St. John Facemaz was an extremely capable woman who had been a member of Mother Celestine's inner circle, particularly during the last year of Celestine's illness. Facemaz had come to the United States in 1854, after failing to obtain an earlier foreign assignment to India. As mistress of novices, she gained a reputation as stern taskmaster and "in the exercise of her authority, she countenanced no half measures."[49] This reputation and her recent French immigration probably provoked the sisters' fears about the direction and future of a community that they had begun to think of as American.

Although Mother St. John's immediate task was to continue the preparations for general governance begun under Mother Celestine, a tragic event made her life and work even more difficult. Seven months after her appointment, a fire destroyed almost all of the Carondelet convent and school. Ill and bedridden at the time, she had been carried out a second-floor window to safety. This devastating blow placed the CSJs once again in financial peril, and Mother St. John had to direct the plans for general government and obtain funds for a major rebuilding project simultaneously.[50]

Archbishop Kenrick played a major role in encouraging and helping to plan the reorganization of the American CSJs. In a major move toward Americanization before her death, Mother Celestine had worked with Kenrick to secure "mutual agreement" with Lyons for a separate American congregation.[51] She had planned to personally visit each CSJ house in the United States to discuss the plans for general government, talking with sisters and bishops in each of the dioceses where CSJs worked. Because of her illness, the visits were never made, and after her death, Mother St. John Facemaz had her hands full trying to calm discontented sisters and deal with the aftermath of the devastating fire. In 1860 Kenrick and Mother St. John were finally ready to proceed with reorganization and establishing a centralized government.

The issues involved were complex and had to do with Americanization, lines of authority, and gender politics. The CSJs' official separation from France necessitated defining new lines of authority in America. The goal was to restructure the congregation and apply for "papal approbation" (i.e., Vatican approval) of the new American constitution. Under the sisters' current French constitution, each bishop, as the supreme authority in his diocese, had the right to impose corrections, confirm elections, appoint or remove the sister superior, and control daily activities of the CSJs under his jurisdiction. The new American constitution proposed the election of a female superior general who would reside at the motherhouse in St. Louis. Similar to a contemporary CEO, she would have authority over all CSJ houses, wherever they were located, and would serve as the official leader of the community throughout the United States. Provincial houses would be created in regions of the country where the CSJs had large concentrations of sisters (north and east). The houses would be tied to St. Louis and the motherhouse under the umbrella of general government, but each province would have authority to train its own novices and operate its own institutions. St. Louis would function both as a provincial house for CSJs in the Midwest and South and as the motherhouse for general government.

In reality, after 1847, when Mother Celestine had sent sisters from St. Louis to Philadelphia, she had been functioning in this de facto role as superior general without possessing constitutional authority. The new constitution would legalize this centralized authority. Naturally, some bishops who had CSJ houses in their diocese fought the centralization movement. They feared not only losing power to a female superior general but, more importantly, losing ecclesiastical power to another male—the archbishop of St. Louis. The location of the motherhouse in St. Louis would make Archbishop Kenrick the immediate ecclesiastical authority for the leadership of the entire CSJ community if it came under general government, and might thus indirectly give him considerable although unspecified influence over houses in the dioceses of other bishops.[52] To gain further autonomy and stability for the community, once the general government was established, Mother St. John planned to present the new constitution to Rome for papal approval. If granted "papal approbation" the CSJs would come under direct Vatican authority, further limiting the control of local bishops. According to Margaret Susan Thompson, the sisters' fear of male interference was not unfounded as "virtually everything sisters did could be affected by the interference of clerics—clerics whose collective mindset was both patriarchal and European."[53]

Amid this gendered web of hierarchy and power, both sisters and bishops struggled with whether to accept this new authority structure. When in April 1860 Archbishop Kenrick and Mother St. John called a meeting of sister delegates from all the dioceses to St. Louis to discuss Bishop Kenrick's proposals and vote on general government as outlined in their new American constitution, battle lines had been drawn. Sisters from St. Louis, St. Paul, Toronto, Hamilton (Canada), Wheeling, Natchez, and Albany dioceses attended; but sisters from Philadelphia, Buffalo, and Brooklyn did not send representatives because their bishops, adamantly opposed to general government, wanted their local CSJs to become diocesan communities completely under their jurisdiction, forever separate from the motherhouse in St. Louis.[54] Male clerics' resistance reflected opposition to what they understood to be a loss of power. Not only did they not want the archbishop of St. Louis to have any authority over them, they strongly resisted a female superior general who would have anything to say about sisters or institutions in their dioceses.

For the sisters the problem was double-edged. Who did they want controlling their communities? Did they want to report to a female superior general in St. Louis (problematic for some), or did they want to be subjected to a male bishop closer to home in their own diocese who, for better or worse, would have complete authority over their local community? General government and papal approbation offered the sisters affirmation of the unity and stability within their young American community—a coming of age of sorts. Most of the sisters had strong ties to each other, the CSJ community, and the motherhouse in St. Louis. On the other hand, local bishops offered them an opportunity to stay in the diocese where they had developed institutions, networks, and local ties. There was a perception that local bishops could provide a new "independent" setting that might have appeared more "American" than the one currently administered by the French-born Mother St. John Facemaz. Writing a few years later, Facemaz described the attraction of "independence" for some sisters, claiming that some CSJs were "seduced by the attraction of a false liberty."[55]

When in the spring of 1860 Bishop Kenrick presented his plan for general government (his "memorandum") to the assembled sisters, he asked for feedback. Based on the sisters' recommendations, he revised the memorandum, incorporating their suggestions on voting, the election of the superior general, and appointment of provincial superiors. After voting to accept the new revised constitution and general government, the sisters elected Mother St. John as the first superior general. In time, more local bishops withdrew their support for the new constitution, and ultimately, St. Louis, Troy, New York, and St. Paul, Minnesota, remained to serve as sites for the motherhouse, Eastern province, and Northern province, respectively. The Carondelet CSJs had lost all institutions and houses in the Philadelphia, Buffalo, Brooklyn, Wheeling, and Canadian dioceses. Iron-handed bishops from these areas told CSJs who favored general government to return to St. Louis because from now on these CSJ communities would be diocesan, severed permanently from the motherhouse and placed under their direct control. CSJ houses were ripped apart as some sisters packed their bags, left their friends, and returned to St. Louis, relinquishing the ties established through years of work and sacrifice in the schools, hospitals, and orphanages they had helped to build. Regional loyalties often influenced sisters' decisions. The Wheeling community was typical: three Virginians and one Marylander chose to stay, while three "nonlocal" sisters chose to return to St. Louis. Those left behind also felt the pain of separation, but some were angry at the Carondelet motherhouse in St. Louis for forcing the issue. In Wheeling, where the number of sisters was cut in half, one nun lamented, "All that had been done before was undone by the action of the Carondelet House."[56]

The loss of the Philadelphia CSJs had to be the most painful. Mother St. John Fournier, one of the eight original sisters who came to America, was superior of this first CSJ mission outside of the St. Louis area. Between 1847 and 1860 the Philadelphia CSJs had thrived under Fournier's leadership, eventually administering and/or staffing ten educational, health care, and social welfare institutions. The decision to remain in Philadelphia must have been very difficult for her. Probably feeling the weight of responsibilities as superior and mourning the loss of her close friend Mother Celestine, Fournier chose to remain in Philadelphia, forsaking the Carondelet community she had helped establish twenty-three years earlier.[57]

It is interesting to speculate what the outcome might have been had Mother Celestine lived to fulfill her plan of visiting all the houses and politicking with sisters and bishops for the change. Also, had her replacement been a more popular choice with the sisters and less of a perceived threat to Americanization, the local bishops' offers of "independence" might have appeared less appealing to sisters caught between loyalty to the motherhouse and regional ties. Ultimately, though, the bishops had the upper hand; gender and hierarchical privilege gave them unquestioned power within the church, particularly in their own dioceses. Even if all the CSJs in a diocese had refused to be part of a diocesan community, the bishop had the authority to send them all packing, forcing them to leave the institutions they had spent years building.

Not all sisters were passive subjects of bishops, however. In the St. Paul province, for example, one sister, through sheer determination, apparently influenced the bishop's decision. In her memoirs of the St. Paul community, Sister Ignatius Cox wrote that Bishop Thomas Grace was against general government, which "caused a great amount of misunderstanding in the community here and came very near severing our relations with the Mother House to which we were all very much attached." Cox gave Mother Seraphine Coughlin credit for convincing Bishop Grace to accept general government. "Our dear Mother Seraphine was wise. . . . [A]s she felt her strength failing she could not endure the thought of leaving her community separated from the Mother House which had been the home of herself and nearly all the sisters then in St. Paul. She pleaded so anxiously and so earnestly with the bishop that in deference to her wishes he withdrew his opposition."[58] Unfortunately, this was the exception rather than the rule; many of the CSJ communities became diocesan, severing ties with the motherhouse in St. Louis. For the next decade some CSJ communities remained unsettled as individual sisters moved about from Carondelet to a diocesan community and back again. Some became founders of new CSJ diocesan communities in other American cities.[59]

Some sisters never got over the pain of the separation and years later understood the ramifications of this "forced" choice. In the early twentieth century one Toronto CSJ wrote, "I re-echo with my whole heart and soul your ardent exclamation—If only there had been union from the beginning what a grand whole we would make! The strongest body of female Religious, I should say, in America. Alas! That St. Louis did not retain its hold on Philadelphia and the latter in turn keep Toronto and we in turn our daughter colonies. Perhaps in God's good time the mistakes may be remedied, even though you and I do not live to see it."[60]

The CSJs were not alone in this dilemma, nor was their battle with male hierarchy unusual. This divide-and-conquer tactic occurred again and again in dioceses throughout the United States. That is why papal approbation was so important to the CSJs and other women's congregations. It was their only defense against local bishops who felt the need to control and constantly interfere in the internal affairs of women religious. Papal approbation also made it possible for geographically separated communities to remain connected to the motherhouse and the original foundation. Additionally, many Catholic sisterhoods felt that submission to male authority in Rome, thousands of miles away, was far preferable to subjugation to a local bishop who could closely monitor and control every aspect of community life.[61]

Armed with a new American constitution and with some of her community still intact, Mother St. John Facemaz headed to Rome to secure papal approbation for the new CSJ constitution. After stopping in France in the spring of 1861 to solicit financial support for the rebuilding of the burned convent, she eventually reached Rome and presented the English translation of the CSJ constitution to a cardinal of the Roman Curia (papal government). However, he refused to accept it for examination, demanding that it be translated into French, Italian, or Latin. Staying up all night to translate into French the sections most important for approval, she presented it again to the cardinal. A Vatican committee deliberated and decided the entire document should be translated before they would even consider the new constitution.[62] Mother St. John completed this task, and in 1863 the sisters received a "Decree of Commendation," which was positive but provisional, requiring a trial period during which the sisters were to continue operating under general government for several years. More letters of support from local bishops, besides Archbishop Kenrick in St. Louis, were also required in support of the new constitution. Throughout the 1860s, bishops who had CSJs working in their dioceses sent a flurry of letters to Rome.[63] Clearly, had the American bishops not supported this effort the CSJs would have had no chance for success with the patriarchal and hierarchical Vatican.

In 1867 an undaunted Mother St. John traveled again to Rome to "remind" the Vatican of the community's request for papal approbation. On this trip she traveled with Sister Julia Littenecker, who, if one were traveling to Rome to convince European clerics to approve a constitution, would be the companion of choice. Born in Germany and educated by the Benedictines, she entered the CSJ community in St. Louis in 1853 at the age of seventeen. A Latin and English scholar, Sister Julia Littenecker spoke six languages, authored devotional books, and was an accomplished musician who was considered an authority on church music and hagiology. She corresponded extensively with members of religious orders in Europe and America and missionaries in China and Palestine—a true woman of the world.[64] With Sister Julia by her side, Mother St. John was ready for anything. The pair exemplified the heterogeneous ethnic mix of Catholicism in nineteenth-century America: a French-born superior appointed by an Irish-born bishop, traveling with a German-born sister to take their American constitution to gain approval from an Italian pope. Their efforts were rewarded with "temporary" approbation, which became final papal approbation ten years later.[65]

In the midst of the internal battles over the new American constitution and general government, the CSJs found themselves spectators and participants in a larger struggle—the American Civil War. When Mother St. John Facemaz returned from her first visit to Rome in 1861, she found St. Louis under martial law. Fearing for the CSJs in the Deep South, she recalled the sisters from Sulphur Springs, Mississippi. The Mississippi academy had lost most of its students when anxious parents requested their children's return before the outbreak of hostilities in the area. Having expected to expand missions in the South, the CSJs reluctantly left their Mississippi convent/school and attempted to return to St. Louis. Union army blockades made train travel in the South difficult, so the sisters had to travel to Louisville, Kentucky, to make railroad connections back to St. Louis. Because of anti-Catholic sentiment, travel to and from Mississippi had never been pleasant, but the nuns found their return trip less frightening than their initial one, during which they were verbally harassed and spit upon. Arriving in Louisville amid hundreds of Union troops, Sister Mary Louis Lynch recalled, "We were looked upon and treated as spies. When we arrived at the dividing line, soldiers in uniform came hurriedly into the car, opened our trunks and baggage, and even examined our lunch basket. They took a sealed letter which Sister [Emerentia Bonnefoy] had written to her home, opened it and examined it carefully." The letter, which was written in French, was passed from soldiers to officers and finally returned undeciphered much to the sisters' private amusement.[66]

In St. Louis and at their boarding school, St. Joseph's Academy, the CSJs needed to maintain neutrality in a divided city. Because of its location in a border state, the academy's student population included both northern and southern sympathizers. Sister Winifred Sullivan, Irish-born but a convert to Catholicism while growing up in Ohio, understood the need for neutrality and tact. As superior at the academy in 1863 she played a diplomat's role, allowing students to demonstrate loyalties on both sides of the issue. In a city occupied by Union troops, the red, white, and blue academy uniforms provided ample cover for private dissenters.[67]

Most scholars argue strongly that the actions of women religious during the Civil War did much to alleviate anti-Catholic sentiments. The war, a four-year struggle with which they could identify and in which they could participate, gave the sisters an opportunity to "feel" and "act" American. Both CSJs and students from the academy in St. Louis provided needlework and sewing for various aid societies that cared for the wounded, and the sisters provided food to poor families whose husbands or fathers were serving in the military. "The number of these families amounted at times to forty who daily received assistance at the convent."[68]

Nursing provided nuns with a visible public activity that broke down stereotypes and earned Protestant admiration both north and south. Since CSJs and other women religious had been operating hospitals prior to 1861, some scholars argue that nuns were the only experienced nurses before the war began.[69] One in five Civil War nurses were nuns, and similar to many other religious orders of women, the CSJs in Philadelphia and Wheeling provided care for soldiers during the war. Protestant prejudice remained strong, and many soldiers who had never seen a nun reacted initially with hostility, fear, and sometimes violence against the sisters. As the war progressed this negative attitude abated, particularly among wounded men and army doctors who worked with the sisters.[70] Wartime activities gained public recognition and commendations for many women religious. Mother de Chantal Keating of the CSJ community in Wheeling received a "bronze medal" from the Grand Army of the Republic in honor of her work as an army nurse. Ever the American and patriot, the Irish-born sister wore her war medal on her habit each Memorial Day until the day she died.[71] The war seemed to solidify the CSJs' American identity, which was reinforced through their continued recruitment of American-born sisters and ongoing rapid expansion, in spite of the loss of the diocesan communities.

Although French-born Mother St. John Facemaz was reelected as superior general in 1866, the community was changing swiftly. American-born Agatha Guthrie was elected assistant superior general, and of the 228 women who entered the community in the 1860s, 46 percent were American-born. With their ranks growing, csjs continued to open missions in other parts of the country and other states, including Illinois, Michigan, Tennessee, Arizona territory, and western Missouri, and in other regions in Minnesota and upstate New York.[72]

By the time of the 1872 election for superior general, the success of the American community seemed assured. In an almost unanimous vote, the csjs placed American-born Agatha Guthrie at the helm of a community in which half of its members had been born in the United States. The csjs had an American constitution and an Americanized customs book that educated and prepared aspiring candidates for community life. In some ways, Mother Agatha Guthrie was the quintessential American superior general, epitomizing what the csjs had become and symbolizing their future. And she had impressive American credentials: Born in Bradford County, Pennsylvania, in 1829, Minerva Guthrie came from a Protestant family whose roots dated back to eighteenth-century Boston, and her grandfather and great uncle fought at Bunker Hill. Enjoying "a well-sung Methodist hymn," she had adopted the religion of her mother until she developed a close friendship with an Irish Catholic woman at a select school in St. Louis where they both were teaching. Baptized and converted to Catholicism, three years later and against her mother's wishes she presented herself at the Carondelet convent clad in "a modish gown of pink." Unabashed as she made her flashy entrance at the convent door, the twenty-one year old received the habit in 1850 and worked at missions in St. Louis, Wheeling, and Troy, New York. After general government was instituted she was appointed as the first provincial superior of the Troy (Eastern) province.[73]

Besides her American credentials, extensive education, and broad experience, Guthrie's personal qualities made her a favorite and effective leader. Known for her commanding presence but also for her sense of humor, she was a "good listener" who provided "clever sallies and a most enjoyable wit" sometimes at the expense of herself and other sisters. Some of Guthrie's sayings have become community legend. She explained away any of her eccentricities by claiming, "It's the Protestant in me." When a young sister, unaware of Mother Agatha's conversion, commented to her, "I think there is always something queer about converts, don't you?," Mother Agatha, without hesitating, deadpanned, "Yes, I do."[74]

Until her death in 1904, Mother Agatha Guthrie, with mostly American-born counselors at her side, offered stability and leadership that continued for thirty-two years. Her election guaranteed the ongoing American transformation of the CSJ community. After struggling for over three decades, the CSJs had come of age, surviving early turbulence and unrest and thriving in their American home. Armed with an American constitution and a general government that provided some autonomy and a partial buffer against clerical interference, they had relinquished their French identity by diversifying their community's ethnicity and class even as they continued their French tradition of service in education, nursing, and social welfare, adapted to the American setting. Although their Catholicism still made them foreign to much of the Protestant majority, their adaptation and service-oriented activities had enabled them to carve a niche in American society and public life that reduced Protestant bigotry and supported the growing Catholic population. It was in this environment that young women entering the CSJ community would be educated and trained, molded to become a part of a larger collective identity and purpose, and primed to be shapers of Catholic culture and American life.

[A] prime attraction of convents was a way of life which gave
women, who would otherwise have had no such possibilities,
an access to effect change, a prominent and active role—in
short, a vocation in the world. Sisterhood was seen as a great
undertaking in the service of an active and enthusiastic faith.
—*A Passion for Friends*

3

Educating the Good Sister

Gender and Religious Identity

For nineteenth- and early-twentieth-century Catholic women, having a
"vocation" or a calling to religious life meant leaving their families,
renouncing their former lives, and embracing a new life of religious identity and consciousness. The adolescents and young women who responded to this "call from God" entered into a female world of ritual,
commitment, and service. They were asked to become "dead to the
world," to vow to live a life of poverty, chastity, and obedience. The community became the mother, the sister, and the teacher who fed, clothed,
supported, and educated them, preparing them for a physical existence of
prayer and service that was to be lived in preparation for the spiritual life
to come. To become a csj the candidates were required to "practice a profound humility, . . . endeavor to act from the supernatural motives of faith,
of hope, and of divine love," and "devote themselves to the service of

their neighbor."[1] For active or "apostolic" communities like the csjs, women joined the order to work actively in the world in education, nursing, or social service, combining religious fervor and ideals with public service.[2] This convent education and culture trained thousands of American sisters who, in turn, spent a lifetime engaged in caregiving activities that shaped the educational and cultural lives of American Catholics in every region of the nation.

Contrary to nineteenth-century Protestant rhetoric describing kidnapped and coerced nuns, American women made their own decisions to enter religious life, and many decided early about their future vocation. Although families varied in their support of daughters who made this choice, some young women "knew" at an early age that this was their calling, while others described a significant person or event that powerfully motivated their decision. Family considerations and connections played an important role for some. For the Littenecker sisters of St. Louis and the O'Gorman sisters of Oswego, New York, joining the csjs became a family tradition when three Littenecker sisters entered in an eight-year span beginning in 1853 and the five O'Gorman sisters entered the csjs between 1862 and 1890.[3] Sister Grace Aurelia Flanagan first experienced convent life in the 1890s, when at age five she began visiting her csj aunt in a Toronto convent. In 1917, Sister Guadalupe Apodaca entered the convent to fulfill her "mother's vocation" since her mother as a young woman had been unable to join a religious community.[4]

For other csjs their decision to enter religious life came from other sources. Some sisters told of an almost mystical experience occurring during mass or at the death of a loved one that influenced their choice. In the late 1890s Sister Charitina Flynn was a student at St. Joseph's Academy in St. Louis when she had a life-altering experience. During chapel one day she distinctly heard a voice say: "I want you to be a Sister of St. Joseph." For weeks she could think of nothing else and finally decided to enter the community, but her widowed mother was adamantly opposed to her daughter's decision. One year later she left her mother's home to teach in another town. Later she visited her mother for the last time and left for St. Louis to enter the community without her mother's permission.[5] Her mother's negative reaction demonstrates the seriousness and permanence that such a decision meant for the candidate and the family left behind.

Besides family considerations and spiritual experiences, interactions with sisters who taught them in school influenced many young women to become csjs. They often saw the life of sisters as an alternative to more

Three members of the Ireland family (*left to right*): Sister St. John Ireland, Sister Celestine Howard, and Sister Seraphine Ireland, St. Paul, Minnesota, 1880s (Courtesy of Sisters of St. Joseph of Carondelet Archives, St. Paul province)

traditional gender expectations and family life. Indianapolis-born Kitty O'Brien became Sister Anselm when life at home and at a university did not appeal to her: "In the fall [1914], I enrolled at Butler University, but regardless of how ardently everyone tried to build up my enthusiasm, I hated it. I felt that I didn't belong. As soon as classes were dismissed I'd run to Holy Angels School and talk with Sister Ethna. There I could feel peace. I was comfortable with her and the sisters. Even at home, no matter how desperately I tried to be a part of all that was happening, my thoughts were somewhere else."[6]

Family life, spiritual experiences, and the presence of alternative female role models provided motivations for many young women of all religious traditions to achieve or pursue an endeavor that at times might have been at odds with more traditional societal or family expectations. In fact, one scholar has argued that by devoting their lives to God, women received "cultural and theological legitimacy in making decisions and expanding work in the public sphere for which they would otherwise have no claim against familial pressure."[7] If one imposes contemporary values and attitudes on these motivations, one may miss the point about the significance of this decision. Women have historically struggled to find a place in reli-

Educating the Good Sister | 69

gious traditions that have elevated men to "divine" status as definers and gatekeepers of religious rituals, symbols, and authority. Women have fought for autonomy and meaning against sacrosanct prescriptions that have attempted to control female behavior in both private and public settings. This seems to have been particularly true when women attempted to claim sacred space or agency in an effort to live out their religious ideals.[8] Between 1836 and 1920 (and beyond), though race, class, or ethnicity may have influenced their choice, women who chose *not* to become traditional wives and mothers and who renounced family interests for a woman-only setting without attachment or subordination to fathers, brothers, or husbands made a singular choice. For Catholic women, an alternative to wife- and motherhood was the convent.

Whatever the defining moment in a young woman's life, most nineteenth- and early-twentieth-century American Catholics, even parents who opposed their daughters' entry, viewed religious life as a "higher" life, which, in effect, provided women with an appropriate alternative to traditional gender expectations. By seeking a higher spiritual existence, girls and women had permission to forgo marriage and focus on a larger life purpose and meaning. Equally important, a religious vocation allowed creative, ambitious, and bright women from working-class or rural backgrounds to obtain education and opportunities that their families could not otherwise provide.[9] Mary Ewens has argued that nineteenth-century nuns "enjoyed opportunities open to few other women of their time: involvement in meaningful work, access to administrative positions, freedom from the responsibilities of marriage and motherhood, opportunities to live in sisterhood, and egalitarian friendships. Perhaps it was this freedom from the restrictive roles usually ascribed to women that enabled them to exert such a powerful influence on the American Church."[10]

In the CSJ community women of all ages and from a variety of urban, rural, ethnic, and class backgrounds came together seeking the new identity and culture provided by religious life. All CSJ constitutions had specific requirements for entry into the community. Each candidate had to complete three levels or stages of formation—as postulant, novice, and professed sister. Although candidates had to be between the ages of sixteen and thirty-five to enter the CSJ novitiate and receive the habit, young women could become candidates or postulants as young as fifteen. The candidates had to be born into a legal marriage and have proof of a Catholic baptism. They should be "virtuous" and "enjoy good health." CSJ postulants were to be free of debt and "old enough to understand well the nature of the state they embrace." By 1884, the required dowry was fixed at $100.[11] The CSJ Profession Book provides intriguing data about the women who joined the order and reveals that at times the prescriptive literature was ignored.

From 1836 to 1920, 3,335 women between the ages of fifteen and fifty-five entered and professed vows as CSJs. Contrary to popular perceptions about religious orders "robbing the cradle" and attracting young, gullible girls to the convent, these entrants averaged 22.0 years of age. This statistic varied little in the eight decades analyzed, with entrants in the 1870s recording the youngest mean age at 20.7 and candidates in the 1910s the oldest mean age at 22.7. Similar to marriage statistics for American women, a significant number of women were between eighteen and twenty-two when they entered the CSJ community, but the majority (57 percent) were between twenty and twenty-nine years of age. As was true of marriage, entering the convent was a lifelong and life-altering choice usually made by young adult women.[12] Foreign-born women who entered the CSJ community were slightly older than American-born women, which may reflect a class distinction prevalent in European convents. Some American communities, unlike European convents, often waived or reduced the required dowry, and sometimes superiors accepted material substitutes in lieu of cash. Foreign-born women who could not afford to join a religious order in Europe found that immigration to the United States eliminated financial obstacles to entering.[13]

The immigrant and working-class status of many American Catholics sometimes made payment of dowry money impossible. Like other American communities, the CSJs ignored this European custom when necessary in order to gain postulants. Concerned about this obvious violation of their newly approved constitution, French-born Mother St. John Facemaz wrote Bishop Kenrick in 1868 about the need to accept postulants without a dowry. Like many other American bishops he understood the problem and told her it would be "undesirable" to discuss the issue with Rome but advised her that the dowry should continue "to be determined by circumstance."[14] Postulant records from the CSJ provinces document that the dowry "problem" occurred in all regions of the country. Some candidates paid one, five, ten, or twenty dollars, but many paid nothing at all. For example, to compensate for their lack of dowry money, the Liengang family of St. Louis "brought over a piano" when their daughter became a CSJ postulant in 1876, while another candidate brought the family sewing machine as "partial dowry." Although some families could afford the dowry, with a few paying thousands of dollars, the CSJ records show that the problem continued for some candidates through 1920 and beyond.[15]

During the earliest years of the community, the CSJ formation process probably varied according to circumstance and need; by the 1870s the method used to shape a new candidate was extremely consistent, varying only with the style and temperament of the postulant and novice mistresses. The three- to six-month postulancy allowed the candidates to observe and interact with the novices and professed sisters at mass, meals, holidays, feast days, and in some work settings.[16] Nineteenth-century postulants retained their secular clothing and were expected to dress "modestly." In the CSJ Customs Book of 1868, the community provided prospects with a list of clothing items to be brought with them and used during the postulancy:

bed and bedding	carpet bag	black dress w/cape
black woolen shawl	2 green veils	1 bonnet, extra dresses
1 dz. chemises	½ dz. towels	24 white handkerchiefs
½ dz. table napkins	½ dz. night caps	½ dz. woolen/cotton hose
4 nightgowns	4 pr. shoes	3 white muslin shirts
white dress	overshoes	flannel underwear.[17]

This was basically a "wish list," since some candidates came with the clothes on their backs and very little else.

After completion of the postulancy, the candidate received the habit (except the crucifix) and her new religious name in a special ceremony of "reception" into the community. The next level or stage of formation, the novitiate, was a highly structured educational experience that assimilated the novices into the community, educated them spiritually, psychologically, and academically, and provided them with a two-year trial period before they took their first vows. Directed by a mistress of novices, the young women were more integrated than postulants into community life; they began to interact with a larger number of professed sisters; and their clothing, behavior, schedules, and activities more closely paralleled professed sisters', although novices performed the major share of domestic duties required by the community. During this apprenticeship period they labored in the kitchen, laundry, sewing room, and throughout the community household, while continuing to receive education through spiritual exercises and classes. The first year of the novitiate was filled with lectures and reading, the study of church history, congregational history, and the

Young postulant dressed as a bride before receiving the habit of the Sisters of St. Joseph, 1880s (Courtesy of the Arizona Historical Society/Tucson, B#4985)

three vows, as well as prayer and religious rituals. Gradually the novices were also taught appropriate "religious" behavior.

Analysis of an early novitiate manual provides an intriguing look at the formation process of CSJ novices. The first section focuses on "General Regulations," which involve the novice's appropriate behavior and religious practices in dressing, washing, eating, and interacting with peers and professed sisters. The second section describes "Things to be Observed During Meditation," where again the focus is on specific practices or behaviors for prayer and meditative activities. The third section, "The Essence or Spirit of the Religious Life," is perhaps the most compelling because it goes beyond behavioral practices and gives the novices a description of the expected and requisite attitudes necessary for a religious vocation. The novice was told that "she cannot expect to be perfect" but should have the "desire of becoming perfect." She had to be "willing to make sacrifices," renounce "gratifications and luxuries of the world," and be willing to participate in "unending labor and toil," being content "with plain and poor accommodations, food, and clothing." Finally, she was told that it was not enough to "possess virtue"; she must "[conform] herself to the spirit of her Order." Clearly the "old" life must be left behind; the "new" life and its challenges must be understood and embraced.[18]

In the second year of the novitiate, the young women were expected to achieve greater proficiency in behaving like religious women (nuns) and were also given a more advanced formal curriculum to prepare them for their future assignments, which most often meant teaching. Sister Winifred Hogan, who entered the St. Paul novitiate in 1879, wrote, "The Novitiate really was the 'House of Study.' We had our regular recitation periods from nine to eleven-thirty in the morning and from two-thirty to four in the afternoon. The curriculum of work consisted of: Christian Doctrine (Perry's Catechism), Reading, Rhetoric, Grammar, Mathematics, Astronomy, Philosophy (Physics without laboratory work), Elocution, Music, Writing, and Drawing." In addition to daily classes the novices took turns reading inspirational or educational material during chapel or meals in the "refectory" (dining room). Sister Winifred called this "an ordeal" because "we could not stand in some obscure corner . . . but we had [to] sit on a high rostrum in the most conspicuous place in the room where the professed members could see and hear us to a greater advantage." Although the listeners were expected to observe silence, this public activity often caused anxiety for the reader and amusement for the audience. One day when she should have read "Examine yourselves and see," Sister Winifred heard herself proclaim loudly, "Examine your *sleeves* and see," much to her embarrassment.[19]

The six-month postulancy and two-year novitiate provided an intensive and powerful life-altering experience for these young women. Cut off from family and friends and enclosed in a self-contained, highly structured environment, they bonded with each other, absorbing community ideals as they worked toward professing vows. The powerful combination of religious ritual, structure, dress, and direct spiritual education molded, shaped, and focused their efforts to fit in and become a part of the larger professed community. This shared experience built an esprit de corps among the novices, although youthful idealism and frivolity could not always be tempered.

As postulants and novices in 1915, Sisters Anselm O'Brien and Cyril Lynch had a common bond: "talent for laughing at almost anything and saying the wrong thing at the wrong time." Periods of "strict silence" were particularly difficult, and Sister Anselm related their dilemma:

Being quite inventive and desperate, it took no time at all until we discovered our own "talking room," the canning cellar. This part of the basement was called the "Catacombs," aptly named, I might add with its dark stone walls and its dampness that chilled your very bones. But [we] weren't motivated by the same fervor as the early Christians, rather it was a fervor for folly as that was the only place where we could really laugh. . . . Unfortunately there were times our laughing drowned out the oncoming footsteps. Often we found ourselves having to ask for a penance for breaking silence.[20]

In reminiscing about her novitiate days, one sister described how her young imagination got the best of her. While caring for one of the elderly nuns, she took ritual practice a little too far. "One night I put candles around Sister Holy Cross' bed and pretended she was dead. The Superior didn't like it. She asked who did it and I said that I did. I said I wanted to give her a bath, and she said it was no way to give a Sister a bath to pretend she was dead."[21] Sometimes the older professed sisters could not protect young novices from "worldly temptations." A superior in the Troy province who endeavored to shield Sister Cecilia Marie Hurley, her young novice, from outside influences normally prohibited her from attending parish activities; on one occasion, however, she decided to take her to the parish play since it was a musical and deemed "safe." Sister Cecelia wrote, "However, there were a few dances, which of course were popular at the time, in the show. Mother was not familiar with them, especially the Charleston. She was afraid I was scandalized. I assured her to the contrary."[22]

Since temptations from the outside world and its influence were minimized if not eliminated, the novices learned to remake themselves and their ideals, assimilating the larger and "higher" aims of religious life. One of the highest compliments a nun could receive was to be called a "Living Rule," which meant that she embodied "The Rule" (constitution), the important document that articulated the ideals and goals of the community and its founders. To form each member into a "Living Rule" was the goal of convent formation, and every aspect of training and environment supported this end. This physical, psychological, and social regime was intended to give candidates the discipline and character to withstand potentially primitive living conditions, loneliness and isolation, and at times grinding poverty and emotional disappointment. Certainly convent training facilitated the group cohesiveness and loyalty required to work for the benefit of others, to build institutions with limited financial resources, and to confront the difficult work necessary to support and ultimately shape American Catholic culture.

A highly structured, educational experience, the novitiate provided a powerful rite of passage for young girls. Anthropologist Victor Turner, utilizing both the Benedictine and Franciscan orders as models for defining and analyzing community process and formation, discusses the stages involved in rites of passage. Incorporating Arnold Van Gennep's work, Turner defines the first stage as the "separation period," where the individual is symbolically detached from her original group; the second stage is "liminality," where the individual experiences a sense of disorientation while she is "in between" groups; and finally, the third stage, called "aggregation," the point at which the society attempts to integrate the liminal person into the new role. Formal and controlled ritual trains the person to accept her new roles and responsibilities. In the convent the desired outcome of the rite of passage was described as "being dead to the world." Turner describes the transition in similar terms, as a process of "death and rebirth" with the individual "fashioned anew." He states that neophytes in many rites of passage dress alike and characteristically are submissive and silent and "have to submit to an authority that is nothing less than that of the total community."[23] The postulant and novitiate periods create these stages of passage and mold the women into their new identity and community as "professed" sisters.

Not everyone who entered the CSJ community between 1836 and 1920 stayed throughout the postulant and novitiate stages to profess vows. Postulant and novitiate records show that sometimes the separation was the young woman's idea and other times the CSJs'. Some entries state that a candidate left because she was "lonely," "homesick," "dissatisfied," or had a "family obstacle." In 1890, twenty-year-old Eva Pherson, of Newport, Kentucky, "went home of her own accord. Cause: loneliness, discontented." Other comments reflect the community's dissatisfaction with the candidate. Illness or a weakened physical condition almost always meant dismissal. The rigorous, demanding life of a nun was not for the physically or emotionally fragile. Ill health, particularly bad eyesight or "sore eyes," was listed on numerous occasions. Seventeen-year-old Rose Gertrude Parker "returned [to secular life] on account of weak eyesight." One candidate in 1906 had "poor eyesight and [was] very nervous." Other comments focused on the candidates not having the "requisite qualities." One had a "hard temper," while another was deemed "very odd." In 1916, one candidate, obviously struggling with the vow of obedience, was sent on her way and labeled "very saucy."[24] The documents demonstrate that this was a mutual selection process and that the two and a half years prior to taking vows provided the candidate and the community with ample time to assess the lifelong commitment and "fit" of each candidate. Although the mistress of postulants and novices knew the reasons that an individual left, the woman's peers were never told. The other novices usually discovered the absence in their group the next morning at mass. Except in private conversations, the names of the excluded would never be spoken again.

Even after the sisters were professed and took vows, convent practices continued to build the sense of community and bonding. All nuns addressed each other as "sister" or as "mother," depending on their office in the community. The leader of the order, or superior general, was always addressed as "Reverend Mother." Historians of women have long realized the importance of nineteenth- and early-twentieth-century boarding schools and other female settings that provided this type of familial nurturing and naming. In these Protestant and secular environments, older girls "adopted" younger ones and were called "mother" by their young peers. Settlement houses created similar bonding relationships, and settlement leaders and colleagues were often fondly referred to as "mother" or "sister." African American churchwomen and other evangelical Protestant groups also utilized the familial terms to denote respect and sisterhood within the group. These female worlds of ritual and interaction provided important environments for molding, supporting, and uniting their members.[25]

In these multigenerational, female environments, secular or religious, younger members cared for older or ill members while the older or mature members provided all manner of educational support, nurturance, and discipline, serving as role models for younger or newer members. In fact, in her discussion of the Chicago settlement community, Hull House, Kathryn Kish Sklar comments on the community's lifelong substitute for family life, stating that "it resembled a religious order, supplying women with a radical degree of individuality from the claims of family life and inviting them to commit their energies elsewhere."[26]

As part of this female support network of postulants, novices, and professed sisters, apprenticeship and mentoring provided important emotional, psychological, and vocational training that formed individual and group identity, enhancing the educational messages implicit in convent education. Apprenticeship was a particularly important part of convent education. After one full year in the novitiate and participation in all the required classes, many second-year novices were expected to begin teaching in the various parish schools or working in a hospital or social service setting.[27] In discussing nineteenth-century women's lives, Carroll Smith-Rosenberg described the apprenticeship experience as a factor that "tied the generations together in shared skills and emotional interaction." The more stable the connection between generations, the more the young accepted the older women's world, expecting and perpetuating a women's support network.[28] The convent environment created and perpetuated this intergenerational bonding and support system, ensuring assimilation for its young members, both novice and professed.

Mentoring provided young sisters with support not only within the convent setting but outside in the public domain. Because the demand for sisters was so great, second-year novices often began teaching, nursing, or doing social service work with very little formal preparation. Older nuns were assigned as mentors to help the young nuns through their early days of fear, anxiety, and unfamiliarity with the work situation. Life at Our Lady of Good Counsel convent on Cass Avenue in St. Louis encouraged mentoring for young teachers in the early twentieth century. Over 100 nuns lived together and taught in twenty-two parish schools. Sister Rose Edward Dailey wrote, "Here the young sisters and many second year novices began their first years of training. It was truly a community of sharing, because here the experienced teachers guided the young sister as she began her apostolate of teaching. . . . Among so many companions, we found many talents."[29] Like the nuns in their convent setting, secular and Protestant women also maintained educational, religious, and organizational environments that provided mentoring opportunities.[30]

Because so much of nineteenth- and early-twentieth-century life was spent in single-sex settings, deep, lifelong friendships were prevalent and seen as quite natural for both men and women. The convent was a place where lifetime friendships formed and where women gave much of their time and energy to each other and worked toward mutual goals. In fact, one scholar has argued that close convent friendships encouraged even greater community achievements. "In a masculinist world and church, a convent community in which women were encouraged to be worthy of each other's and God's love was a powerful motivation for many achievements that nuns have wrought from the early monastic period to the present."[31] Historians of women have described the "homosocial bonds" of nineteenth-century women's friendships that defined relationships along a broad continuum of lifetime sharing and caring among family members or close friends.[32]

However, even in the less judgmental atmosphere of same-sex friendships in nineteenth- and early-twentieth-century America, convent culture warned novices and professed sisters against "particular friendships." A sister was not to be exclusive in her ties to any one sister. Special friendships occurring in a close, communal setting were seen as detrimental to community, potentially divisive, and often an impediment to the vows, not just of chastity but also of obedience. Under a vow of obedience, sisters were often transferred from one mission site to another, and good friends could be separated indefinitely depending on the needs within the community.[33] Writing to a newly professed sister in 1907, Mother Elizabeth Parrott of Los Angeles advised the young nun to "have *no particular* friendships. . . . Now is the time the instructions you received during your novitiate will be called upon to guide you."[34]

Since most Americans prior to the 1920s viewed women as less sexual than men, same-sex friendships rarely had the taint of sexuality that would be associated with them later in the century.[35] Like Protestant and secular women, particularly those who spent time living or working closely together, sisters in the convent setting found that religious life offered an opportunity for enduring friendships and longtime companions. Even with the "warning" against special friends, convent archives document many close ties between sisters who lived and worked together for decades.[36]

Although secular comparisons are intriguing, the religious community utilized a very direct method of education that clearly distinguished it from secular and Protestant women's communities and organizations. As religious women, novices and professed followed very stringent guidelines concerning prayer, mass, and other spiritual exercises. As if in a time warp, American nuns worked in the contemporary public culture but were still expected to participate in a strict schedule of religious exercises, many dating from the Middle Ages.[37] Mary Ewens provides insight on how sisters might have reconciled outdated, centuries-old practices with their active lives in American society: "An authentic spirituality, common sense, and a sense of humor enabled [sisters] to separate the essential from the nonessential. Practices that were anachronistic or silly were looked upon as God's will for religious. That was reason enough to carry them out, however unreasonable they might have seemed to an outsider."[38]

Along with the long, and sometimes physically demanding spiritual exercises, prayers, and meditations before and after a strenuous work day, the novices and professed participated monthly in the "Chapter of Faults." This activity required each novice and professed sister to publicly confess minor transgressions, ways that she had failed to live "The Rule" (i.e., breaking silence, temper display, etc.), to her superiors and peers. If she did not confess or if her confession was deemed incomplete, other community members were encouraged to reprimand her by stating her transgressions in front of the entire group. After acknowledging her mistakes the sister was to "listen with humility to the correction . . . and accept the penance imposed." Similar to public shaming techniques used by colonial Puritans and eighteenth-century colleges, the "Chapter of Faults" provided a powerful incentive for appropriate behavior and an opportunity for sisters to display humility through open confession. The attitude that no one was perfect or above correction included the community superiors as well.[39] This "public shaming" supplemented the required private confessions of transgressions that sisters made weekly to the priest confessor assigned to the convent.

Much of the sisters' training and experience reflected aspects of both traditional gender and religious ideology. Gender ideals associated with Victorian womanhood demanded that women be passive, self-effacing, and self-sacrificing in order to prove their "natural" femininity and to counter and temper their more "naturally" outgoing, self-centered masculine counterparts. As Colleen McDannell and other scholars have noted, Catholic women, particularly in middle-class families, embraced traditional ideas of Victorian womanhood and domesticity.[40] Individuals, male or female, who joined a religious community were trained to embrace humility by subsuming the self within the larger community, working toward the greater good of others. However, unlike male religious, women religious, socialized from childhood in appropriate female behavior, received a double dose of instructions on humility, self-sacrifice, and passivity, since these behaviors were expected and reinforced in both patriarchal secular society and within the context of religious life.[41] The CSJ Rule, Customs Book, Spiritual Directory, and Novitiate Manual consistently maintained the importance of these behaviors, and approximately one-third of the "Maxims of Perfection" stressed the need for humility, self-effacement, and self-sacrifice.[42]

For nuns this meant avoiding "singularity" or the appearance of standing out in any way. Similar to the silent woman behind the man, individual nuns were subsumed within the community. Special talents were to be hidden to avoid pride or any temptation to receive individual accolades for activities. According to CSJ historian Patricia Byrne, for a sister to appear "singular" would be "a serious transgression of good convent manners."[43]

Consequently, most sisters have left sparse records of their personal achievements or thoughts. csjs involved in nursing during wars or epidemics or other dramatic events have rarely written about their feelings or accomplishments unless they had been asked by superiors to do so.[44] Uniformity of dress, manners, and attitudes insured absorption into the community rather than individuality. Priests, especially members of religious orders such as the Jesuits and Franciscans, were also encouraged to take on selfless and self-obliterating behaviors, but as males they received quite different messages from secular society.[45]

Unfortunately, this "requirement," coupled with similar gender messages, prevented nuns from taking ownership of their talents, their work, and their major contributions to Catholic culture and American life. The Maxims of Perfection instructed, "Let your actions be hidden in time, and known only to God. . . . [R]ejoice more when in the eyes of the world it appears that His glory is promoted by others rather than by yourself."[46] In effect this prescribed avoidance of recognition gave male clerics permission to ignore sisters' efforts and at times take credit for their achievements. A good nun would not challenge such expectations. Struggling with religious hierarchy, male privilege, and patriarchal interference, women religious had to appear to acquiesce or remain detached while attempting to control their institutions, maintain their community's autonomy, or even receive simple acknowledgment and recompense for their services. As in the gendered struggles of many Protestant and secular women, sisters could assert themselves only on behalf of others—an acceptable "feminine" trait that women have historically utilized in efforts to gain agency in a patriarchal society.[47]

On the other hand, nuns also utilized religious traditions and symbols to subvert gender limitations and expand their possibilities. In her discussion of the relationship between gender and religion, Carolyn Walker Bynum writes that all human beings are "gendered" and that "no participant in ritual is ever neuter."

> Religious experience is the experience of men and women, and in no society is this experience the same. Gender-related symbols, in their full complexity may refer to gender in ways that affirm or reverse it, support or question it. . . . [M]en and women of a single tradition—when working with the same symbols and myths, writing in the same genre, and living in the same religious or professional circumstances—display certain consistent male/female differences in using symbols.[48]

For example, Protestant women, drawing material from the Bible, have utilized the "androgynous" qualities of Jesus and St. Paul's epistle, "there is neither male nor female: for ye are all one in Christ Jesus," as ways to attack gender limitations and claim "moral authority" and female agency in their various churches, schools, and philanthropic endeavors, legitimizing their presence and influence in the private and public domain.[49] Madeleine Sophie Barat, founder of the Religious of the Sacred Heart, certainly understood the potential influence of women on religion and society when she wrote in the early nineteenth century, "More than ever, the hope of salvation will be in the weaker sex. The men of our time are becoming women; transformed by faith, the women can become men."[50]

Like Protestant women, nuns used their own religious symbols and tradition to create new identities that, as Bynum notes, had the potential to reverse or minimize gender limitations. As nuns, women had the prerogative to identify with male gender and status in certain ways. Names and titles often expressed gender oxymorons. Many sisters' religious names came from male saints or martyrs. A demure, tiny nun became Sister St. John or Sister George. The 1860 CSJ Constitution refers to the superior general as the "Mother General," blending female nurturance with the status of a male military title.

Emulation of male role models also expanded gender prerogatives. Through the prescriptive literature, CSJs were encouraged to emulate the lives of male saints, to welcome the most severe deprivations and even risk martyrdom if necessary. Their CSJ patron and male role model, St. Joseph, provided incentives for patience, stoicism, and hard work. Most importantly, to justify sisters' behavior and at times create space for their endeavors, CSJ prescriptive literature encouraged them to emulate Jesus and his "sacrifice" for others. Although the Virgin Mary is venerated, the CSJ prescriptive literature encouraged CSJs to model themselves after Jesus; the literature is strangely silent on emulation of Mary. Part of the formation process included self-discipline and the willingness to forgo physical comfort, individuality, and other human needs. The goal was shared sacrifice and the development of "Christ-like virtues."[51] This emulation of Jesus' work took nuns into the public domain to succor the needy, wherever they were found.

Even symbols specifically associated with females could be perceived in ways that evoked power and influence. Although committing one's life to virginity and becoming a "bride of Christ" symbolized a "safe" alternative to heterosexual marriage, it also signified a direct connection to the "divine spouse," a role no mortal man could attain. Additionally, this elevated status set nuns apart and effectively "transferred allegiance from worldly men and the larger expectations of women's roles as wives or mothers."[52] In her study of nuns across two millennia, Jo Ann Kay McNamara writes that this "independent" existence has often been perceived as a perennial threat to male control and power over women's bodies and behavior. In response, the patriarchal church has attempted to control these "loose" women with regulations and/or cloistered convents, while secular officials, particularly in Protestant America, denigrated the commitment to convent life, convinced that women could not freely choose to become nuns—that coercion must be involved.[53]

Utilizing two thousand years of history and tradition, CSJs also learned about and identified with female saints and religious women who challenged prescribed gender roles. European convents produced some strong, female role models who defied patriarchal privilege and took on "male traits" by asserting their right to become scholars, mystics, and spokespersons for their faith. They used the convent to write, think, and live autonomous lives even at the risk of punishment. St. Teresa of Avila, one of only two women designated as a "Doctor of the Church," engaged in theological discourse when this was forbidden to women, and she is a particularly important role model for CSJs. Complimenting her brilliance, one of her male admirers stated, "She is a man." Comments made about her frequently describe her as "a virile woman," "a manly soul," and "endur[ing] all conflicts with manly courage." Living in sixteenth-century Spain during the Spanish Inquisition, Teresa walked a tightrope of gender and religious orthodoxy.[54]

In addition to the utilization of religious symbols and traditions to modify some gender limitations, another important factor that dominated convent formation and had the capacity both to suppress and to encourage female autonomy was the profession of three vows—poverty, chastity, and obedience.[55] Although the vow of poverty could be used to justify lack of payment or underpayment of their services, it also aligned CSJs with the majority of their constituency, the Catholic immigrant population. The vow of poverty justified harsh living conditions and gave CSJs the strength to endure significant physical and financial deprivations in more primitive areas of the country. The vow of chastity prohibited sexual thoughts or behavior, but it also provided a buffer against male sexual advances as well as heterosexual marriage, and allowed sisters access to isolated settings on the frontier and other male-dominated milieus with less fear of scandal or unwanted sexual attention. They used this vow as many Protestant women utilized the ideology of "passionlessness" to gain moral superiority, public space, and agency over their bodies and activities.[56] Lastly, the vow of obedience provided a double-edged sword of submission and strength. Although holy obedience provided a hierarchical structure in which both female and male dictators could flourish, it also created a barrier to clerical control, particularly for communities that had "papal approbation" like the CSJs. Female superiors and superiors general stood between most individual CSJs and male clerics. When the superior general wanted to say "no" to a bishop she could ultimately withdraw her sisters from his diocese or use communication with Rome (which took weeks, months, and sometimes years for an answer) as a method to stonewall or ultimately refuse a demanding bishop.

Even with uniformity of dress, schedule, values, and training, two factors had the potential to divide a religious community or limit its influence. Differences in class and ethnicity provided challenges for the CSJs as they did for other communities in the nineteenth and early twentieth centuries. European convents maintained a class consciousness that continued with communities like the CSJs that transplanted to the United States. From the beginning this attitude was problematic, for it clashed with American ideals of egalitarianism and equality. Besides the dowry issue discussed earlier, this class consciousness was evident in the convent practice of a two-tiered membership—choir and lay sisters.[57] Choir sisters wore a veil and participated in activities that required some education such as "teaching and works of charity." Lay sisters wore a "cap of black taffeta without veil or band." They had minimal education and were "chiefly devoted to manual labor and to domestic duties" in the community. Lay sisters had no voice in community elections and ranked below the choir novices.[58]

Although one of the six original sisters who came from France in 1836 was probably a lay sister, Bishop Rosati had encouraged the group to discontinue the lay dress because of its unpopularity with American Catholics who viewed the lay habit as a marker of servant status within the religious community.[59] Even without the distinctive clothing, it appears that sisters were working as lay sisters in the 1840s and that the lay habit was reintroduced in the early 1850s. The memoirs of Sister Febronie Boyer indicate that she was a lay sister and that the lay habit was reinstated. Sister Febronie entered the CSJ community in 1848. She was raised by her father in Old Mines, Missouri, where she was a baptized and confirmed Catholic but without the benefit of any formal schooling. She came to the convent at age fifteen, having never seen a nun. "When the community found that I could [recite] the 'Veni Creator' they rejoiced thinking they had received a great scholar and were disappointed that I knew very little." Ultimately, she was given charge of the kitchen, although she had never seen a stove. Sent to Cahokia, Illinois, at the request of Mother Celestine, she was supposed to study when her work was finished in the kitchen. The more class-conscious sisters in Cahokia refused to give her time to study or to allow her to learn to write. Sister Febronie said that once the lay habit was reintroduced, some of the first sisters who received it left the community soon after.[60]

Although the CSJs did not abolish the distinction between choir and lay sisters until 1908, Americanization had its effect in modifying or blurring the distinction between the two classes of sisters. In the 1847 French constitution, the lay sisters are referred to as "servants." Even though the lay habit was reintroduced in the 1850s, the first American constitution in 1860 demonstrated that the sisters understood the limitations of this distinction. No longer called "servants," the lay sisters, although expected to do domestic work, could, "if necessary . . . be otherwise employed."[61] The reality of the situation was that they were desperately needed to work as teachers and caregivers for young children. Likewise, the choir sisters could also "be otherwise employed," and in the primitive conditions of their nineteenth-century missions, CSJ choir sisters often found themselves engaged in the lower status jobs of cleaning, cooking, and other domestic chores. Even Sister Febronie's duties went well beyond domestic work. During her seventy years as a CSJ, Sister Febronie worked as a teacher of religion, chapter councillor, local superior, and procurator as well as cook, laundress, and housekeeper.[62]

The demands of the American environment, both practical and ideological, eventually forced the CSJs to discontinue this classist distinction. During the General Chapter meeting of 1908 and with strong encouragement from Archbishop John Ireland of St. Paul, who labeled the practice "Un-American," and "antiquated and practically meaningless," the CSJs abolished it, although for many years it remained a sensitive issue until lay sisters were "integrated" fully into the community.[63]

A less significant class-related problem brought regional rivalry and discord. In 1866, Mother Assissium Shockley was appointed as the provincial superior in the Eastern province of Troy, New York. Born of a family whose origins dated back to the Revolution, Mother Assissium was well educated and not easily intimidated. After her appointment as provincial superior she began a massive building project to erect a provincial house/novitiate, even though the Eastern province had little money and only small numbers of recruits. Apparently her building ideas were considered too extravagant by the motherhouse in St. Louis, but she forged ahead, acquiring most of the money through her own fund-raising abilities. Undaunted by opposition from St. Louis, Mother Assissium felt that "the bone of contention seems to have been the introduction of the modern improvements which up to that time were not seen in any of our convents." Clearly the sisters in New York had access to more "modern conveniences" in the late 1860s than their counterparts west of the Mississippi, who probably had different understandings of "poverty" and "humility."

Mother Assissium's class-sensitive superiors in St. Louis were not the only ones stirred up by her plans. The local Know-Nothing Party, fueled by anti-Catholic sentiment, also responded to her ambitious building project. Spurred on by this visible and audacious symbol of "popery" rising on the Troy hillside, their annual event of burning St. Patrick in effigy on the frozen Hudson River took on new meaning with the new novitiate and large statue of St. Joseph looming nearby. Trouble was anticipated the day of the dedication, but Mother Assissium had loyal defenders at the ready. "A number of Catholic men headed by a brawny butcher with a meat axe" confronted the "bigots," and Mother Assissium, the novitiate, and "St. Patrick" were all saved from the torch.[64]

Despite the heterogeneous ethnicity of American Catholicism, ethnic rivalries abounded, and convents and religious orders were not spared from this potentially divisive issue. For some orders of religious women, ethnic problems caused divisions and at times impeded a community's ability to recruit postulants. Some of these orders, particularly Irish and German, retained their homogeneous ethnic identity, and some German orders, hoping to maintain linguistic and cultural purity, expected their English-speaking postulants to learn German upon entrance.[65]

As discussed earlier, part of the reason that the CSJs survived and continued to grow was that they were able to Americanize quickly, particularly in the linguistic transition from French to English. Margaret Susan Thompson points out, for example, that, unlike many communities of women religious, the CSJs and the Sisters of the Holy Cross in Indiana, both from France, were able to provide a "melting pot" of ethnic heterogeneity very early in their American foundations.[66] As evidenced by their American constitution and customs book, the CSJs nonetheless saw a danger of ethnic and class division and took steps to limit problems by adding a clause, not present in the earlier French constitution, to their vow of obedience: "[Sisters] should detest the spirit of independence, of nationality, and of faction, that, laying aside all worldly considerations of personal qualities, and of advantages, which they enjoyed in the world, all pretensions to privileges and favors on account of talents, natural or acquired [they may] labor with perfect union of will to procure the glory of God and the salvation of their neighbor."[67] The CSJ Customs Book of 1917 told sisters that "to question novices and postulants with regard to their station in life, their family or similar subjects . . . is in direct opposition to the religious spirit, which we are obliged to inculcate in word and manner."[68]

In a community diversifying as quickly as the CSJs, attempts to eradicate ethnic and/or class prejudices were necessary to insure unity and avoid, as much as possible, ethnic infighting. By the 1870s, American-born outnumbered foreign-born sisters, and over the next fifty years this trend continued. The American-born/foreign-born ratio remained two to one until the 1910s, when 90 percent of all new candidates were born in the United States. Between 1836 and 1920, the nationality of foreign-born sisters remained diverse and represented nineteen countries. The largest groups came from Ireland, Canada, Germany, and France, but the community also included women from countries as disparate as England, Russia, and Mexico. Although the number of American-born CSJs of immigrant parentage is impossible to assess, an informal analysis of the CSJ Profession Book documents the preponderance of Irish and, to a lesser extent, German surnames.[69]

Further analysis reveals some interesting provincial or regional differences among foreign-born sisters. St. Louis, St. Paul, Troy, and either Tucson or Los Angeles were the geographic headquarters of the four regional provinces.[70] Not surprisingly, the vast majority (72 percent) of Canadian-born members entered the St. Paul province and all French-born sisters entered either in France or in the St. Louis province, where the community began. Three-quarters of all German-born entered in St. Louis, which reflected the city's large German population. The rest of the German-born sisters entered in either St. Paul or Troy. Mexican-born women entered in Tucson, Los Angeles, or St. Louis. All fifteen Russian-born sisters entered the Troy province between 1906 and 1919. Lastly, the large Irish-born contingent entered in all four provinces, but half of the 632 Irish women entered in St. Louis, with St. Paul and Troy also boasting large numbers of recruits from Ireland.[71]

As was the practice of many religious communities in the United States, the CSJs took recruiting trips to garner candidates to help handle the heavy demands of their missions in America. Sisters from St. Paul went to Canada and Ireland to secure recruits, and sisters from Troy and St. Louis made numerous visits to Ireland. In 1898, thirty-seven of the fifty-five postulants in St. Louis had been recruited from Ireland, and eight more entered the following year.[72]

Sister Ailbe O'Kelly was seventeen when she and four friends left Ireland in 1911 with two CSJs who had come to recruit from Troy, New York. Full of life and ready for adventure, the adolescents could hardly be contained by the sisters. Spending their first night in a hotel before boarding the ship to New York, the girls amused themselves by dropping chicken bones on unsuspecting passersby and quickly dropping to their knees to say the "Third mystery of the Rosary" when one of the sisters came to check on them. Later, on shipboard they played pranks on passengers and crew. "We had more fun on that boat," Sister Ailbe recalled. "Everyone thought we were let loose out of an orphanage. . . . [The older nun] was so worried about us. We were having so much fun; I think she thought we were going to fall overboard." After a brief stop in New York City, where the girls "thought the people were crazy" because they were "running and wouldn't wait for nobody to pass or move or anything, [they] were glad to get on the train [to Troy]."[73]

Thousands of young women like Sister Ailbe came to the United States to enter the convent, and many others entered religious life after emigration from Ireland. What made Irish women such good candidates for religious life in the United States? Historian Hasia Diner's book *Erin's Daughters in America* provides some insights into this phenomenon. Diner states that Irish emigrant women outnumbered their male peers and many migrated in "female cliques," as did Sister Ailbe. The young women hoped to escape economic and social factors that made their future life in Ireland a grim prospect. Women left Ireland because "they could not find a meaningful role for themselves in its social order [and] American opportunities for young women beckoned. . . . Ireland became a place that women left."[74]

Other aspects of Irish culture made a religious vocation particularly appealing for these young women. The Irish married later, and gender segregation and celibacy were far more common in Irish culture than in other European countries. The Catholic church, clergy, and women religious were highly respected in Ireland. Irish orders of nuns were rarely contemplative but functioned as activists, working in the everyday world of

Forty-five Irish "recruits" who came to the United States to join CSJ communities in St. Louis and Troy, New York. This is a shipboard photograph of their arrival on the *Pennland* in the port of Philadelphia, 1898. (Courtesy of Sisters of St. Joseph of Carondelet Archives, St. Louis province)

teaching, healing, caring for destitute women and children, and administering all types of social services. Nineteenth-century Irish women were at the forefront in founding new religious orders in Ireland and the United States. As Diner writes,

> These young women, the daughters from the thousands of small farms that dotted the countryside, the daughters of the survivors of the great Famine, saw themselves not as passive pawns in life but as active, enterprising creatures who could take their destiny in their own hands. Although possessed of a profound religiosity that belittled what people could do for themselves to alter the course of human events, the Bridgets, Maureens, Norahs, and Marys decided to try just that.

Irish women were prime candidates for religious orders in the United States, and recruiting trips, undertaken by many religious orders, proved to be fruitful endeavors.[75]

Although the Irish recruitments were successful and the young women seemed to integrate easily into the CSJ community, race remained a barrier to CSJ diversity. The nineteenth- and early-twentieth-century CSJs taught and interacted with Native Americans and African Americans, as did most other Catholic sisterhoods and Protestant churchwomen, but they never made an attempt to integrate their order by receiving Native American or African American women. They did successfully recruit Hispanics, however, which proved problematic nevertheless.

In 1892, Sisters Julia Littenecker and Monica Corrigan visited Mexico to discuss opening a school and to recruit Mexican women into the community. Although the CSJS were making inroads in Arizona and California, ethnic prejudice and the impoverished circumstances limited their recruiting efforts in the Southwest. The Arizona novitiate became the home for six Hispanic novices, but Anglo parents, who did not appreciate the "foreign aspect and primitive conditions," sent their daughters east to St. Louis for their novitiate. After fourteen years, having recruited only a handful of new vocations, the novitiate closed.[76]

Sisters Julia and Monica were unsuccessful in negotiating a CSJ school in Mexico, but they returned to St. Louis with fourteen Mexican girls and women who entered the postulate in 1892. Cultural differences proved to be too much for five, who returned within the year to Mexico.[77] Struggling to make a success of their Western missions and needing a novitiate in the West, the CSJS decided in 1899 to reopen the Western province. After a three-year study the novitiate opened its doors in fast-growing and ethnically diverse Los Angeles. This locale proved to be a wise choice because the new novitiate steadily gained candidates each year, including some Hispanic women from CSJ Arizona missions.[78]

The ethnic heterogeneity of the CSJS made them popular with priests and bishops whose ethnic parishes often preferred sisters of a similar ethnicity. Nineteenth- and early-twentieth-century American Catholic life revolved around the ethnic parish, and the parochial school provided the focal point. Ethnic rivalries abounded, and clergy and sisters had to be savvy about working with individuals with a variety of national loyalties.[79] In 1911, when Sister Mary Eustace Huster told her mother that she wanted to enter the CSJS, her German-born mother refused permission because she did not want her daughter in an "Irish Order." Her mother relented when a CSJ explained that "we have sisters of different nationalities including German and we need sisters who could teach German."[80] This ethnic adaptability and diversity enhanced the CSJS' influence as they were called to serve in small towns and urban centers throughout the United States.

In a way the CSJS had the best of both worlds. By the late 1800s, their ethnic diversity opened doors in many parts of the country, but the pre-dominance of Irish among them provided them with distinct advantages that contributed to their growth and influence and gave them access to power in both the secular and religious worlds. Many Irish American men were attracted to politics and the church. By the turn of the century, many major cities were controlled by Irish political machines that doled out monies for city and state charitable institutions, many of which were run by nuns. Additionally, American Catholic life was heavily influenced by Irish culture because a large majority of the male hierarchy were born in Ireland or of Irish descent. In 1900 half of American Catholics were of Irish descent, but 62 percent of the bishops were Irish, and so were a large number of parish clergy. Among the diocesan clergy of St. Louis, Ger-mans outnumbered the Irish but eleven of twelve clergy promoted to the episcopacy between 1854 and 1922 were Irish.[81] Clearly, power in the church came from Irish connections, and this gave the Irish-dominant CSJs added influence and clout.[82]

Although Irish women flooded into the CSJ community, a few notable sisters born in Ireland or of Irish parentage struggled with the regime and became mavericks or free spirits who left the Carondelet community or founded their own orders. In the 1860s, Irish-born sisters Blanche Fogerty and George Bradley remained angry over the introduction of general gov-ernment and both left the Carondelet community. Sister Blanche asked to be transferred to the Wheeling community, which had become diocesan and separate from Carondelet. Two years later, still resisting centralized authority, she left the Wheeling community and the Catholic Church, "obstinately refusing to accept the dogma of Papal Infallibility."[83] Sister George, a former provincial superior of the St. Paul province, left the community in 1868 with four other sisters who were also disgruntled with general government. She pursued a different track: she left her current community and, at the request of a bishop in another diocese, established a new diocesan foundation with herself as superior general. American bishops were in such dire need of sisters that they encouraged these "unat-tached" and sometimes disaffected nuns to come and work in their dio-ceses. Sisters might leave a particular community, but they could remain vowed religious and start over in a new setting as founders and/or members of a diocesan order. In Sister George's case she became the founder of the Sisters of St. Joseph of Cleveland and one of her companions, Sister Aurelia Bracken, eventually founded a community in Lewiston, Idaho.[84]

Sometimes sisters left to "escape" conflicts with their female superiors, but just as often they left because of battles with male clergy and bishops. Sister Stanislaus Leary, born in New York to Irish parents, had been the first CSJ postulant in Canandaigua, New York. At the time of general government and the split with Carondelet, she chose to stay in the Buffalo diocese. When the Rochester diocese was formed in 1868, she became the superior general of this CSJ diocesan community. In the early 1880s she and Bishop Bernard McQuaid had a "misunderstanding" over some property willed to the sisters. In 1882, he deposed Mother Stanislaus and ordered the sisters to elect another superior. Ignoring the bishop's directive, the sisters voted Leary back into office, but he immediately overruled their vote and installed his own candidate as superior. In a diocesan community, Mother Stanislaus had no alternative but to accept the bishop's decision or leave the community she had led for fourteen years. She left the diocese and went on to found two CSJ diocesan communities and assisted in the foundation of two more.[85]

The case of maverick Sister Mary Herman Lacy (a.k.a. Sister Margaret Mary Lacy) perhaps best illustrates the gendered politics that encompassed the life of a woman religious. Unlike other CSJs who left a community, she had no intention of starting her own foundation, but a series of clashes with members of the male hierarchy resulted in her founding two diocesan communities and helping to found a third. By all accounts Lacy was well educated and multilingual, with considerable business acumen. Physically attractive and assertive, she had an independent spirit and enthusiasm that attracted young postulants. The chronology of events leading up to each founding is difficult to sort out, but her gendered power struggles are evident in various sources. Accounts of two events that precipitated her leave-taking survive. Both incidents probably occurred in the early to mid-1870s, and both involved her challenges to male authority.[86]

While serving as superior at the Cathedral School in Albany, New York, Lacy became embroiled in a dispute among the clergy of the diocese. Her biographers believe that she, as well as several priests, may have been trying to protect a well-liked bishop who had alcohol problems from the attempts of his coadjutor, Bishop Francis McNierney, to have him removed from office. McNierney, who won the dispute and became bishop, ordered Lacy out of his diocese for her insubordination and strong verbal support of the former bishop. Soon thereafter, Lacy was involved in another conflict that also demonstrated her independence, confidence, and unwillingness to be bullied as well as the sexual double standard regarding insubordination.[87]

After working a few years in the Midwest, Lacy returned to New York. While a superior in Albany, she visited a CSJ friend who was a superior in Kansas City. During the visit she was told of rumors that her friend was being "too friendly" with a local priest. Satisfied that the rumors were false, Lacy ignored them until the Kansas City bishop, John Hogan, summoned CSJ superior general Agatha Guthrie to Kansas City, demanding to know why nothing had been done in response to these rumors. After being reprimanded by the bishop, Mother Agatha was told that Sister Mary Herman Lacy had also known about the "scandal." Summoned from her convent in Albany to Kansas City, Lacy met with Bishop Hogan, her accused CSJ friend, and Mother Agatha Guthrie. All were "exonerated" (including the accused priest) except Sister Mary Herman Lacy. Her sin had been to verbally challenge and infuriate the bishop. Apparently during the meeting with the bishop, she made an impassioned argument on her friend's behalf, quoting canon law and directly challenging the bishop's authority. To placate the bishop, Mother Agatha removed her from office and sent her to "rest" until matters calmed down.[88]

Frustrated, Lacy left the CSJs and became a postulant in the community of the Religious of the Sacred Heart in Brooklyn. Unfortunately, during her postulancy, Bishop Hogan of Kansas City happened to pay a visit to the Sacred Heart Convent. He pretended not to recognize her, but as soon as he returned to Kansas City he wrote the bishop in New York, who forced the Sacred Heart sisters to dismiss her. After that she disappeared, and what she did next is disputed by community historians. She appears to have traveled about, stopping with various CSJ diocesan communities that took her in for periods of time.[89]

Records indicate that in 1880 she began a diocesan community in Watertown, New York, renaming herself Sister Margaret Mary. Her community struggled economically, but some of the sisters went on to establish a new foundation in Tipton, Indiana.[90] Battling illness, disappointment, and dissension within the Watertown community, she left Watertown and founded a community in Kalamazoo, Michigan. Soon after her arrival she and Father Frank O'Brien, the parish priest who had invited her to Kalamazoo, clashed. He began interfering in the internal affairs of the community and demanding her unquestioned obedience to his wishes. As a ruse, he sent her on "vacation" with his biological sister and upon her departure deposed her as superior, appointing another sister who would follow his orders. Unaware of his actions, she wrote letters to her community informing them of her whereabouts and activities. Father O'Brien intercepted her letters to the sisters, told them she had run off, and ordered her locked out of her convent when she returned. O'Brien accused Lacy of "disrespect to priests and ecclesiastical (male) superiors . . . criticizing and making light of them generally." Frantic to get her community back she attempted to contact O'Brien, but her letters went unanswered. Unable to comprehend her assertiveness and lack of submission to his authority, Father O'Brien lamented her "queer way of acting" as if *she* were in charge, not himself or the bishop. Ultimately, he wrote her and accused her of insanity:

> I believe, what I have had reason to presume for a long while, that you are insane, and a proper course of treatment at the Asylum is what you stand in need of. If, however, you are sane, no explanation is necessary. The vile language of your letters must be atoned for and the proper penance received and performed. When you express a desire to do this in the proper language of a lady, not to say religious, I will then, and only then, consent to an interview.[91]

Out of desperation Lacy agreed to a mental examination, and the doctor found her exhausted, emotionally stressed but totally sane. She was ordered from the diocese by the bishop and was told that if she returned she was to be treated as "an intruder." Ill, exhausted, and emotionally spent, she wrote Mother Agatha Guthrie, her former superior, who allowed her to return to the Carondelet community in St. Louis and eventually resume her original rank.

The saga of Sister Mary Herman Lacy provides a portrait of the limitations experienced by American nuns. The need for sisters and their labor in nineteenth-century dioceses opened doors for individual autonomy and the creation of new religious communities. However, this "liberation" went only so far since women's power and authority could be limited by male clerics and bishops, particularly in diocesan communities. Like their Protestant and secular counterparts, women religious who challenged male authority often found themselves ostracized and labeled "unladylike" and their very sanity questioned. The entrenched male hierarchy of the American Catholic Church provided a formidable obstacle for nuns who either lacked the political savvy to maneuver through this gender and hierarchical minefield or who simply chose not to play the game.

Religious identity and gender created space for women religious within the parameters of nineteenth-century American life. Convent culture and education provided messages that challenged gender ideology even as they reinforced and maintained it. Similar to their Protestant and secular counterparts, women religious lived in a world of ambiguities that gave meaning and value to their lives and work at the same time that it limited their opportunities. Women who were members of religious communities like the CSJs became a powerful, trained workforce (numbering 90,000 by 1920) who lived in female settings across the country, teaching, nursing, and caring for hundreds of thousands of Americans, both Catholic and Protestant.[92] Convent training and education prepared them physically, mentally, and spiritually to relinquish individual needs and identity in favor of community identity and cohesion. Trained to persevere even in the most difficult of circumstances, they placed themselves on the cutting edge of institution building in the American West and throughout the nation in schools, hospitals, and social welfare settings.

We were quite far from the church and there were not as yet any streets or roads in St. Paul. All they had done was to cut down trees in a row and leave all the stumps. . . . Once the snow came we would sink in two or three feet, or we would walk over it as if it were ice. It was on one of these mornings that the hungry wolf tried to get a piece or all of my body. — Mother St. John Fournier

4

Expanding American Catholic Culture

The Trans-Mississippi West

When the first CSJs arrived in St. Paul, Minnesota, in 1851, the town was a small frontier community, isolated in winter by the frozen and impassable Mississippi River. After spending the previous four years in the "civilized" confines of Philadelphia, Mother St. John Fournier and her companions learned to thrive and develop new skills in the rugged, primitive environment typical of much of the American West in the nineteenth century. As the federal government claimed land from Native American and Hispanic peoples through military campaigns and treaties, women religious, like Protestant and secular women, traveled west and helped build towns and cities in many areas of the United States and its territories.

Although male religious orders, particularly the Jesuits and Franciscans, had been in the trans-Mississippi West for centuries, the influx of white settlers, especially immigrants, created new opportunities and new demands for services. Responding to the opening of lands for white settlement, Protestants and Catholics jockeyed for moral and cultural influence, hoping to save the bodies and souls of Eastern transplants, European and Asian immigrants, Hispanics, and native peoples who populated much of the American West. Lyman Beecher's *A Plea for the West* stirred many Protestants to "save the West from the Pope" and work toward fulfilling the nation's manifest destiny through the spread of Anglo-Protestant influence and culture. Calling the Catholic Church "the most skillful, powerful, dreadful system of corruption . . . slavery and debasement to those who live under it," Beecher skillfully used fear to galvanize Protestants to fund "introducing the social and religious principles of New England" to Westerners.[1] Hoping to promote their own religious and cultural influence in the West, Catholics, with contributions from European philanthropic associations, aspired to support "the growth of the Roman Catholic Church in Protestant and heathen countries, and more specifically, . . . Catholic missions in the United States."[2]

Both Protestant and Catholic women participated in this battle for the minds, hearts, and souls of the multiethnic peoples of the trans-Mississippi West. Scholarship in Western women's history has provided new insights into the gendered and multicultural dimensions of life west of the Mississippi River.[3] However, nuns have remained mostly invisible in more recent Western history and in Catholic histories of the West. Discussing the historiography of Western women and religion, some scholars have noted, "The study of religion has led scholarship in two different directions: the first an examination of the church as an institution and as a community; the second a reading of personal conversion and vision. Within these parameters, whether as witches or as missionaries, women have generally been placed within the framework of American Protestantism."[4]

The experiences of nineteenth-century women religious are critical to understanding the interaction of gender, ethnicity, religion, and class in the American West. American sisters were some of the first white women brought in to "civilize" newly forming towns and other areas of settlement. Male clerics, who usually preceded the sisters' arrival and often had large territories to cover, frequently functioned as itinerant clergy, forced to travel vast distances to serve Catholic parishes and communities.[5] The sisters came in larger numbers and were important shapers of American Catholic culture and public life because they worked directly with the people on a daily basis, administering and staffing some of the first religious, educational, health care, and social service institutions in isolated frontier settings that included both Protestants and Catholics. The scarcity of clergy meant that women religious often functioned as surrogate priests at baptisms, at religious services and ceremonies, and at the death bed. They trained the children, helped the poor, nursed the sick, and buried the dead.[6]

The sisters' ability to accommodate and adapt to rugged, and sometimes dangerous, frontier conditions enabled them to provide much needed educational and social services to men, women, and children in a variety of Western settings, counteracting the often hostile, anti-Catholic attitudes prevalent in nineteenth-century America. Mary Ewens states that "it might well be shown that sisters' efforts were far more effective than those of bishops or priests in the Church's attempts to meet these challenges. It was they who established schools in cities and remote settlements to instruct the young in the tenets of their faith, who succored the needy . . . who changed public attitudes toward the church from hostility to respect."[7] Using their religious beliefs, convent training, and vows, the sisters, by their early presence in the American West, were at the forefront of the development and expansion of Catholic culture.

The work CSJs did to build institutions in three diverse geographic locations and milieus in the West illustrates their adaptability and influence there. First, St. Paul, Minnesota, and Kansas City, Missouri, provide representative examples of the urban West and how the sisters shaped American Catholic culture in settings that began as frontier camps and grew into important regional centers. Second, the sisters' greatest challenges may have been in the Southwest, specifically Arizona and California, where they experienced cross-cultural interactions with Hispanics and Native Americans. Finally, the predominantly male, Rocky Mountain mining communities of Central City and Georgetown, Colorado, supplied their own obstacles.

Urban West

Both St. Paul and Kansas City were "frontier towns" in the mid-nineteenth century. In each place the CSJs were called by local clergy to open a school and provide an early visible presence of American Catholic culture. The sisters, though challenged by the journey and the physical deprivations, poverty, and isolation of the first few years, filled a variety of needs in these ethnically diverse settings. By the end of the nineteenth century, as economic, commercial, and transportation advantages placed St. Paul and

Kansas City on a course for growth, prosperity, and regional prominence, the csjs were deeply rooted in St. Paul and adjoining Minneapolis, in Kansas City and western Missouri. Through their successful participation in town building and a variety of educational, health care, and social service institutions csjs made important contributions to American Catholic culture and public life in the urban West.

In the fall of 1851 four csjs left St. Louis and traveled by steamer to St. Paul to open a school. Although St. Paul (formerly known as "Pig's Eye") is located on the eastern bluffs of the Mississippi River, it had few "Eastern" amenities. During the long winter months the frozen river made travel impossible, and the closest supply station was 500 miles away in Dubuque, Iowa. The territory had been organized in 1849, and agricultural lands were opened to whites in 1851. The newly appointed bishop, Joseph Cretin, described the territorial capital as having "two printing shops [and] three Protestant churches, although Catholics are in the majority." He described the 3,000 souls in the St. Paul diocese as a mixture of "Catholics, heretics and infidels."[8]

To meet the people's needs Bishop Cretin sought French- and English-speaking sisters who were willing to come to the northern and isolated setting to work with a variety of ethnicities, including Native American. Turned down by other groups of nuns, Bishop Cretin invited the csjs, whose ethnic profile and variety of work experience would fit well in his new diocese.[9] With the opening of agricultural lands, Minnesota and the St. Paul/Minneapolis area soon attracted large numbers of people, including Germans, Scandinavians, and Irish. In addition to this population explosion, the twin cities experienced significant economic and commercial growth between 1865 and 1900 and soon became a shipping, transportation, industrial, and agricultural hub for the region.[10]

Similar to the first convent/school in St. Louis, the first csj home in St. Paul had a prominent location on the bluffs overlooking the Mississippi River; but it had little else to recommend it. Sister Francis Joseph Ivory described their "small frame shanty" and "privations of the most severe kind": "We had a small stove on the first floor—the pipe of which was set upright through the roof, around this opening we could count the stars; the rain storms were frequent. When the rain poured down through the roof, we (like the man in the gospel) would take up our beds and walk, but only to rest in the water on the second floor. As there was only one well in the place, and this was generally locked, we often had a long wait for our coffee in the morning.[11]

In spite of the physical deprivations, the sisters persevered, opening the first Catholic school in the territory, St. Joseph's Academy, and also began teaching at the Winnebago Indian Mission, 100 miles north of St. Paul. In 1854, with the large influx of immigrants, the CSJs moved boldly to open the first hospital in St. Paul and the state, although they had actually begun nursing in the city and caring for orphans during the outbreak of cholera a few years earlier. Within three years of arriving in St. Paul the sisters had established an academy, an Indian school, and a hospital/orphanage; and as Minneapolis began expanding across the river, the CSJs extended their activities in both communities, providing multiple services to the two cities and the region.

Over the next six decades as the twin cities grew and prospered, the CSJs became leaders in education, health care, and social service.[12] By 1920 they created and/or staffed fourteen parish schools (plus catechism classes in twelve other parishes), three academies, a music and art conservatory, two hospitals, two orphanages, and a women's college. The CSJ contribution to American Catholic culture and service in St. Paul/Minneapolis encompassed thousands of schoolchildren and hospital patients and hundreds of art/music students, orphans, and young women in secondary and post-secondary education.[13]

Kansas City, Missouri, also began as a "glorified frontier camp" that, according to one historian, even prostitutes avoided in the 1850s. The town was best known as a "jumping off spot" for the Overland and Santa Fe Trails and as a haven for proslavery renegades who made intermittent border raids into "Bleeding Kansas." In 1861 the town's 4,000 inhabitants were joined by Union troops, who established a military outpost after the outbreak of the Civil War. Kansas City boomed after the war when the town won the rights to the economically strategic railroad bridge over the Missouri River that connected the city to Kansas and Western markets; the town's future seemed assured. Like St. Paul in the late nineteenth century, Kansas City grew as a transportation hub and as a center for social, commercial, and economic interests. The addition of the railroad stockyards in the 1880s established the city as the regional center of agricultural markets.[14]

Predicting economic prosperity and an influx of settlers, Father Bernard Donnelly, a local priest, called the CSJs to serve the fast-growing Catholic population. But, however promising the future may have seemed, in 1866 when five CSJs arrived to begin a school, led by forty-two-year-old Sister Francis Joseph Ivory, Kansas City was still a "cow town." Upon arrival, the sisters found unpaved dusty or muddy streets, ugly wooden buildings, numerous saloons, open drunkenness, and frequent fights among a rough and transitory population that included many thieves and gamblers.[15]

Pennsylvania-born Ivory, who had fifteen years earlier founded the St. Paul mission, was an important member of many "advance teams" to new mission sites because of her strong physical endurance, education, interpersonal skills, and her ability to speak English. Arriving in Kansas City by train in 1866, Sister Francis Joseph utilized her years of experience in beginning new missions. Within weeks, she had acquired free railroad passes for the sisters and quickly raised funds for the convent/school. "We took possession of the walls as the house was not furnished," she wrote. "Our first possession was a cow—We got up an entertainment, and in one night cleared Thirteen Hundred Dollars thus we were able to furnish the house in necessaries. Providence came to our aid, that we had no difficulty in getting along on temporals." The sisters' school, St. Teresa's Academy, opened that fall with 150 pupils (girls and small boys) and for the next twenty-five years was the only Catholic school providing more than an elementary education for girls in Kansas City. Although other religious orders had institutions in western Missouri, nuns in habits were still a novelty in Kansas City. As Sister Francis Joseph humorously recalled, once when a group of them were traveling across town, "the people thought we were the Circus."[16]

As was true of CSJ institutions in St. Paul, those in Kansas City grew with the city's population and prominence. In 1874 the sisters opened St. Joseph's Hospital, the first private hospital in Kansas City and one of the earliest in the trans-Mississippi West. Having cared for orphans in all their institutions, they established a separate orphan home for girls in 1880.[17] By the early twentieth century, the sisters had expanded their teaching activities into a number of ethnically diverse parish schools, educating Irish, Germans, Hispanics, and a growing Italian population.[18] By 1920, when Kansas City's population had grown to more than 300,000, the CSJs had established or were staffing many successful institutions in Kansas City, St. Joseph, and Chillicothe. Serving thousands of women, men, and children, Protestant and Catholic, they conducted twelve parish schools, two academies (elementary and secondary), an orphanage for girls, a hospital, and a junior college for women.[19]

The CSJs in St. Paul and Kansas City are good examples of the important role women religious played in town building in the trans-Mississippi

Young girls feeding the chickens at St. Joseph's Orphan Home for Girls in Kansas City, Missouri, 1910 (Courtesy of Sisters of St. Joseph of Carondelet Archives, St. Louis province)

West. In both cities, CSJs established institutions that were among the first in the city and/or state. Like Protestant and secular women who formed organizations and groups to promote schools, health care, and social services, sisters provided labor, time, and monies by caring for children, the sick, and the poor of society. To these raw frontier towns the sisters "brought higher education with its appreciation of culture and the arts, as well as practical science," particularly in the education of girls.[20] Many historians of the West have described the importance of Eastern capital, government subsidies, and the migration of families in creating the urban West, thereby rejecting the myth of the rugged, lone male riding into the sunset, unencumbered by family and society, and "winning" the West. Clearly, institutions such as churches, schools, hospitals, and orphanages helped support frontier families by providing much wanted and needed community services. The sisters' and Protestant women's organizations were important builders and caregivers that helped these towns thrive and grow into urban centers.[21]

Even with gender and religious ideology supporting women's active work, nuns, like their Protestant counterparts, often needed the support of influential males to make their institutions a reality in the gendered and patriarchal world of nineteenth-century America. Similar to Protestant women who utilized the monetary and political connections of male relatives and friends, the sisters benefited from networking with clerics who had the political clout and influence to serve as "town boosters" in the secular realm and as advocates of the sisters' projects in promoting Catholic culture in their cities. In both St. Paul and Kansas City, csjs had male advocates with the power and foresight to provide invaluable economic, political, and social support for their endeavors.

In St. Paul, Archbishop John Ireland played a leading role in csj successes, encouraging, if not propelling, the sisters into prominence and power. Even before his sister Seraphine took over the leadership of the St. Paul province in 1882, Bishop Ireland had provided extensive monetary and political advantages that made the csjs the preeminent female religious group in St. Paul for decades. Nationally and internationally known, John Ireland brought thousands of Catholic immigrants to Minnesota and interacted with an extensive network of powerful men in business, government, and the clergy.[22] Besides providing financial support for the csjs he helped them secure new mission sites and institutions, sometimes by removing the competition.[23]

Father Bernard Donnelly, a local priest, also proved to be a strong advocate for the early Kansas City csjs, although he had little of Archbishop Ireland's national clout. Donnelly was a trained civil engineer whose skills were utilized by early town builders and developers.[24] A savvy businessman whose vision and planning helped shape Catholic growth and influence in Kansas City, he invited the csjs to become the first female religious order in the city and helped provide for their monetary needs, at times using his personal funds to support the academy, and later the hospital and orphanage. For over two decades his shrewdness and foresight supported the csjs' institution building and strengthened the Catholic community and its recognition in Kansas City.[25]

Religious and gender ideology and the support of influential males provided an effective combination for justifying and encouraging women's presence and work in the public domain. And the types of community services that women provided were often seen as a responsibility of the church as well as a continuation of nurturing activities that women performed in their families. Furthermore, since religious affiliation was such an important marker of nineteenth-century life, the religious rivalry between Catholics and Protestants may have aided the proliferation of female institution building. The animosity and suspicion between Catholics and Protestants made separate institution building desirable and often necessary as each group "competed" for clients. Certainly Catharine Beecher and other Protestant educators utilized gender ideology and fear of Catholicism to raise funds for female seminaries to train Protestant teachers to "save the West" from teaching orders of nuns whose success they both respected and feared.[26] In discussing women's push to establish "female moral authority" in the American West, Peggy Pascoe describes the difficulty Protestant women had when they encountered women whose "influence emanated from . . . sources" other than their traditional roles as wife and mother. The behavior and activities of nuns were particularly problematic for women who viewed Protestantism as elevating to the status of women. Through their eyes nuns were degraded as women and "a Catholic embarrassment." According to historian Mary Ryan, Protestant women saw themselves as benevolent "guardians of immigrant children, often of Catholic background."[27]

Likewise, American Catholic clergy and sisters utilized the threat of Protestant proselytizing and bigotry to secure thousands of dollars from European and American philanthropic sources and to justify the need for sisters and their work. Hoping to acquire CSJs for a Western school, one cleric wrote to Reverend Mother Agatha Guthrie asking her to help him save the children from "our arch-enemy and his helpers . . . and accept that school and prevent it from dropping into Protestant control."[28] Such inflammatory rhetoric as well as the real competition that existed between Protestants and Catholics opened doors for nuns and Protestant women to help fund, staff, and administer educational and caregiving institutions. From their initial journey to St. Paul and Kansas City in the mid-nineteenth century until 1920, the CSJs contributed with other women religious to the building of urban centers throughout the West. The CSJs expanded and shaped Catholic culture in locations such as Fargo and Grand Forks, North Dakota; Denver, Colorado; Tucson, Prescott, and Yuma, Arizona; and San Diego, Oxnard, Los Angeles, Oakland, and San Francisco, California.[29]

Southwest / Indian Mission Schools

In 1870 the CSJs moved into a second Western locale that provided physical, educational, and interpersonal challenges unlike any previous missions. On April 20th a band of seven csjs left the motherhouse in St. Louis to travel to Tucson, Arizona Territory, to open a school. This move would open Arizona and eventually California to the sisters, allowing them to continue their institution building in newly expanding towns and cities and on Indian reservations. More importantly, however, it gave the csjs opportunity to work in what one historian has called a "frontier of interactions" or a "cultural crossroads" among the various multicultural groups in the Southwest.[30] Besides encountering a plethora of European, and to a lesser extent, Asian immigrants, the sisters established institutions that put them in touch with a variety of Native American and Hispanic populations in settings where race, class, religion, and gender collided in a myriad of intercultural and cross-cultural interactions.[31] Although the csjs were certainly not the first group of women religious in the Southwest, their experiences provide a good representation of the journeys, deprivations, activities, and accomplishments of other American nuns who worked in the region.[32]

Sister Monica Corrigan's journal offers intriguing insights into the csjs' thirty-seven-day odyssey to Tucson by train, ship, and overland trek. The seven sisters traveled by train from St. Louis to San Francisco, where they boarded the steamer that took them down the coast of California to San Diego. From there they rode and walked for twenty days to reach Tucson. Along the way Sister Monica recorded sights, events, and feelings about her experiences. As in the accounts of many women who traveled west before and after her, it is her personal perspective that fascinates and gives the reader the opportunity to see the West through her eyes.[33]

Before making her historic journey, Sister Monica (born Anna Taggert) had taken a unique path to the convent. Born in Canada to Anglican parents, she eloped with John Corrigan, a Catholic, and moved to Kansas City, Missouri. In 1866, she found herself a widow at twenty-three, her husband and two children dead from diphtheria. Utilizing the college training in mathematics that she had received in Canada, she began teaching at St. Teresa's Academy and within a year had converted to Catholicism and joined the csjs. After taking vows in 1869, she was sent with five French-born nuns and an Irish-born lay sister to Tucson the following spring. Although her newness to religious life kept her from being appointed superior of the Tucson-bound sisters, she was chosen for this difficult assignment because the csjs "needed a woman with more worldly knowledge than many of the others had. Having been in Canada, at the university, and married and a widow, her experience was wide."[34]

The train ride began April 20, 1870, with stopovers in Kansas City and

Sister Monica Corrigan (*third from right*) and her sister companions who journeyed to Tucson in 1870. The sister in the center wears the lay habit. (Courtesy of Sisters of St. Joseph of Carondelet Archives, St. Louis province)

Omaha, Nebraska. West of Omaha the sisters encountered four Protestant missionaries and their wives in the dining car, and Sister Monica noted, "Whether owing to our presence or not we do not know, but religion was the principal topic of conversation. . . . Everyone maintained his own opinion and proved it from the *Bible*, agreeing only on one thing, Catholicity is intolerable."[35] Later in the journey while traveling through Utah, Sister Monica, having some sense of her own preconceived notions, expressed her sentiments about another religious group—Mormons: "They are a degraded looking set, but perhaps it is prejudice that makes me think so." Winding their way through the chasms and gorges on the narrow train tracks through the Rocky Mountains, an excited sister urged Sister Monica to "wake up and take notes" as the "silent" passengers "enjoyed the scenery" but prayed to survive "dangers, terrors, and perils of the place."

Upon reaching San Francisco the CSJs lodged with the Sisters of Mercy, who fortified them with provisions for the sea journey, which included "some crackers and a couple of bottles of liquor." After four days on the ocean battling seasickness, the sisters arrived in San Diego, where they stayed for three days preparing for the final twenty-day trek to Tucson. On May 7th, the seven sisters and their male driver headed east in their covered "spring wagon" into the desert. The heat, desolation, and unknown "terrors" of the desert must have frightened them considerably. French-born Emerentia Bonnefoy, superior of the group, was nearly "inconsolable" when she heard "wolves" howling the first night, fearing that they would eat her and "all of our crackers and tea." Trying to calm her down, the driver said, "to her great consolation and our amusement, that there was no danger as wolves in this country had no teeth." Mother Emerentia was less assured when she was awakened one night by screams from the driver and Sister Martha Peters, who in the darkness had been tending the fire and mistakenly grabbed the sleeping driver's leg thinking it was a log. Mother Emerentia's trials continued when, walking ahead of the wagon one morning to pray, she became lost. The sisters and driver became very concerned and went looking for her. When the driver finally spotted her, he began running toward her and yelling to attract her attention. "When Mother saw the man in pursuit of her, not recognizing him, she was terribly frightened, and ran too, as fast as she could."

At times the sisters stayed at ranches or lodges along the way, but even this "luxury" had its challenges. In an environment where males far outnumbered females, the sisters found themselves in difficult situations. At one ranch a group of men proposed marriage to them, and at another they had to fight off a group of drunken men who "annoyed us very much." At a later stopover, the sisters were forced to share a "stable" with "40 men" who were boarding for the night.

The greatest challenge of the twenty-day trek was the terrain itself and the accompanying physical deprivations and dangers. Sister Monica described the difficult trials they endured—trials that at times may have challenged their faith and resolve. They came upon "thousands" of dead cattle and sheep and a spot where only a month earlier a stage had been buried in a sudden sandstorm, leaving the seven passengers entombed inside. Probably to allay fears and anxieties, the sisters "sang nearly all the time," alternately walking and riding. Dressed in their woolen black habits and veils, they were poorly equipped for the extreme heat and rugged terrain of desert and mountain crossings. An exhausted Sister Monica wrote, "For several miles, the road is up and down mountains. We were obliged to travel on foot. At the highest point it is said to be four thousand feet above the level of the sea. We were compelled to stop here to breathe. Some of the Sisters lay down on the roadside, unable to proceed any farther. Besides this terrible fatigue, we suffered still more from thirst." Blistered by the "scorching sunbeams" and unaccustomed to walking in desert terrain, one sister suffered even more physical discomfort: "One of the sisters happen to wear 'low' shoes. Her feet and ankles were badly scratched, her stockings bloody and sticking to her. On removing her stockings, there were 22 bleeding sores produced by cactus thorns that had worked their way through her stockings."

Relieved to see Fort Yuma, the Colorado River, and water ahead of them the sisters faced another near disaster. To expedite the river crossing they were told to stay in the wagon, which would be secured to a raft for crossing. During the crossing, when the raft carrying their wagon tipped as one of the horses fell, Sister Monica managed to leap to safety. She watched in terror while her six companions teetered over "17 feet of water" before two men with ropes could stabilize the carriage.

When they reached Fort Yuma they were joined by Father Francisco, who had been sent by Bishop Salpointe to accompany them to Tucson. To avoid the heat during the final leg of their journey, the group began traveling more at night; Martha Peters, the Irish-born lay sister, shared some of the driving duties to allow the driver and Father Francisco time to sleep. Approximately seventy-five miles west of Tucson, sixteen soldiers, "some miners," and "citizens" arrived to accompany them through "Apache territory." Once they were within three miles of the city on the evening of May 26th, they were given an exuberant welcome: "We entered the city about 8 o'clock P.M. As we approached the crowd increased . . . some discharging firearms, others bearing torches. The city was illuminated, fireworks in full play, balls of combustible matter thrown in the streets through which we passed, many of them exploding, bells ringing. At every explosion, Sister Euphrasia made the sign of the cross."[36]

The culmination of this incredible journey resulted in the first of many csj institutions in the Southwest. During the next fifty years csjs built and/or staffed schools, academies, hospitals, and orphanages in medium and large cities throughout Arizona and California. Because of the distance from the St. Louis motherhouse, the csj presence and successful institution building spawned a novitiate and a new Western province, its headquarters originally in Tucson and later relocated to Los Angeles. Besides "urban" successes during the first fifty years, the csjs also dramatically expanded their work with Native Americans in both Arizona and

California. They participated in "contract schools" funded by the federal government and worked with the Bureau of Catholic Indian Missions (BCIM) by staffing boarding and day schools. Although they had already administered and staffed some schools for Native Americans in Minnesota, Michigan, and Wisconsin, the CSJs experienced some of their most difficult challenges in the more primitive and isolated settings of the American Southwest.[37]

In 1869, before the CSJs arrived in the Southwest, as part of President Grant's peace policy a board of Indian commissioners, composed of wealthy, mostly Protestant laymen, was created in an attempt to monitor government subsidies to Native Americans more effectively and provide a more consistent educational system for Indian children. Many religious denominations agreed to provide supplies, furnishings, buildings, and other educational necessities to Indian children in return for a fixed annual per capita appropriation from the federal government. To counteract "federal prejudice and to augment their native evangelical apostolate," Catholics created the Bureau of Catholic Indian Missions to fund and oversee Catholic mission schools.[38] When monies became available for these "contract" or government schools, the BCIM lobbied Washington for funds, assisted and helped finance Catholic Indian schools, and attempted to protect Catholic mission schools from "Protestant" interference.[39] As part of this Catholic push to increase and expand work with native tribes, religious orders like the CSJs were asked to send sisters to staff the schools.[40]

The CSJs' work with native tribes in the Southwest began with Papago and Pima children, south of Tucson at San Xavier del Bac Mission in 1873.[41] Four other Indian mission schools followed: Fort Yuma Government School in Yuma, California (1886), St. Anthony's Indian School in San Diego (1886), St. Boniface Indian School in Banning, California (1890), and St. John's School in Komatke, Arizona (1901).[42] Although these schools differed in size and longevity and had varied financial resources and native support, they were typical of many schools run by nuns and provide insights into the cross-cultural interactions of race, class, religion, and gender.

The CSJs had come to the United States with a mandate to work with Native Americans, but funding for this work had always been problematic. By far the greatest share of monetary support given to the BCIM and directly to Catholic sisterhoods for work among American Indians came from one woman—a nun, Mother Katharine Drexel. A Philadelphia heiress who entered the convent in 1889, Drexel founded her own

CSJs and Native American students at San Xavier del Bac Mission in the 1890s (Courtesy of the Arizona Historical Society/Tucson, B#109,287)

order—the Sisters of the Blessed Sacrament for Indians and Colored People in 1891.[43] In her book *The Catholic Philanthropic Tradition in America*, Mary Oates states, "As Catholics generally ignored appeals for Indian schools, Drexel was nearly singlehandedly subsidizing them when government funding ceased entirely in 1900. She channeled most of her donations through the [BCIM], concerned that if the extent of her personal largess became known, grassroots contributions would decline even further and the church would be publicly embarrassed."[44]

Even with the millions of dollars provided by Mother Katharine Drexel, CSJ Indian missions and most missions staffed by women religious barely survived, and living conditions, for both the Indians and the sisters, certainly reflected the deprivations of life at the mission schools in the Southwest. Arriving at Fort Yuma, one sister described the CSJs as "children of 'holy poverty'. [The] Government does not supply furniture nor rations to the employees of these schools. They have to supply themselves."[45] Sisters at San Xavier del Bac "shoveled bat dirt and debris" from their convent/school and begged boxes from Tucson merchants to use as desks for students. Battling with desert creatures for living space, Sister Bernadette Smith described several days and nights of burning pans of sulfur in their sleeping quarters "to oust the centipedes, scorpions, tarantulas . . . which had nested there for years. As a result they began to fall half dead upon the floor from the dried mud which formed the ceiling. When one of these things would fall, the Sister who saw it first would call out its name, then we would run and get a broom or stick and finish him only to find another one soon again."[46]

Letters and memoirs of sisters who worked at the missions described the poverty of the Indian people and the constant "begging" done by the sisters to secure funds and clothes. "The Indians were very poor. . . . [W]e frequently suffered from shortage of food. . . . We had no horse, cow, goat—not even a chicken. There was no well and the water had to be carried quite a distance."[47] Sisters at government schools often faced similar shortages while waiting for promised government supplies to materialize. One sister recalled, "In answer to our request for fifty pairs of overalls for the boys, it was not unusual to receive one hundred pairs in the shipment. Then, at other intervals, our petitions would be of no avail."[48] At St. John's School the children had only one change of clothing, if that, and during their weekly baths "whatever shawls we had or anything that could be called a covering we put on them . . . until their clothes were dry."[49] CSJS used their vow of poverty to justify and deal with their own deprivations, but the poverty and the deplorable living conditions of the people often interfered or took precedence over the activities in the schoolroom.

When the CSJS were not addressing the daily needs of the children and adults on the reservation, they taught the basic academic curriculum used at most Indian schools in the nineteenth and early twentieth centuries. Like mission schools run by Protestants and secular groups, the sisters' schools reflected the prevailing stereotypes held by white Americans in regard to educating Native American children. Viewed as "uncivilized," and "undisciplined," Indian children were subjected to a strict routine with the goal of inculcating white, middle-class values that included "proper" ideas about dress, speech, manners, and work habits—all perceived to be lacking in native cultures. A daily regime of religion classes, vocational skills training (domestic and industrial), and basic education in the three R's formed the core of Indian mission education.[50] Sometimes music and art were part of the curriculum, and the entire structure of the day was interspersed with military drills or calisthenics to insure discipline and wean children, particularly boys, away from "Indian time" and lack of submission to authority.

Vocational classes reinforced gender stereotypes of Victorian America. The sisters taught the academic basics to both sexes and domestic skills to girls; male religious or a priest taught the older boys vocational skills. If no male clerics were available to work with young males, laymen were hired to teach farming, military drill, and discipline.[51]

Many historians have documented the misguided and unsuccessful aspects of this ethnocentric curriculum, regardless of whether it was taught by Protestants or Catholics. Children who succeeded in gaining basic skills and who assimilated some white middle-class values often became alienated from their families and culture only to be rejected again by white society. Many children succeeded in absorbing white culture while at the school but at the end of the term simply returned home to resume their former cultural practices.[52]

Although the CSJs adhered to the prescribed curriculum, when it came to certain cultural and religious practices some sisters clearly showed a degree of admiration for and acceptance of native culture. The nuns attended some Indian social activities and were fascinated with their dances, music, and native games. Sister Marsina Power was enthralled watching the women of San Xavier play a ball and stick game. She admired the colorful clothing, free-flowing hair, and athletic prowess of the Papago women. Sister Marsina attended dinner in Papago homes and described the women as "good cooks" who extended "exquisite courtesy" to strangers.[53] At times the sisters were more than spectators. When picnicking with the schoolchildren, Sister Bernadette Smith wrote, "I took part in their modest little dances which they had taught me. We went in a line one after the other with a certain step and carrying a little branch of a bush."[54] Some sisters also made every attempt to learn the language of the people in order to prepare them better for spiritual guidance and conversion. Mother Mary Aquinas Duffy learned the Papago language in two years, and Sister Mary Thomas Lavin served as an interpreter so a local priest could provide instruction for engaged couples who were to be married in the church at Fort Yuma.[55]

Working toward the goal of Indian conversion, the sisters also may have benefited from both their visible role as "holy women" and the symbols, rituals, ceremonies, and sensuous aspects of Catholicism. Jacqueline Peterson and other historians have hypothesized that the various Catholic statues, rituals, and symbols that so offended Protestant eyes might have been accepted more readily by Native Americans, who sometimes chose to "graft" Catholic rituals onto their traditional religious customs. Although

Native American religious practices are highly diverse, Peterson writes, "It is likely that American Indian peoples responded most positively to Christianity when a convergence of religious symbolism or ceremony revealed itself." She adds that "rosaries" and other "power objects" could "add to the store of sacred paraphernalia revered by American Indian people without disrupting traditional beliefs."[56]

Some CSJs seemed to feel that motivation and fervor might be more important than perfecting the aesthetics of religious practice. As preparation for one Catholic observance, a young man named Venancio was asked to decorate the "Blessed Mother's altar for the month of the Holy Rosary." Venancio was devoted to honoring the Virgin Mary and had spent many hours in the church, caring for the altar and statues. However, the sisters were somewhat surprised when they saw his approach to honoring Mary. "When we gathered there the first day . . . the statue of our Blessed Mother was painted yellow. She had a little straw hat on her head and the ribbons were tied under her chin. The altar was banked with flowers, which were hard to get, all put in tomato cans as we had no vases. This was Venancio's way of doing honor to our Blessed Mother."[57]

The CSJs reported some religious conversions and intercultural successes, but their greatest contribution may have been in their humanitarian activities—the spiritual, material, and medical sustenance they provided for children and adults, particularly on the poverty-stricken reservations. The sisters shared much of the poverty as well as many tragedies of the people and did what they could to alleviate suffering. The sisters baptized, held services for, taught religion and catechism classes to, and officiated at funeral services for Native Americans who adopted Catholicism and some Christian spiritual practices. With a shortage of priests, particularly in the Arizona missions, the sisters filled a surrogate role. At St. John's the sisters had no priest for two Sundays a month, so they would hold "services for our Indians by reciting the rosary and singing hymns."[58] In San Xavier and Yuma death and hardship came often, and when asked, the sisters would "baptize the dying babies . . . sprinkle the home-made coffin containing the dear one, say some prayers, and then go to the grave with the sorrowing ones, speak words of consolation to them. This was done for the older people as well as for the little ones when Father could not be present."[59]

Although the majority of Native Americans living on reservations were not Christian, many of them came to the sisters for assistance in time of need.[60] The sisters assumed a "political" and fund-raising role to secure donations and materials to meet the daily needs of children and adults. They wrote family and friends and cajoled local merchants for money, resorted to "begging" to secure funds or material goods, and served as intermediaries between Native Americans and local whites. As a buffer between hostile whites and native peoples, the sisters may have served as what Peggy Pascoe called "intercultural brokers, mediators between two or more very different cultural groups," thus keeping ethnic hostility and rivalry to a minimum.[61] Taking on this mediator role sometimes meant resisting unwanted government interference. At Fort Yuma, Mother Ambrosia O'Neill corresponded constantly with Washington to secure supplies and had continual confrontations with "inspectors" sent from the Interior Department to check on the "government nunnery" and school. For example, she resisted one inspector's demand that she enforce harsher discipline practices with the children and parents: "He thought we should punish them or lock them up in prison when they disobeyed."[62]

Additionally, the sisters functioned as the only "doctors" during epidemics, and the Native Americans often came to ask for help during these times of illness or disease. During the 1887 measles epidemic at Fort Yuma the people "flocked in great numbers to the mission, begging help from the Sisters." In San Xavier the sisters crawled on hands and knees into native homes that were "so dark inside that it was necessary to feel until you found the sick person." Sister St. Barbara Reilly performed many medical duties during her work at the missions. "The job didn't end at nightfall for a summons might and did come at any time."[63]

One of the more fascinating aspects of the csj experience in their Indian mission work revolves around the construction of gender roles and how religion, race, and class impacted the sisters' activities and experiences. Clearly, the sisters' educational and humanitarian roles crossed gender lines—they functioned as priest, politician, and doctor. More than Protestant women missionaries, they may have expanded gender parameters. Operating in an all-female group, often without the assistance of priests, the sisters were not as restricted by gender stereotypes. Historians tell us that Protestant women also felt a strong call to work among the Indians, but for most that meant marrying a missionary. Most Protestant churches refused to send single women alone or in groups to an Indian mission, which was viewed as too dangerous for them. Single Protestant women usually joined a married couple, living and working with them at the mission.[64] Additionally, Protestant women missionaries carried a double burden of work and responsibility. As a wife and/or mother, a

Protestant woman missionary was responsible for her home duties as well as her teaching or working with native women. Nuns had no such conflict of interest or family responsibilities; they had no need to divide their energies and time between private and public work. Their entire purpose for working at the mission was to focus on the needs of the people.

Even without the additional burden of family responsibilities, CSJs and women religious could not ignore the limitations of gender. The CSJs' fourteen-year experience at the Fort Yuma Government School provides further illustrations of challenges and complications that they faced when gender, race, religious, and class prejudices interacted and boundaries blurred.

Pressured for months by the BCIM to staff the newly formed government school in Fort Yuma, California, Reverend Mother Agatha Guthrie had refused. Primitive conditions, dangerous terrain, and some past difficulties with mission priests caused her to decline. Father Zephyrin Engelhardt of the BCIM, in a twelve-page letter, utilized both religious and gendered discourse to plead his case. He implored her to "make it *impossible* for *Protestants* to gain a strong foothold among [the tribe]. . . . If that school gets into Protestant hands and those Indians become non-Catholic, I do not think Our Lord would overlook that matter." He also assured her that the sisters would not have to work under some "narrow-minded man." He went on to say, "It would be a blessing if no priest were in charge. . . . [T]he priest is not necessary to carry on the school work there." And in a last attempt to play on gender he compared the sisters' work to a that of a "mother, tenderhearted and soothing."[65]

Engelhardt's appeal and a preliminary visit to Yuma by her experienced and multilingual assistant, Sister Julia Littenecker, convinced Mother Agatha to change her mind.[66] Five CSJs, led by Sister Ambrosia O'Neill, arrived in 1886 to take over the school located at a former army post at Fort Yuma. O'Neill had an exceptional position because she was also appointed as "Superintendent" of the school, a job almost exclusively held by men in Indian mission schools.[67] Her initial contact with the tribal chief, Pascual, and the Yuma people seemed friendly, and they began calling her "El Capitan" out of respect for her rank. Local whites, however, expressed opposition to the nuns immediately. A Mr. A. Frank led the attacks, which were expressed in local gossip and the newspapers. Writing to St. Louis, Mother Ambrosia quotes Mr. Frank as saying that "it was against the laws of the country for a woman to hold an office, and more especially a religious one. . . . [H]e thinks we are deceiving Washington . . .

and he would like to know why I did not write my name Sister instead of Mary O'Neill."[68] Two months later letters to the editor appeared in the *San Francisco Argonaut* about the "governmental nunnery" at Fort Yuma that some whites found "galling in the extreme."[69]

With the blessing of the elderly and ailing Chief Pascual, the sisters had little conflict with the tribe. When Pascual died and a new chief, Miguel, was elected, however, intratribal conflicts erupted. Unlike Pascual, Miguel openly opposed Christianity and began withdrawing the children from the sisters' school. Father J. A. Stephan, during a routine visit for the BCIM, attempted to intimidate the new chief. Treating Miguel as a naughty child, Stephan gave him "a good scolding" and threatened to have the "great Father in Washington . . . take the children by force and place them in an Eastern school."[70]

Although angry and insulted, Miguel appeared to soften his resistance for a while, but after two epidemics (measles and typhoid) and increased government indifference, he blamed the CSJs when he failed to be re-elected chief in 1893. In an attempt to punish the sisters and assert his authority, he took thirty older girls, ages twelve to seventeen, from the convent school and sold them as prostitutes to white men, profiting five to twelve dollars a girl.[71] The CSJs were devastated, and conflict continued to escalate. As further revenge, Miguel had planned to murder Mother Ambrosia, but Yumans loyal to the sisters hid her outside the fort and repelled the attack against the convent. Miguel and eight co-conspirators were arrested and sentenced to jail in Los Angeles.[72]

Faced with dwindling support in Washington, the CSJs at Fort Yuma received less and less material and financial assistance from the government in the 1890s. Interestingly, the CSJs viewed this as hostility from the "Protestants and Republicans," who they feared would remove them from the school. In reality, the federal government was moving away from providing political and financial support for any church-run Indian schools.[73]

Driven by growing shortages of food and supplies and residual anger at the sisters, Miguel's son, Patrick, set fire to the school. Patrick's arson attempt probably resulted from more than family revenge since a "group of Yuma Methodists" paid legal fees for Patrick's defense and arranged for Miguel to be present during the trial.[74] Discouraged and frightened, the CSJs resigned at the end of the school term in 1900 when the government discontinued funds. Frustrated with their never-ending struggle with the political and power dynamics of gender, race, class, and religion, the sisters withdrew after a fourteen-year effort.

The sisters, like many Protestant missionaries, gave years of their life to a cause they firmly believed in, providing educational and humanitarian aid to native peoples. Although the devastating impact of federal policy and the ethnocentricity of whites cannot be denied, the CSJs had strived to do and be what their religious ideals had required of them. Their vows and their sense of charity, particularly in humanitarian assistance, guided their actions; and although they certainly made every attempt to indoctrinate the native peoples in white culture and religion, they also made extraordinary attempts to support and assist them, particularly during times of illness and suffering.

Colorado Mining Frontier

As the CSJs continued to work in the urban West and in the multicultural Southwest, they found themselves faced with a different set of challenges—the Colorado mining frontier. Responding to an invitation to open a school in the Colorado territory, Reverend Mother Agatha Guthrie sent an advance team of sisters to look over the prospective site. By April 1877, an anxious but determined Sister Perpetua Seiler was in the midst of what proved to be exasperating negotiations with Bishop Joseph Machebeuf to secure a building and create a school in Central City, Colorado. Writing to her superior in St. Louis, she said: "Dearest Mother, I fear that your patience will be sorely tried by my epistles. . . . This is the most complicated and harassing affair I was ever commissioned to undertake. . . . Pray for your wanderer. Do not be uneasy. Am trying to do right."[75]

Sister Perpetua's two-month correspondence with Mother Julia Littenecker describes the beginnings of what proved to be a physical and spiritual odyssey for herself, her companion, and the CSJs. But over the next forty years the CSJs became firmly entrenched in the rugged mining communities of Central City and Georgetown, Colorado, where they created and maintained educational, health care, and social welfare institutions.[76]

The CSJs' arrival in Colorado in 1877 predated that of most organized Protestant women's groups, but other nuns had been in the territory since 1864.[77] Similar to preparations for establishing other new mission sites, two sisters were sent to Colorado as an advance team that "networked" its way across the country. Traveling by train from St. Louis to Denver, the two stopped off in Kansas City, where they stayed with CSJs who were teaching at St. Teresa's Academy. There they left trunks filled with potential lottery prizes to be shipped to Colorado later to be used as a way to make money for the new institutions. When they reached Denver, the sisters boarded at St. Mary's Convent as guests of the Sisters of Loretto.[78]

In Colorado, Sister Perpetua Seiler and her young travel companion, Sister Angelica Porter, served as representatives from the St. Louis motherhouse and negotiated directly with Bishop Joseph Machebeuf for purchase of a building and creation of a school in Central City. Machebeuf, a well-known cleric with a reputation as a shrewd businessman, was assisted by attorneys, investors, and advisers in administering diocesan finances and institutions. On the surface, Sister Perpetua appeared to be greatly overmatched. Little is known of her except that she was born in Lyons, New York, in 1837, and her letters give evidence of many years of formal schooling.[79] From March 25 to May 2, 1877, she engaged in hard-nosed bargaining with Machebeuf and was forced to play the middle ground between him and Father Honoratus Burion, the parish priest of Central City.[80] Sister Perpetua's letters to St. Louis document the bishop's constant bickering, mood swings, financial ploys, and last-minute pressures to strike a better deal for the diocese at the sisters' expense. After her first meeting with Machebeuf she wrote, "One dreaded interview with the Bishop is at last over. He is indeed a hard man to deal with." Seiler firmly held her ground on the price, interest rate, and payment schedule, refusing to assume additional debts incurred by the parish priest and bishop or to offer the motherhouse property as collateral.[81]

Assuming a role frequently required of other nineteenth-century nuns, Seiler negotiated contractual agreements, traveled to Central City, inspected the building, talked with local parishioners, kept counsel with an attorney and banker in Denver, and set up a soliciting trip that encompassed three states and hundreds of miles. She had to make some important decisions without the advice of her superiors since the mail rarely came consistently or quickly enough to provide complete communication with St. Louis. In fact, she shrewdly used the geographic distance and her vow of obedience to resist and eventually refuse demands made by the bishop. After a particularly grueling two-hour negotiating session, Sister Perpetua wrote Mother Julia that she refused the bishop's demands by reminding him of her vow of obedience to her own superiors. This tactic proved useful at those times in the negotiations when the bishop became most demanding.[82] After the deal was finalized, she wrote: "The opening is a good one for us in the state, but I am truly sick of it all. Have done everything I could to make all come out right; can now do no more. All our prayers and fatigue have been offered for this end." Later, feeling much relieved and confident after her difficult five weeks of negotiations, Sister Perpetua suggested that "someone possessed of great tact, prudence and skill in business and virtue to be at the head of the Central City house. Neither of them [Burion and Machebeuf] are hard to deal with, by those who know how to handle them."[83]

Like their Protestant counterparts, women religious learned how to subvert patriarchal power in an acceptable but effective way, passing on their strategies for other women to emulate. Sister Perpetua's letters to Mother Julia show that she clearly knew what she was doing and enjoyed outmaneuvering the bishop. On the day the contract for the Central City properties was to be signed, Bishop Machebeuf had asked that a clause be added to it. Seiler agreed immediately, realizing that the bishop's clause had no affect on the amount paid by the csjs. She wrote Mother Julia, "The lawyer had a good laugh at the simplicity of the Bishop. And I know you will have another when I tell you that [the bishop] . . . invited me to take up my abode [in Central City]." Clearly the bishop was not in the position to make such a request, and Sister Perpetua once again refused by telling him she would be guided by obedience to her own superiors.[84]

In discussing power relationships between men and women, Carroll Smith-Rosenberg discourages historians from viewing women as "victims" or as "co-opted spokespersons for male power relations." Historically, nuns have been seen as both. Smith-Rosenberg believes that one who takes this kind of approach "fails to look for evidence of women's reaction, of the ways women manipulated men and events to create new fields of power or to assert female autonomy. . . . But if we reject the view of women as passive victims, we face the need to identify the sources of power women used to act within a world determined to limit their power, to ignore their talents, to belittle or condemn their actions."[85] Sister Perpetua Seiler clearly understood the gender dynamics in her interactions with the economically, politically, and religiously powerful bishop. However, it was her gender and her identity as a woman religious that allowed her to appear to acquiesce even as she manipulated the bishop to achieve her ultimate goals. The source of her power came from her identity as a woman and a vowed religious in an all-female community. Publicly, she was polite, demure, and submissive, but she was shrewd in handling the male cleric, who had both his gender and his religious office to buttress his authority.

After signing the contract, Sister Perpetua and Sister Angelica traveled for six to eight weeks with the U.S. Cavalry and the paymaster on a fundraising mission to all the military outposts in northern Colorado, Wyoming, and South Dakota. Traveling in potentially dangerous territory only one year after the Little Bighorn battle, they toured Indian reservations, observed native dances, and visited and solicited money from officers and enlisted men. They stayed in the company of the post commander (Catholic or Protestant) and his wife on each stop of the journey. They camped, slept in a tent, and traveled on trains, stagecoaches, ambulances, and freight wagons to their various destinations. To find suitable lottery prizes, they dug for gems and crystals, hiked mountains, explored caves, and panned river beds. Clearly the frontier environment presented the sisters with a range of experiences unknown to most secular or religious women in the nineteenth century.

Like her predecessor Monica Corrigan, Sister Angelica Porter kept a diary of their journey with the army. Although Angelica made it clear that Perpetua required her to keep the journal, she wrote with emotion and childlike wonder of the sights and adventures of her Western travels on the rugged terrain. On a trip to Crystal Cave, the sisters, accompanied only by another woman and her young son, rode in freight wagons up a mountain before beginning their journey on foot. After picking strawberries, flowers, and prairie apples, the sisters entered the cave. Sister Angelica wrote, "[We] descended a very steep side of mountain[,] could scarcely support ourselves and keep from falling. Reached cave after great difficulty. Were first ladies ever in it. Picked crystals and explored it with torch light." Nineteen years old and Canadian born, Sister Angelica gave a poetic description of the mountain sights around her on their perilous climb: "Saw bone of huge animal miners had found in earth. Named a large rocky peak 'The Way to Heaven' on account of difficulty of ascent. Remarkable! Saw a rainbow formed by the reflection of sun on water leaking from flume, crossing the Gulch, the water fell like rain."[86] Even Sister Perpetua, after her difficult financial dealings in Denver, appreciated the wonders and isolation of the West. On an early soliciting trip, while camped on the Powder River with the military payroll company, New York–born Perpetua pondered the spiritual significance of the frontier setting as she wrote of her feelings to Mother Julia: "The scenery here is picturesque and beautiful. Our tents are camped on the brink of the stream, which is lined with cottonwood trees. . . . There is to me something sublime in the thought that we have bent the knee in prayer in these far off wilds . . . in the wilderness in the midst of 40 armed soldiers."[87]

Although steeped in religious and spiritual metaphors, the sisters' accounts of their adventures are similar to those of other women traveling in the West.[88] As Catholic nuns, they also utilized their vows of poverty, chastity, and obedience to interpret their life experiences. Like many women in the frontier West, they experienced homesickness and at times stringent physical deprivations and difficulties, but seen in religious context, these hardships could be welcomed as God's blessing and an opportunity to serve God in a more humble and edifying way—the goal of every CSJ. Certainly, the sisters utilized their religious worldview and vows to calm their fears and justify their physical or emotional challenges. Their faith helped them accept and persevere in extraordinarily difficult circumstances in an isolated and potentially life-threatening environment.[89]

After five months the advance team successfully completed their negotiations and solicitation and had prepared the way for CSJ teachers, and later, nurses, to be sent from St. Louis to create and maintain the new Colorado institutions. In turn, the nuns who settled there adapted their roles, institutions, and social interactions to the specific needs and circumstances of the diverse mining communities of Central City and Georgetown.[90]

In the 1860s and 1870s Central City functioned as a mining and commercial rival of Denver. The majority of the male population worked in mining or as suppliers to the mines. In fact, Central City's Gilpin County encompassed one of the most famous gold districts in Colorado. By the 1870s, the merchant class was attempting to attract families and encourage the arrival of clergy and the building of churches and schools. For any mining town this was desirable as the way to acquire long-range stability for the community.[91]

Central City was the site of the first Catholic parish outside of Denver to be established by the Denver diocese, and Georgetown was the site of the second. Its large Catholic population and wealthy patrons could well afford to support a private academy. When four CSJs arrived in 1877 to open Mt. St. Michael's Academy, St. Mary's of the Assumption Church boasted 700 parishioners from throughout Gilpin County. Central City called itself the "richest square mile on earth," and the townspeople built the CSJ academy on a hilltop overlooking the city; the $30,000, two-story, Gothic revival structure included a bell tower and a large Celtic cross that could be seen for miles. For forty years academy children daily climbed the 150 steps up the hill to Mt. St. Michael's. When the population of the town peaked in 1900 at 3,114, six sisters were teaching 120 students, Protestant and Catholic, in the academy.[92]

In 1880, the CSJs accepted the call to Georgetown to open a parish school and a hospital. With silver prices escalating in the late 1870s and 1880s, Georgetown became the "Silver Queen" of the mining towns, and the census of 1880 revealed what would be the population peak for the mining community: 3,294.[93] In contrast to other mining towns, free-wheeling dance and gambling halls, saloons, and brothels occupied a "quieter" place amid public outcries for churches, schools, and civic reforms in Georgetown. In a community where families predominated, parents worried about the "moral well-being" of their children and the variety of bad influences present in most mining communities, where 90 percent of the population moved on within ten years.[94] The large contingent of Catholic families had created Our Lady of Lourdes parish in 1866, which boasted the largest and finest church in Georgetown. Unlike the private academy in Central City, where tuition ranged from $1.00 to $2.50 a month, the parish school, opened in 1880, was free to all Catholic children, and 100 boys and girls were reciting lessons by 1885.[95]

Protestants and Catholics alike welcomed the opening of the CSJ hospital in 1880. Before it opened, local women in Georgetown, as in other mining communities, bore the brunt of nursing care; women who ran boardinghouses and wives of miners often found themselves nursing not only their husbands but other "unattached" men.[96] Although the sisters' first hospital in Georgetown was located in a former residence, the Demin House, in 1883 the lay board of Protestants and Catholics created a new brick facility. The new hospital, staffed by two doctors and eight nun-nurses, included a large ward and eight private rooms. Most of the patients were miners who paid $.50 a week to use the hospital at any time. Sometimes mining companies paid in advance for all their employees' hospital stays. Over 90 percent of the patients were males between the ages of twenty-one and sixty-five, and the typical hospital stay was three or four days, or with serious injuries, two to three weeks. The surviving patient lists describe a variety of injuries, accidents, and diseases.[97]

In the mining communities of Central City and Georgetown, the CSJs faced two potential barriers that had to be overcome for them to create and successfully maintain their Colorado institutions: anti-Catholic sentiment and class and ethnic rivalries. In Central City, where the CSJs established their first school, some anti-Catholic attitudes surfaced as the nuns prepared to initiate their mission in the territory. Earlier, the Sisters of Charity of Leavenworth, who began a school in 1874, left Central City ill and disillusioned, having received no remuneration for their three years of

Our Lady of Lourdes School, Georgetown, Colorado, late 1890s (Courtesy of Sisters of St. Joseph of Carondelet Archives, St. Louis province)

service. In her correspondence to the motherhouse, Perpetua Seiler wrote that the sisters were "withdrawn because they were not happy here." Local gossip included rumors about conflict between the priest and sisters and an unaccounted for infant staying in the rectory. One sister had "left the order under suspicious appearance." In a later letter, Sister Perpetua assured Mother Julia that the accusations were false: "There has been no public scandal given here" and the "sisters bear a good name."[98]

The csjs worked hard to establish their good name and reduce anti-Catholic attitudes. Sister Perpetua's letters to St. Louis mention the importance of performing duties for "the honor of Religion." The sisters' efforts in Central City appeared to be successful. The academy was filled with students, and community support boomed. The sisters would recall later their successful fund-raising fairs and plays and townspeople throwing money into a big kettle in front of the Teller Opera House on Eureka Street. One account of this incident claimed that thousands of dollars were collected within a few days.[99]

Even in Georgetown, which had a large Catholic population, religious bigotry surfaced. A local Methodist was appalled at the "gambling" by which "Catholic ladies raised considerable money with raffles." He went on to describe Catholics as "different" because of their "strange statues and paintings" and because "they had to get up real early on Sunday mornings and go to Mass. Of course, this was compensated for by their being allowed to play ball on Sunday afternoon, and use strong drink, and be forgiven once a week by the priest for all they might have done amiss."[100]

Many in the mining town were grateful for the sisters' attention, however, and "reconciled" their anti-Catholic sentiments. Newspaper clippings from Georgetown referred admiringly to the "Sister's Hospital." In describing the community effort to keep the hospital financially solvent, the *Georgetown Courier* stated, "The makeup of the [hospital] committee speaks for itself and plainly shows that neither religious beliefs nor nationality enters into the matter in any way whatsoever." The writer went on to say that the sisters kept the hospital in a "far more efficient manner than a private concern can."[101] Mr. Thomas West provided a personal testimonial in the July 5, 1888, *Georgetown Courier*. Mr. West said he expected his hospitalized Protestant friend would receive "scant attention" and be charged higher prices; however, he assured the local readers that he had witnessed "kindly" care at the hands of the sisters.[102] Clearly, the CSJs in Colorado functioned in an educative role that softened Protestant attitudes toward nuns and Roman Catholics in general.

The CSJs also played a pervasive role in caring for and ministering to the large majority of immigrant Catholics in both mining areas. Religious and ethnic familiarity helped integrate the sisters into the Colorado mining communities they served and enabled them to reduce divisive ethnic rivalries that often prevailed in larger urban settings such as Denver.[103] Either by design or necessity, the CSJs sent a large percentage of foreign-born sisters into Colorado. Of the twenty-two CSJs who served in Georgetown, 40 percent were foreign-born, and their ethnicity matched well with the Georgetown Catholics, who were predominantly German, Irish, Italian, and French.[104] It is clear from the sisters' records that they also considered ethnicity an important marker of identity and recorded a patient's birthplace as well as age and other data. Records from the Georgetown hospital provide a representative sample of the heterogeneous mixture of patients. In the thirty-three years of the hospital's existence, the approximately 1,500 patients admitted for care came from eighteen countries and eighteen different states in the United States. The majority of foreign-born patients were miners who came from England and the predominantly Catholic countries of Italy, Germany, and Ireland.[105]

In contrast to Georgetown, over half of Central City's immigrants were non-Catholics from Canada, Wales, and England (largely Cornish). The forty-year roster of csjs who worked in Central City included 26 percent foreign-born, ethnically matched with the Catholic population that consisted mostly of German-, Irish-, and, later, Italian-born miners.[106] It is also plausible that many of the American-born sisters in both locations were second generation and therefore capable of relating to ethnic, cultural, and language differences within the towns.

Compared to middle-class Protestant women, the sisters bonded and blended well with the local communities ethnically; but equally important, most csjs and other women religious came from working-class backgrounds similar to those of the people to whom they ministered. Additionally, as a result of their vow of poverty, the sisters knew firsthand of the deprivations and needs of the many Catholic and non-Catholic immigrants and families. Although elevated spiritually in the eyes of their parishioners, their lack of financial security kept them on a par materially with the people they served. Their own poverty helped the csjs avoid a tendency to patronize the needy, which was characteristic of some Protestant women's groups.[107]

By 1917, the mining boom was over, and the csjs withdrew from Central City and Georgetown; the communities could no longer support the csj institutions. The growing population in Denver and surrounding areas had expanding needs, which the sisters met by establishing additional schools and other institutions there. Their forty-year ministry on the mining frontier demonstrates the significance and importance of their activities and provides one of many examples of the religious community's ability to adapt to life in the American West.

The csjs' presence in the urban West, Southwest, and the Colorado mining frontier helped to preserve, sustain, and shape American Catholic culture in the trans-Mississippi West. In all three environments their support networks and institutions provided important services to men, women, and children. Gender ideology, particularly "domestic ideology," supported the role of both Protestant women and Catholic women religious. In his discussion of "domestic ideology" in the American West, Robert Griswold defines it as "a shared set of ideas about women's place [that] also bound non-related women to each other." He goes on to state that domestic ideology strengthened bonds of sisterhood among women by "offering women a cultural system of social rules, conventions, and values—a moral vocabulary of discourse—that gave meaning to their daily behavior and to their friendship with other women."[108] Although Catholic sisters and Protestant churchwomen defined their religious missions in different ways and at times competitively, both used gender ideology as an impetus and justification for expanding their influence and providing necessary social services in the American West.

The isolated and primitive conditions of the frontier, particularly during their early years there, gave sisters additional autonomy and influence. Clearly the travel and business activities of the advance teams thrust nuns into all kinds of social, legal, and economic situations. Long-distance travel by land and sea in isolated and potentially dangerous environments and interaction with secular and clerical males forced them to adapt their behavior and develop much more flexibility and spontaneity than was required by daily convent routine in established areas of the country. The CSJ Customs Book of 1868 provided very explicit direction about avoiding "unnecessary" conversation and involvement with seculars. It told sisters to avoid "levity" and interactions with laymen that were not of spiritual benefit.[109] The sisters' journals and correspondence demonstrate that secular interaction, encompassing the federal government, local businesses and authorities, and a vast range of ethnically diverse women and men, was not only necessary but also constant and ongoing. The sisters' conversations certainly ranged well beyond religious edification.

CSJs established women's support networks and institutions that educated the young and cared for the physically and spiritually needy. Gender ideology limited them, even as it provided a justification for their educational and nurturing roles, but their vows of poverty, obedience, and chastity may have allowed more latitude in their behavior and provided them with ways to avoid male influence and unwanted attention. Like many secular and Protestant women who traveled west, CSJs challenged and appreciated the rugged terrain of the frontier even as they fought off homesickness and fear. Its physical isolation and deprivation provided constant reminders of their mortality and their call as religious women. Present in larger numbers than male clerics, the CSJs and other women religious lived and worked daily with the people they served. Creating and/or staffing parish schools, Indian missions, private academies, colleges, hospitals, and orphanages, they expanded and shaped Catholic culture and American life throughout the trans-Mississippi West.

[F]or more than 100 years, [parochial] schools were identified with the sisters who lived in the local convent, taught in the classrooms furnished by the parish, supervised children on the playground, and carried out additional functions within the parish. In fact, by many of the local citizens, the schools in the Catholic parish were referred to as the sisters' schools.
—*They Came to Teach*

5

Promulgating the Faith

Parochial Schools and American Catholic Identity

Probably no other institution in the nineteenth or twentieth century had a more pervasive and long-lasting impact on Catholic culture and identity than the parochial school. The massive Catholic school system familiar to most contemporary Americans, both Catholic and non-Catholic, was the centerpiece and anchor for parish life and activity. So important did the parochial schools become in the nineteenth century that many bishops encouraged priests from poorer parishes to use their limited funds first for a school and later for a church.[1]

American sisters provided the lion's share of the labor force, and even Catholic children who attended public schools received their religious training after school or on Saturdays from the nuns.[2] The sisters' role in parish education was extensive. They served as teachers (for grades K–12), principals, fund donors and fund-raisers, sponsors for religious organizations, choir directors, coaches, and social workers in a hierarchical and male-dominated church that often exploited and devalued their labor and contributions. Consequently, their experiences provide an intriguing and complex portrait of nineteenth- and early-twentieth-century Catholic parish life that was permeated by the interactions and power struggles of class, ethnicity, and gender.

When the CSJs arrived in St. Louis in 1836, the American common school movement was in its infancy, and state-supported, tuition-free, and coeducational public schools would not become a reality for most children until later in the century. In colonial America, schools, with few exceptions, had been a privilege for elite white males.[3] After the Revolutionary War and in an attempt to live up to its egalitarian principles, Americans in the new democracy debated the importance of schooling and, specifically, *who* should be educated, *what* should be taught, and *how* schools should be funded. Race, class, and gender provided major barriers to education for the vast majority of children well into the nineteenth century. The few schools available were either church-supported, public-supported, or some combination of the two.[4]

From the late 1830s until the end of the century, common schools developed in a very uneven pattern across the United States, and access to education was often determined by the state legislature's and local community's interest and willingness to provide funds. Although historians of education continue to debate its objectives and outcomes, the common school movement reflected concerns that were both political and ideological.[5] "It was argued that if children from a variety of religious, social-class, and ethnic backgrounds were educated in common, there would be a decline in hostility and friction among social groups" and that teaching a "common political and social ideology" would enhance national identity and unity. Schools could become instruments of government policy to educate people for democracy and ameliorate any "foreign" (antidemocratic) tendencies.[6]

As the Catholic population grew with the influx of German and Irish immigrants prior to the Civil War, Catholic parents wanted their children to take advantage of this new American system of "mass education." However, for many Catholic parents and clergy the "common" school appeared to be an overtly "Protestant" school. The curriculum included the use of the King James version of the Bible, Protestant hymns and prayers, and blatant anti-Catholic statements. The term "popery" appeared throughout textbooks, and even when Protestant public school committees attempted to purge offending passages from their texts they seemed to have difficulty recognizing their own biases. For example, in one "revised" New York textbook a historical character, who was a "zealous reformer from Popery," was killed when "trusting himself to the deceitful Catholics."[7]

The battle over the public schools permeated urban politics in many Eastern states. In New York City and Philadelphia public emotions spilled over into high-profile political debates and, in some instances, riots. In 1843, four years before the CSJs came to Philadelphia, thirteen people died and a Catholic church was burned to the ground during the Philadelphia Bible Riots. Although Catholics saw themselves as loyal Americans, Protestant extremists viewed the Catholic challenge to the "Protestant" culture of the public schools as "un-American." As Jay Dolan has stated, "Because they attacked the public school, Catholics were perceived as assaulting the basic Protestant ideology that inspired not only the school, but also the nation. Thus, to attack the school was to attack God, nation, and government."[8]

In the First and Second Plenary Council meetings of American bishops in 1852 and 1866, education was actively discussed, and both councils "recommended" that "in every diocese" a school be built next to every church.[9] In actuality, bishops were divided on the issue. Some sought separate Catholic schools, others hoped to work out "state-supported Christian free schools," both Catholic and Protestant, and a few still hoped for some compromise plan with the public schools. Even when public schools became more secularized in the late nineteenth century, controversy continued because many bishops felt that even though public schools were less "Protestant," their secularization now made them "Godless." Consequently, by the Third Plenary Council meeting in Baltimore in 1884 a majority of American bishops had taken a strong separatist stand. The council, in turn, "commanded" the building of a school within two years for all parishes, threatened that priests could be removed from the parish if they did not comply, and asserted that parents were "bound to send their children to the parochial schools."[10] As some historians have noted, this landmark decision spurred "probably . . . the largest project undertaken by voluntary associations in American history." The labor and low wages of nuns subsidized the cost of schools considerably and "made feasible an otherwise financially impossible undertaking."[11]

Even after the 1884 mandate and even with sisters subsidizing the schools, financial limitations made school building impossible for some

St. Vincent de Paul School, first CSJ parochial school, St. Louis, Missouri (Courtesy of Sisters of St. Joseph of Carondelet Archives, St. Louis province)

parishes, and some bishops and priests continued to try "alternative" arrangements with public school educators, who often had similar financial constraints. Some of these alternative plans were modeled on a plan begun in 1873 in Poughkeepsie, New York. In the "Poughkeepsie Plan" the town board of education "rented" the Catholic school during school hours, controlled the curriculum, and paid the teachers. This arrangement allowed Catholic teachers to teach Catholic children secular subjects during the regular school hours and religion classes after school when the building returned to church control, therefore avoiding a church-state conflict.[12] The CSJs were involved in a number of compromise plans with the public schools, some of which barely lasted a few months, while others continued for years.

In 1883 sisters in Troy, New York, crossed the Hudson River in a rowboat or walked across the frozen river to teach at St. Brigid's School in Watervliet (West Troy). By 1886, the parish had built a residence for the CSJ teachers and a new school with eight grades and an academic (secondary) department. Because the public school facilities were inadequate, the town board of education "leased" St. Brigid's School and renamed it West Troy Union Free School. The city paid rent and maintenance costs and awarded standard teaching contracts to the CSJ teachers. The sisters were appointed under their secular names, which they used to sign legal documents and reports. By the mid-1890s this arrangement was being challenged by some local citizens who did not want the sisters teaching in a public school. At a hearing in 1897 the New York State Board of Education decided that each sister was "a duly qualified teacher" and that "no prayers or religious exercises were held during school hours" so the school board was within its rights to establish the arrangement. However, the main objection of the local citizens, that the women wore religious garb, was upheld. The CSJs could continue to teach only if they no longer wore their habits. Of course the sisters refused and they were fired at the end of the 1887 school year.[13]

Bishop John Ireland introduced a similar plan in 1891 in Faribault and Stillwater, Minnesota. The Dominican Sisters were teaching at Immaculate Conception school in Faribault, and the CSJs were teaching at St. Michael's in Stillwater. In both cases the parochial schools were struggling financially, and under the new arrangement both schools acquired badly needed public funds. However, success at both sites was short-lived and within two years the Faribault-Stillwater plan was discontinued. Attacked by both Protestants and Catholics, the plan failed for many reasons, including the controversy surrounding Bishop Ireland's "liberal" views on Americanization.[14]

Once again, however, the nuns' habits seemed to be a major source of contention for Protestants. Although all religious symbols (e.g., crucifixes and religious pictures) had been removed from the schools and the sisters were deemed good teachers, the visible presence of nuns in habits seemed to undo some Protestants, who labeled the Faribault-Stillwater plan "a clever trick . . . to capture the public schools for the Church of Rome."[15] The CSJs in Stillwater were the subject of a lengthy newspaper article published in the *Minneapolis Journal* on January 9, 1892. The local reporter, who visited the classrooms, provided his readers with a detailed description of the nuns' habit. The reporter also quoted a Protestant minister who found the habits "particularly obnoxious," and the article concluded with a cartoon of a CSJ in habit.[16]

Another, longer-lasting conflict involving the CSJs in the Minnesota public schools occurred at St. Mary's in Waverly in 1893. As in Faribault and Stillwater, the plan placed nuns in a school funded by public tax dollars. Although controversy began as usual, the local citizens seemed less alarmed by the presence of teaching sisters and the arrangement with the public school continued until 1904. While sisters in some states had fewer problems than the CSJS experienced, "anti-garb laws" and negative reactions to the religious habit would continue to limit American nuns' participation in public schools into the twentieth century.[17]

As the barriers between church and state increased in the 1900s, the Catholic school system continued to define itself as a separate entity. The parochial school statistics from 1880 to 1920 clearly illustrate not only the growth of the parish schools but also the financial difficulty parishes experienced in creating a Catholic school system in the United States. In 1880, six million American Catholics supported over 2,000 parochial schools with 400,000 students. By 1920, seventeen million Catholics had created approximately 6,000 schools with 1.7 million children enrolled. Although these numbers are significant and the growth rate is evident, these schools existed only in about 35 percent of Catholic parishes.[18] Fortunately for the parish schools, as the Catholic population grew so did the number of American sisters. The phenomenal increase of women religious in the United States made the growth of parochial schools possible. In 1850, fewer than 2,000 sisters lived in the United States, but by 1890 over 32,000 women had taken vows, and by 1920 the number had risen to over 90,000. One historian has estimated that between 1866 and 1917, more that 50,000 American nuns devoted their entire lives to teaching in parochial schools.[19]

The CSJS, like many women religious, taught in a wide variety of parochial schools throughout the United States. Between 1836 and 1920, CSJS taught in nineteen states in all regions of the country. Beginning with their first school in 1836, they had established 155 parochial schools by 1920. Over 57,000 European American, African American, Hispanic, and Native American students were enrolled.[20]

Besides teaching racially and ethnically diverse students, the CSJS also created schools for the education of deaf children. Beginning in 1837, with the arrival of two sisters trained in the latest French methods for teaching sign language and working with deaf students, the Carondelet CSJS created schools in St. Louis, Buffalo, and Oakland, California, and they were indirectly responsible for institutions conducted by other Sisters of St. Joseph, who traced their earliest beginnings and training methods to the St. Louis sisters. As some of the earliest trained teachers of the deaf in the United States, they taught classes for children and adults that included religious instruction, academic course work, and vocational education.[21]

Although CSJs taught in a wide variety of private and select schools and academies and in many of their orphanages, staffing parish schools engaged the largest number of sisters. Throughout the nineteenth and early twentieth centuries, the Catholic school system included a diverse mix of schools that were funded by parishes, male and female religious orders, dioceses, or some combination of sources. Additional confusion was created by the variety of names used to identify these schools. Depending on the region of the country, the need of the parish, or the whim of their creators, these schools might include a mixture of elementary and secondary and sometimes postsecondary levels, and might be indiscriminately called academies, parish schools, parochial schools, high schools, institutes, and sometimes colleges. For example, in the Midwest and Western part of the country, the CSJs used the label "academy" to refer to their private or select schools, which were boarding and day schools for Catholic and Protestant young women. In reality these schools often included a mixture of young boys and girls of all ages from the parish. St. Mary's Academy in Los Angeles provides an example of the eclectic nature of some of the early CSJ schools. In correspondence to Reverend Mother Agatha Guthrie in St. Louis, Father A. J. Meyer defined his ideas on the nature of St. Mary's Academy: "I agree with you in calling the school an academy, for besides there being a great deal in a name, your school will be it in reality; we must also consider it a parish school, where all the girls in the parish can go, even as you so kindly mention, the poor, for we must never neglect them . . . and besides we must have room for our little boys."[22]

The schools in the CSJ Eastern province (Troy, New York) provided a somewhat different profile. By 1883, the Troy province no longer had private or select schools in New York, but the label "academy" or "institute" continued to be used for elementary and secondary parish schools. St. Bernard's Academy, the parish school in Cohoes, New York, served an even broader purpose: the sisters taught night classes to accommodate children and adults who worked in the city's factories. Sister Flavia Waldron reminisced with another CSJ about teaching a full day with parish children and then beginning night classes: "Don't you remember the crowds of girls we had to teach at night after teaching all day? My eyes were nearly blind when we got through. Sisters Dominic and poor De Sales used to teach big young men with beards in the basement. It used to be ten o'clock before they got home. Then we had to do our washing and ironing on Saturday and take our turn to sit up with Mother Philomene every night until she died."[23]

Music class at St. Peter's School, Troy, New York, 1888 (Courtesy of Sisters of St. Joseph of Carondelet Archives, Albany province)

Parish schools often taught a variety of students at different skill levels, but their main purpose was to educate children, regardless of socioeconomic standing, in the tenets of the Catholic faith and provide a basic education similar to that of the public schools of the time period. Fearing the Protestant and secular influences of the public schools, Catholics wanted the parish schools to imbue children with a Catholic identity, immerse them in Catholic culture, and save their souls while educating them in the basic skills necessary to survive in American society.

As was the case in the public schools, the parish school structure and curriculum varied from school to school and could be affected by funding, geographic location, availability and expertise of teachers, parental support, and sometimes ethnicity and class. Gender segregation also reflected the availability of teachers and the variety of students to be taught. In the public schools coeducation became the accepted norm by the mid-nineteenth century, although sex-segregated schools lasted longer in urban centers in the East and South, where competition with private schools was most intense.[24] When it was financially feasible, most Catholic parochial schools continued the European tradition of separation of the sexes. In St. Louis, CSJs taught in St. Anthony's parish, which had three parish schools located in two buildings—one building for elementary school boys and

one building for elementary and high school girls. Boys and girls were segregated in separate schools where possible; but more likely, funding limitations required that they reside in the same building but in separate rooms
or wings. Describing the physical layout of his school, a Los Angeles priest
assured the new CSJ teachers that "the building is so arranged, that the little
boys having their separate yard, can go to their room without ever coming
in contact with any girl."[25] However, in the primitive conditions of St.
Anthony's School in Minneapolis "one school room was closed from
motives of economy, and the boys and girls were taught in the same room,
and by the same teacher."[26]

Class size was also determined by the availability of funds and teachers.
Although many nineteenth-century classrooms in cities were large, on the
average Catholic schools were probably even larger than public schools.
CSJs in the Troy, New York, province focused strongly on parish education. By 1920 they were teaching in twenty-three parish elementary schools
and sixteen high schools in the Albany and Syracuse dioceses. They taught
over 15,000 students a year; the average class size varied but ranged
between thirty-seven and fifty-two students, although at times individual
classes could include as many as sixty or seventy pupils. The smaller numbers were more typical of secondary classes, and the largest class sizes normally occurred in the primary grades.[27]

The sisters' concern about such overcrowding was countered by the
pressures of local priests and their own desires to serve the parish and provide education where it was needed. At Francis de Sales School in Denver,
Father Donnelly constantly pressured the CSJ leadership for more teachers.
"I recognize the wisdom of your suggestions about not overcrowding the
school. . . . I would prefer to take only the third, fourth and fifth grade . . .
but I expect this will not be possible as there is so strong a demand to have
the younger ones cared for by the sisters."[28] In Oakland, Father J. B.
McNally was more direct in his demands, blaming the school's declining
reputation and his poor health on the lack of CSJ teachers: "Now my Dear
Mother, you are expected to fill your part of the Contract—viz. to supply
teachers for the girls and all the boys up to receiving the sacraments. So far
you have not done your part. I am much annoyed. I am grieved and trou-
bled at having to provide lay teachers who give no satisfaction, who are
helping to give the school a bad name (unintentionally) and all this failure
at an expense that is crippling my energies."[29]

The CSJs may have had little control over crowded conditions, large
classes, and the constant demand for "more sisters," but in the area of cur-

riculum they were the experts. Before coming to the United States the csjs had taught school for almost two centuries in France. One of the items the original sisters brought with them in 1836 was the *School Manual for the Use of the Sisters of St. Joseph*.[30] In the 1840s, Sister Mary Rose Marsteller, a native-born Virginian, "Americanized" the French version of the manual by incorporating in it "the standard methods of her day." She also "added a full secondary course, with mathematics, rhetoric, German, and the natural sciences of botany, physics, chemistry and astronomy." Course work in French, vocal music, Latin, and history were retained from the earlier manual, but she added instrumental music and ornamental subjects (needlework, tapestry, etc.). In 1884, a team of teachers from all csj provinces worked to update and publish the first English version of the manual. In 1910, it was revised again to keep it current with changes in curriculum and teaching methodology.[31]

Used widely by many other religious orders who did not have specific teaching guides, the csj manual provided an in-depth look at the content and methods utilized by sisters teaching throughout the country. It also serves as an excellent example of the type of teaching manual written by other orders of women religious.[32] Other than the obvious inclusion of religion, the parochial school curriculum closely paralleled public school courses of study. Reading, arithmetic, grammar, history, geography, nature study, and writing formed the core of the elementary curriculum.

Although the often stilted, rote, and drill-oriented approach typical of nineteenth-century pedagogy can be found in the 1884 version of the manual, what astonishes the contemporary reader is the presence of many "modern" approaches in teaching methods. In contrast to the French version of the manual, which defined the importance of "conformity in teaching methods and disadvantages of using diverse methods," the introduction to the 1884 American manual stressed the importance of flexibility and new ideas and discouraged uniformity of approach. "It was considered, that to restrict the teachers to particular ways of conducting the different studies, would be to close the door to future improvements, as new ideas and suggestions on these subjects are constantly appearing. . . . These suggestions are not intended to trammel the teacher in the exercise of a wise discretion, but are given simply as aids to those who may need them."[33] The French version of the manual focused extensively on teacher control and the need to "inspire respectful fear" in children to "make them submissive." Teacher control was valued in the 1884 Americanized manual, but the teaching strategies were much more child-centered and the pedagogy extended well beyond lecture and recitation. Excerpts from the American manual reflect this change in approach:

> Teaching chronological tables is not teaching history. . . . Encouragement inspires confidence, and children, more than others, need it. . . . Begin each new lesson with conversation on objects or pictures illustrative of the reading lesson to awaken interest and develop an idea. . . . Where the text-book routine—assigning pages and hearing recitations—belongs to a past age, you must teach. . . . The chief object of teaching should be to elicit thought.[34]

Also interesting to contemporary readers is the manual's use of the feminine pronoun. The sisters' long tradition and centuries-old commitment to female education is obvious since all discussions and examples in reference to students used a feminine pronoun. The 1910 revision of the manual continued to use feminine pronouns even though American CSJs had been teaching boys for decades.

The CSJs also produced some of their own textbooks for use in elementary schools. Within six years of the publication of the American CSJ teaching manual in 1884, CSJ educators published two language arts and one geography/history text. The books incorporated "modern" strategies of what are currently termed "whole language" and "integrated curriculum" approaches in language arts. The authors' intent was to "improve the difficulty we find in procuring from children written ideas." Similar to the CSJ manual's preference for feminine pronouns, the frequent representation of females in stories and pictures was a unique feature of these books.[35]

When the sisters used other textbooks, they probably ordered them from the fast-growing Catholic textbook industry. Interestingly, except for the books published for religious instruction, these publishers created schoolbooks that looked remarkably similar to those used in public schools. In his systematic analysis of nineteenth-century Catholic and public school textbooks, Timothy Walch identified three fundamental themes in both public school and Catholic school books. Both public and parochial school books stressed patriotism and the superiority of the United States over other nations, the educational value of nature, and a conservative code of social behavior. Walch's careful analysis shows that nineteenth-century schoolbooks, Catholic or public, taught "docility, diligence, and patriotism in children." The main difference between public and parochial texts appeared in how patriotism was taught. Both textbooks emphasized that America was "a nation of God's chosen people." However, Catholic texts supplemented this theme with examples of specific contributions and the importance of Catholics to the American experience—a Catholic "great men" approach to history. According to Walch, this partisan approach taught young Catholics "to render their spiritual loyalty to the Catholic Church and their temporal loyalty to the United States." Consequently, nineteenth-century Catholic school textbooks mimicked public school textbooks in subjects and themes, but their additional emphasis on Catholic contributions clearly helped develop a Catholic identity in "Protestant" America. Likewise, the sisters' presence as teachers of religious *and* secular subjects provided a visual and constant model of how to be both Catholic *and* American.[36]

Immigrant parents wanted the sisters to teach their children to be successful Catholics and Americans, but ethnic identity played an important role in the development of Catholic parishes and subsequently the parish school. Although communal living, religious identity, and Americanization motivated CSJs to downplay ethnicity and class in the convent, the sisters had to work within a variety of ethnic or national parishes. The ethnic parish became the vital center of Catholic life, where parishioners hoped to worship in their native tongue and recreate their "old world" social, cultural, and religious institutions, protecting or insulating them not only from anti-Catholic sentiments but also the antiforeign bigotry prevalent in nineteenth-century America. One historian asserts that one of the major reasons for the success of a separate Catholic school system was "the commitment of Catholic immigrant groups to hand on the faith according to their own cultural traditions."[37]

However, within the vast pluralism of American Catholicism, different ethnic groups had varying commitments to parochial schools, and regional location as well as the size of the parish affected parents' support of Catholic schools. Germans, with the added incentive to maintain linguistic purity, were avid supporters of parochial schools. Like their German Lutheran counterparts, they felt that if their children lost the language, they would also lose the faith.[38] In Minneapolis and Kansas City, two CSJ strongholds, more than half of all German Catholic children attended parochial schools. French Canadian and Polish immigrants also sent their children to the parish schools in large numbers. Irish parents were less motivated than German parents to build parish schools probably because their children spoke English and could more quickly integrate into the public school system. Also, Irish American children who attended public schools, particularly in large Eastern cities, often had female teachers who were daughters or granddaughters of Irish immigrants, so the ethnic connection was maintained.[39] Italian American and Mexican American parishes had the fewest parochial schools, and their children attended in very small numbers. Neither group had developed a strong parish-centered tradition, and the lack of parish schools reflected this pattern.[40] Few African American children had the opportunity to attend Catholic schools, and by 1918 only thirty-eight African American parishes had a school.[41]

Besides ethnicity, geographic location and the size of towns and cities affected the creation of parish schools. Children in urban areas in any region of the country attended parish schools in larger numbers than children in rural communities. Midwestern states such as Ohio, Illinois, Indiana, Missouri, and Wisconsin had larger numbers of parish schools particularly compared to New England and the Southwest. There were fewer Catholics in the Deep South than in other parts of the country, but their scarcity probably encouraged more parish schools as their church-to-school ratio was often higher than in Northern dioceses. For Catholic parents in the South, parish schools provided their children with a strong Catholic identity amid an overwhelming, and at times disapproving, Protestant majority.[42]

The CSJs taught in all regions of the country and in urban and small-town settings where their ethnic diversity and adaptability made them highly sought-after teachers.[43] With more non-English-speaking Catholics immigrating to the United States in the late nineteenth and early twentieth centuries, parishes formed around ethnic groups, particularly those defined by language differences. Parishioners demanded priests and teaching sisters who had appropriate fluency to preach and teach in the church and school. Many parents of various ethnic backgrounds wanted separate parish schools not because they necessarily feared the secularization of public schools but because they wanted to maintain their linguistic and cultural traditions. This merging of American educational principles with "old world" language and culture created many parish schools that were truly bilingual and bicultural.[44]

CSJs made every attempt to match sisters' ethnicity to parish ethnicity when possible, particularly when staffing a parish school where linguistic compatibility was important. In 1851, French- and English-speaking CSJs were invited to teach in St. Paul, Minnesota, because of its large French Canadian population. A few years later, with the German population expanding, Sister Radegunda Proff was sent from St. Louis to "run the

German school" at Assumption parish in St. Paul, and two other German-speaking CSJs staffed St. Boniface School in Hastings, Minnesota.[45] Beginning in the 1880s, German-speaking CSJs in St. Louis staffed what became the city's largest parish school, St. Anthony's. At St. Joseph's School in Schenectady, New York, when the CSJs could not provide enough German-speaking sisters, they used a team-teaching approach: Irish-born Sister Ailbe O'Kelly learned to say prayers in German, but when it came time to teach reading in German, she traded places with another sister so she could teach spelling in English and this German-speaking sister, Honorata Steinmetz, could teach the reading class.[46]

Sisters Agnes Orosco and Isabel Walsh used a similar strategy in a Spanish-speaking school in Florence, Arizona. Mexican-born Orosco was fluent in Spanish and taught classes in music and religion. Walsh learned the prayers in Spanish and taught them to her English class after being tutored by Orosco in the appropriate Spanish equivalents. Sister Agnes and the other five Spanish-speaking sisters who entered the CSJ community in the 1870s played a prominent and important role in helping the CSJs staff bilingual schools in Arizona and California. However, there were never enough bilingual sisters for all the CSJ schools. At St. Augustine's School in Tucson, Sister Serena McCarthy had to find her own solution to a language dilemma. In her classroom of 100 Spanish-speaking boys, she found a seven year old who was bilingual, and from his perch atop her desk he translated her instructions to his classmates.[47]

Ethnic parishes were prevalent throughout the nineteenth and early twentieth centuries, but the pluralism of American Catholicism and funding limitations made multi-ethnic parishes a common exception in some locations. In 1858 an eclectic group of American-, Irish-, German-, and French-born CSJs staffed the school at St. Mary's in Oswego, New York. Initially a French priest and a French Canadian populace dominated the parish, but the growing presence of English-speaking Catholics facilitated two separate congregations that shared the same building and occupied the church at different hours on Sundays.[48]

In the 1880s, sisters in Waverly, Minnesota, taught children of seven different nationalities in the parish school. CSJs in the upper peninsula of Michigan taught in schools that contained a mixture of French Canadian, Italian, Irish, and German students whose fathers worked in the mining industry around Lake Superior. At St. Joseph's School in Hancock, Michigan, classes were taught in English and, if needed, explanations or elaborations were given in French or German.[49] At St. Patrick's parish in

Sister Francis Joseph Ivory and her class, St. Mary's Academy, Glens Falls, New York, circa 1900 (Courtesy of Sisters of St. Joseph of Carondelet Archives, Albany province)

Mobile, Alabama, the nuns initially taught white children, but in 1894, they also staffed the Creole school in the same parish.[50] In 1904, when the CSJs came to St. Patrick's School in Los Angeles, they adapted to a multi-ethnic parish where sermons were given in German but confessions were heard in French, Spanish, Italian, and English, as well as in German.[51] In the ethnic and multi-ethnic parish schools, the CSJs taught in a Catholic culture that took many forms, and over time, as ethnicity blurred, the American and Catholic identity remained.

The financing and control of parochial schools also provide an intriguing view of how class, gender, and hierarchical privilege interacted and at times clashed in shaping the newly formed school system. As new parish schools were built more sisters were called to staff them. Where parish schools had existed prior to the 1884 mandate, lay people had sometimes been the first to staff them or had shared teaching duties with nuns. This was particularly true for the CSJs in the Troy province who taught in the dioceses of Albany and Syracuse.[52] The main reason for the shift away from lay teachers to nuns was mostly economic but also a continuation of European traditions of education. Some religious orders, like the CSJs, had been teaching girls for centuries, and they came to the United States specifically to continue that tradition. Therefore, the American sisters were seen as "natural" teachers for girls and, because of the great need for teachers, young boys. More importantly, they contributed a lifelong dedication to teaching and worked for little recompense, making parish education affordable. Clearly the main reason that parochial schools survived financially was because the sisters subsidized them through their low salaries, which averaged around $200 for a ten-month period, an amount that rarely increased over decades.[53]

Public school teaching became a female occupation in the nineteenth century for many of the same ideological and economic reasons that sisters taught in parochial schools. Women were seen as natural teachers of young children because teaching was viewed as an extension of their maternal role in the home. As males began leaving the teaching field to pursue other job options and the number of schools rapidly increased in the nineteenth century, women, who had few job options, willingly moved in to fill the void. More importantly, male administrators and school boards saw women teachers as an economic bargain, paying them one-third to one-half the salary given to males.[54]

Many American nuns would have been delighted to receive this "reduced" salary since they were typically paid one-third less than what a female public school teacher earned. Caught in the double-bind of their gender and their religious ideals of poverty, charity, humility, and service, American sisters received salaries from parish schools that rarely met their basic living expenses.[55] Although male religious orders also took a vow of poverty, they received higher salaries than the sisters. Experiencing a centuries-old tradition of devaluing women's work, European sisters had fared no better.

Underpaying and devaluing the work of sister-teachers continued in the American milieu, and as late as 1912 the practice was justified by Catholic educators, because "women could live more cheaply and consequently with a lower salary [since] the living expenses of women are not so high as those of men."[56] At St. Mary's, a wealthy parish in St. Paul, CSJs earned $250 per year while the parish agreed to give $450 per year for each Christian Brother and to provide an additional $200 for "outfitting, traveling and incidental expenses of the Brothers."[57] At St. Mary's Institute in Amsterdam, New York, the two male teachers each earned $600 for the year, the lay female teacher earned $300, and each CSJ earned $250, even though three of the six CSJs had thirteen to nineteen years of teaching experience and one of the male teachers had taught for only one year.[58]

The financial report of 1914 from St. Vincent's convent in Los Angeles reflects the low compensation sisters received and indicates the ways that they supplemented their income. Twelve sisters taught over 500 children and received a combined yearly salary of $2,100. However, their expenses for the year totaled over $3,000. Using strategies similar to those of other women religious to supplement their income, the CSJs alleviated the deficit by selling books, begging for donations, and taking on private pupils. Over one-fourth of their yearly income came from teaching music lessons.[59] Sister Rose Edward Dailey, reflecting on her many years in the parish schools of St. Louis in the early twentieth century, wrote: "Our salary as teachers was twenty-five dollars a month . . . [and] some of the pastors, from then flourishing parishes, took the sisters for granted and [did] not pay the sisters' salary for years. This is hard to believe when all parishes were engaged in Social Justice and were doing intensive study of writings on [the topic]."[60] Financial records from other CSJ institutions demonstrate this pervasive practice of "taking the sisters for granted." At St. John's parish in Kansas City the financial accounts from 1882 to 1904 list in detail all monies paid to pastors, assistant pastors, building funds, choir directors, organists, and janitors as well as contributions sent to male colleges/seminaries, the Society for the Propagation of the Faith, "Peter's Pence," and the "Holy Land Fund." Not one dollar was recorded for CSJ teacher salaries.[61]

In many parishes the CSJs were promised accommodations as part of their salary. Sometimes they materialized and other times not. In 1883 Father J. B. McNally wrote Mother Agatha Guthrie to thank her for agreeing to send CSJs "without any expense to me, ready, able, active, energetic, zealous and ardent" to teach in his parish school in Oakland. Then he asked her to "advance some cash for your *own benefit* as well as for the sake of religion" to help him build the school and convent even though it is clear from the letter that she had already refused an earlier request for money. He wrote: "Try if you possibly can to aid me materially, as the Sisters of Notre Dame have done in a neighboring parish. I don't plead poverty, for we have done wonders in a short time and we don't owe anyone anything. I only fear that the strain may be felt too keenly by my faithful people. . . . I think that you'll be pleased if you will send on at least

Senior class, St. Joseph's Institute (St. Patrick's School), Oakland, California, 1893 (Courtesy of Sisters of St. Joseph of Carondelet Archives, Los Angeles province)

$5,000 so that the building might be more grand and imposing and commodious."[62]

Father McNally was unsuccessful, but other pastors did receive monetary assistance to finance the sisters' housing. CSJS at St. Mary's Academy in Hoosick Falls, New York, did share expenses in the furnishing of their convent. The financial records show that the CSJ Troy province provided a very generous share for the convent interior, spending over $2,000, compared to the parish's $724 contribution.[63]

For nineteen years sisters at Ascension parish in Minneapolis waited for their convent to be built next to the school so that they would not have to endure the eighteen-block walk to and from school. With only their woolen shawls to protect them, they battled the fierce Minnesota winters and accompanying frostbite by walking backward or taking turns walking in front to protect the rest of the sisters from the frigid winds. The pastor refused to close the school even during blizzards. In 1916 parishioners intervened on behalf of the sisters by refusing to pledge money to help the pastor build a gymnasium for the school until the sisters had their convent.[64]

In the early 1900s the sisters in Oxnard, California, probably had some of the most unusual accommodations. Their convent was so small and the halls so narrow that when the portly Bishop Montgomery came to bless it, he remarked that "one has to go outdoors to turn around." The four-room cottage had no bedroom space so two sisters slept in the bathroom, one in the small room across from the chapel, and one in the tiny kitchen. When entertaining the provincial superior, Mother Elizabeth Parrott, the sisters covered three wash tubs with boards, linens, and bouquets of flowers and served Mother Elizabeth her "first full course meal in a laundry." The school accommodations had their own problems. Sister Liboria Wendling reminisced, "Before the new school was completed three sisters taught school in an abandoned restaurant. It was not unusual during the day to have patrons throw open the doors expecting to be served a hot meal. . . . The reason for the mistake was a simple explanation. No one had ever had the courage or gymnastic ability to climb atop the roof and remove the huge sign which spelled out in bold letters the single word '*restaurant.*'"[65]

In light of their limited support from many parishes and local pastors, how did the csjs finance their work in parish education? In addition to making ends meet through private music and art lessons, fairs and fundraisers held in the parish, food and monetary donations from parishioners, and extremely frugal living, the csjs used a method to earn money that they had earlier found helpful in France and one very typical of many religious orders of women. In many nineteenth-century parishes the sisters opened private, or select, secondary academies for girls that catered to wealthy families, Catholic or Protestant, who had the means to pay tuition for their daughters' education. This select school was the "cash cow" that enabled sisters to work in parish education and receive little or no compensation. It is important to remember that these schools were often the first type of school that women religious opened when coming to a new setting, and their success often determined whether sisters could "afford" to staff schools for poor children and/or parish schools. Americans' sensitivity to class made these schools problematic at times, but they were vital to many religious communities' existence and financial survival.[66]

The csjs in the Troy province, probably at the request of the bishop, discontinued their select schools in 1883, which forced them into low-paying parish teaching positions without the means to supplement their income. A letter from the csj provincial superior in Troy in 1911 that informed local parishes about the necessity for a salary increase for sisters illustrates the financial sacrifice the Troy province made when it gave up its select academies twenty-eight years earlier. Reminding the pastors of the fifty years of csj service in the Albany and Syracuse dioceses, she told them that "it is impossible to make ends meet . . . without practicing an economy detrimental to the health and strength of our Sisters." She continued,

> Our mortality is abnormally high and as teaching is a severe drain on vitality we can only hope to counteract it by abundant nourishment. . . . As a matter of record it is proper to recall that some years ago all the larger parishes had their select schools which were a source of revenue. To strengthen and develop the parochial schools and discard artificial distinctions which tended to divide members of the same [parish], these select schools were surrendered at a pecuniary sacrifice to local convents.[67]

Her request was actually very modest since she asked for $25 per month for elementary and $30 per month for secondary teachers—salaries that CSJs were already earning in other parts of the country and that were still significantly lower than what female public school teachers earned in 1911.

Besides struggling with limited financial support, Catholic nuns faced a problem that permeated every aspect of their work and community: the threat of patriarchal interference and control of the schools. In many CSJ settings the local pastor was the principal in name only and left the curriculum and day-to-day decisions totally in the sisters' hands. However, if he chose to exercise his clerical privilege, the local parish priest had the authority to interfere in every aspect of decision making including scheduling, class size, numbers of students, grade levels, curriculum, sisters' salaries and accommodations, budgets, and personnel decisions regarding individual sisters whom he favored or disfavored depending on the circumstances. In each diocese the bishop had ultimate control over all parish schools, and if the bishop and the parish priest disagreed the sisters could be caught in the middle with little recourse.

In 1909 CSJs had to battle both a parish priest and the bishop in a clash of egos and power that typified the ethnic and gender politics involved in their work. At St. Patrick's parish in Denver, the sisters became caught in a power struggle between a popular Irish-born priest, Joseph Carrigan, and a powerful French-born bishop, Nicholas Matz. Father Carrigan wanted to build a new church at St. Patrick's and began to do so against the express orders of Bishop Matz. The flamboyant Carrigan, who had connections at city hall, used his political influence and the Denver newspapers to make his case against the bishop. The battle raged publicly for months, and a series of letters document how the sisters were pressured by both clerics to acquiesce to their divergent demands concerning the parish school and the instruction of schoolchildren. This was humiliating for the CSJs, who hated the publicity and their constant presence in the newspapers, which they felt tarnished their hard-won reputation in Denver.[68] Gender was an important factor in this incident, not only because both men used patriarchal and hierarchical power to bully and threaten the CSJs, but also because religious communities of women had to guard their "reputation" as carefully as any individual secular woman or group of women. If the sisters' reputation was sullied in any way, rightly or wrongly, this threatened the viability of all their institutions in Denver and their ability to recruit young women to the order.

For months both clerics sent letters and telegrams to St. Louis pressuring the Reverend Mother for the community's unqualified support. Frustrated by what he perceived as a lack of CSJ cooperation, Father Carrigan labeled the CSJ superior in Denver "hysterical" and demanded her removal, while Bishop Matz sent veiled threats demanding obedience from the CSJs and hinting at possible repercussions for all CSJ institutions in the diocese.[69] Sister Marguerite Murphy, the superior at St. Patrick's convent, held her ground waiting for instructions from her superiors in St. Louis. Her vow of obedience enabled her to refuse both men until her female superior, Reverend Mother Agnes Gonzaga Ryan, sent advice. Finally Ryan took matters into her own hands. She withdrew all the sisters from St. Patrick's parish and stated that she would not let them return until the matter was settled between the men. This strategy was sometimes adopted by communities of women when "voting with their feet" seemed the only way out of an untenable situation. Ryan wrote the bishop that she was not justified "in allowing sisters to go through so much [when] there is a great scarcity of sisters" and they are needed in other places.[70] For three years, Ryan continued to refuse the bishop's demand for their return to St. Patrick's, using the one powerful leverage she had—withholding needed services. Some scholars have argued that historically women's power has rested on control of "goods and services" and is expressed through the "withdrawal of their services."[71] For women religious, the ability to control or withhold the many services they provided was key to any autonomy within the highly patriarchal Catholic Church that badly needed their labor. The nuns used their vow of obedience to their female superiors and their "Holy Rule" as leverage against male clergy. And like other women, they found that it was sometimes easier to leave a situation than continually battle with patriarchal authority.[72]

For American sister-teachers, and female teachers in general, the issues of autonomy, control, and professionalization became of paramount concern in the late nineteenth and early twentieth centuries. Although American women had gained a profession, they were neither able to control it nor make it their own. As large urban public schools began to centralize and move away from local political control, women teachers' destinies were increasingly in the hands of male administrators hired by school boards. One scholar has noted that, "from the earliest days of the development of the urban school systems, women teachers were being given lessons in subservience. . . . These men knew exactly the kind of educational system they wanted—ordered, disciplined, with decision-making following the model of the business corporation. Thus the reformers elevated the superintendency to a position of great prestige, and spoke of the new systems of education as 'scientific.'"[73] Some scholars have argued that this model mirrored the patriarchal family comprised of father-administrator, mother-teacher, and children-students. Calling it "scientific," "modern," and "efficient" was simply a way to confer new status on a very old system of male dominance and privilege.

As many states and large cities began standardizing curriculum and graduation requirements, instituting grading policies, and establishing requirements for teacher certification, Catholic educators began to make efforts to "create a complete system of Catholic training" that paralleled the public school system.[74] Under the direction of the Baltimore Council of 1884, Catholic educators hoped to create a unified system that would allow children to attend Catholic schools from elementary school through college if they so desired. Standardization, bureaucracy, male supervision, and centralization, all features of the public school system, fit well within the goals of the Catholic hierarchy and educators who strove for more uniformity and control of an ethnically divided church.[75] The archdiocese of New York selected the first diocesan school board, superintendent, and board of examiners in the 1880s, and other large dioceses soon followed its lead. Between 1904 and 1911 Catholic educators, mimicking public school educators, created a Catholic Education Association, the *Catholic Educational Review*, and a department of education at Catholic University; they also established a separate Sisters' College at Catholic University to provide education courses and degrees for nuns.[76]

As part of the move toward standardization and uniformity, Catholic educators called for the creation of more secondary schools. Although the majority of American children did not enroll in high schools until after

1920, earlier there was a move to provide secondary education on the East coast. By the 1880s, the CSJs in parish schools in New York began to work toward obtaining a charter for their secondary schools and helping their secondary students pass the regent's exam, which would admit them to state-funded institutions of higher learning in New York. This accreditation required a uniformity of curriculum and a specific level of competence in core subjects; but more importantly for Catholic schools, accreditation conferred a special status on an institution since it demonstrated its competitiveness and comparability with the public schools. One year after CSJs came to teach at St. Mary's in Amsterdam it became the first Catholic school to be chartered in the New York regent's system.[77]

Although all the CSJ secondary institutions in New York became chartered over the next few decades, sisters often battled with older parish priests who resented the state intrusion. Sister Blanche Rooney, striving to achieve recognition for her school, found the leverage she needed to convince a local priest in Saratoga to allow the school to be chartered. When Sister Blanche informed the cleric that one of the daughters of a prominent man in the parish had to go to another high school to complete her exams in an "accredited" school, he finally agreed to apply for the state charter. Sister Petronilla McGowan related that the sisters often had to first convince the parish priest and then deal with the anti-Catholic bias of some of the secular examiners in Albany. The sisters worried that their students' papers were scrutinized more carefully than others since some of the examiners showed open "hostility" toward these schools and referred to them as the "old saint schools."[78]

The requirements of two school systems, public and Catholic, often presented conflicting demands for teaching orders of women religious. As nuns struggled to meet both secular and religious expectations, they were often compared unfavorably with public school teachers in regard to their training and expertise. In the period after World War I this negative comparison had merit. At that time demands for teachers to acquire more formal schooling were escalating, and public school teachers were often able to meet additional state requirements more easily than the sisters. Catholic schools usually did not require their teachers to obtain state certification, and teaching orders were under enormous and increasing pressure from bishops and local pastors to place their young nuns in classrooms, even with inadequate training. The cost of a formal college education for large groups of young sisters was also prohibitive for many congregations. As a result many young nuns entered classrooms with minimal preparation in the early and mid-twentieth century and were clearly at a disadvantage if compared to public school teachers.

However, when examining the training and expertise of female teachers prior to 1920, the comparison between sister-teachers and public school teachers provides a different picture. In fact, we would argue that sister-teachers were as skilled, if not more skilled on the average, than their public school counterparts.[79] As the urban public school system developed in the late nineteenth century, young women were needed to fill the teaching ranks of often overcrowded classrooms in the many ethnic ghettos proliferating in cities across the country. Although deemed an opportunity for women, teaching was not viewed as a high-status occupation, and many young teachers were placed in situations where they had little training and even less understanding of the immigrant children flooding urban schools. Charged with the important work of teaching American language and culture, women teachers were often treated no better than "factory hands" by an increasingly elite male administration.[80]

With a growing system of administrative controls and standardization, public school administrators hoped to hire young, single females who would obey without question, follow a prescribed curriculum, work for less money, and view teaching as temporary since their ultimate goal was expected to be marriage and motherhood. In reality, most women became teachers in the public schools because they needed the money, wanted meaningful work, and had few job options. If they chose to marry, most states *required* them to resign immediately. In 1900 the average female public school teacher was twenty-six years old or younger and worked for about five years before marriage. Only a few attended state-run normal schools, some attended summer institutes held on college campuses or took a year's training in high school, but "most simply met the requirement to have completed a year of school beyond the grade they wished to teach."[81] As late as 1921 only four states required a high school diploma and thirty states had no scholarship requirement at all to obtain a teaching certificate. Even in New York, a state that often was a leader in teacher training, the state commissioner of education in 1912 lamented that "the lack of preparation of teachers is one of the greatest evils of our school system."[82]

Unlike their secular counterparts, sister-teachers often spent decades of their lives in teaching, gaining experience and expertise. The choice of religious life meant that their personal and professional aspirations became one, and without a family to care for they could focus on their life's work as religious women and teachers of children. In the nineteenth century, prior to the development of professional nursing and social work, the best educated of the sisters were expected to teach and the very brightest were groomed to teach at the secondary level. Many sisters who came from European teaching orders were well-educated women who brought a strong tradition of teacher training and experience to the United States. On-the-job training and mentoring played a key role in training sister-teachers for decades. Besides using their teaching manuals, the sisters acquired ideas and expertise from others in the community, learning theory and practice simultaneously under the direction of an older member of the order.[83] Stepping into her first classroom amid disorder and chaos, Sister Mary Eustace Huster was relieved when an older, experienced nun "stayed with me for two days to give me some valuable pointers for teaching and discipline." Later, as one of 120 sisters teaching at sixteen parochial schools and living at the Cass Avenue convent in St. Louis, Huster had extensive opportunity to work informally with other sisters who taught the same grade and who "provided a great deal of help." Over her sixty-two years as a teacher of every elementary grade, she was able to reciprocate as a mentor for many elementary sister-teachers who came after her.[84] Reflecting on the mentoring activities of CSJ teachers and other sister-teachers in Minnesota, Sisters Annabelle Raiche and Ann Marie Biermaier write,

> Oral tradition within each community has preserved stories about older, more experienced sisters who faithfully coached and encouraged younger members during their initial months and years in the classroom. . . . [M]entoring sessions occurred in the community rooms of convents everywhere in Minnesota. . . . Night after night, sisters helped one another to prepare the next day's lessons and exchange ideas about the most effective ways of fostering the intellectual development of the students.[85]

Even as sisters began taking more formal classes, this tradition of on-the-job training and mentoring continued for decades. Living in large convents and sharing daily work experiences with other sister-teachers provided a constant support system that few public school teachers had. Night or day, the sister-teacher had experienced teachers close by to answer questions, give advice, or provide support.

Although the vast majority of states required little formal education of public school teachers prior to 1920, the trend toward more preparation was evident, and to enable Catholic schools to compete, women religious began to work toward increasing their formal training. Many religious communities developed "normal schools" within their novitiate programs where lay professors, experienced sister-teachers, or clergy educated the young novices in pedagogy.[86] By the late nineteenth century, CSJ provinces in St. Paul, St. Louis, and Troy developed programs to improve the education of their prospective teachers. This training varied in quantity and quality because the provincial superiors always had to choose between providing more time and training for their teachers or yielding to pressure from clergy who demanded more teachers for parish schools. As early as 1876 St. Paul CSJs had a "practice teaching school" at St. Joseph's School, where postulants and novices did the teaching. By the early 1880s CSJs in St. Paul had created a "House of Study" for novices. Sister Winifred Hogan described a varied curriculum that included Christian doctrine, reading, rhetoric, grammar, mathematics, astronomy, physics (without lab work), elocution, music, writing, and drawing. Older sisters who specialized in each area taught the classes. Lay professors from local colleges in St. Paul and special guest speakers were hired to provide lectures to the novices and "inservice" training for sister-teachers already teaching.[87]

Having outside speakers and lay professors provided CSJ sister-teachers with excellent opportunities to hone their skills and receive current educational information. However, as women religious, the sisters walked a tightrope as they updated and perfected their skills without appearing to be a part of the "secular world." In 1894 Sister Adele Hennessey used the Cass Avenue convent to hold a citywide teaching institute for sister-teachers from various orders in St. Louis. She and the CSJs were criticized by "Catholic editors and others who looked with disfavor on the experiment."[88] This was the perennial dilemma. The teaching orders were supposed to provide an unlimited supply of superb teachers who were as good if not better than public school teachers; yet, they were also expected to minimize training to get more sisters in the classrooms faster and to avoid secular contact. They contended with a set of mutually exclusive expectations that set them up for criticism in whatever they did.

However, the CSJs consistently sought advice from public school educators, particularly if they felt it would improve their teaching strategies. The 1884 CSJ teaching manual listed helpful sources for teachers in methods and subject matter. The suggested books were from publishers not found within the Catholic publishing industry, and the most highly recommended source throughout the manual was the book *1,000 Ways of 1,000*

Teachers: Being a Compilation of Methods of Instruction and Discipline Practiced by Prominent Public School Teachers of the Country. Clearly, the csjs were less afraid of secular influence than some of their Catholic critics.[89]

By the early twentieth century most larger teaching orders of nuns, like the csjs, had a formal process of training that included three components: on-the-job training and mentoring, teacher preparation classes taught in the novitiate sometimes by lay educators, and college classes in secular and Catholic institutions.[90] As had happened with the nuns' earlier attempts to obtain professional preparation, sisters received an ambivalent response from Catholic clerics when they attempted to obtain more formal college training. After criticizing the sisters both for being ill-prepared for their jobs and for taking course work at secular institutions, the hierarchy now told them that they could attend the newly created "Sisters' College" affiliated with Catholic University, an all-male institution. The first summer institute was held in 1911, and that fall undergraduate and graduate degree programs were initiated for sister-teachers.[91] Actually, some of the sisters had already been attending college classes for years. Having been excluded from all-male Catholic colleges and with few Catholic women's colleges available, many had taken course work on Saturdays and during the summers at nearby state universities or private colleges.[92]

Although finding time and opportunity to attend college classes was problematic, an even larger issue involved the costs of tuition and housing. Low-paying parish teaching did not even cover living expenses and certainly not the costs of a college education. Many csjs in Kansas City, St. Joseph, and St. Louis attended the University of Missouri in Columbia. To minimize cost and for greater convenience, the csjs opened Sacred Heart convent and school in Columbia in 1912 to provide housing for the many sisters who attended summer classes.[93] Sisters in the St. Paul province completed course work from the College of St. Catherine (a csj institution), the University of Chicago, or the University of Minnesota. In 1921, over 100 csjs were enrolled at Moorhead State Teachers College in western Minnesota.[94]

Some New York csjs attended Columbia Teachers College, and when Mother Odilia Bogan requested a higher teacher's salary for csjs in 1911, her rationale involved more than money for living expenses. Citing the sisters' "competition with state schools" and having to work "under the Regents" standards that were "growing progressively more exacting and advanced," she wrote, "To equip our teachers for these conditions we are obliged to provide exceptional training both technical and scientific at weighty expense. To illustrate: for two summers we have had four Sisters at Columbia taking courses, to be followed by the same number this summer. This year four will go to Catholic University. We have but one regret —that our limited means do not permit us to care for a larger number."[95] Pushed by state requirements and a desire for quality teachers but limited by time and money, CSJs and other sister-teachers were in a religious, professional, and financial quandary that forced them to subsidize and improve their skills in parish schools, the very work setting that created a tremendous drain on their financial and personal resources.

When given the opportunity, sisters flocked to summer institutes, and Sisters' College at Catholic University was successful from its inception. During its first summer in 1911, 255 sisters from twenty-three congregations in thirty-one states registered for the all-day, five-week session. Sisters of St. Joseph had the third largest attendance of any congregation.[96] Nuns who wrote about their feelings concerning the summer session probably expressed sentiments of many of the sisters who attended. One sister wrote of "how good it was to feel that we no longer stood alone and unchampioned." Another sister thanked the college for "withdrawing its barriers" but shared her past frustration by stating, "The exigencies of the times are making such demands upon the teaching sisters as to strain their endurance to the snapping point."[97] One has to wonder whether male academics really understood the difficulty of obtaining a college degree while teaching full time. One well-known Catholic educator told sisters, "Let it not be said that our teachers have not the time for [higher education], that they are overburdened with classes or administrative duties. The busiest teachers, it will be found generally have the most time for study and writing. . . . It is not a question of time or opportunity, so much as ideals and atmosphere."[98] Obviously this academic had never spent long days in a classroom of sixty first graders while attempting to earn his degree on weekends and summers.

Some sisters completed their undergraduate degrees at Sisters' College after accruing large numbers of credit hours at secular institutions. Anti-garb laws had often barred them from completing teaching degrees at a state colleges because the sisters could not complete the final hours of student teaching. The sisters in Minnesota were forced to quit or continue to take hours without receiving a degree because they were unable to wear their habits in a public school and were barred from student teaching in a parochial school.[99] In Wisconsin, sisters could not attend normal schools because prospective teachers had to sign an agreement to teach in the public school.[100] Since they had already accrued well over the 126 credit hours required for graduation, CSJs and other sisters receiving B.A. degrees at Sisters' College needed only to complete a year of residence or approximately twenty credit hours to receive a degree. The list of graduates and their years of experience and past course work illustrates the dilemma for American sisters. Two CSJs, Sisters Mary Pius Neenan (St. Louis) and Mary Rosina Quillinan (Troy), were typical of the types of B.A. graduates in the first class of 1913. Both had over fourteen years experience in the classroom and had accrued hundreds of college credits before coming to Sisters' College to receive a diploma from Catholic University.[101]

Although Sisters' College helped the nuns acquire degrees and advanced education, financially it was a mixed blessing. Stretched to the maximum to send a few sister-teachers each year, communities of women religious not only paid tuition but were also asked to help finance the institution by building a separate residence for their order and paying a "ground rent sufficient to defray the expense of the upkeep of the grounds." Desperate for the opportunity to obtain degrees and accustomed to subsidizing all manner of church institutions, twenty-five women's communities agreed to build houses on the campus.[102]

The CSJs and other American sisters contributed to the workforce and financial subsidy that made the parochial schools possible in the nineteenth and twentieth centuries. Their work provided an important linchpin for American Catholic culture and identity for generations of children. Expanding on their European tradition of teaching, CSJs had to adapt to an American setting that required an ability to handle ethnic, linguistic, class, and gender differences while they attempted to maintain autonomy in a religious and educational setting that was moving toward more centralized authority and control. In many ways their struggles with male authority and their second-class status mirrored the difficulties of women in the public school system. However, their status as women religious, their traditional role as teachers, and the necessity of their services helped provide them with limited control in a patriarchal church and society. Nevertheless, at times they were caught between the demands of church and state and could please neither. It was in their role as educators of young women in secondary academies and colleges that they achieved more autonomy and expanded the parameters of gender in Catholic culture and American life.

Fill your minds with great things and there will be no room for trivialities. . . . She who would be woman must avoid mediocrity!—Sister Antonia McHugh

6

Educating for Catholic Womanhood

Secondary Academies and Women's Colleges

As dean of the College of St. Catherine, the first CSJ institution of higher education in the United States, Sister Antonia McHugh personified a generation of women academics who challenged their young female students to move boldly into the mainstream of American life in the early twentieth century. The CSJs had been in America for almost seventy years when the College of St. Catherine opened its doors, and during this time they had developed a solid reputation in female secondary education, particularly through the creation and administration of their private academies. Created, staffed, and financed by many orders of women religious, academies or select schools provided some of the earliest secondary education for girls and young women in cities and towns throughout the country. These institutions also laid the foundation for the development of most Catholic women's colleges in the early twentieth century.

Steeped in European tradition, female academies existed as early as the eighteenth century in territory that was to become the United States. Both Catholics and Protestants established some of the earliest boarding school academies, sometimes called seminaries, and many of these institutions were established by women.[1] In 1727 Ursulines came to New Orleans and opened a convent academy attended by both Protestant and Catholic girls. Later in the century other female academies were opened by private individuals in Delaware and Pennsylvania.[2] A few other academies existed for short periods of time, but it was the rhetoric and idealism of postrevolutionary America that provided justification for more education and the increase of both Protestant and Catholic female academies.

Urging Americans to live up to their egalitarian principles and hoping to develop a justification for female education based on the concept of "Republican Motherhood," both male and female educators openly discussed the need for and purpose of education for girls. The postrevolutionary debate on women's education reflected some European ideas on the importance of women's roles as mothers and educators of children, but it also had a decidedly American spin. Including both conservative and liberating aspects, "Republican Motherhood" argued that all citizens needed a broad education to maintain the new democracy and insure its survival for future generations. American mothers would be expected to train their sons for democratic citizenship and as future participants and leaders in the governance of the republic. This concept combined women's "natural" role as mothers with their new "political" role as participants in a democracy.[3]

Another factor influenced the growth and development of female education in the United States, particularly for Protestants. The Second Great Awakening swept the country in the late eighteenth and early nineteenth centuries, and the revivals and religious fervor associated with it provided further impetus for female education. Young Protestant girls and women flocked to these gatherings that often lasted days or weeks. Promoting youthful conversion and the individual's right to choose church membership as a matter of conscience, the religious movement encouraged many Protestant women to assert their moral and religious influence beyond the home. Although the ideal of the Christian wife and mother reinforced the need for women's education, Protestant women were also motivated to make their presence felt through social action outside the home, particularly as teachers. The western expansion of the United States and the growth of schools provided the stimulus for combining patriotic and

Christian ideals to justify the education of women as future mothers and teachers.[4]

Female academies and seminaries became the primary training ground for women teachers in antebellum America, and the academy continued to be the major institution of women's higher learning until the 1870s. These academies and seminaries were located throughout the country, but most of the earliest and notable academies were located in New England. Although some of them were administered and directed by men, the list of Protestant women founders reads like a who's who of nineteenth-century women educators and activists. Some of the more influential founders and/or leaders include Emma Willard (Troy, N.Y.), Zilpha Grant (Derry, N.H., and Ipswich, Mass.), Mary Lyon (South Hadley, Mass.), and Catharine Beecher (Hartford, Conn., Cincinnati, Ohio, and Milwaukee, Wisc.). The seminaries in Troy, South Hadley, and Hartford "became prototypes for women's institutions in the Midwest and Far West as well as the South."[5]

For the CSJs and other European communities that transplanted themselves to the United States, teaching girls of all ages had been a part of their heritage for centuries, and many American-founded communities opened female academies soon after their inception.[6] Seven of the first eight orders of women religious in the United States opened a convent school for girls. The fact that so many early graduates of Catholic academies were Protestants indicates that Catholic academies for girls fit nicely into the gender ideology of the dominant Protestant culture and benefited from the cultural and social debates on improving female education. However, the convent academies also had another role. As schools operated by a religious minority, the academies also helped to preserve the faith of Catholic girls and women to help them persevere in an American Catholic culture that was marginalized and at times actively persecuted. By 1820 there were ten convent academies, and by the time the CSJs began St. Joseph's Academy in St. Louis in 1840 there were approximately forty convent schools administered by many different orders of nuns. This number increased to over 200 by 1860, and by 1880 over 500 convent academies were scattered throughout the United States.[7]

Although convent academies continued to open in the twentieth century and provide a primary setting for Catholic girls' education, by the 1880s the growth of parish, diocesan, and private high schools provided additional opportunities for secondary education.[8] With few exceptions, regardless of the setting, nuns created and/or staffed the vast majority of these schools. As a result of convent academies and the sisters' focus on female education, Catholic girls, like their Protestant and secular counterparts, attended secondary schools in larger numbers than their male peers in the nineteenth and early twentieth centuries.[9]

Similar to other institution building, the proliferation of female schools—in this case academies and seminaries—was probably increased by the nineteenth-century competition and rivalry between Protestants and Catholics because it justified expanding women's education and role for both groups. The success and growth of convent academies and schools in the first half of the nineteenth century, particularly in the Old Northwest and the trans-Mississippi West, provided added incentive for Protestant educators to increase funding for their academies and to train young women in New England academies to teach in the West. Although teacher graduates of Emma Willard's and Zilpah Grant's seminaries had been heading west for years, it was Catharine Beecher who founded the National Board of Popular Education (NBPE), a formal organization that sponsored Protestant seminary graduates to teach in Western schools. The religious intent was obvious. Before being sponsored by the NBPE, teacher applicants had to prove membership in an evangelical church and describe their conversion experience. Similar to a young Catholic woman's calling to religious life and a "vocation," these "women teachers shared one common 'pull' factor, their sense of mission to bring Protestant evangelical religion and education to the West."[10]

Fearing Protestant proselytizing and alarmed that ethnic Catholics were sending their children to "Protestant" schools and Sunday schools, Catholic clergy clamored for sister-teachers to open convent academies and parish schools. Four years before the CSJs became the first group of sisters in St. Paul, the NBPE had sent a Baptist woman, Harriet Bishop, to open a "citizen's school" in 1847. In a letter to the *New York Evangelist* Bishop stated the importance of educating the French Canadian (Catholic) children who in her opinion were neither "American" nor "Christian."[11] It is understandable that Bishop Joseph Cretin brought CSJs to St. Paul to offer Catholic parents an alternative to the "citizen's" school. Clearly, battle lines were drawn and gender and religious ideology guided the fate of both Protestant and Catholic female academies, giving them added purpose and incentive.

The sisters' success with their academies was both feared and admired by leading Protestant educators, particularly Catharine Beecher. Daughter of a well-known minister and anti-Catholic spokesman, Lyman Beecher, she spent her life attempting to create a place for women in the social, professional, and religious realm of public life. Referred to by one admirer as "a kind of lady-abbess in educational matters" she disseminated lists of Catholic academies in the West in order to frighten male clergy and others into supporting her efforts.[12] At the same time, she presented a plan to create a "Protestant parallel to the Catholic pattern," establishing a web of interlocking social institutions of family, school, and church—with women in the central role. Beecher proposed that Protestant women be given the same "social support for their religious and moral activities as Catholic nuns received from their society." Utilizing nineteenth-century gender stereotypes but also sounding like she could have been quoting from a convent novitiate manual, Beecher emphasized women's need for "self-denial and self-sacrifice." However, so as not to offend her Protestant listeners, she carefully differentiated the Catholic form of self-denial, which, in her view, was "selfish" and aimed "to save self by afflictions and losses," from her Protestant version, which was not a means of "personal salvation" but a means to "save society." To fund this national program Beecher again used her own interpretations of American Catholic culture —an interpretation that American nuns would have found amusing. Lamenting how self-sacrificing Protestant women had been rebuffed in their efforts to do public service, she stated, "Had these ladies turned Catholic and offered their services to extend that church, they would instantly have found bishops, priests, Jesuits . . . to counsel and sustain; a strong public sentiment would have been created in their favor and abundant funds would have been laid at their feet."[13]

Although there were the obvious differences of religious doctrine, the goals of most antebellum academies, Protestant or Catholic, were the same: to combine religious and gender ideology in preparing young women for life—a life that was to include religious and moral behavior and obligations, domestic and maternal responsibilities, and social and cultural influence. Course work that developed mental discipline, intellectual enjoyment, physical health, teacher preparation, and aesthetic accomplishments certainly fit well into this religious and gender paradigm.[14] Within those broad goals, however, curricula did vary from one academy to another and from one region of the country to another.

Beginning their American foundation in St. Louis may have provided csjs with advantages and incentives to provide a broad-based and diverse academy curriculum. When the sisters opened their first convent academy in St. Louis in 1840, they had to compete with a large number of existing academies, both Protestant and Catholic, that had established reputations.[15] Nikola Baumgarten argues that although European-based sisterhoods had their own heritage and traditions as educators of young women, curricula in many academies in St. Louis "reflected the preferences of Emma Willard, Catharine Beecher, and other celebrated New England educators who tried to adapt the male course as far as possible without overstepping the boundaries of woman's sphere." Her analysis of the Sacred Heart Academy and other St. Louis academies documents the influence of these New England educators and their ideas on women's education in the Midwest, particularly concerning curricular offerings.[16] To compete effectively, the CSJ academy had to reflect similar ideals.

Besides conforming to high standards on curriculum, the CSJs utilized another strategy to enhance their academy's reputation. In the early and mid-nineteenth century, academies begun by French sisterhoods like the CSJs appealed to many wealthy parents who hoped to provide their daughters with a "proper French education." St. Joseph's Academy was popularly referred to as "Madame Celestine's School."[17] Profiting from their French heritage and hoping to compete with the nearby and highly respected Sacred Heart Academy in St. Louis, the CSJs moved quickly to upgrade the academy. American-born and highly educated, Sister Mary Rose Marsteller expanded and "Americanized" the secondary curriculum in the 1840s. As a result of her work, their first select school, St. Joseph's Academy, offered French, Latin, German, sacred and profane history, geography, mathematics, rhetoric, botany, physics, chemistry, and astronomy, as well as a variety of music and ornamental courses.[18] This school and curriculum served as a prototype for future CSJ academies that opened later in other parts of the country. Between 1840 and 1920 the CSJs would establish secondary academies in eleven states in every region of the country, from New York to California, Minnesota to Alabama, and throughout the Midwestern states.[19]

When the CSJs came to a new town or city one of their first acts was to advertise their convent academy. In 1858 the sisters in Oswego, New York, advertised their "Select School for Young Ladies," where they "will teach all the branches generally taught in the best academies." The sisters also offered "private lessons in French, music, embroidery, painting, etc. to young ladies who may desire." A sympathetic editor at the *Palladium Times* added an additional plug for the sisters, probably meant for his Protestant readers: "The Sisters of St. Joseph are a similar order to the Sisters of Charity, but are more especially trained for teaching and are highly accomplished, both in the common and higher departments of study. Their system of instruction is thorough and complete, and pupils will make rapid progress under their efficient oversight and direction. The accommodations at the house of the Sisters are ample and convenient for study and the comfort of pupils."[20]

The formal curriculum changed over time in response to educational trends and the expectations of American parents. As private, tuition-driven institutions, CSJ schools had to be responsive to what was educationally credible but also marketable to middle- and upper-class families. By midcentury, course work in "ornamentals" (i.e., painting, needlework, music), which had been standard fare in many New England academies also, was declining, and some scholars have argued that it never maintained the strong place in the academy curriculum that some historians have believed. Although the ornamental arts were clearly present in both Protestant and Catholic academy catalogs, in many instances they were electives and separate from the standard curriculum and required special fees. If parents wanted their daughters to take these courses, they often paid extra and sometimes steeper tuition rates than for the basic curriculum.[21]

CSJ academy catalogs support this interpretation, and although academies staffed by nuns were not all the same, the CSJs probably are representative of the larger religious communities that were active in female secondary education and had convent academies in urban centers.[22] In their earliest academies in St. Louis, St. Paul, and upstate New York, CSJs offered private lessons in music, art, needlework, etc., always for an extra fee. By 1860 in CSJ academies in both St. Louis and St. Paul, the cost of music, drawing, and painting was not only extra, but it also exceeded the cost for standard tuition and board for the entire year. This practice of separating the fine arts from the traditional curriculum and its higher fees continued in all CSJ academies through 1920.[23]

Another aspect of antebellum curricula that has only recently been explored concerns the existence of science courses in female academies. In her comparative study of girls' and boys' academies, Protestant and Catholic, historian Kim Tolley systematically analyzed academy curricula in all regions of the United States in the early nineteenth century. She concludes that while most boys' academies emphasized a classical curriculum, particularly Latin and Greek, girls took many classes in botany, chemistry, natural philosophy (physics), natural history, and physiology. Science courses were viewed as a way to improve "mental discipline" and as a good substitute for the more prestigious "classical curriculum" prevalent at antebellum boys' schools. Since girls were not expected to go to college and therefore did not need Greek and Latin to fulfill entrance requirements, science was substituted as appropriate course work for future "wives, mothers and teachers." Tolley states that many Catholic girls' academies "Americanized" by adding this science curriculum and by upgrading mathematics courses so that by the 1860s algebra and geometry were as common in girls' academies as boys'. In essence, science courses are what sometimes took the place of the ornamental courses in the standard curriculum.[24] CSJ academies reflected this pattern since those of the late 1840s and 1850s offered courses in botany, physics, chemistry, and astronomy, and by the 1860s, courses in both algebra and geometry were available. To differentiate this course work from either a classical or ornamental curriculum, CSJ catalogs sometimes referred to their standard curriculum as the "English Scientific Course."[25]

By the early twentieth century, academy course work reflected a new trend in girls' secondary education—the move toward vocational or practical education. Commercial courses in typing, bookkeeping, and stenography as well as a renewed focus on domestic or home economic skills became a part of the secondary curriculum. American educators, concerned about the utility of a liberal arts education and convinced that education should not be the same for all students, utilized gender, race, and class stereotypes to create vocational or practical programs to supplement or replace courses in the formal secondary curriculum. Academy education diversified in response to this ongoing trend in coeducational public high schools; some CSJ institutions added vocational courses as electives, while others gave young women a choice of three tracks: college prep, commercial, or domestic. Although music and art continued to play a large role in academy curricula, the subjects were never perceived as "vocational" or "practical" but as additional options, particularly for the wealthier students who could afford the extra fees.[26]

CSJ academies in different parts of the country varied in their course listings, probably in response to the expertise of available faculty and the market demand within the town or city. In St. Louis, St. Joseph's Academy offered a two-year commercial track and a four-year college prep track. Academies in Kansas City; Peoria, Illinois; Green Bay, Wisconsin; and Jamestown, North Dakota, offered commercial courses as electives, although St. Teresa's in Kansas City also provided a two-year domestic science curriculum. Academies in Arizona and California focused on college prep courses with selected elective courses in more vocational areas. CSJs in Minneapolis/St. Paul had three academies by 1907. St. Joseph's Academy offered three different tracks: a classical, an English scientific, and a commercial curriculum; St. Margaret's Academy (formerly Holy Angels) offered a college prep and a commercial track; while Derham Hall limited students to college prep course work.[27]

Although the formal curriculum of the convent academy changed over time and responded to societal attitudes on gender, its "hidden curriculum" remained amazingly constant through 1920. The "hidden curriculum" is the term educators use to describe the attitudes, behaviors, and activities that are part of educational institutions but not part of the formal course work. Although most CSJ academies began with a mixture of boarders and day pupils of elementary school age (girls and boys) and girls of high school age, by the late nineteenth century few boys remained and some academies accepted only females who had completed "grammar school." The mixture of boarders and day students remained in most academies, and the girls and young women, most between the ages of thirteen and nineteen, lived in an environment where the daily schedule of convent life was followed in many respects. Academy boarders spent twenty-four hours a day under the care of the nuns, and even local girls, who returned home each evening, spent most of the day within the convent milieu, experiencing the routines and life activities of the sisters. Mass, prayers, meals, uniform dress, celebrations and funerals, restricted hours, study, and recreation activities placed the girls in constant contact with nuns and convent life.[28]

Interaction with the sisters was particularly intense in the early years of many academies, where a mixture of sisters, boarders, day students, orphans, and sometimes "outsiders" had limited living space and mingled in most daily activities. Academy students visited the poor with the sisters, served as "English" interpreters for French-speaking sisters in some business transactions, and helped in times of emergency. For example, when a steamer was wrecked on the icy Mississippi River just below the convent and academy at Carondelet, the sisters and academy students raced to the scene with others from the village to bring "bottles of wine and good brandy, and bandages" to the 200 stranded passengers, thirty of whom were housed at the convent that evening.[29] An early student of St. Joseph's Academy in St. Louis described spring and fall picnics, when all the sisters and students, including the students from the deaf institute at the convent, trekked into the surrounding woods. "Our most pleasant excursions were to the Red bridge crossing the Meramec River . . . going as early as possible

Physics class, St. Teresa's Academy, Kansas City, Missouri, late 1880s (Courtesy of St. Teresa's Academy Archives, Kansas City, Mo.)

and carrying our lunches with us. Boarders, orphans, mutes, then became filled with joy and the woods were a perfect bedlam until we reached the bridge; there Grandpa and Grandma Pauponet came to greet us, and we lived like kings for that day as they gave us freedom to their garden orchard and hen nests."[30]

The early French-born CSJs probably bonded easily with the boarders since they also experienced homesickness and loneliness. Sisters seemed to enjoy amusing the students with "horrid ghost and fairy tales" and taking part in the students' recreation, at times forgetting piety and religious demeanor. One snowy winter two French-born sisters helped the students build a "hand sled," although they had never seen "a sled going down a hill with no one leading it." Sister Philomene Vilaine became so fascinated watching what she had deemed "impossible," that one student "coaxed her to seat herself on the sled and was going to push her down the hill when [Mother Celestine] who had been watching from the upper window came on the scene and terminated our sport."[31]

Later in the century well-established CSJ academies provided a more formal structure and separation between the sisters and students, but the convent environment and sisters' influence remained. Kate Hogan, who was accompanied by her mother to the CSJ academy in St. Paul in 1876, reminisced about her first glimpse of convent life:

> As we approached the stately old [building], with its round windows peering out of the gables on the roof, like the eyes of a monster, a feeling of awe came over me. . . . Thoughts and visions of Medieval Monasteries came to my mind, the descriptions of which I had read in story books. I dreamed of a foreign land, for I was getting farther and farther away from home, my courage was abandoning me and only that my attention was arrested by arriving at the door, I might have disappointed my mother's expectations.

In fact, discovering the "mystery" of the nuns' lives sometimes became a student obsession. Hogan and her friends talked constantly about the sisters' lives; their fascination is reflected in Hogan's description of the doorway that separated the academy from the sisters' living quarters: "This was reserved entirely for the Sisters and no student ever crossed its sanctified threshold. Its mysteries were never fathomed and years passed without any of the girls even getting a peep into that secret cloister or knowing just what the 'Nuns did when they were by themselves.' "[32]

Some girls and young women found the academy life austere, repressive, and stifling, while others thrived, emulating and admiring their favorite sisters. It is in the realm of student life and activities that convent academies were probably most distinctive from other secondary settings for girls. Based on an analysis of nineteenth- and early-twentieth-century academy catalogs and student handbooks, some historians have determined that convent academies had more student supervision and regulations compared to other secondary educational settings. By the early twentieth century, even as Americans' ideas about women's public behavior became more flexible, Catholic secondary academies, still based on the convent model and ideal, remained more conservative than other types of schools concerning students' vacations, correspondence, daily schedules, and extracurricular activities.[33] That a St. Paul student caused a "scandal" when her male cousin stopped to talk to her on the street during an academy outing is a reflection of this. Students at another CSJ academy realized they had breached convent propriety when, hoping to provide a special Thanksgiving drama production for the sisters, they decided to reenact the balcony scene from Romeo and Juliet. With the provincial superior and professed sisters seated in the front rows, the curtain opened. Seeing "Romeo," with a painted mustache and skirt pinned tightly to her legs to resemble pants, gazing at Juliet was "too much" for the provincial superior, who "left the hall[,] and the production was at an end."[34]

Some students played pranks to break the monotony and found ways to display their displeasure with convent rigidity. Resetting clocks and disrupting convent schedules, raiding neighborhood orchards, and making ridiculous "English" retorts to French-speaking sisters added merriment to the predictability of their lives.[35] Students not only competed for academic prizes but also "vied with one another as to who could play the biggest pranks or have the most fun." Being "smart, efficient, fearless, and daring" marked a student for "greatness" in the eyes of her peers and insured her acts would be a part of an academy tradition passed on to the next class. At times the students openly resisted when convent practices were not to their liking. Students in St. Paul, for example, returning from a school vacation, found out that their beloved music teacher had been recalled to the St. Louis motherhouse, never to return. In protest, some rebellious music pupils refused to practice and were determined " 'never to look at a piano again' or 'take another music lesson.' "[36]

Although rules governing student behavior were at times restrictive and formulaic, in the area of religious tolerance and religious freedom the convent academies demonstrated remarkable flexibility and openness. From the time of the earliest convent academies in the United States, non-Catholic girls enrolled in large numbers. All denominations of Protestant girls, Jewish girls, and girls without a religious affiliation enrolled in the sisters' schools, although the numbers diminished in the late nineteenth century when other educational institutions became available. Trying to survive among a Protestant majority and needing the money for their own subsistence, Catholic sisterhoods went to great lengths to demonstrate religious tolerance and to encourage non-Catholic enrollment. Academy prospectuses, catalogs, and advertisements boldly told the American public that religious diversity was respected and usually that the only religious requirement for non-Catholics was church attendance on Sunday. The catalog for St. Teresa's Academy in Kansas City is typical of other CSJ catalogs. Under "Purpose" it states: "There is no interference with the religious convictions of non-Catholic students, but all, irrespective of religion are required to be present in the Chapel at Sunday services." In Prescott, Arizona, at St. Joseph's Academy the CSJs added an additional clause to avoid any appearance of proselytizing: "Non-Catholic pupils are not permitted to study Christian Doctrine without the written permission of parents or guardians." The sisters in Tucson placed an advertisement in the

1881 City Directory to make their point about their academy's religious policy. They told readers, "As an indication of the tolerant spirit and . . . [to discourage] prejudice in this city, we will mention the twenty-nine children of Jewish parents" who attend the school. In Peoria, Illinois, a turn-of-the-century Protestant writer reported to his readers that at the CSJ Academy of Our Lady of the Sacred Heart, "pupils of all denominations are admitted, and except the religious instruction to the children of Catholics, all are treated alike."[37]

Protestant enrollment at CSJ secondary academies was typical of many female academies taught by women religious in the nineteenth century. In some cases non-Catholic parents were lured by the reputation of the French sisterhoods; for others it may have been the only choice for secondary education for their daughters, and for others the restrictive and close supervision of students appealed to many parents who saw the convent as a "safe" environment for their daughters.[38] Indeed, it is because of Protestant enrollment and the nuns' willingness to accept non-Catholic students that antebellum popular debate over the "Catholic plot" to convert America so many times focused on convents. Convent academies were seen as breeding grounds for such a takeover because they "captured the future mothers" of the nation. One antebellum writer warned readers that these converted Protestant daughters "will educate their children for the special service of the Pope of Rome, and their Catholic sons will become our rulers, and our nation a nation of *Roman Catholics*."[39] Regardless of the rhetoric, many non-Catholic parents sent their daughters to the sisters' academies, and in turn, convent-educated Protestant girls were often some of the fiercest defenders of the sisters against anti-Catholic bigotry.[40]

In reality the sisters did have a powerful tool of conversion at their disposal—themselves. Even with the restrictions of academy/convent life, many students thrived in the environment in which they were immersed, and, in some cases, the sisters became their surrogate mothers, confidants, and role models. In many ways, what was taught at the convent academy was not that far removed from the gender and religious socialization young girls received before entering the sisters' school. Most nineteenth-century American girls came to the academy from a white, middle-class culture already comfortable with gender-segregated activities and religious piety and practices. Living daily in a safe, supportive female atmosphere with habit-clothed religious women who practiced meaningful work outside the confines of marriage and motherhood certainly turned some Protestant girls and young women toward thoughts of conversion and possible religious life. Being present at religious celebrations, interacting with young postulants and novices, and watching some of their Catholic friends choose religious life made an impression. An academy student who watched her first "reception ceremony" provides a unique perspective on how many adolescent academy girls may have been affected by such a solemn and powerful ceremony:

> When the bridal train appeared headed by the little girls out of the "E" class carrying the baskets containing the religious dress, we were all on edge, for among the group of postulants to be received were Mary Werden, Lizzie Mackey and Annie Doherty who were employed on the boarders' side and we knew them better than the others. The singing was beautiful . . . resounding throughout the chapel, as the white-robed group moved slowly up the center aisle. . . . [I]t could never be forgotten.[41]

The CSJs, like many religious orders, have some well-known converts who were exposed to convent/academy life and became a force within the community. Converts Reverend Mother Agatha Guthrie, who held the highest position in the community for thirty-two years, Sister Monica Corrigan, who was a major force in the Southwestern missions and a self-appointed archivist, and Sisters Giles Phillips and Kathla Svenson, leaders in nursing and hospital development, are notable examples of women who decided to become not only Catholics but CSJs. The story of nineteenth- and early-twentieth-century American CSJs would be very different without the presence and activities of these women.[42]

If some Protestant girls were tempted by conversion or religious life, certainly Catholic girls, many taught by nuns in their younger years, saw the sisters as viable role models who presented them with an acceptable alternative to traditional domesticity and a meaningful life option that was viewed by many Catholics as a "higher" life choice. Friendships and attachments to sisters and peers who chose religious life certainly influenced some young women, and the secondary academies were indeed a recruiting ground for religious vocations. Moving from an all-female academy setting to convent life proved to be a natural transition for many. Many CSJs recall friends who joined the community together and how their own attachments to sisters who taught them influenced their decision to enter the convent.

Although CSJs were successful in attracting diverse populations of girls to their schools and later to religious life, the financing of these institutions continued to provide challenges for the community, particularly in the early years. Bishops and priests initially invited the CSJs to create academies in their parishes, but the sisters soon learned that the financial support and accommodations the clergy offered were often limited and overstated. The CSJ archives are replete with stories of "misunderstandings" between clergy and the CSJs who traveled to a new mission and "promises" unkept by the clergy. In 1871, on a bitter cold day in January, a group of CSJs came to Chillicothe, Missouri, to open an academy in the recently vacated Redding Hotel. However, what the local priest, Father Abel, had not told them was that the hotel had been uncared for and recently abandoned with "bare wall and heaps of debris" on every floor. Sitting on her trunk in the "bar room" of the dilapidated hotel, the superior, Mother Herman Lacy, "gave vent to her feelings." After working until nightfall to clear some of the debris, the sisters requested a lamp from Father Abel and were aghast when he also offered "a revolver for protection."[43] Sisters at Hancock, Michigan, spent their first year in their "promised" convent/academy in a building whose walls had not dried before winter arrived. Sister Justine LeMay wrote that every morning the walls were covered with frost, "very nice to look at, but not so nice to feel, for when it melted, the water ran down in streams."[44] Sister St. Barbara Reilly, who moved from the amenities of St. Louis to work in the academy in Tucson, learned quickly that candles, not gas, provided the light and eight buckets of sprinkled water "polished" the hard, dirt floor.[45]

Although the CSJ academies in New York were "plush" compared to those in other parts of the country, most academies survived and thrived with a mixture of funds generated from a variety of sources. Though the CSJs came to create academies at the request and often pleading of the clergy, clerical support varied widely and often diminished once the sisters arrived. For example, Father Bernard Donnelly in Kansas City had a three-story, brick building waiting for the CSJs when they arrived in 1866, but he did not have the means to continue financial support. Once classes began that fall, funding and financial obligations became the sisters' responsibility and they began supplementing their income as they had in other towns by selling scapulars, dead habits, raffle tickets, books, scrap iron, old bottles, old rags, embroidery, and needlework.[46] By the late nineteenth century most CSJ academies were financially secure, but the nuns were always scrambling to supplement their successful academies' incomes to help finance other, poorer institutions like the parish schools.

Typical of other CSJ academies, financial records from Our Lady of Peace Academy in San Diego recorded income generated through loans (many from women), donations, fairs, tuition, board, and private lessons in art and music.[47]

Art and music lessons continued to be major sources of income for the sisters, and large urban academies in all parts of the country offered extensive course work in both areas. "Conservatories of art and music" were usually housed within larger CSJ academies in St. Louis, Troy, and Los Angeles, but the St. Paul province took a different approach. In 1884 they opened a separate facility strictly for the visual and performing arts. Taking advantage of a national trend in the late nineteenth century to bring "the arts to American cities," Sister Celestine Howard conceived of the idea of founding a conservatory whose profits would help fund other financially struggling CSJ institutions. St. Agatha's Conservatory in St. Paul became the first arts school in Minnesota, offering children, adolescents, and adults the opportunity to take a wide variety of course work in art, music, drama, and dance.[48] Sister-teachers of the arts were trained in major American universities, and a few were trained in studios, galleries, and conservatories in Europe. National and international artists performed and sometimes served as adjunct teachers at the conservatory, which became a stopping point for artists touring the Midwest. St. Agatha's Conservatory achieved public recognition and provided large financial dividends for the St. Paul province. By the early 1920s, the conservatory was not only debt free but often generating $1,000 a day in revenue.[49]

CSJs also resorted to a traditional method of fund-raising used by many European religious communities—begging. Some American-born sisters abhorred the humiliating task, but many probably took a philosophical approach similar to that of Pennsylvania-born Sister Francis Joseph Ivory: After being "introduced" to "begging in the markets," she found it distasteful but stated, "[I]t seems you can get used to anything."[50] In the Rocky Mountain states and the Southwest, railroad camps, mining camps, and military posts were targeted because they had large concentrations of men who had regular payroll schedules. The sisters arrived on payday before the men's paychecks could be used for "entertainment purposes." Although the sisters appealed to the men's benevolence, the miners and railroad workers were also reminded of how they benefited from the sisters' hospitals and their children benefited from the sisters' schools. Sister Monica Corrigan, who made many "begging trips" throughout Arizona, had a particular flair for this activity, and stories of her exploits—including crawling into mine shafts and boarding railroad cars, soliciting from car to car on a moving train—abound.[51]

Another CSJ method of generating revenue was more indirect but demonstrated the sisters' understanding of the American entrepreneurial and competitive spirit. Since the academies were so dependent upon tuition and board for their survival, it was not unusual for CSJs and other women religious to make recruiting trips to adjoining states looking for prospective students. Academies in the Midwest often attracted boarders from many neighboring states, and just as they had made recruiting trips to Ireland and Mexico to secure new members, CSJs sent groups of sisters to recruit students for their academies.[52] Newspapers advertised when the sisters would arrive and where interested parents could contact them. Although these trips were beneficial for the academies, the sisters had to deal not only with stiff competition from other religious orders but also with gender and hierarchical politics. Whether on begging trips or recruiting trips, sisters had to receive "written permission" from the local bishop to solicit or recruit in his diocese. A letter from Bishop Matz to General Superior Agnes Gonzaga Ryan illustrates the obstacles the sisters faced. Chastising her for allowing CSJs to recruit in Colorado Springs without his permission, Matz told her to "withdraw these sisters immediately" because he did "not approve of Sisters leaving their convents to canvass for pupils in this manner." The bishop went on:

> However, the chief cause for objection in this case lies in the fact that the Sisters secured rooms in the Antler's Hotel and advertised this fact extensively in the press. This course of action caused adverse comment and reasonably so, since there are in the locality four houses of Sisters and many respectable Catholic families in which the Sisters could have received hospitality. . . . [T]he sisters failed to call on the local pastor of Colorado Springs, they were noticed in public parties sightseeing and spent evenings on the public veranda of the hotel.[53]

When it came to financing private academies and conservatories, the sisters knew that there would be little or no financial support from parish or diocesan coffers. But this had one advantage: although CSJs had to survive on their own, they struggled less with patriarchal control than sisters in parish, health care, or social service institutions who had to deal more directly with the whims of parishioners, local pastors, bishops, and male boards. However, owning and controlling an institution was not easy for any women in nineteenth- and early-twentieth-century America. Married women had few if any property rights, and single women had difficulty securing loans and transacting business in the male world of bankers and attorneys. Protestant bankers had even less desire to deal with foreign-born nuns who needed loans to create Catholic academies. In these circumstances the early sisters relied heavily on male clergy to handle legal matters, which often meant that CSJ properties were deeded in the names of individual sisters, local pastors, or bishops. This ambiguity regarding ownership invariably caused problems, and the archives of women religious are replete with "horror stories" of properties lost and devastating financial losses and injustices.[54] Women religious were perennially caught in a bind of trying to survive financially and to control their institutions while attempting to live their ideals of poverty, obedience, humility, and charity. Since gender socialization reinforced religious ideals of self-sacrifice, self-effacement, and submissiveness for women, American capitalism and entrenched patriarchal authority made the sisters easy targets for exploitation, unfair treatment, and criticism.

Even with a deed in hand, women religious were still subject to patriarchal control and pressure, particularly if it came from a bishop. St. Teresa's Academy in Kansas City provides an example of the vulnerability faced by many communities of sisters.[55] The academy property was deeded to the CSJs in 1867. In 1907, when the CSJs decided to sell it and acquire a larger space in the fast-growing southern portion of Kansas City, Bishop John Hogan intervened and flatly stated they could not sell because the property belonged to the diocese. Frustrated and clearly angry, the superior general in St. Louis, Agnes Gonzaga Ryan, argued with the bishop, but to no avail. She wrote the superior at St. Teresa's, Sister Evelyn O'Neill, lamenting, "There is no use! You might just as well give up the idea of a new building and a new site. I'll never go near him again." However, Ryan did give O'Neill permission to talk to the bishop and encourage him to acquiesce by offering to buy him a building to use as a girls' school for the parish. The bishop still refused, maintaining that the academy belonged to the diocese, not the CSJs. Apparently, although the sisters had a legal deed to the property, a second deed, written nineteen years later, gave them permission to sell the property only with the bishop's permission. Undaunted, O'Neill wrote the bishop a letter "placing before him frankly the facts as I saw them":

1. According to land prices in 1866, the entire St. Teresa's block was worth $50 when given to the CSJs.

2. The first convent was crude, having been built by unskilled laborers and could not have cost very much.

3. The CSJs met all expense of grading and paving the streets around the block. This included areas around the Cathedral.

4. The CSJs paid all the general and special taxes on the academy for 40 years.

5. The CSJs, with no help from the Cathedral parish, maintained the parish girls' school for 40 years.

6. The CSJs paid half the cost of the parish boys' school.

7. The CSJs kept high standards for St. Teresa's and had ungrudgingly provided untiring efforts for 40 years.

8. The CSJs had added to the original building, put a stone coping around the grounds and had paid for all repairs and upkeep for 40 years.

9. Only now, because of keen injustice, have the CSJs expressed any mercenary nature.

Bishop Hogan responded with a letter indicating that he would release the deed if the CSJs would indeed purchase a replacement building in the "location of his choice." Aghast that he still required more from them but determined to act quickly, Mother Evelyn set out to find a replacement building before he could change his mind. Recalling the incident years later, she said, "Even now it seems unfair. We had saved the Cathedral Parish during those forty years far more than anything that had been given us."[56] In hindsight, the CSJs had a "legal" right to the property, but in 1907 it would have been unthinkable for a nun to challenge a bishop in court—such was the power of gender and religious hierarchy.

Even with all the financial difficulties and the debates on the appropriate education for young women, CSJ secondary academies thrived, educating thousands of young women and influencing American Catholic culture and public life. In the early decades of the twentieth century, the CSJs moved further into women's education by creating opportunities for higher education. For the majority of Catholic sisterhoods, secondary academies played a significant role in the creation of women's colleges since most of the Catholic women's colleges that opened prior to 1920 began as an extension of secondary academies.[57]

Throughout the nineteenth century, the debate over women's education continued, although it changed over time. The development of the common school provided basic, coeducational education for young girls, and Catholic parochial schools, although often sex-segregated, provided similar educational opportunities for young females. By the late nineteenth century, adolescent girls were attending secondary institutions, public and parochial, in larger numbers than males.[58] However, even as more women began attending colleges after 1870 the debates over the appropriateness of higher education for American women continued well into the twentieth century.

In the 1870s, one of five college students was female, and by 1920, 47 percent of all college students were women.[59] These numbers were a result of the hard-won battle fought among American educators, physicians, theologians, social scientists, politicians, feminists, and the general public. Issues involving women's nature, women's place, biological determinism, psychological gender differences, divine or natural law, race suicide, and public morality all contributed to the discussions. Middle-class and wealthy Americans of various religious persuasions entered into the fray, and although Catholic colleges for women developed later than other women's colleges, coeducational institutions, and Catholic men's colleges, the gender aspects of the debate were strikingly similar.

From 1870 to 1900 opponents of higher education for women focused on biological and sometimes theological arguments. They viewed female education as a direct challenge to the traditional place of women in American society and in the patriarchal, Judeo-Christian family. Even in polite circles, the womb took center stage. A group of physicians and psychologists writing between 1871 and 1904 warned of the dire physical consequences awaiting women who attended colleges, particularly coeducational institutions. Former Harvard professor Dr. Edward Clarke labeled women's higher education as "a crime before God and humanity" and so damaging to the "female apparatus" that American males would have to "import European women to be mothers of the race."[60] Charles Darwin concluded that motherhood disadvantaged females and that through natural selection they gradually fell behind the male.[61] The medical and psychiatric establishment published "scientific data" proving that women had smaller brains, so mental and physical breakdown was assured. According to psychologist G. Stanley Hall, women were subject to "over-brain work." The "womb doctors" claimed that the uterus was a great power that dominated a women's mental and physical life, resulting in a weak, submissive, and generally inferior person.[62]

By the early 1900s coeducation had become the norm in collegiate settings, particularly in the Midwest and West, where public institutions welcomed women students whose tuition helped keep the colleges solvent.[63]

Contrary to decades of dire predictions, women, who now constituted almost 40 percent of the college student body, maintained good health as well as scholastic parity and in some cases superiority to males. Male college administrators and faculty fearful of the "feminization of academia" began worrying about having "too many women" on campus and the resulting "unfair advantage" to males.[64] Consequently, the biological doom argument was replaced with cultural and theological warnings that women in higher education resulted in "mannish" females, "effeminate" men, flirtations, promiscuity, early marriages, lack of marriages, dissatisfied wives and mothers, assertive females, emasculated males and/or sexually uncontrollable males, and other potential violations of "divine law." Although most of these sometimes contradictory fears coalesced around gender ideology, "race suicide" was also predicted, since college-educated white women not only married less frequently but had fewer children as well. This argument was not only taken seriously by many but also had the support of President Theodore Roosevelt, who publicly attacked the birth control movement and "selfish women."[65]

As a result of decades of debate and the increasing enrollment of women in higher education, American colleges and universities provided diverse solutions to what one educator at Catholic University labeled "a rather difficult problem."[66] By the early decades of the twentieth century American higher education consisted of a mixture of public and private institutions that included single-sex colleges, coordinate colleges (e.g., Radcliff and Harvard), coeducational colleges with gender-segregated curricula, and coeducational institutions with identical curricula.[67] Although the Catholic Church strongly espoused single-sex institutions taught by male and female religious, just as it did for younger students, the burgeoning Catholic middle class still wrestled with the feasibility of higher education for women and how it affected women's traditional role of wife and mother in the Catholic home. Although placed within Catholic theological and social discourse, the debates about women's higher education were similar to those taking place in the larger public domain and included liberal and conservative factions, with Catholic hierarchy found on both sides of the issue. Even though the vast majority of the clergy and laity tended to be conservative on this issue, proponents of women's higher education did have some outspoken advocates in the hierarchy.[68]

Regardless of the volley of rhetoric within Catholic circles, by the mid-1890s, three factors forced open the door to the creation of Catholic women's colleges. First, Catholic laywomen were already attending college in state or secular institutions, which was deemed a threat to the faith and found unacceptable by many conservative clerics and laity. Second, nuns, who were increasingly required to obtain college course work and degrees to meet professional state accreditation in education, also were attending secular institutions. Third, no existing Catholic college or university admitted women, except in small numbers for summer or off-campus sessions. In 1895, when Catholic University opened the college to laymen but continued to bar laywomen and nuns, the sisterhoods, with the help of supportive bishops, began to take matters into their own hands.[69]

When the College of Notre Dame of Maryland began offering the first four-year program for women, graduating its first class in 1899, other sisterhoods followed. Aided by a small but powerful group of bishops and male clergy, the Sisters of Notre Dame de Namur opened Trinity College in 1900. Unlike most other Catholic women's colleges, Trinity did not evolve from a sisters' secondary academy. Modeling its curriculum and structure after some "Seven Sister" colleges (e.g., Vassar, Wellesley), the nuns created it to function as a "coordinate college" to Catholic University in Washington. Terrified of having women students within a half a mile of Catholic University, the conservative Catholic press "charged that women students would present a danger to the university men" and might have the audacity "to apply to the university's graduate school."[70] Desperate to provide formal college training for their sisters and motivated to continue their legacy of education for Catholic girls and women, sister-sponsored colleges expanded rapidly in the early twentieth century. Although the quality of the institutions varied widely, by 1918 fourteen women's colleges were listed as accredited by the Catholic Education Association, and almost all were located in the East and Midwest.[71]

Although the history of Catholic women's colleges occurs mostly after 1920, the first two decades of the twentieth century laid the foundation for many colleges that would follow. Attempting to create viable institutions for a sometimes skeptical and reluctant clergy and laity, these early colleges (pre-1920) struggled to secure funding, students, academic credibility, support of clergy, and trained faculty. The first CSJ institution of higher education, the College of St. Catherine, provides a representative example of an early sisters' college that dealt successfully with these problems and established itself as a premier women's college in the Midwest.[72]

After decades of hope, planning, and struggle, the College of St. Catherine—the first Catholic women's college in Minnesota—opened its doors to seven students in St. Paul in 1905. The creation of the college was

Latin class at the College of St. Catherine, circa 1912 (Courtesy of the College of St. Catherine Archives, St. Paul, Minn.)

to be the crowning achievement for the Northern CSJ province, which had established the first Catholic parochial school and secondary academy for girls in Minnesota in the 1850s. Critical to this endeavor was the Ireland family. Discussions about a women's college began a few years after Sister Seraphine Ireland became a CSJ provincial superior in 1882. She was joined in her educational goals and endeavors by her first cousin, Sister Celestine Howard, and later by a younger sister, Sister St. John. When older brother John became the bishop of St. Paul in 1884, this foursome "was nowhere more bold and successful in realizing its ambitions than in the advancement of Catholic education in general and women's education in particular."[73]

Bishop Ireland, along with Bishop John Lancaster Spalding, was a prominent proponent of Catholic women's education at the national level. Touting that he was "a firm believer in the higher education of women," Ireland drew the ire of conservatives but continued to push for a CSJ college in his diocese: "I covet for the daughters of the people . . . the opportunities of receiving under the protective hand of religion the fullest intellectual equipment of which woman is capable. In this regard I offer my

Educating for Catholic Womanhood | 181

congratulations to the Sisters of St. Joseph for their promise soon to endow the Northwest with a college for the higher education of young women; and I take pleasure in pointing to this college as the chief contribution of their community to religion during the half century to come."[74] Ireland's clout propelled the CSJs into the educational forefront in St. Paul, and unlike many other bishops who resisted higher education for women and the efforts of women religious to create women's colleges, he constantly encouraged the endeavor. With Mother Seraphine's vision, Sister Celestine's financial acumen and Bishop Ireland's financial, social, and political networks, the college became a reality.[75]

Hoping to use their successful secondary academies as a springboard for student recruitment, the CSJs began formulating the plans for the college in the late 1880s. An editorial in the *Northwest Chronicle* in 1891 described the proposed college, and the author's comments clearly demonstrate familiarity with the ongoing debates concerning women's higher education. Lamenting the "past narrow sphere of woman," the writer asserted,

> [T]he education of the future must be as broad as the wide field opened up to the gentler sex. We are not here discussing the physiological questions regarding the underdeveloped and therefore uncomplicated state of the average woman's brain as compared with man's; we [do] accept the fact that the world thought fit to throw open to women almost every field of industry and intellect and therefore, Catholic women should be prepared to take part in this new and enlarged sphere. . . . There may be misdirected or one-sided education; there is no such thing as too much education.[76]

St. Catherine's, which promised a curriculum that "will comprise all the branches that are usually taught in colleges for boys," pledged to "secure the aid of outsiders who are specialists" in various curricular areas.[77] Unfortunately, a national economic recession, hitting particularly hard the Midwestern farm belt, placed the CSJs' future college and their academies in financial peril for over a decade. Resorting to traditional fund-raising techniques, the St. Paul CSJs peddled copies of the *Catholic Home Calendar* to raise funds and begged for donations. Similar to many early women's colleges in the East and some coeducational institutions, the projected CSJ college needed private endowments to provide support and financing.[78] Bishop Ireland signed over rights to his book of essays *The Church and Modern Society*, and the sisters hit the streets again, peddling it door-to-door, eventually selling 20,000 books and garnering $60,000 in royalties. Encouraged by Bishop Ireland, Hugh Derham, a local wheat farmer, donated another $20,000. The first building on campus, Derham Hall, was named after him.[79]

From the beginning the sisters aspired to create a high-quality institution. In addition to their vigilance and hard work in fund-raising, in 1903, in a highly unusual move for Catholic sisterhoods, the CSJs sent two sisters to tour European institutions of higher learning for women. On this fact-finding mission, Sister Hyacinth Werden, traveling with Sister Bridget Bohan, kept a diary and extensive notes about their travels, which also included stops at art galleries, museums, music halls, and other tourist attractions. Their favorite European institution, St. Ann Stift, the Catholic sisters college of Munster in Westphalia, Germany, became a model for St. Catherine's.[80]

Although the doors opened in 1905, St. Catherine's functioned only as a junior college, since early students either ended their education in one or two years or completed it at the University of Minnesota. Sisters not only struggled with financing but worked hard to attract students, sending pairs of sisters as far away as Montana to recruit. These activities directly challenge the stereotype of the demure, passive, and "otherworldly" nun. Knowing they were in a competitive and difficult economic market and understanding that they had to "sell" a women's college to conservative, middle-class Catholics, they ran advertisements in local secular and Catholic newspapers. This personal recruiting not only was the most effective advertisement; it also placed sisters squarely in the public arena:

> They went to and from the coast on the Northern Pacific and Great Northern railways on passes granted by the railroads on the assumption students would come back as paying fare. Each pair of sisters carried fifty dollars in cash to cover six weeks' travel expenses. They stopped in a fair-sized town along the way, staying without cost in convents or hospitals and in the homes of students or alumnae. They visited the homes of those who had inquired about the college or who were known as prospective recruits by students or alumnae from the town.[81]

Additionally, when coming to a new town, sister-recruiters would go to the local priest and acquire the names of adolescent girls in the parish. Margaret Shelly described how Sister Bridget Bohan arrived to talk with her father on the family porch in 1909 and the next thing she knew, "I was routed out to St. Catherine's."[82]

Through the sisters' extensive recruiting efforts, in 1911 the college had nineteen students, and when two students returned for their junior year, St. Catherine's finally had its first graduating class in 1913. In 1914 Sister Antonia McHugh was appointed the first dean of the college, and her energy and drive pushed the school into a more competitive arena. Educated at the University of Chicago with an M.A. in philosophy, she began moving the college from obscurity to recognition as a high-quality liberal arts college for women. McHugh's attendance at Chicago during the first decade of the twentieth century exposed her to preeminent women faculty in a variety of curricular areas. Historian Karen Kennelly credits the high-powered, academic atmosphere at the University of Chicago for much of McHugh's belief that "women could accomplish great things, and that college for women could and ought to be a gathering of scholars, great men and women, so wholeheartedly dedicated to the spread of knowledge that they drew students into a mutual striving for learning."[83]

After her appointment as dean, McHugh began to change St. Catherine's curriculum to emulate the University of Chicago's curricular offerings. Although Chicago was a coeducational institution and beginning to struggle with whether to have an identical or gender-segregated curriculum, she definitely moved St. Catherine's toward a "male curriculum." Upgrading work in mathematics, history, English, and French, McHugh made drastic revisions in the sciences by strengthening courses in chemistry, botany, and geology, while downplaying physiology, hygiene, and other gender-specific curricula offered at other women's colleges.[84]

Together with solidifying the curriculum, McHugh pushed for more sisters to receive graduate degrees. She and a few other sisters in the early years of the college already held advanced degrees, and by 1920 thirteen CSJ faculty had completed M.A. degrees from the University of Minnesota, Columbia University, and the University of Chicago. This trend continued in the 1920s with sisters studying in Europe and completing the Ph.D. in some fields. The college lay faculty held M.A.'s and Ph.D.'s from European universities, the University of Minnesota, and Northwestern, Chicago, and Columbia Universities.[85] Because of McHugh's networks at Chicago and Minnesota, the enhanced curriculum, and the faculty's advanced degrees, national accrediting agencies began to recognize the college. Between 1916 and 1920 the College of St. Catherine was accredited by the North Central Association, the National Education Association, the National Catholic Educational Association, and the Association of American Colleges. By 1920 its 218 students, from nine states, Canada, and France, also were

Art class at the College of St. Catherine, circa 1915 (Courtesy of the College of St. Catherine Archives, St. Paul, Minn.)

made eligible for membership in the American Association of University Women.[86] Never one to miss a public relations coup, Sister Antonia's recruiting brochures now touted the College of St. Catherine as "the only college for women in the Northwest belonging to the North Central Association, which places it educationally on a par with Vassar, Wellesley, and Smith."[87] Although the message was more rhetoric than reality, the intent was clear. This CSJ college not only wanted to provide opportunities to Catholic women, it wanted to compete in the larger public realm of American academic life.

Besides the College of St. Catherine, two other CSJ institutions had begun by 1920. In Kansas City, Sister Evelyn O'Neill pushed to begin college courses at St. Teresa's Academy, and in 1916 the junior college was established. From the beginning St. Teresa's Junior College was established as an extension of the secondary academy course work, and it would be decades before this institution became a four-year college. In the fall of 1920 the sisters in the New York (Troy) province opened the College of

St. Rose in Albany, New York. Encouraged by Bishop Edmund Gibbons, who hoped to "free our young women ... from the necessity of going far from home to pursue their studies in a Catholic college," Sister Blanche Rooney formulated plans for the new college.[88] Within the next five years csj colleges began in St. Louis (Fontbonne College) and Los Angeles (Mt. St. Mary's College). By 1925 the csjs had created four colleges and one junior college in four different regions of the country.[89]

Although these five colleges had somewhat different goals, purposes, and levels of support, csj institutions and other colleges begun by women religious had some common aspects. Most colleges begun by nuns placed a severe strain on community finances. As had been true of their private secondary academies, women religious had to finance almost the entire cost of creating and maintaining these institutions. Eventually the colleges became sites to train young sisters inexpensively, particularly for the parochial school system, but the training was never fast enough to meet the demands and pressures from parish clergy. Some clergy resented these colleges and felt that they took money, energy, and the best teachers away from the parish schools. Accusing the sisters of selfishness and wasted energy, other clergy felt higher education was unnecessary, was wasted on females, and overprepared the nuns for parish school teaching. Like some male public school administrators, some clergy preferred young, inexperienced, and compliant sisters to staff their schools. Time taken for professional development was time away from serving parish children. Additionally, to staff their secondary academies and colleges most sisters had to complete graduate work at secular colleges, an expense that strained community coffers. Although only the brightest of the sisters were groomed for college faculty, the csjs spent years and thousands of dollars to prepare sisters adequately. It was a huge investment made on each prospective faculty member.

Lastly, the sisters' move into higher education often challenged their convent training and religious ideals. Taught to be humble and self-effacing and to avoid singularity, sisters had to compromise if not reject these values to complete M.A.'s and Ph.D.'s in secular institutions that challenged them to compete, excel, and strive for individual awards and accomplishments. Ironically, just at the time that csjs discontinued their classist distinction between choir and lay sisters in 1908, it was necessary for some sisters to be singled out and propelled into positions of academic prominence and achievement if they were to accomplish their goals in women's higher education. Formal education, not socioeconomic level, became a new source of tension within the community. Sisters who earned graduate degrees created a new distinction, and at times it must have been difficult to mesh the religious goals of uniformity and solidarity with the "special status" awarded to college faculty.

In the early days of the College of St. Catherine, "one group within the community thought that sisters would be tempted to pride if they held academic degrees. They considered that it was sufficient preparation to pursue the courses, without being presented for graduation honors." Young Sister Antonia McHugh thought "this was worse than nonsense—she was sure that those who had this notion were too fearful of failure to make the effort to achieve standards." Fortunately for her, Bishop Ireland agreed and proceeded to send sisters to obtain advanced degrees at the University of Chicago.[90] Sister Evelyn O'Neill, however, received a different response from the motherhouse in St. Louis as she struggled to run a secondary academy and take advanced course work in hopes of establishing a college in Kansas City. This problem was not an issue of "pride" but an illustration of the "choice" many nuns were forced to make between daily teaching duties and working toward individual professional development and graduate degrees. Sister Evelyn O'Neill was chastised by Reverend Mother Agnes Gonzaga Ryan in 1913: "I am convinced you are doing too much [studying] and wish you to discontinue at once. . . . Stop all study immediately—this is a direct order; please understand it so; meant to give your mind the relief it needs. If you think it well for the sisters to keep on you may let them do so although I believe if they gave more time to class work and less to personal improvement during the year it would bring better results at the school."[91] This struggle both to perform community work and to obtain higher education and the battle between humility and achievement would continue well into the twentieth century and was resolved only with the changes brought about by Vatican II in the 1960s.

By the 1920s, CSJs who came from France in 1836 to teach American girls had established girls' secondary academies, high schools, and colleges in every part of the United States. Using Protestant and secular academies and colleges as an impetus and meshing American ideas about female education with their own heritage and religious ideals, CSJs expanded their educational outreach to and influence on females, from young girls to college women. Their nineteenth-century secondary academies touched the lives of Catholic and non-Catholic girls and laid the groundwork for Catholic women's colleges. The CSJ movement into higher education set a precedent for growth and achievement through the twentieth century and marked the sisters, along with other women religious, as important shapers of Catholic culture and American life.

The most visible and impressive aspect of the Catholic response to the social problems of the age was the founding of hospitals and orphanages. The people most responsible were women religious. . . . Care of the sick and of orphans was an area that attracted their attention from the very beginning.—*The American Catholic Experience*

7

Succoring the Needy

Nursing, Hospitals, and Social Services

Besides the founding of parochial schools, academies, and colleges, women religious created and staffed the vast majority of Catholic hospitals, orphanages, and other social service institutions in nineteenth- and twentieth-century America. Although most religious communities initially focused their work on education, the needs of the American milieu quickly moved them into continuing a European tradition in the care of sick and needy adults and children. The CSJs were similar to other Catholic women's communities in that they began these activities soon after arriving in the United States, but they are unusual among women's orders in that they functioned in all three areas: education, health care, and social service. Within thirteen years of coming to the United States the CSJs were active in all three settings.[1]

Although the history of the development of hospitals and orphanages is separate and distinct, in the early days of most new missions to American cities, the CSJs often provided nursing services and care for orphans in the same building. The early CSJ convents, academies, and hospitals routinely cared for abandoned infants and children, but epidemics and wars created a dual need for more hospital and child care since many children were orphaned or abandoned during these citywide or national crises. Between 1836 and 1920, the sisters' nursing activities during epidemics and two wars spawned the development of CSJ hospitals in every region of the country but the Deep South.

Nursing and Hospitals

Although the CSJs had been *hospitalières* in France for centuries, nursing in America for most of the nineteenth century was not considered work for "ladies." In the Victorian mind, women were the primary caregivers for ill family members but nursing a nonrelative male was considered obscene, degrading, and compromising to feminine virtue. In fact, with the exception of nuns, nursing was usually relegated to working-class women who performed manual labor and provided minimal care in the early almshouses for the infirm poor. Working-class and poor American women comprised the majority of nurses or patients in antebellum hospitals.[2]

Even without the social prohibitions of gender, nursing was also tedious, emotionally and physically exhausting, and dangerous, particularly when epidemics of highly contagious diseases and/or devastating war wounds required nurses to endure long hours, tedious bodily care, emotional and physical stress, and a high risk of death. Antebellum hospitals were viewed as places to die and places where the indigent were sent because they had no family to care for them. For women religious the religious ideal of "charity to the neighbor" provided them with the physical and emotional strength needed to carry out the necessary work. Viewed within a spiritual context, nursing gave sisters the opportunity to tend to the physical and spiritual needs of their patients and, if necessary, face martyrdom for their efforts. Also, their vow as celibate women allowed them to ignore some prescriptive gender prohibitions and, to a limited degree, nurse males or anyone who needed their assistance. In Europe and the United States, the constitutions and customs manuals of most religious communities had specific mandates and instructions for visiting and caring for the sick.[3]

Although historically care for the sick has been viewed by some as a "religious calling," the nursing profession received a boost and a renewal of the tie between religious commitment and nursing in the mid-nineteenth century with the accolades given Florence Nightingale and her nurses during the Crimean War. Twenty-four of her thirty-eight nurses were from Anglican and Roman Catholic religious orders. In Europe and the United States their well-publicized success brought recognition and a heightened public interest in nursing as a vocation and intensified the religious commitment of sisters to nursing. Some antebellum Protestant women looked for ways to participate in their own "religious communities" devoted to their "calling" to care for the sick. Lutheran and Episcopalian women, although attacked for their "Catholic tendencies," became deaconesses, staffed some hospitals, and managed to establish small numbers of sisterhoods in the United States.[4]

The CSJs' entry into American health care began more as spontaneous responses to "nursing opportunities" (epidemics, disasters, and wars) than as a systematic plan for sister-run hospitals. In fact, the creation and staffing of CSJ hospitals often resulted from the successful nursing done by sisters in their convents, in private homes, and in "isolation camps" during citywide epidemics. During the early decades of the CSJ mission in St. Louis, the sisters provided nursing care after devastating floods, riverboat accidents, and chronic cholera outbreaks prevalent in Mississippi River ports. Although the Sisters of Charity had a hospital by 1828 in St. Louis, the CSJs also nursed cholera victims during outbreaks in the 1840s, 1850s, and 1860s.[5]

When the CSJs moved outside of St. Louis, their nursing activities expanded as well. In the late 1840s sisters began nursing cholera victims in Philadelphia, where the CSJs staffed their first American hospital from 1849 to 1859. In the early 1850s the sisters sent to Toronto, Canada, Wheeling, (West) Virginia, and St. Paul, Minnesota, also provided nursing during epidemics. CSJs were specifically called to Wheeling to staff the first private hospital that opened in the city in 1853.[6] Likewise, within a year of their arrival in St. Paul, the CSJs began nursing cholera victims. In 1854, they officially opened St. Joseph's hospital but had been providing nursing since their arrival.[7]

Other Catholic sisterhoods also began health care work in antebellum America. A decade before the Civil War, twelve different religious communities staffed hospitals, both private and public, and many other religious orders gained nursing experience from their work during citywide epidemics. By 1861, sisters in seventeen congregations had created and/or were staffing approximately thirty hospitals in the United States. With this background, communities of women religious were the most experienced nurses in the country when war began, and their services were utilized by both Union and Confederate armies.[8]

In her book on sister-nurses during the Civil War, Mary Denis Maher states that the sisters brought four important contributions to Civil War nursing: tradition and experience, skills and religious commitment as a model for others, a willingness and ability to adapt to the needs of unpredictable situations, and written regulations for nurses, patient treatment, and personal discipline. CSJs in Philadelphia and Wheeling became part of the group of over 600 sisters from twenty-one different Catholic women's communities, representing twelve separate orders, who served during the Civil War. One in five army nurses was a nun. The sister-nurses staffed military hospitals and hospital ships, performed battlefield triage, operated "pest" hospitals for soldiers with contagious diseases, and turned their convents into makeshift hospitals.[9]

When the war began the CSJs in both Philadelphia and Wheeling had almost a decade of hospital experience behind them. The Philadelphia sisters helped staff a military hospital and later the hospital ships the *Commodore* and the *Wilden*. With the hospital ship anchored in the middle of the river, the sisters would be sent in small boats to gather the wounded from the battlefield before transporting them back to the ship. An account by a Sister of Charity described the ordeal that sisters experienced on hospital ships: "[We] ministered to the men on board what was properly known as a floating hospital. We were often obliged to move further up the river, being unable to stand the stench from the bodies of the dead on the battlefield. This was bad enough, but what we endured on the field of battle while gathering up the wounded is beyond description."[10] To avoid attacks from Confederate gunboats, hospital ships used the sisters' presence as deterrents to battle. On one occasion, naval officers on a ship floating downriver near Richmond assembled the Philadelphia CSJs on deck to alert a Confederate battery of its peaceful mission. Firing began before the Confederates recognized the sisters, and flying bullets narrowly missed Mother Monica Pugh. Later in the war, CSJ teachers from the academy in McSherrystown, Pennsylvania, found themselves within a few miles of a major battle. In its aftermath, they loaded their wagon "with bandages and homemade remedies for emergency aid" and headed for the wounded at Gettysburg.[11]

CSJs in Wheeling, West Virginia, were already running a hospital when the war began. After the battle of Harpers Ferry, 200 wounded soldiers were brought to the sisters' hospital. To make room, the csjs sent the orphans to another location and agreed to make the hospital available for wartime nursing. By 1864 the csj Wheeling hospital officially became a "post hospital"; field tents were added, and the Union army paid the sisters $600 a year rent and commissioned the sisters as paid army nurses.[12] The sisters treated both Confederate and Union soldiers and "prepared the corpses for burial and made the shrouds." With the scarcity of food and the inconsistency of government supplies and money, the csjs were forced to beg in the markets. In February 1865, frustrated with the government's unpaid bills, Mother de Chantal Keating headed to Washington to personally plead her case. Taking an "orphan girl, an insane soldier, and his keeper" with her, Irish-born Keating (in habit) probably caused quite a stir roaming the halls of the War Department; however, within two weeks the csjs finally received their overdue government funds.[13]

The anti-Catholic attitudes of nursing superintendent Dorothea Dix caused friction between her and the Catholic sisterhoods during the war, but nuns made a strong positive impression on many doctors, soldiers, and some Protestant women nurses. Most doctors appreciated the nuns' discipline, skills, and discretion. For soldiers who had never seen a nun in habit, their first experience was at best comical and at worst hostile. Some hid under blankets and refused to let the sisters touch them, others asked the nuns if they were men, and a few even spit, cursed, or struck the sisters. However, by the end of the war secular newspapers, government officials, and popular fiction lauded the nuns' discipline, selflessness, and dedication to duty.[14] The fact that sister-nurses were perceived differently from secular women by society was not lost on one Protestant woman frustrated with Victorian gender barriers that limited her participation as a nurse. Critical of people who deemed nursing unladylike for Protestant women but acceptable for nuns, she wrote, "A very nice lady, a member of the Methodist Church, told me that she would go into the hospital if she had in it a brother, a surgeon. I wonder if the Sisters of Charity have brothers, surgeons, in the hospitals where they go? It seems strange that they can do with honor what is wrong for Christian [sic] women to do. Well, I cannot but pity those who have such false notions of propriety."[15] The nursing activities and notable service of women religious during the Civil War had a major effect on diminishing anti-Catholic sentiment in the United States. Their religious identity also modified gender limitations, and their highly visible presence in nineteenth-century public life helped make inroads for the acceptance and expansion of the role of other American women in the field of nursing.[16]

After the war the CSJs and other Catholic sisterhoods continued to expand their health care mission. Soon after the CSJs arrived in Kansas City in 1866, they opened a "neighborhood clinic" for indigents when a cholera epidemic struck the city. Eight years later and after a smallpox epidemic in 1872, the CSJs opened St. Joseph's Hospital, one of only two hospitals in the city, in 1874.[17] CSJs also nursed the sick during the yellow fever epidemics that devastated Memphis in the 1870s. Although they were there as parochial school teachers, they became nurses during the years that the Memphis population was dying by the thousands. In fact, in 1878, during one of the last major outbreaks, six of the nine Memphis CSJs were in St. Louis for a retreat. Fearing for the lives of the remaining sisters, Reverend Mother Agatha Guthrie planned to bring them back to St. Louis, but the three sisters pleaded to stay in Memphis to nurse. Guthrie acquiesced and agreed to send three more sister-nurses, who volunteered from St. Joseph's Hospital in Kansas City, to help the Memphis CSJs during the crisis. Since no passenger trains were allowed to enter Memphis because of the epidemic, the three CSJs reached the isolated city by riding twenty-five hours in the caboose of a freight train.[18]

During the late nineteenth and early twentieth centuries, sister-run hospitals, and American hospitals in general, expanded to serve a variety of special populations.[19] In 1878 and 1880 CSJ hospitals were created to serve the needs of railroad men and miners in Prescott and Tucson, Arizona, and Georgetown, Colorado. Although the Prescott hospital and eventually the Georgetown one failed when the railroads pulled out and the mines closed, the sisters had provided health care for large groups of single men, many without families or female caregivers, who worked in accident-prone work settings and environments.[20]

Like their academies, CSJ hospitals accepted non-Catholics, a policy that was important enough that it was recorded in the CSJ Manual of Customs. The section providing instructions for "Sisters Employed in Hospitals" states, "If the patient be a Protestant, his religious convictions are respected, and he is not refused the consolations which his conscience may prompt him to ask. All will endeavor to show him the greatest courtesy and respect."[21] An early-twentieth-century brochure advertising the CSJ hospital in St. Paul contained the following sentence in its first paragraph. "The Hospital is in no sense a sectarian institution, as people of all creeds and nationalities receive alike the best that modern nursing is capable

Horse-drawn ambulance in front of the circular tuberculosis sanatorium at St. Mary's Hospital, Tucson, Arizona, 1900 (Courtesy of the Arizona Historical Society/Tucson, B#110,385)

of supplying."[22] Although all CSJ hospitals served Catholics and non-Catholics, the hospitals in the West, because of their scarcity, were particularly diverse. Ledgers from the hospital in Georgetown, Colorado, from 1880 to 1914 recorded a patient population that was 90 percent male and was Catholic, Protestant, and Jewish. During the thirty-four years of the "Sisters' Hospital," the approximately 1,000 patients represented eighteen countries and eighteen states.[23]

In the late nineteenth century, hospitals sponsored by ethnic and/or religious groups proliferated and formed a large segment of American hospitals. The CSJs took over hospitals to serve the Menominee Indians in Wisconsin and the Catholic populations in Lutheran-dominated Minneapolis and Winona, Minnesota. Various Protestant denominations and ethnic groups organized locally to provide their special populations with hospital care. At the turn of the century in a competitive and growing market, linguistic, ethnic, racial, and religious compatibility became important factors in hospital care with which women religious hoped to serve the physical, emotional, and spiritual needs of patients.[24] Kansas City, Missouri, provides a representative microcosm of late-nineteenth and early-twentieth-century urban health care and the highly "segregated" character of urban hospitals. Although a municipal hospital began first in Kansas City, followed by the csj hospital in 1874, other groups created institutions catering to particular patrons. At a locale dubbed "Hospital Hill," university and college hospitals were established in addition to the hospitals and clinics created by city funds and private interests such as the Wabash Railroad, the Missouri Pacific Railroad, the Red Cross, homeopaths, osteopaths, African Americans, German Americans, Swedish Americans, the Christian Church, the Episcopal Church, the Lutheran Church, the Scaritt Bible School, and Catholic religious orders.[25]

As sister hospitals and other hospitals continued to expand nationwide, the csjs were brought back into military nursing with the Spanish-American War. When the war began, 282 women religious, including 11 csjs, were inducted into wartime nursing. The csjs served with the Second Division of the Volunteer Army, first at Camp Hamilton, Kentucky, then Camp Gilman, Georgia, and eventually in Matanzas, Cuba. The eleven csj nurses were from the sisters' hospitals in Minneapolis, St. Paul, and Kansas City. The csjs found army life very different from convent life, but they learned to live in their "convent tent" and, adjusting their schedules, they "soon learned to obey taps and bugle calls." Although less intense than during the Civil War, distrust and animosity between secular nurses and sister-nurses abounded. Mother Liguori McNamara, the csj superior there, related in a letter to the St. Louis motherhouse that the secular nurses "are watching every move we take," but to avoid sexual scandals some doctors wanted sisters in all the wards "as [our] presence is a check to the [secular] nurses and doctors."[26] Indeed the sisters seemed to draw night duty, serving as a deterrent to romantic liaisons between secular nurses and doctors or patients. Besides the tension with secular nurses, McNamara also wrote about the competition between the three religious communities. Somewhat resentful that a Holy Cross Sister was given "command" over the csjs and the Sisters of Charity, McNamara privately referred to her as "Major Lydia." Another csj described the "segregation" in the nurses' dining room. "We all dine in the same room but at different tables. The Holy Cross nuns of course have a table for themselves. The [secular] nurses are seated at another table and poor St. Joseph and Saint Vincent's daughters (Sisters Of Charity) have a table together."[27]

Even with the periodic tension, the sisters seemed to enjoy themselves and had "many hearty laughs" as they dealt with "army rumors" that changed "every two seconds" and learned to "fight and steal" supplies

csj nurses and soldiers in the military hospital at Matanzas, Cuba, 1899 (Courtesy of St. Joseph Health Center Archives, Kansas City, Mo.)

since "it is the only way to get along." The csjs also worked closely with young soldiers who served as hospital aides to care for thousands of soldiers in camp, many of whom were suffering from typhoid or malaria. The sisters became very protective of the young men, refusing to report them when they fell asleep on night duty. To spare them time in the guardhouse on "bread and water," a sister would go "running into the wards" when a doctor made night rounds to alert the "poor lads" who found it "impossible to keep their eyes open" after midnight.[28] When the sisters returned from Cuba in 1899, their wartime experience was utilized to open new hospitals and deal with epidemics in other parts of the country.

In late 1899 some sister-nurses, including Sister Liguori McNamara, headed to Hancock, Michigan, after their return from Cuba to take over a newly created hospital abandoned by the Franciscans, using their government war salaries to finance the venture. When smallpox broke out during the first year, the sisters again found themselves in an "isolation camp." Harassed nightly by fearful and angry townspeople who wanted the sisters and their patients far from town, two sisters with wartime nursing experience moved with the ill patients to an isolated shack on the edge of the city. For over a month they were quarantined with their patients, coming out of the building only to receive food that was left on a fence post at a safe distance from the house.[29]

Likewise in 1918, with many doctors and nurses participating in the war effort, the widespread influenza epidemic strained the space and staffs in

Catholic sister hospitals as it did in all American hospitals. Sisters volunteered to staff some "emergency hospitals," even as they nursed the adults and children in their social service institutions and provided some home care nursing. CSJ hospitals in densely populated areas such as St. Paul, Minneapolis, Kansas City, and New York State struggled both to meet the war needs and to handle the flu crisis. Although CSJs did not nurse in World War I, many of the graduates of their nursing schools did.[30]

By the end of the decade, the CSJs had added additional hospitals in North Dakota and upstate New York. Of the sixteen hospitals founded by the Carondelet CSJs after their arrival in 1836, ten remained under their sponsorship, serving approximately 17,000 patients a year in 1920.[31] If hospitals founded by diocesan and daughter communities were also included, the Sisters of St. Joseph had founded thirty-five hospitals nationwide.[32] Although they had come to St. Louis originally to teach, they had become full participants in the nation's health care system. Beginning with "nursing opportunities" that placed them and other Catholic sisterhoods on the front lines during epidemics, disasters, and wars, they had parlayed their learned expertise into creating major health care institutions that over time served both Catholics and non-Catholics. However, two factors had dramatically changed their nursing activities during their first eighty-four years. First, hospitals and women nurses had become an accepted feature in American health care, and sister-nurses and sister-run hospitals formed an important part of the national scene. In the vanguard of early-nineteenth-century nursing and hospital care, sister-run hospitals in the twentieth century remained a visible symbol of American Catholic culture and its growing prominence in American public life. Second, as large numbers of trained doctors and nurses utilized advanced technology and staffed the growing number of American hospitals, schooling for all medical personnel became more rigorous and regulated. As in the arena of education, by the early twentieth century, sisters had to make adjustments to meet the growing demands of formal nurses' training.

During much of the nineteenth century, the sisters' discipline, dedication, and hands-on experience helped compensate for lack of formal training in nursing care. Dressed in habit and avoiding "singularity," sister-nurses responded well to the regulation, routine, and stoicism sometimes necessary for handling what could be highly charged, emotional situations, particularly during a crisis. But they were not the heartless "machines" that some Protestant nurses had labeled them during wartime.[33] Undoubtedly sisters were frightened and often repulsed by their nursing duties as they battled their own natural reactions and sometimes insufficient training. Throughout most of the nineteenth century, training was achieved through on-the-job experience, mentoring, and, later in the century, in-house teaching by doctors. Sisters recorded some of their difficulties and recognized the problems of mastering both the medical skills and emotional aspects of the job. Mother St. John Fournier had to help her young novices and sisters through the initial training in their Philadelphia hospital in the late 1840s. She wrote, "Our Sisters were so afraid of the dying that I had to stay with them during the night. If there was a festering sore to dress the Sister would faint. Little by little these poor children got accustomed to working for the sick and the dying."[34]

Arriving in Memphis to teach at St. Patrick's school in 1873, two CSJs found the Memphis sisters in the midst of a yellow fever epidemic. The new arrivals "were both deathly afraid of the fever on hearing of its ravages" and asked to remain in the convent while the other CSJs went to nurse the victims. Two days later when the doorbell rang the sisters were afraid to answer it, fearing it was a plague-stricken person needing their assistance. After repeated rings, Sister Mary Walsh opened the door to a local priest who asked her to nurse a dying parishioner and his family. After a "goodly number of tears, with fear and trembling," Sister Mary agreed to care for the patient.[35]

At St. Mary's Hospital in Tucson, Sister Mary Thomas Lavin, who was volunteering for night duty, spent an anxious evening worrying that some of the critically ill patients might die. To allay her fears she checked on them often. As one patient explained the next morning, "Every time I opened my eyes there was Sister standing over me with her lantern and pitcher of water. I never had so much water in my life."[36] Spanish-American War nurse Mother Liguori McNamara had eight very experienced CSJ nurses with her at the military camps and in Cuba, but she openly fretted about the lack of experience of two members of her group. The need to respond to the rigorous demands of army doctors and to compete with other sister-nurses and secular nurses put her under pressure to perform—and perform well. Alerting the Reverend Mother in St. Louis to her concern that even her most experienced nurses had to work hard to "hold our own" to meet the needs of the hundreds of disease-stricken soldiers, she wrote, "I do not think it advisable to send any more Sisters for the present. . . . Unless they are trained and well-trained, there is no use for them here."[37]

Before the 1870s there had been no formal nurses' training programs in the United States and nuns were the most experienced group of nurses in the country. However, by 1873 the need for better preparation of hospital personnel led to the introduction of formal nurses' training at hospitals in New York City, New Haven, and Boston. The first Catholic nursing school was opened in 1886 by the Hospital Sisters of St. Francis in Springfield, Illinois. CSJ hospitals experienced the same pressures as other hospitals from doctors, patients, and state accrediting boards to upgrade the preparation of nurses. They also began to have difficulty obtaining a sufficient number of sisters to fill the staffing needs of their fast-growing health care institutions. To meet these demands CSJ- and other sister-run hospitals began creating formal schools of nursing that included training not only for sisters but for laywomen as well.[38]

Religion, gender, and the experiences of nursing in the Civil War strongly affected the early training schools for nurses. Historians note that these early secular nursing schools maintained a blend of "religious, domestic, and military ideals identified with the 'calling' to nursing."[39] Likewise, the early application forms and informational brochures for CSJ nursing schools are reminiscent of those connected to entry into a religious community and the training of postulants and novices. When in 1915 Hulda Olivia Larson applied for admittance to the CSJ St. Michael's Hospital Nursing School in Grand Forks, North Dakota, she was expected to be between twenty and thirty years old, have a common school education, be in good health, and provide three character references. The young female applicants were provided with lists of rules, regulations, textbooks, curriculum, clothes to bring, and behavioral expectations. They received a modest room and board and a small monthly stipend to defer uniform or other school expenses. After a two-month probationary period they were allowed to wear the "training-school uniform" but "not allowed to wear laces, ribbons or jewelry while on duty." Subject to dismissal at any time for "inefficiency or misconduct," candidates had to complete three years of course work and on-the-job training successfully before they would receive their diplomas.[40]

The sisters at St. Joseph's Hospital in St. Paul began the first CSJ school of nursing in 1894, followed closely by hospitals in Minneapolis and Kansas City.[41] CSJs who nursed during the Spanish-American War or graduates of nursing schools often began nursing programs for CSJ hospitals, and some of these sisters had high levels of formal training at institutions such as Bellevue Hospital, Columbia University, and Mercy Hospital Chicago. Two older, highly educated converts played leading roles in the early days of csj schools of nursing. Swedish-born Sister Kathla Svenson received her training at Augustana Hospital in Chicago before she entered the community at age thirty-five. She served as director of the St. Mary's School of Nursing in Minneapolis and helped prepare the first three sisters from the hospital to pass the Minnesota State Board Examinations in 1914 to become registered nurses.[42] Sister Giles Phillips, daughter and sister of Protestant ministers, received her training in Kansas City and later at Columbia University. She entered the community at age twenty-nine and soon after became director of nursing at St. Joseph's Hospital and later at the csj hospital in Hancock, Michigan.[43] These highly trained and experienced sister-nurses often moved from one csj hospital to another to train new nurses and share expertise. This sharing of experience provided a consistent and rigorous curriculum for csj nursing schools, an important advantage over other nursing schools since the first standard curriculum for schools of nurses was not published until 1917.[44]

Training and teaching nurses was one of many collaborative endeavors between male doctors and sister-nurses. The nuns taught the textbook courses and nursing methods and the doctors provided lectures in their specialty areas. The growing specialization of health care, the sisters' primary role in administration, the increasing revenue of the larger hospitals, and the expanding prestige of doctors provided a certain autonomy and power for hospital sisters that went beyond the gender politics of the male doctor–female nurse dyad. Doctors and sisters worked in a parallel but interdependent universe with doctors controlling the medical staff and policies and sisters providing the nursing, training of nurses, housekeeping, and most administrative duties. In the 1920s at St. Mary's in Amsterdam, New York, the administrative and staffing contribution of the csjs was significant and typical of most sister-run hospitals. Nuns functioned as hospital superintendents, pharmacists, nursing supervisors and faculty, pediatric supervisors, emergency and operating room supervisors, blood bank and floor supervisors, lab and x-ray technicians, cooks, laundry supervisors, seamstresses, bookkeepers, and clerks. Sister Austin Dever's role was probably the most unique since she supervised the main office and "cared for the chickens." All these roles were filled by sisters who took no salary and were the sole owners of the hospital.[45]

Clearly, doctors and sisters needed each other for the hospital to remain medically accredited and financially viable. When doctors in Kansas City felt they needed a new hospital and updated equipment in 1914, the physicians had to convince the csjs to fund it. A series of letters from doctors in Kansas City to the superior general in St. Louis provides interesting insights into the deferential discourse between doctors and the nuns who sponsored the institutions. Calling the doctors at St. Joseph's Hospital "twenty conscientious, faithful servants" and "your staff," Dr. J. D. Griffith pleaded with the female superior, "We beg of you a conference."[46]

The control and autonomy exerted by CSJs and other sisters working in hospitals extended to leadership in secular, national nursing and hospital associations. Early CSJ nurse educators in Arizona, Minnesota, and Missouri held offices on their respective state boards of nursing, the National League of Nursing Education (NLNE), and the Catholic Hospital Association (CHA).[47] In fact, in 1914 fourteen CSJs from the St. Paul province met with Father Charles Moulinier, a regent of the medical school at Marquette University, to discuss founding a national Catholic organization to push for professionalization and higher standards for Catholic hospitals. The CHA began a year later, and the sisters held many prominent positions in the organization, which provided a "unique forum for women religious representing the communities engaged in health care."[48]

Although Moulinier expected the CHA to be a "sister's organization" and felt a sister should always be its president, conservative critics had narrower interpretations of what the nun's function was in the medical community. Compared to sisters in national educational and social service organizations the hospital sisters had unprecedented influence, but patronizing and sexist attitudes hampered the sisters' autonomy in the CHA and in their hospitals. In the early years of the CHA, conference discussions and written debate were dominated by male clerics who obsessed about whether sisters should attend night meetings, take courses from seculars, receive training in obstetrics and massage therapy, wear "washable" habits, use labor-saving devices, and join secular accrediting boards that "graded" Catholic hospitals and nursing schools. Male clergy were particularly concerned with sisters' participation in the secular and female-dominated National League of Nursing Education. Catholic hospital historian Christopher Kauffman places conservative critics of the CHA in two camps: One group feared that the CHA was "chasing after modern ways and secularism," while another feared a loss of Catholic identity, since "this whole movement with its Protestant and Jewish lecturers, will gradually turn over our hospitals to control of non-Catholic bodies, such as the American Medical Association."[49]

When sister-nurses' activities could mean life or death for patients, nuns sometimes found themselves trapped in a choice between "modern science" and medieval religious practices. In practical terms it could mean a choice between staying with a patient or making it to prayers on time or between assisting in an operating room or avoiding the sight of the male body. At times, "holy obedience" was indeed challenged even when directives came from the highest authority. Representatives from the Vatican, who were concerned about the work of sisters in American hospitals, attempted to investigate the activities of sister-nurses. In 1909 superiors of women's communities received a letter asking whether hospital sisters were performing activities "not altogether becoming to virgins dedicated to God." The Vatican prelate was particularly interested in whether men were patients, whether the sisters did bandaging or gave baths, massages, or "other personal services," and whether sisters assisted in operations, "especially on the bodies of men." A superior in the St. Paul province penned a very diplomatic letter in response. Telling the cleric that the sisters did have male patients, never gave massages, and performed only "slight bandaging now and then," she described the operating room: "At times Sisters may be found in the vicinity of the operating rooms, so as to see that whatever is needed is duly provided: but . . . nothing is done or allowed that could conflict with the strictest rules of religious modesty."[50] In reality, some sisters had received special training as operating room nurses, and archival photographs reveal that for some sisters being in the "vicinity of the operating room" clearly meant standing over the operating table next to the surgeon. CSJs and other hospital sisters, like their peers in education, tried to find a balance among the sometimes conflicting demands of their ideals and identity as nuns, to preserve autonomy within their own institutions, and to work toward professionalization in secular American society.

Orphanages and Other Social Services

Besides the emphasis on teaching and nursing, the European and American CSJ constitutions document the importance of care for orphans, the poor, and specifically young girls and women. Caring for orphans, both girls and boys, began immediately after the sisters' arrival in St. Louis, and it became an important aspect of the CSJ mission to the United States. Early orphan care was usually provided at convents and hospitals as the CSJs expanded across America in the nineteenth century. When monies became available, separate institutions were built to house the growing number of Catholic immigrant and poor children needing assistance.

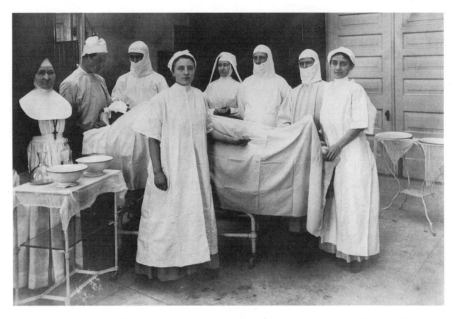

Surgery, St. Mary's Hospital, Minneapolis, 1908 or 1909 (Courtesy of Sisters of St. Joseph of Carondelet Archives, St. Paul province)

Although the csjs' main focus in social service became orphanages, between 1836 and 1920 they, like many other Catholic sisterhoods, also staffed charitable institutions that provided for widows, working women, women with dependent children, infants, and pregnant women and offered child day care. Creating an independent system parallel to Protestant charities, Catholic sisterhoods developed a large network of charitable institutions that spanned the United States.[51]

Historians of women have documented the importance of gender ideology in the benevolent activities of Protestant and secular women, arguing that gender construction gave distinct opportunities to create women's culture and public activities even as it set limits on them.[52] In much the same way that female nursing moved from the home to the public domain, public female benevolence reflected women's family role as providers of physical and emotional nurturing. Historian Anne Firor Scott writes that women realized that power and influence resided in collective action and therefore formed all manner of voluntary organizations "that lay at the very heart of American social and political development" in the nineteenth century. "[W]omen's associations were literally everywhere, known or unknown, famous or obscure; young or ancient; auxiliary or freestanding; reactionary, conservative, liberal, radical or a mix of all four; old women, young women, black women, white women, women from every ethnic group, every religious group had their societies."[53]

Although women's public activities and goals became more secularized in the twentieth century, for most of the nineteenth century, Protestant women used religious ideology as well as gender to justify their presence and influence in public charitable work, particularly when that work involved assisting women and children.[54] Some of the first philanthropic organizations and activities begun by Protestant women focused on expanding women's "natural" duties into the public domain. With increases in immigration and the growing problems of urbanization and industrialization, nineteenth-century Americans debated, as Europeans had for centuries, how best to differentiate between the "deserving" and "undeserving" poor.[55] For some Protestant women this meant expressing their anti-Catholic sentiments. Emphasizing their "natural" role in child care, many Protestant women's organizations focused on "saving children" from a "Popish" religion that became synonymous with poverty and intemperance. This attitude "underpinned the cultural authority of a multilayered middle class over the poor, the non-Protestant and the fallen."[56] As one historian summarized, "In the name of a Protestant Christ, nineteenth-century women's activists sought to contain the sexuality of working-class women and to remove Catholic children from 'undesirable' homes and place them as apprentices on Protestant farms."[57]

Such actions alarmed Catholic clergy and mobilized the Catholic sisterhoods to expand their mission by creating more Catholic orphanages in the United States. As historian Maureen Fitzgerald notes, "Nuns' efforts to counteract the influence of the 'child-savers' became the single most important strain of Catholic charitable work through the rest of the century."[58] In her extensive study of Catholic philanthropy in America, Mary Oates states that early in the nineteenth century Catholics saw Protestant benevolent agencies as "mainly proselytizing forums" and Protestant institutions as "dangerous." In response to overt proselytizing but also to demonstrate patriotism and social responsibility within the mainstream Protestant culture, the Catholic Church, mainly through the work of the nuns, began a massive institutional approach to charity. Sister-run charities, particularly Catholic orphanages, became a highly visible response to the social problems of nineteenth-century America and "represented an original development in American philanthropy in general." Oates explains,

Given the rhetoric of the day concerning women's proper sphere and [nuns'] exclusion from clerical offices in the church, their prominence in its voluntary sector was a phenomenon remarked upon by Protestant and Catholic alike. Although mainstream suspicion of them lingered, . . . their public vows, distinctive dress, ecclesiastical approbation, and essential social mission brought them considerable status within the church and, to a lesser extent, in the wider society as well.[59]

Fitzgerald not only agrees with Oates but argues, quite convincingly, that Catholic sisterhoods in New York City and other large urban centers had a major impact on some cities' welfare systems.[60] Certain characteristics of Catholic religious life made this possible. Unlike most Protestant women who initially learned the skills necessary for collective action in small religious or charitable organizations and usually had to balance these activities with their duties to their families, the sisters had to their advantage a centuries-old tradition of female collective living and activity, a large mobile workforce, disciplined and narrowly focused goals, and the ability to react quickly to the needs of a given situation. Responding to the problems of a growing immigrant, working-class population and coping with the aftermath of wars and epidemics, women religious, incorporating both gender ideology and religious ideals, were "natural" providers for orphaned children.

For the CSJs, the creation and maintenance of orphan asylums formed the mainstay of their social service in the United States. The sisters' activity peaked in the 1890s when they staffed twelve orphan and half-orphan asylums in six states; by 1920, they were maintaining nine different establishments that cared for over 1,200 children. These institutions were located in large and medium-sized cities in New York, Minnesota, Illinois, Missouri, and Arizona.[61] In their orphanages the sisters attempted to fill the role of "parent," "protector," "nurse," "teacher," and sometimes "child advocate." In a brochure describing St. Joseph's Orphan Home for Boys in St. Louis, the CSJs advertised that they "endeavored to supply a mother's care." Their activities placed them in the public arena that included the court system, city hospitals, parish schools, social service agencies, and private families. The CSJs requested references for prospective adoptive parents and at times required payment from biological parents who wished to leave their child temporarily in the sisters' care.[62]

Records from CSJ orphanages document that children were brought there by parents, relatives, police officers, clergy, or court order, or simply abandoned on the premises. The CSJ orphanage in Tucson, the first in Arizona, had no admission requirements other than that the child must be three years old and without a "natural protector or guardian."[63] Nineteenth-century records clearly show that almost half of the children the sisters cared for were "reclaimed" or "taken" by one of the parents or relatives after a few months or sometimes a few years. St. Bridget's Half-Orphanage had a very transitory clientele: the average stay was one year. Between 1872 and 1875, St. Bridget's admitted 186 children, and of these 86 were "claimed by relatives."[64] Clearly the sisters' orphanages served as a backup child care facility for parents who needed temporary assistance. Correspondence between Chicago clerics described the plight of working-class Catholics and how sister-run orphanages attempted to support these families during hard times: "These poor people try to put their children . . . where they will be able to see them frequently and bring them clothing and other necessaries."[65]

Consequently, the nineteenth-century orphanage was sometimes used as a temporary care facility when a parent was ill, financially burdened, or simply unable to cope with child care. CSJ orphanage records reveal the irony in the contemporary discussion of the "breakdown of the family" and nostalgia for the bygone days when families "took care of their own." Sometimes children were brought to the orphanage because they were ill or handicapped and the parents would not or could not care for them. In 1910, for example, two days after five-year-old twins and their seven-year-old sister were admitted to the sisters' care, they were rushed to the hospital. Scarlet fever, small pox, pneumonia, and measles were common conditions for abandoned children.[66] The CSJ Home for the Friendless in Chicago accepted children who were "neglected, ill-treated, or abandoned by parents or guardians . . . [or] whose mother is ill and whose father's resources are insufficient to provide the necessary care for the little ones."[67] The records for the girls' home in Kansas City listed the specific family situation for eighty-one children admitted during one year: 16 percent had both parents living, 23 percent had both parents deceased, 26 percent had only a father living, and 35 percent had only a mother living. The fact that more children had a single mother probably said less about parenting commitment than the economic realities of working-class women trying to care for a family in a gender- and class-biased wage system. The sisters were no Pollyannas concerning their surroundings, and they peppered the ledger with additional comments about the girls' families, such as "parents divorced," "mother insane," "parents separated and worthless."[68]

From the earliest days the CSJs functioned as caseworkers by attempting to find homes for the children who had no known relatives. Although the sisters interviewed and required references from prospective adoptive parents, problems still arose and children could be "passed around" or returned if the adoptive parents decided they did not want the child. For example, Nellie Wolf Thompson, who was abandoned by her parents, was five when she came to a CSJ orphanage in 1892. Five months later she was adopted by Mrs. Edmund Hoffman, who twenty-two days later left her at the "city hospital." Nellie was then transferred to the "children's hospital" and returned to the CSJ orphanage after nine months.[69] By the early twentieth century most Catholic sisters were working with state agencies to screen prospective parents more effectively. After 1907, the Minnesota sisterhoods worked with the State Board of Control and had two sisters present at court placement hearings for all Catholic children. They also initiated a three- to six-month probation contract with the adoptive parents to make sure the placement was a good one.[70]

The sister's role as protector and nurse more often meant daily care and protection from harm. Fires were always a major fear in orphanages, particularly those housing small children. The fast action of sisters in Troy, New York, for instance, saved the children, all eight years old or younger, when the St. Joseph's Infant Home burned to the ground. Smelling something hot, and though no flames were visible, the sisters awoke the children and called the fire department. The youngsters were dressed, told they were going on "an excursion," and marched or carried out of the house into a freezing December night.[71] Probably the most dramatic fire and escape came in the Chicago Fire of 1871. A CSJ orphanage located on lakefront property housed over 200 children and eighteen CSJs. Sister Incarnation McDonough wrote a firsthand account of the sisters' evacuation: "Each sister took in her arms two infants. The larger boys and girls took charge of the smaller ones, and we formed a close line of march . . . to hold on to one another. We started walking northward not knowing where we were going. Mad rushing people, some jumping through windows to save their lives, the hurrying of horses and vehicles, made it almost impossible to keep together. The greatest difficulty was crossing the streets." The large group wound its way through the city, led by Mother Mary Joseph Kennedy, and as they were attempting to cross a street two teams of horses came rushing toward them from both directions. Seeing the children, one driver halted, but the other driver would not. Sister Incarnation wrote: "Mother stepped up and took the horses by the bridle, while he continued to beat them. Passersby, seeing the situation, tore the driver from his seat, and gave him what he richly deserved. While this was going on, we seized our opportunity and got across."[72]

The gender and age of children often determined which sister-run institutions they would be placed in. As in parochial schools, gender segregation was important; some CSJ orphanages cared for only one sex, while others had both boys and girls. Compared to some religious orders, the CSJs were unusual in caring for boys. Girls who were not adopted often stayed until age sixteen or seventeen, but boys were usually transferred to a home operated by male brotherhoods or moved into a home or work setting by age fourteen.[73] The CSJ orphanages show an interesting pattern of gender segregation and differences among the four provinces. In large Midwestern cities in the St. Louis and St. Paul provinces, single-sex orphanages were the norm, but in Arizona, with small numbers of children, and in New York, with large numbers of children, CSJ institutions housed the sexes together but on separate floors or wings of the facility.[74]

Catholic orphanages, which were attacked by critics as warehouses where children received no individual care, varied widely in both numbers of children and numbers of sisters available to care for them. CSJ records indicate that critics may have overstated this problem. Although complete CSJ records are not available, data from the 1880s to 1920 from cities in New York, Arizona, Missouri, Illinois, and Minnesota provide some interesting insights into the sister/child ratio of these institutions. The number of children varied, but most CSJ orphanages each housed from 60 to 200 children. The data on numbers of sisters are remarkably similar in that most CSJ orphanages regardless of size averaged one sister per eleven children. In some orphanages in Missouri, Illinois, and Minnesota the ratio was even better, with one sister per eight children.[75]

In addition to the daily care of these children, CSJs provided the children with elementary school classes and vocational training. Sometimes the children were sent to a nearby parochial school, but many times the sisters maintained an elementary school in the institution. Providing basic education and teaching gender-specific work skills were considered important means to make the children self-sufficient and employable when they left the orphanage. A recent study states that most orphanages "provided educational advantages beyond the reach of most nineteenth-century families."[76]

As caregivers and educators, the CSJs also cared for the spiritual needs of their orphaned children. A publication for a CSJ home for boys states,

An immigrant child as brought to Aemilianum Orphan Asylum (*left*) and later in orphan's uniform (*right*), Marquette, Michigan, circa 1880 (Courtesy of Sisters of St. Joseph of Carondelet Archives, St. Louis province)

"Religious instruction is given the prominence due to it, as the only foundation of our holy religion."[77] Besides descriptions of baptisms, confirmations, and prayer activities, the sisters recorded their success as role models for religious life. In 1883, Sarah, Mary, Peter, and Teresa Dunn were brought to a CSJ orphanage after the death of their parents. Years later an entry in the orphanage record book states, with obvious pride, that three of the four children entered religious life. Peter went on to become a monsignor and started an orphanage in St. Louis.[78]

The traditional orphanage was the mainstay of CSJ social service activity between 1836 and 1920, but the sisters established other institutions that attempted to provide specific support to single women and single women with families. The CSJs came to Philadelphia to take over an orphanage, but within three years they not only had engaged in hospital work but had created St. Ann's Widows' Home by 1850. The aim of the widows' home was "to take care of poor widows and even of single old ladies from the age of forty or fifty 'til their death." Apparently there was a great need for this kind of facility. As one sister wrote, "The house can accommodate only thirty-six; it is always full and there is always a number waiting for empty places."[79] In 1885, the St. Louis CSJs opened another facility for women only, the Home of the Immaculate Conception for Working Women. The establishment was unique in that it served as a convent for sister-teachers, a housing facility or "night refuge" for young single women, mostly Irish, and an employment bureau for domestic servants.[80]

Two facilities that opened in the twentieth century show the CSJs moving into different types of social service that were precursors to their post-1920 activities. A large-scale social service institution was established in Chicago in 1912 when two CSJ orphanages were consolidated and a "Home for the Friendless" was created by the diocese and run by the CSJs. More akin to a settlement house or contemporary shelter than a traditional orphanage, the well-financed institution was to be a "temporary refuge for homeless women and children." Referring to a "comparatively new line of charitable work," the early documents described a large campus facility that included living quarters, infirmary, laundry, school, and playgrounds. It accommodated "mothers with young families who have been abandoned or left destitute . . . women, young girls and children without protection . . . women and girls who are traveling and find themselves in a strange city without friends or money [and] children who are neglected, ill-treated or abandoned by parents."[81] An even more "modern" establishment was created in 1917 in one of the poorest sections of Albany, New York. CSJs staffed the Masterson Day Nursery, which provided day care facilities for preschool and school-age children of working mothers who needed a place for their children to play safely and receive meals. During one year it provided approximately 15,000 meals to the preschool children who stayed all day and to schoolchildren who came for lunch and after-school care.[82]

Historians have credited nuns with providing a support system for Catholic women and girls that particularly benefited the great numbers of Irish girls and women in large cities. Male clerics, preferring to focus on children instead of adult women, often resisted efforts by nuns to establish and maintain support institutions for women only.[83] According to historian Hasia Diner, Catholic sisterhoods, particularly Irish orders, provided an extensive national network that "sustained Irish women from childhood to old age [and] services available to women exceeded those available to men."[84]

Unlike sisters who worked in hospitals, CSJs and other sisters involved in social service did not actively participate on secular state charity boards or Catholic bureaus of charity. When only eight nuns attended the first National Conference of Catholic Charities in 1910, the sisters were heavily criticized. Since sister-nurses who created policy and actively participated on external boards including the Catholic Hospital Association were criticized *because* of their involvement, this reaction presented an interesting gender paradox. Attacked by laity and male clerics, sisters who had been encouraged and at times pressured to build social service institutions to support Catholic children and the poor, and who had done so at a great personal and financial cost, were now told their ideas and institutions were "old fashioned" and not sufficiently "scientific." The sisters were depicted as "out of touch" and too easily "hoodwinked" by the undeserving poor.[85]

Lack of money and education as well as fear of losing autonomy to central Catholic charity boards kept sisters away from the national organization. Sisters in social service had little opportunity for higher education and consequently less interaction with other secular professionals or new trends in the field. By 1910 the few sisters selected for higher education were often chosen because of the type of work they were expected to do in the community. Teaching positions at the secondary and postsecondary level still received only the brightest sisters who were given some of the best educational opportunities affordable, but the need for well-trained sister-nurses to supervise all areas of the hospitals insured that larger numbers of them also obtained college degrees. Consequently, with limited funds and the increasing demands of professionalization in the twentieth century, the education of sisters in social service took a backseat to the need to educate sisters in education and health care.

Financing and Networking with Laity

Sisters involved in health care and social service institutions faced challenges in maintaining financial stability and networking with male and female laity. In both hospitals and social service institutions sisters provided most of the labor, rarely received salaries, and had the major responsibility for funding. Although the hospitals became financially profitable in the twentieth century, solicitation trips and begging were important components of early fund-raising for both hospitals and orphanages. Sister Monica Corrigan traveled throughout Arizona to acquire funds for the hospitals in Prescott and Tucson as well as the CSJ orphanage, and her escapades on a pack mule caught the attention of Jessie Benton Fremont, the governor's wife. According to Fremont, Sister Monica "was riding alone through the sage brush and rocks up into the mines, soliciting money for the proposed hospital, and killing snakes with a manzanita cane."[86] The spirited and indomitable Corrigan seemed to catch the interest of the public, and her solicitation activities promoting a type of "health insurance" received a lot of "good press." The *Arizona Miner* always reported her comings and goings and in 1881 wrote,

> Mother Monica of Prescott branch of the sisters of St. Joseph, got back safely, after a trip of seventeen days through the mountains . . . along the grade over 100 miles, visiting every camp, talking kindly, ministering angel that she is, to the workers [about] forming an association, the object of which is to have sick and wounded people along the road brought here to the hospital, and attended to, as only ladies of her order can attend to suffering mortals.[87]

Twenty years later Sister Angelica Byrne, accompanied by "an orphan girl," traveled over the same territory seeking funds to rebuild the burned out Tucson orphanage. Catching free rides in the caboose of freight trains, she took soliciting trips, returning to Tucson every six weeks to deposit her earnings. Four years later she had acquired the $16,000 to rebuild.[88]

CSJs and other nuns used some creative methods to support their hospitals. In Colorado and Arizona they sold monthly "subscriptions" to individual men or to railroad and mining companies. These individual and group subscriptions functioned like contemporary "insurance" policies guaranteeing that for a monthly or yearly sum an individual would have hospital care and a bed should he have an accident or become ill.[89] At St. Joseph's Hospital in St. Paul, for $100 per year individuals could maintain a "perpetual bed" for themselves or whomever they chose "to send when a vacancy occurs."[90] Although some of the hospital work was charity, much of it was provided to paying customers—an advantage that CSJ hospitals had over orphanages. Hospitals charged on a sliding scale for private rooms or wards; sisters in orphanages rarely received public monies or were salaried and had to rely on the donations of relatives or benefactors. With the advancement of technology, the middle-class acceptance of hospital care, and the growing prestige of male doctors, the profit and status of hospital work increased while institutional care for children began to fall out of favor in the twentieth century. As in contemporary America, child care was never a high status occupation or a lucrative one.

Parishes and dioceses rarely provided the major share of funding for hospitals or orphanages; more often it was "seed" money and occasional donations at later dates. Like the schools, many of these institutions began when a parish priest or bishop acquired a building, secured some support from Catholic and sometimes Protestant laity, and asked a group of women religious to staff it. If the CSJs agreed to staff a hospital they immediately, or within a few years, purchased the property, took on additional expenses to renovate and equip the building, and eventually filed to receive corporate status, with sisters serving as the board of directors. For example, for CSJ hospitals in Grand Forks, North Dakota, and Georgetown, Colorado, businessmen in the towns worked with local Catholic clergy to provide some property and an initial investment before asking the sisters to take charge of the facility.[91] In Amsterdam, New York, Father William Browne purchased property and a building for a hospital. Parish records indicate that Browne "gave" the hospital to the CSJs, but he actually sold it to them for $7,000, and they invested an additional $10,000 to transform the three-story building into a twenty-seven-bed hospital in 1903. Nine years later they spent $35,000 to add rooms, a sisters' residence, and a chapel.[92] With few exceptions, the sisters financed the buildings, the cost of care and equipment, and maintenance. Sometimes they even provided the manual labor. For instance, to help lower renovation costs at St. Mary's hospital in Amsterdam, New York, Mother Matilda Donovan, the hospital superintendent, rose very early each morning, pinned up her skirts, climbed a ladder, and painted the porch and trim "between 4:30 and 6:30 A.M. before the neighbors were awake."[93]

Sometimes orphanage and hospital administrators joined forces in fairs, raffles, and other fund-raising events. In Tucson, Arizona, and Troy, New York, CSJ hospitals and orphan asylums were located in close proximity and sometimes shared a common superior and finances. In 1889 the *Tucson Daily Star* advertised the upcoming "grand raffle at Reid's opera house on New Year's Day" to support St. Mary's Hospital and the St. Joseph's Orphan Home.[94] St. Joseph's Infant Home and its maternity hospital in Troy shared receipts from a "Patriot and Field Day" that was held in 1909 to help the sisters "pay off the loan" for both institutions.[95] CSJ orphanages in Minneapolis, St. Paul, Tucson, Troy, and Kansas City saved money by having a trained sister-nurse at the orphanage treat sick children; or, in cases of serious illness children could be sent to a nearby CSJ hospital at no cost. This practice provided significant financial benefit since epidemics, childhood diseases, and the high incidence of ill, abandoned children were chronic problems in orphan homes.[96]

Financially sisters' social service institutions were in a much more precarious position than hospitals: unlike hospitals that eventually generated profits for the CSJs, child care and social service institutions were lucky to break even. Although many social service institutions had a lay male board of directors, CSJs often assumed the financial burden. At St. Mary's Home in Binghamton, New York, the bishop placed Mother Bernard Walsh in control of finances in 1888, after the male board of trustees accrued a $60,000 debt.[97] At the CSJ boys' orphanage in Minneapolis, the male board of directors initially gave the sisters a salary, later reduced it, and finally did away with it completely. By the 1890s, their quarterly meeting "concerned itself chiefly with matters concerning the physical plant, leaving the active management and burden of support almost entirely to the Mother Superior and her staff."[98] At times the sisters were salaried "employees," at times not paid at all, or expected to raise most of the funds themselves. In St. Louis and Kansas City, a portion of Catholic cemetery funds helped finance orphanages, but even this yearly stipend was not secure. Father Bernard Donnelly, for example, had earmarked money from the St. Mary's cemetery fund to help support the girls' orphan home in Kansas City; however, a few years after Donnelly's death, when Bishop John Hogan wanted the money for other diocesan purposes, he simply cut the monthly stipend in half, and the sisters were expected to make up the difference.[99]

The survival of most CSJ orphanages depended on the sisters' free labor and their ability to acquire old clothing, supplies, and donations for their yearly expenses. Sisters from St. Mary's Home in Binghamton went to "factories and from door to door begging" and once a year traveled in a large wagon asking local farmers to donate vegetables for the children.[100] Although it was the exception not the rule, one social service institution the CSJs staffed had solid, if not ample, funding. The diocesan-owned Home For the Friendless in Chicago was a favorite of Bishop Quigley. In this case the sisters were salaried employees and the bishop insured that funding and monies from male and female lay groups provided for the needs of the institution.[101]

An important and changing component for sisters in the nineteenth and early twentieth centuries was their interaction with Catholic laity. The remarkable aspect of Catholic philanthropy was that the massive network of charitable institutions was built by a working-class, immigrant population. Both hospitals and orphanages benefited from parish fairs, male and female benevolent organizations, special collections, and personal acts of charity. Catholic laywomen have historically supported and many times worked alongside sisters as benefactors, public advocates, organizers of parish fund-raisers, and lay staff in schools, hospitals, and social service institutions. Ladies' aid societies, rosary and altar societies, the Queen's

Toddlers at lunch, St. Joseph's Infant Home, Troy, New York, circa 1910 (Courtesy of Sisters of St. Joseph of Carondelet Archives, Albany province)

Daughters, St. Margaret's Daughters, citywide Catholic Women's leagues and associations, and Catholic hospital guilds were examples of organized female groups that supported sister-run institutions and provided food, crafts, and monetary contributions for fairs and other fund-raising events.[102]

Other laywomen worked directly with the sisters. CSJs in Minneapolis worked closely with Julia Casey, a "baby-mother" who cared for homeless infants and unmarried mothers. The babies were baptized at the CSJ orphanage, and Casey worked closely with the superior, "caring for as many as twelve babies at a time." Casey also accompanied the superior on soliciting trips, served as a cook for parish fairs, and chaperoned the orphan children on special outings.[103] Catholic laywomen in Kansas City who were unable to achieve diocesan or private support for a small "maternity hospital" that provided care for poor pregnant women and "discarded" babies turned to the CSJs for assistance in 1907. As a way to establish obstetric training for St. Joseph's Hospital and serve the needs of poor women, the CSJS sent student nurses to assist the employed matrons with births and infant care at the "hospital." Besides the hands-on experience, students apparently also received a strong message about gender and class in American society. A former student recalled the "heartbreaking experiences" of witnessing the high infant mortality rate and the "little pine boxes stacked on the latticed porch at the end of the hall . . . until evening when the city wagon came to take them out to a place where the city buries its outcasts and where they were all put into one unmarked grave. We have seen eight or ten go out in one single day. We nurses got the experience we went there to get, but the price we paid can never be estimated."[104]

Laymen also supported the sisters' activities through their more visible public roles as benefactors, laborers, professionals, and as members of boards, particularly for social service institutions. Because of gender politics and hierarchical and paternalistic attitudes, the sisters' associations with laymen were at times problematic, particularly where there were male boards of sister-run institutions. Sisters who cared for orphans and staffed other social service institutions had much less autonomy than hospital sisters. They struggled for funding and often had to wrestle with lay or diocesan boards and battle with laymen over control and autonomy.

The history of the Catholic Boy's Home in Minneapolis provides a microcosm of the many types of tensions that resulted from gender politics. In 1878 Bishop John Ireland and a group of Catholic laymen established a corporation and officers to begin a new boys' orphanage in the city. Deciding to take "ultimate responsibility for construction and maintenance of the institution," the laymen asked the CSJS to staff it. From the beginning the CSJS were expected to share expenses, although the mother superior was never invited to the board meetings and was expected to submit written financial and statistical reports. Board members made inspections to "investigate the condition of things," and eventually there were "clashes of authority" between the female superior and the laymen, who accused her of "usurping functions of the board." Wanting to reassert their authority but obviously intimidated by the religious status of the nuns, the board members agreed to "visit the asylum in a body" to acquaint the "Matron" with "business principles." Even after the visit of the "irate gentlemen," the mother superior continued to exercise authority; in response, the men terminated the sisters' salaries. The superior then billed the board $1,200 for services rendered in 1888. Frustrated, the laymen asked Bishop Ireland to intervene with the sisters.

The board members continued to struggle to fund the institution adequately, so they asked their wives to organize fund-raisers for the orphanage. The laywomen organized many successful "orphan's fairs," and the proceeds along with the sisters' soliciting provided the major funding for the institution. Looking for a way to cut costs and fearing the sisters were being duped by irresponsible parents, the board wanted to take control of the admission policy. They requested that the superior refuse to take children who had any living relatives and that she send the board monthly acceptance reports for their perusal. Incredibly, when a physician requested money for "electric treatments" for one of the boys who had a "hip disease," some board members asked the doctor to consider amputation of the limb to limit the cost. By 1894 board attendance had dwindled so severely that Bishop Ireland and the remaining laymen dissolved the corporation and transferred control to the diocese.[105]

The twentieth-century trend toward diocesan centralization and control by bishops as well as the secular expansion of state and city charity boards and accrediting agencies effectively limited the participation and activity of Catholic laity. In the early twentieth century American bishops began to consolidate their authority within their dioceses, which, in effect, reduced the autonomy and control of the laity over their benevolent activities and monies. Mary Oates has stated that bishops tended to be suspicious of organizations they did not direct and that any organization that wished to be termed "Catholic" had to obtain episcopal approval. Although diocesan centralization may have been financially expedient, it also had a dampening effect on local lay interest and initiative. In essence, it placed all benevolent societies, male or female, in an auxiliary role and gave bishops and priests leadership and monitoring authority over charitable institutions within the diocese.[106]

Besides accepting clerical control, local laity who had helped support Catholic hospitals and social service institutions for a century had to submit to the authority of the "cult of professionals" and their move toward "scientific charity." To gain respectability in the Protestant mainstream, Catholic charity boards attempted to mimic centralization practices by forcing laity and communities of women religious to subordinate and centralize their activities under diocesan or national boards controlled by clergy and educated laymen. This had a particularly limiting effect on Catholic laywomen, who had worked extensively to support local charities and who found themselves not only restricted by gender but by educational status as well. Laywomen who had worked closely with the sisters on many projects were ignored and their activities marginalized as highly educated professionals, business men, and clergy provided the "public voice" for Catholic charity.[107]

Struggling to work within the growing professional world of health care and social service, CSJs and other sisters were also affected by diocesan centralization and the growing control of secular and Catholic accrediting boards. Perennially dealing with the dichotomy between religious self-effacement and humility and secular professionalization and achievement, nuns struggled to live in both worlds within religious and gender constraints that, at times, must have seemed irreconcilable. The sisters' various roles in hospitals, particularly as superintendents and supervisors, their financial independence, their working relationship with male doctors, their increasing educational status, and their stronger presence on both Catholic and secular professional boards helped them maintain more control and autonomy over their hospitals.[108] Sisters in social service, on the other hand, struggled with funding limitations, lack of educational opportunities, and their growing dependence on institutional boards comprised of laymen or priests. These factors made them more vulnerable than hospital sisters to limitations imposed by secular regulations and paternalistic Catholic charity boards that more and more relegated the sisters to nonpaid or low-paid "employee" status similar to that of parish school teachers.

By 1920 the activities of American sisters had made a significant impact on the expansion of American health care and social service. Although they would never rival the CSJs' and other sisters' contributions in education, sister-run hospitals, orphanages, and support services for women and families provided an extensive support network and "safety net" for immigrant and working-class Catholics in the United States. A centuries-old tradition of collective living, a vowed life, and a variety of charitable activities made American women religious natural players in the expansion of female-dominated institution building in the nineteenth century. The sisters' expanding activities in health care and social service helped support and shape Catholic culture and American life well into the twentieth century.

Epilogue

The six French Sisters of St. Joseph who disembarked in St. Louis in 1836 brought with them almost two centuries of tradition and experience in education, health care, and social service. For the next eighty-four years, through their efforts and those of the American- and foreign-born sisters who joined them, the CSJs, like thousands of other Catholic women religious, worked and lived at the center of Catholic culture and American life. Their story is one of survival, growth, risk taking, entrepreneurship, travel, and adventure as well as one of poverty, suffering, bigotry, loss, exploitation, and compromise.

The size, geographic extension, and diverse activities of the CSJ congregation make it an excellent example of nineteenth- and early-twentieth-century American sisters who numbered over 90,000 by 1920.[1] Nuns educated, nursed, and cared for generations of immigrant and working-class Catholics in every part of the United States. Catholic sisterhoods gave American women an alternative to marriage and motherhood, an opportunity for lifelong meaningful work, and a way to live out their spiritual ideals within an all-female community that shared similar goals and values. The travels and work experiences of sisters far exceeded the opportunities open to most nineteenth-century American women, Catholic or Protestant. Their religious identity provided them with the opportunity to go beyond gender barriers and produced the impetus and opportunity for them to be builders and shapers of Catholic culture and American life.

The nuns' impact on American Catholic culture was powerful and pervasive, particularly when one considers the linguistic, ethnic, and socioeconomic diversity of the Catholic population. Consistently outnumbering priests and male religious, sisters were everywhere, serving as visible symbols, spiritual educators, and active caregivers of the church, particularly in the nineteenth century when Catholics in more isolated settings rarely saw a priest. The CSJS' daily activities took them into homes, schools, hospitals, orphanages, and other settings that formed a support network spanning the country.

Although supposedly "sheltered from the world" the sisters were clearly in the public domain. By the mid-nineteenth century, American Catholics formed the largest religious denomination in the United States. Often the focus of anti-Catholic bigotry, nuns interacted with a variety of people, and this direct interaction with non-Catholics, particularly in the American West, in hospitals, and in their select academies, decreased hostile sentiments and behavior. The sisters' activities and institution building had a direct impact on the larger society and touched the lives of generations of Americans.

Using gender and their religious convictions to build their own institutions, Protestant churchwomen envied, resented, admired, and competed with nuns. Consequently, both groups of churchwomen ultimately expanded the gender and religious parameters in Victorian America in an attempt to justify female-defined space, influence, and activity in the public domain. Like their Protestant and secular peers, women religious sometimes challenged patriarchal authority in an attempt to maintain autonomy and control over their activities. Also like Protestant women, they had mixed success in this endeavor. If power and influence are demonstrated by an ability to act and create, the evidence suggests that American sisters possessed power, influence, and the ability to shape Catholic culture and American life. However, unlike white, Protestant women who honed their political skills and established a "public voice" on social issues involving women and children, nuns did not. Limited as members of a minority religion composed of mostly working-class immigrants and by "convent manners" that emphasized humility, obedience, selflessness, and public silence, nuns demonstrated their influence but rarely gave voice to it.

Lack of a public voice, which was also problematic for Catholic lay-women, and sometimes laymen, in a male hierarchical church has been a factor in rendering the influence of women religious unremarked and invisible. Not only has "Father" or the "beloved Bishop" been credited for many of the sisters' achievements, but twentieth-century stereotypes have buried the nuns' major accomplishments in either negative caricatures of rigid, ruler-wielding drones or in romantic and syrupy discourse describing passive and self-sacrificing martyrs. Both of these stereotypical extremes have been perpetuated by ignoring the strength, creativity, and risk-taking behavior that marked many of the CSJs' and other sisters' activities. "Passive minions" or "self-sacrificing handmaidens" could not have created, financed, and/or administered the vast number of educational, health care, and social service institutions that were an accepted part of American Catholic culture by 1920. The complexity of the sisters' lives and the breadth and significance of their activities belie these outdated and belittling stereotypes.

Post-1920

By 1920 the CSJs and other women religious were victims of their success and the increasing stability of the American Catholic Church. As shapers of American Catholic education and culture, they were now part of a large successful church that was moving more into the American mainstream and middle class. In fact, during the first two decades of the twentieth century, religious and secular factors coalesced, forcing sisters into a more subservient role than they had played in the nineteenth century—a role that would not change until the 1960s and the Second Vatican Council.[2] As a result of papal decrees in 1900 and 1901, the CSJs and other active sisterhoods were elevated to a "higher status" in the church. Their "simple" vows, which gave them lay rather than religious status, no longer excluded them from the ranks of "real religious," despite lack of cloister and "solemn" vows. However, this "elevated status" also brought more interference from Rome and the American male hierarchy. Episcopal control was strengthened over diocesan women's communities, and even orders with papal approbation like the CSJs were forced to standardize their internal organization, impose partial cloister, and restrict sisters' travel.[3] In addition to this change in religious status, by 1908 the Vatican no longer considered the United States a "mission territory" and the entire American church came under traditional Vatican authority. The 1917 change in canon law reified this tightening of control by Rome, demanding that sisterhoods align their constitutions to comply with Vatican perceptions of gender and religious life. One historian describes the changes: "After the first World War, sisters, who had worked energetically and with freedom, were slowly curtailed in their activities and made to conform to a role and lifestyle which defined them as demure handmaidens, delicate, withdrawn brides of Christ who were not quite human."[4]

Restricted in their travel and their interaction with seculars, family, and the outside world, limited in their autonomy and control over their missions, their flexibility as to religious exercises, and their ability to re-elect superiors, and hampered by new regulations, the sisters found their decision-making abilities and autonomy greatly diminished. Canon law had not been codified in 600 years, so the 1917 code required "the application of its prescriptions to the minute details of daily life [that] became a science engaging a whole corps of priest experts."[5] Every five years superiors of Catholic sisterhoods had to submit responses to a detailed Vatican questionnaire, which measured how well the community was following the new canon law. Innovation, risk taking, and responding to the contemporary needs of the people, which were trademarks of the sisterhoods prior to 1920, were discouraged in favor of rigidity, uniformity, regulation, and following "the letter of the law." The vow of obedience became the overriding concern.[6]

As part of this transformation process in the early twentieth century, American bishops honed their skills in the corporate world and began to centralize ecclesiastical and financial power within their dioceses. Catholic historian Jay Dolan writes, "Clericalism had become the standard, and the pastor, now enjoying a relatively long tenure in office, ruled as lord and master of his parish, where the lay people were left to pay, pray and obey."[7] Demanding more of sisters yet often ignoring the professional aspects of teaching, nursing, and social work, some priests and bishops saw these skills as "natural womanly instincts" and treated sisters as unpaid "housekeepers" of the church and its people.[8] The mavericks and free spirits who had helped expand women's communities and sisters' work in the nineteenth century could no longer leave an unpleasant or difficult situation with a superior or bishop and hope to be accepted in another diocese.

As historians of women have so often noted, opportunities for women expand when their labor is needed during times of crisis or during the early stages of growth and expansion of an organization or movement. When the crisis is over or the new organization becomes stable, women see their influence and power eroded and diminished, co-opted by a return to male dominance. Although for different reasons, American Protestant women and secular women's organizations also experienced some erosion of power in the early twentieth century when many previously all-female organizations became coed and males were placed in leadership positions formerly held by women.[9]

Although the sisters maintained their woman-only communities, control within the institutions they had created and/or staffed had significantly shifted to the male hierarchy. The American sisters who had once been builders and shapers in the world of education, health care, and social service found themselves in the quandary of needing formal education but lacking the time, support, autonomy, and funding to maintain parity with the secular professionalization in their fields. The proliferation of local, state, and national boards and accrediting agencies, secular and Catholic, often imposed contradictory demands on the sisters. Nuns were further isolated and marginalized with the centralization of Catholic boards and agencies that relied on clerical or male spokesmen to interact with secular agencies. The parochial schools, the sisters' greatest gift to the church, exploited them in ever larger numbers. At the very time that educational, social, economic, and political opportunities were expanding for women in American society, the Catholic sisterhoods were reined in and put under more stringent controls than their nineteenth-century predecessors.

After 1920 communities of women religious calcified under the weight of ecclesiastical hegemony. For the next forty-five years, Catholic nuns labored under what one historian has labeled "The Great Repression" and another "A Virtual Ice Age."[10] The irony is that young American women continued to enter religious communities in large numbers even though convent life after 1920 was far more dissonant with contemporary American society and gender expectations than ever before. This, however, is another story that needs prudent research and analysis, particularly considering the dramatic changes brought about by the Second Vatican Council in the 1960s, the ensuing decrease in religious vocations, and the more activist, and in some cases feminist, attitudes of contemporary American nuns. The years after 1920 have proven to be very different from the pre-1920 period, but they are equally fascinating and deserve careful analysis in the context of modern and postmodern American society.

Notes

Abbreviations

AAD	Archives, Archdiocese of Denver, Colorado.
AASL	Archives, Archdiocese of St. Louis, Missouri.
ACSJC-AP	Archives, Sisters of St. Joseph of Carondelet, Albany Province, Latham, New York.
ACSJC-G	Archives, Sisters of St. Joseph of Carondelet, Generalate, St. Louis, Missouri.
ACSJC-LAP	Archives, Sisters of St. Joseph of Carondelet, Los Angeles Province, California.
ACSJC-SLP	Archives, Sisters of St. Joseph of Carondelet, St. Louis Province, Missouri.
ACSJC-SPP	Archives, Sisters of St. Joseph of Carondelet, St. Paul Province, Minnesota.
BCIM-AMU	Bureau of Catholic Indian Missions, Archives, Marquette University, Milwaukee, Wisconsin.
CSCA	College of St. Catherine, St. Paul, Minnesota, Archives.
SJHA-KC	St. Joseph's Health Center, Archives, Kansas City, Missouri.
STAA	St. Teresa's Academy, Archives, Kansas City, Missouri.

Introduction

1. Memoirs of Sr. St. Protais Deboille, ACSJC-SLP. This is the only written record by one of the original six founders who came from Lyons, France, to St. Louis, Missouri, to begin the American foundation of the Sisters of St. Joseph of Carondelet (CSJ). Until recently, their sailing vessel was thought to be the *Heidelberg,* but microfilmed passenger lists recorded at the port of New Orleans on March 5, 1836, definitely show the sisters came to New Orleans on the *Natchez* (Port of Havre, France), and the sisters' names and ages were recorded as follows: Antoinette Fontbonne (age thirty), M. A. Fontbonne (age twenty-three), Maria Chapellon (age twenty-five), Margaret Boute (age twenty-five, although this is probably a mistake since the CSJ records indicate an August 19, 1804, birth date, which would make her thirty-one), Maria Vilaine (age twenty-four), and Clodine Deboyne [Deboille] (age twenty-one). See also "Passenger Lists of Vessels Arriving at New Orleans,

1820–1902," No. 259, Roll 13, Washington, D.C., National Archives Microfilm Publications.

2. After the attack in Charlestown, other convents in Baltimore, St. Louis, Galveston, and other locations were subjected to mob violence and harassment. Mary Ewens, *The Role of the Nun in Nineteenth-Century America* (New York: Arno Press, 1978), 70–73, 146–60. See also Ewens, "The Leadership of Nuns in Immigrant Catholicism," in *Women and Religion in America*, vol. 1, ed. Rosemary Radford Ruether and Rosemary Skinner Keller (San Francisco: Harper and Row, 1981), 101–4. For an excellent analysis of the Charlestown attack see Jeanne Hamilton, "The Nunnery As Menace: The Burning of the Charlestown Convent, 1834," in *U.S. Catholic Historian* 14, no. 1 (Winter 1996): 35–65. In the anti-Catholic atmosphere of early-nineteenth-century America, Protestants often assumed that women who entered the convent were either kidnapped or coerced. The term "escaped nun" was used arbitrarily and referred to women who left the convent as well as to nuns in habit who traveled in the public domain.

3. The term "religious" when used in reference to a member of a religious community (i.e., a group of individuals who live together as sisters or brothers and publicly profess religious vows) is a *noun* and "women" would designate the gender of the group. Although the term "nun" specifically refers to a member of a religious order whose chief purpose and work is to worship in a cloistered setting, it is popularly used to refer to any woman religious. Therefore, throughout this book we will use the terms "sister," "nun," and "woman/women religious" interchangeably.

4. Exact numbers are difficult to assess, partly because the sisters were marginalized by the church and their numbers were rarely documented as carefully as male clergy. Also, communities sometimes divided, and *how* each group was counted and at what period of time can make significant differences in final tallies. For statistical information on nuns see Mary Ewens, "Women in the Convent," in *American Catholic Women: An Historical Exploration*, ed. Karen J. Kennelly (New York: Macmillan, 1989), 17–47. Using a variety of Catholic directories published between 1817 and 1920, Ewens estimates that between 1830 and 1900, 106 new communities organized: 23 American, 8 from Canada, and 75 from European foundations. For a detailed analysis of individual communities in the early twentieth century see Elinor Tong Dehey, *Religious Orders of Women in the United States* (Hammond, Indiana: W. B. Conkey, 1930), and Evangeline Thomas, *Women Religious History Sources: A Guide to Repositories in the United States* (New York: R. R. Bowker Co., 1983). George C. Stewart's *Marvels of Charity: History of American Sisters and Nuns* (Huntington, Ind.: Our Sunday Visitor, Inc., 1994) painstakingly chronicles numbers of communities and their institutions compiled from multiple sources, including Elinor Tong Dehey's *Historical Statistics of the United States*, the *Official Catholic Directory* (New York: P. J. Kenedy, 1912–20), and a variety of nineteenth-century Catholic directories (under multiple titles) published by Creagh, 1822, 1840, and 1850; Dunigan, 1860; Sadlier, 1870 and 1880; and Hoffmann-Wilzius, 1890 and 1900. Stewart's "Sister-Population Statistics, 1830–1990" (Appendix F in Stewart, *Marvels of Charity*), researched by Catherine Ann Curry, currently seems to be the most thorough and accurate source for statistics on Catholic sisters.

5. Stewart, *Marvels of Charity*, appendixes C and D; *Official Catholic Directory* (1920).

6. Although most Catholic history continues to focus on institutional history and male clerical achievements and women's history continues to focus on the experiences of Protestant and secular women, there are some notable exceptions. See Jo Ann Kay McNamara, *Sisters in Arms: Catholic Nuns through Two Millennia* (Cambridge: Harvard University Press, 1996); Marta Danylewycz, *Taking the Veil: An Alternative to Marriage, Motherhood, and Spinsterhood in Quebec, 1840–1920* (Toronto: McClelland and Stewart, 1987); Ewens, *Role of the Nun*; Susan Carol Peterson and Courtney Ann Vaughn-Roberson, *Women with Vision: The Presentation Sisters of South Dakota, 1880–1985* (Urbana: University of Illinois Press, 1991); James J. Kenneally, *The History of American Catholic Women* (New York: Crossroad, 1990); and Mary J. Oates, *The Catholic Philanthropic Tradition in America* (Bloomington: Indiana University Press, 1995). For some recent anthologies on women and religion that include discussions on American sisters see *In Our Own Voices: Four Centuries of American Women's Religious Writing*, ed. Ruether and Rosemary Skinner Keller (San Francisco: HarperCollins, 1995), 17–60; Kennelly, *American Catholic Women*; and Joseph M. White, ed., *The American Catholic Religious Life* (New York: Garland Press, 1988).

7. Danylewycz, *Taking the Veil*, 96; Ewens, "Leadership of Nuns," 107; Margaret Susan Thompson, "Discovering Foremothers: Sisters, Society, and the American Catholic Experience," in White, *American Catholic Religious Life*, 275; Mary J. Oates, "'The Good Sisters': The Work and Position of Catholic Churchwomen in Boston, 1870–1940," in White, *American Catholic Religious Life*, 195–96.

8. Ann Braude, "Women's History *Is* American Religious History," in *Retelling U.S. Religious History*, ed. Thomas A. Tweed (Berkeley: University of California Press, 1997), 87–107. For further discussion on Catholic domesticity see Colleen McDannell, *The Christian Home in Victorian America, 1840–1900* (Bloomington: Indiana University Press, 1986), 52–76, and Ann Taves, *The Household of Faith: Roman Catholic Devotions in Mid-Nineteenth-Century America* (South Bend, Ind.: Notre Dame University Press, 1986).

9. James J. Kenneally, "Eve, Mary, and the Historians: American Catholicism and Women," in *Women and American Religion*, ed. Janet Wilson James (Philadelphia: University of Pennsylvania Press, 1980), 191–206; Oates, "'Good Sisters,'" 177. Patricia Byrne states that the sisters themselves reinforced this perception with their lack of expressiveness concerning even dramatic events in their lives. The CSJs who went to Cuba as nurses in the Spanish-American War never discussed their experiences. Byrne states that "their reticence was likely inspired by a desire to avoid 'singularity'—a considerable transgression of convent manners." Quoted from Patricia Byrne, "Sisters of St. Joseph: The Americanization of a French Tradition," *U.S. Catholic Historian* (Summer/Fall 1986): 263.

10. Leslie Woodcock Tentler, "On the Margins: The State of American Catholic History," *American Quarterly* 45, no. 1 (March 1993): 104–27. Tentler states, "The Catholic sisterhoods are without numerical equivalent in the nineteenth and twentieth centuries as alternatives for women to marriage and family life" (107). For a fascinating discussion of female friendship and friendships in the convent setting see Janice Raymond, *A Passion for Friends: Toward a Philosophy of Female Affection* (Boston: Beacon Press, 1986), 78–82.

11. Ewens, "Leadership of Nuns," 101. Using Catholic directories, Ewens states that by the late nineteenth century, sisters outnumbered male church workers in almost every diocese that kept records and that "there were almost four times as many nuns as priests by the century's close."

12. Most active or "apostolic" communities of women religious (as compared to contemplative orders that were cloistered and focused on prayer) provided one or more of three types of service: teaching, nursing, or social services (particularly in orphanages and homes for women). The CSJs engaged in all three activities, and between 1836 and 1920, 3,335 women entered the order. The Sisters of St. Joseph of Carondelet Profession Book, ACSJC-G (hereafter referred to as CSJ Profession Book), records chronologically the name and demographic information for each woman who entered the community and took final vows of profession. By 1920, the order had placed sisters in nineteen states in every region of the country and had created and/or maintained over 200 educational, health care, and social service institutions. These numbers are compiled from the "Summary of Community Statistics" in General Chapter Reports (1869, 1875, 1881, 1887, 1893, 1899, 1908, 1914, 1920), ACSJC-G. The states represented and the number of institutions changed over time with the advent of central government in the 1860s and the subsequent loss of some CSJ communities that came under diocesan control. By 1920, if all Josephite communities that have roots in the original Carondelet foundation are included, these sisters had worked in twenty-five states and Canada.

13. "Motherhouse" is the name given to the place where each religious community has its central base or government. Typically, the main convent of the community is located there and all postulants and novices are trained within this setting.

14. "Summary of Community Statistics," General Chapter Report (1920); Mary Lucida Savage, *The Congregation of St. Joseph of Carondelet: A Brief Account of Its Origin and Its Work in the United States, 1650–1922* (St. Louis: Herder Book Co., 1923), 319–28. A more recent CSJ history and useful secondary source is Dolorita Maria Dougherty et al., eds., *Sisters of St. Joseph of Carondelet* (St. Louis: Herder Book Co., 1966).

15. Braude, "Women's History," 89.

16. There are some excellent studies that demonstrate the ways that Protestant women have utilized their religious beliefs to expand their control and influence. Some examples are Peggy Pascoe, *Relations of Rescue: The Search for Female Moral Authority in the American West, 1874–1939* (New York: Oxford University Press, 1990); Kathryn Kish Sklar, *Catharine Beecher: A Study in American Domesticity* (New York: W. W. Norton, 1976); Nancy F. Cott, *The Bonds of Womanhood: "Woman's Sphere" in New England, 1780–1835* (New Haven: Yale University Press, 1977); and Ruether and Keller, *Women and Religion in America* and *In Our Own Voices*. See also Ruth Bordin, *Women and Temperance: The Quest for Power and Liberty, 1873–1900*, 2nd ed. (New Brunswick: Rutgers University Press, 1990). For an excellent discussion on religion in the lives of African American women see Evelyn Brooks Higginbotham, *Righteous Discontent: The Women's Movement in the Black Baptist Church, 1880–1920* (Cambridge: Harvard University Press, 1993). For an extensive bibliography of journal articles on women and religion see *Journal of Women's History* 3 (Winter 1992): 141–78.

17. Tentler, "On the Margins," 107–8.

18. Besides the works cited earlier that document the direct impact of religion in the lives of Protestant women, other scholars describe women's organizational activities that were grounded in their Protestant worldview but articulated in a more "secular" public culture of reform and activism in the nineteenth and early twentieth centuries. Examples include Kathryn Kish Sklar, *Florence Kelly and the Nation's Work: The Rise of Women's Political Culture, 1830–1900* (New Haven: Yale University Press, 1995); Anne Firor Scott, *Natural Allies: Women's Associations in American History* (Urbana: University of Illinois Press, 1992); Lori D. Ginzberg, *Women and the Work of Benevolence: Morality, Politics and Class in the Nineteenth-Century United States* (New Haven: Yale University Press, 1990); Nancy A. Hewitt, *Women's Activism and Social Change: Rochester, New York, 1822–1872* (Ithaca: Cornell University Press, 1984); and Mary P. Ryan, *Cradle of the Middle Class: The Family in Oneida County, New York, 1790–1865* (New York: Cambridge University Press, 1981).

19. Assessing ethnic diversity was not an easy task. In the eighty-four years covered by this study the CSJs had many foreign-born sisters who entered their ranks. Approximately 32 percent were foreign-born, coming from nineteen different countries. Although exact data is impossible to acquire, it can be speculated that many second-generation immigrant daughters also entered the order. The Catholic population, particularly by the end of 1920, was also extremely ethnically diverse, and although many parishes coalesced around an ethnic population, the CSJs were sent all over the country into a myriad of ethnic communities. For a discussion of this Americanization process see Byrne, "Sisters of St. Joseph," 241–72.

20. "Decrees of the General Chapter, 1908," ACSJC-G. In 1836, when the sisters came from France, the community, like most other European-founded religious orders, continued the practice of differentiating sisters into "choir" or "lay" sisters, with the latter group performing domestic chores, wearing a different style habit, and not having full community privileges. In the late nineteenth and early twentieth centuries, most religious orders eventually discontinued the practice because it clashed with American egalitarian ideals. See Margaret Susan Thompson, "Sisterhood and Power: Class, Culture, and Ethnicity in the American Convent," *Colby Library Quarterly* 25, no. 3 (September 1989): 149–75.

21. Ewens, "Leadership of Nuns," 101. In discussing anti-Catholic hostility Ewens gives major credit to the sisters and their activities. She states: "It might well be shown that sisters' efforts were far more effective than those of bishops or priests. . . . It was they who established schools in cities and remote settlements . . . and succored the needy . . . [they] who changed public attitudes toward the church from hostility to respect."

22. The CSJ Constitution (1860 and 1884) and the CSJ Customs Book (handwritten, 1868), ACSJC-SLP, delineate the specific types of activities that were appropriate and when for postulants, novices, and professed. By the late nineteenth century, CSJs, like many other orders, began to add more formal education, particularly for those who would be teachers or nurses; however, this varied among the four CSJ provinces. A good overall secondary source on the education and the historical changes in American sisters' education, particularly prior to World War I, is Bertrande Meyer, *The Education of Sisters* (New York: Sheed and Ward, 1941), 3–49.

23. Mission records for each CSJ document the types of work settings and location of all assignments throughout her religious life. The assignments were usually based on need, and it was not unusual for a sister, particularly in the nineteenth century, to have served in nine or ten different locations, working in two or sometimes three different roles (education, health care, and social service) during her career.

24. We do not mean to denigrate the efforts of Protestant women's organizations or downplay their importance. However, we would argue that there was greater socioeconomic disparity between many members of Protestant women's organizations and their recipients compared with Catholic nuns and their clientele. Because nineteenth-century ideology frequently associated the "poor and the needy" with biological or social inferiority, this attitude oftentimes led benefactors to feel superior to or patronize those they aided. In spite of the institutional wealth of the Catholic Church, nineteenth- and twentieth-century activities of women religious were often minimally funded, and nuns (more so than male clerics) lived a life comparable to that of the community they served.

25. Correspondence between Rev. Mother Agnes Gonzaga Ryan and Fr. Peter J. Geraghty, September 21 and 25, 1911, ACSJC-SLP.

26. Gerda Lerner, *The Creation of Patriarchy* (New York: Oxford Press, 1985), 215–16, and *The Creation of Feminist Consciousness: From the Middle Ages to 1870* (New York: Oxford University Press, 1993), 58–74, 227–46.

27. For information on non-Catholic sisterhoods see Thomas, *Women Religious History Sources*. Thomas's book includes information on Lutheran, Episcopalian, Methodist, Mennonite, and Orthodox orders of sisters and deaconesses. See also Catherine M. Prelinger, *Episcopal Women: Gender, Spirituality and Commitment in an American Mainline Denomination* (New York: Oxford University Press, 1992).

Chapter One

1. Patricia Ranft, *Women and the Religious Life in Premodern Europe* (New York: St. Martin's Press, 1996), 104. The Catholic Church convened the Council of Trent in 1545 to clarify doctrine and enact administrative and disciplinary reforms in response to the Protestant challenge.

2. Judith Combes Taylor, "From Proselytizing to Social Reform: Three Generations of French Female Teaching Congregations, 1600–1720" (Ph.D. diss., Arizona State University, 1980), 192–93, 197–98, and 706–26.

3. Monks and nuns with solemn vows had to accept cloister and a kind of civil death that made them unable to contract a valid marriage or exercise any property rights. They could be dispensed only by the pope. Simple vows had none of these effects. Catholic sensitivity to scandal about the conduct of nuns because of Protestant criticism of previous abuses was a major reason for Trent's insistence on solemn vows for all women religious. Solemn vows also gave more security to upper-class families by protecting the "honor" of their daughters and preventing them from returning to the world where they might marry and claim a larger share of the family property. See Ruth P. Liebowitz, "Virgins in the Service of Christ: The Dispute over an Active Apostolate for Women during the Counter Reformation," in *Women of Spirit:*

Female Leadership in the Jewish and Christian Traditions, ed. Rosemary Ruether and Eleanor McLaughlin (New York: Simon and Schuster, 1979), 132–52.

4. Elizabeth Rapley, *The Dévotes: Women and the Church in Seventeenth-Century France* (Montreal: McGill-Queen's University Press, 1990), 31.

5. *Parlements* were royal courts of appeal that also performed more general administrative duties such as registering royal decrees. There were *parlements* at Paris, Toulouse, Grenoble, Bordeaux, Dijon, Rouen, Aix, Rennes, Pau, Metz, Besançon, and Douai. Robin Briggs, *Early Modern France* (Oxford: Oxford University Press, 1977), 230. See also Taylor, "From Proselytizing to Social Reform," 405, for discussion of social attitudes toward women religious.

6. "Tertiaries" are lay members of a religious order; "beguines" were women religious who belonged to communities without an approved religious rule; "Sisters of the Common Life" lived in community like nuns but did not take vows. For a discussion of these and similar groups see Elisja Schulte Van Kessel, "Virgins and Mothers between Heaven and Earth," in *Renaissance and Enlightenment Paradoxes*, ed. Natalie Zemon Davis and Arlette Farge, vol. 3 of *A History of Women*, ed. Georges Duby and Michelle Perrot (Cambridge: Harvard University Press, 1995), 137–38; Jo Ann Kay McNamara, *Sisters in Arms: Catholic Nuns through Two Millennia* (Cambridge: Harvard University Press, 1996), 391–92; and Ranft, *Women and the Religious Life*, 82–86.

7. Merry E. Weisner, *Women and Gender in Early Modern Europe* (Cambridge: Cambridge University Press, 1994), 196.

8. Ephesians 5:22; 1 Timothy 2:11 (Revised Standard Version).

9. St. Thomas Aquinas, *Summa Theologiae*, ed. and trans. Edmund Hill (London: Blackfriars, 1964), vol. 13 (1a.90–102):39.

10. Mary Daly, *The Church and the Second Sex* (Boston: Beacon Press, 1985), 97; Rapley, *Dévotes*, 4.

11. Women's economic and legal position in early modern Europe is described in Olwen Hufton, *The Poor of Eighteenth-Century France 1750–1789* (London: Oxford University Press, 1974), 38–41; Merry E. Weisner, "Spinning out Capital: Women's Work in the Early Modern Economy," in *Becoming Visible: Women in European History*, 2nd ed., ed. Renate Bridenthal, Claudia Koonz, and Susan Stuard (Boston: Houghton Mifflin Company, 1987), 221–49; Marilyn J. Boxer and Jean H. Quataert, "Overview," in *Connecting Spheres: Women in the Western World, 1500 to the Present*, ed. Boxer and Quataert (New York: Oxford University Press, 1987), 35–36; Rapley, *Dévotes*, 12–15; and Natalie Zemon Davis, *Society and Culture in Early Modern France* (Stanford: Stanford University Press, 1965), 124–51.

12. Robin Briggs, *Witches and Neighbors: A History of European Witchcraft* (New York: Viking Penguin, 1996), 8. See also B. P. Levack, *The Witch-Hunt in Early Modern Europe* (London: Longman, 1987), and Alan C. Kors and Edward Peters, eds., *Witchcraft in Europe, 1100–1700: A Documentary History* (Philadelphia: University of Pennsylvania Press, 1972).

13. Rapley, *Dévotes*, 19–22. The theory known as Gallicanism, developed in the thirteenth century, claimed for France the right to resist all but very restricted forms of papal intervention within its jurisdiction. Gallicanism was vigorously upheld by the French state courts (*parlements*), and it served as a convenient excuse for French clergy

and government officials, including the king, when they wished to ignore papal decrees. Taylor, in "From Proselytizing to Social Reform," and Rapley both describe French clerical support enjoyed by the early secular congregations.

14. Economic and social conditions in seventeenth-century France are described in Briggs, *Early Modern France*, 35–61; John Lough, *An Introduction to Seventeenth-Century France*, 1–59; Pierre Goubert, "The French Peasantry of the Seventeenth Century: A Regional Example," in Trevor Aston, *Crisis in Europe: 1560–1660* (New York: Basic Books, 1965), 141–65; and Robert Jutte, *Poverty and Deviance in Early Modern Europe* (Cambridge: Cambridge University Press, 1994), 21–82.

15. Quoted in Lough, *Introduction to Seventeenth-Century France*, 19.

16. Rapley, *Dévotes*, 79.

17. A well-known example of Tridentine spirituality is the Society of Jesus, founded by St. Ignatius of Loyola and approved by the pope in 1540. The Jesuits were "completely focused on the thought of greater service to God, to Christ, to His Church and to the souls He redeemed." Joseph de Guibert, *The Jesuits: Their Spiritual Doctrine and Practice: A Historical Study*, trans. William J. Young, ed. George E. Ganss (St. Louis: The Institute of Jesuit Sources, 1964), 73.

18. Briggs, *Early Modern France*, 168. France had 120 bishoprics and almost 30,000 parishes with curés, along with a great number of vicars and unattached priests.

19. H. Outram Evennett, *The Spirit of Counter-Reformation*, ed. John Bossy (Cambridge: Cambridge University Press, 1968), 72–76; Robin Briggs, *Communities of Belief: Cultural and Social Tension in Early Modern France* (Oxford: Oxford University Press, 1989), 364–80; Henry Kamen, *The Iron Century: Social Change in Europe, 1550–1660* (New York: Praeger, 1971), 231–39.

20. Taylor, "From Proselytizing to Social Reform," 102.

21. The *dévots* were pious laymen or laywomen (*dévotes*) and in the early seventeenth century also a religious party who represented the "Catholic" interest in politics in contrast to the more pragmatic policies of the king and his ministers. After losing influence at court in the 1630s they became critics of society and began attacking libertines, atheists, and actors and many aspects of popular culture. Aristocratic and influential, they were disliked by many for their excessive religiosity and ridiculed by Molière in *Tartuffe* (Rapley, *Dévotes*, 75).

22. The Ursulines were founded in Italy in 1535 by Angela Merici to educate young women. They took no vows, lived at home, and were originally not intended to be a religious order. After Angela's death, changes occurred, and by 1582 they were living in community as a religious congregation. In 1612, a bull of Paul V added cloister and solemn vows.

23. Rapley, *Dévotes*, 51.

24. Ibid., 34–41, 48–60; Ranft, *Women and the Religious Life*, 101–6, 14–17.

25. Rapley, *Dévotes*, 39, 58–59, and 107.

26. Taylor, "From Proselytizing to Social Reform," 216.

27. Since men also wanted to participate, de Paul experimented with a "mixed" confraternity but had to give it up. He explained that the men wanted to control all aspects of administration but "the women will not tolerate it" (Taylor, "From Proselytizing to Social Reform," 225).

28. Rapley, *Dévotes*, 85–86.

29. Ibid., 93.

30. Taylor, "From Proselytizing to Social Reform," 192–93, 197–98.

31. A typical example is the community of Filles de Sainte-Geneviève, founded in Paris in 1636 by Mademoiselle Blosset after ill health forced her to give up the life of a cloistered nun. She began a school for young girls that soon had 300 pupils receiving instruction from her community of schoolmistresses (Rapley, *Dévotes*, 96).

32. Emmanuel S. Chill, "Religion and Mendicity in Seventeenth-Century France," *International Review of Social History* 7 (1962): 413; Rapley, *Dévotes*, 78; Kamen, *Iron Century*, 408.

33. Taylor, "From Proselytizing to Social Reform," 706–26.

34. The date of the first CSJ foundation cannot be established with certainty. Sources mention a foundation made in Dunières in 1649 and indicate that another existed before 1647. Much information about pre-revolutionary religious communities has been lost, since all of them were suppressed during the Revolution, their property confiscated, and many of their records destroyed. In many cases only partial histories can be pieced together from scattered and fragmentary surviving records. See Rapley, *Dévotes*, 247–54.

35. Patricia Byrne, "French Roots of a Women's Movement: Sisters of St. Joseph, 1650–1836" (Ph.D. diss., Boston College, 1985), 107–8, 7–38. In early modern France the term "hospital" referred to multipurpose institutions that cared for the sick, the indigent elderly and infirm, orphans, abandoned children, and various other groups, and sometimes distributed home relief. "General hospitals" were a new type of penal institution created in the seventeenth century to incarcerate the poor and discipline them through work. "*Hôtels-Dieu*" were primarily engaged in care of the sick, but they usually received foundlings also. For information on strategies hospitals used to manage the problems of poverty see Muriel Joerger, "The Structure of the Hospital System in France in the Ancien Régime," in *Medicine and Society in France, Selections from the Annales*, vol. 6, ed. Robert Forster and Orest Ranum (Baltimore: Johns Hopkins University Press, 1980), 104–36; Colin Jones, *The Charitable Imperative: Hospitals and Nursing in Ancien Régime and Revolutionary France* (New York: Routledge, 1989), 174–76; Chill, "Religion and Mendicity," 400–425; Hufton, *Poor of Eighteenth-Century France*, 133–76; and Jutte, *Poverty and Deviance*, 136–37, 75–77.

36. Byrne, "French Roots," 37–41. The anonymous "grouping of women" could have been the early community at Le Puy, but verification for this is lacking. Marius Nepper, who researched the life of Médaille and the origins of the CSJ community, believes that the first foundation was in Saint-Flour, but Marguerite Vacher questions this. See Nepper, *Origins: The Sisters of Saint Joseph*, trans. Research Team of the Federation of the Sisters of St. Joseph, U.S.A. (Erie, Pa.: Sisters of St. Joseph, 1975), 16, and Vacher, *Des "régulières" dans le siècle: Les soeurs de Saint-Joseph du Père Médaille aux XXVII et XXVIII siècles* (Clermont-Ferrand: Adosa, 1991), 45.

37. Missionaries usually preached and evangelized among "heathens" in distant lands, but home missions began in seventeenth-century France after the clergy discovered large numbers of peasants, adults and children, who knew virtually nothing of their religion and had never received the sacraments. Vincent de Paul's Congrega-

tion of the Mission was founded in 1625 to meet this need, and other orders also were involved, including the Jesuits. Rapley defines a home mission as "an organized descent by a group of preachers upon a community, a period of intensive exhortation and instruction which ended only when everybody had received the sacrament of penance" (*Dévotes*, 80).

38. Byrne, "French Roots," 40; Ignatius of Loyola, *The Constitutions of the Society of Jesus*, trans. George E. Ganss (St. Louis: Institute of Jesuit Sources, 1970), 262–63.

39. Nepper, *Origins*, 8. The necrology was a compilation of brief biographies of deceased members of the Jesuit order. Jesuits usually maintained their distance from communities of active women religious. The precedent was set by St. Ignatius himself in connection with a Jesuit benefactor who obtained papal approval to found an order of women as a female version of the Jesuits. Ignatius believed the need to supervise the order's affairs was distracting him from more "important" duties, and he successfully petitioned the pope to suppress the enterprise and forbid similar efforts in the future. The Jesuits were equally hostile when Mary Ward, who founded the Institute of the Blessed Virgin Mary in 1609, modeled her order after them. See Weisner, *Women and Gender*, 196–98. McNamara comments that while the Jesuits consistently rejected partnership with virtuous women, they took a special interest in the conversion of fallen women (*Sisters in Arms*, 468). For an account of St. Ignatius's dealings with women see Hugo Rahner, *St. Ignatius Loyola: Letters to Women* (New York: Herder and Herder, 1960).

40. Ranft, *Women and the Religious Life*, 114–20; Rapley, *Dévotes*, 50, 61, and 84.

41. Byrne, "French Roots," 39, 108.

42. Ibid., 109–10; Vacher, "*Régulières*," 56–57.

43. The four basic texts written by Médaille for the early Sisters of St. Joseph were the *Règlements*, probably the earliest rule; the *Constitutions*, a later, more developed rule outlining the purpose, activities, community life, government, and devotions of the congregation, which, with relatively minor revisions, became and remained the basic guide for the Carondelet CSJs until the early twentieth century; the *Eucharistic Letter*, an exposition of the spiritual ideals proposed for the early sisters; and the *Maxims of Perfection*, a series of 100 short maxims that briefly summarized Médaille's basic spiritual advice for the CSJs.

44. Evennett, *Spirit of the Counter-Reformation*, 40.

45. Nepper, *Origins*, 74.

46. Jean-Pierre Médaille, *Constitutions for the Little Congregation of the Sisters of St. Joseph*, trans. Research Team of the U.S.A. Federation of the Sisters of St. Joseph (Erie, Pa.: Sisters of St. Joseph, 1969), 12, 34, and 64, in ACSJC-G.

47. Jean-Pierre Médaille, *The Little Design, the Règlements, the Eucharistic Letter*, trans. Research Team of the U.S.A. Federation of the Sisters of St. Joseph (Erie, Pa.: Sisters of St. Joseph, 1973), 5–6, in ACSJC-G.

48. Nepper, *Origins*, 58.

49. Ibid., 86–87.

50. Médaille, *Eucharistic Letter*, 30.

51. Taylor, "From Proselytizing to Social Reform," 344–45.

52. Byrne, "French Roots," 38–39; Vacher, "*Régulières*," 57–58.

53. Briggs, *Early Modern France*, 168. In seventeenth-century France the king had the right to nominate bishops, and his choices were usually accepted by the pope.

54. Vacher, *"Régulières,"* 55.

55. Rapley, *Dévotes*, 115.

56. Byrne, "French Roots," 111–12.

57. Vacher, *"Régulières,"* Annexe 5.

58. According to Byrne, dowries typically ranged between 300 and 500 livres in the Lyons and Le Puy dioceses in the seventeenth century but increased to about 1,800 livres at Le Puy by the late eighteenth century. This supports Vacher's comment that the sisters' social level seemed to rise in the course of the eighteenth century. It did not approach that of the aristocratic women who entered traditional cloistered orders, where dowries of 7,500 to 8,000 livres were usual. Byrne, "French Roots," 285–86; Vacher, *"Régulières,"* 321.

59. Intensified religious persecution under Louis XIV, culminating in the revocation of the Edict of Nantes in 1685, meant that after that year French Protestants had to choose either conversion or emigration if they wished to avoid severe penalties.

60. Information about the CSJs' work in institutions and parishes and their working and living conditions is from Vacher and Byrne unless otherwise noted.

61. Byrne says the Le Puy community reported 2,896 livres in revenue and 5,100 in expenses in 1787 ("French Roots," 281).

62. Byrne, "French Roots," 114.

63. Hufton, *Poor of Eighteenth-Century France*, 151, 154.

64. Byrne, "French Roots," 134.

65. Details about Mother Jeanne Burdier's accomplishments as superior and later developments in Vienne are from Vacher, 213–51.

66. Byrne, "French Roots," 131–33. Byrne's account of the legal battle in Sauxillanges is based on an article by A. Achard in the *Revue d'Auvergne* (1904). Records of the sisters' response to Arnauld's allegations may not have been available to Achard since Byrne does not include this information.

67. Letters patent gave a religious community or institution the status of a legal corporation with rights to control property and act in legal matters. The crown's policy in granting them was vague, and few pre-Revolutionary CSJ communities managed to obtain them. Taylor, "From Proselytizing to Social Reform," 397; Byrne, "French Roots," 276.

68. Rapley, *Dévotes*, 176.

69. Médaille, *Constitutions*, 10.

70. Quoted in Rapley, *Dévotes*, 169.

71. The discussion of seventeenth- and eighteenth-century girls' education in France is based on Rapley, *Dévotes*, 142–66, and Martine Sonnet, "A Daughter to Educate," in *A History of Women in the West*, vol. 3, *Renaissance and Enlightenment Paradoxes*, ed. Natalie Zemon Davis and Arlette Farge (Cambridge: Harvard University Press, 1993), 101–16.

72. Vacher, *"Régulières"*; Byrne, "French Roots."

73. The revocation of the Edict of Nantes required Protestant schools in France to close, and subsequent royal edicts made elementary education, including religious

instruction, compulsory (theoretically) for all children, in effect forcing Catholic education on the nominal converts (Briggs, *Communities of Belief*, 200).

74. Rapley, *Dévotes*, 157.

75. Sonnet, "Daughter to Educate," 117–21.

76. Ibid., 114; Vacher, *"Régulières,"* 326.

77. Kathryn Norberg, "Prostitutes," in Davis and Farge, *A History of Women in the West*, 3:460–65; Weisner, *Women and Gender*, 101; Wilma Pugh, "Social Welfare and the Edict of Nantes: Lyon and Nîmes," *French Historical Studies* 8 (1974): 369–72.

78. Médaille, *Constitutions*, 11, 30.

79. Vacher, *"Régulières,"* 254–59. "Penitent" was the term commonly used for repentant prostitutes but also for unwed mothers or girls who had been seduced, even if they had no responsibility for what had happened to them. In general, "penitent" referred to women who had lost respectability but were not considered incorrigible.

80. Ibid., 322–34.

81. Quoted in Byrne, "French Roots," 119, 126.

82. For the origins of the Revolution see Georges Lefebvre, *The Coming of the French Revolution*, trans. R. R. Palmer (Princeton: Princeton University Press, 1947), and William Doyle, *Origins of the French Revolution* (Oxford: Oxford University Press, 1988). For later developments and the Napoleonic period see Norman Hampson, *The Terror in the French Revolution* (London: Historical Association of Great Britain, 1981); J. McManners, *The French Revolution and the Church* (London: S.P.C.K. for the Church Historical Society, 1969); F. Markham, *Napoleon* (New York: New American Library, 1963); and P. Geyl, *Napoleon: For and Against* (New Haven: Yale University Press, 1963).

83. Byrne, "French Roots," 161.

84. Ibid., 163.

85. The CSJs executed during the Terror were Marie-Anne Garnier and Jeanne-Marie Aubert (possibly the former Sister Saint-Alexis), who were guillotined with two other women, a layman, and a priest at Le Puy; and Antoinette Vincent, Marie-Anne Sénovert, and Madeleine Dumoulin, guillotined with four priests at Privas. Ironically, the victims at Privas were executed shortly after the fall of Robespierre, when the Terror was almost at an end.

86. Byrne, "French Roots," 186, 201.

87. The French census of 1808 reports a total of 439 sisters of St. Joseph in 66 houses in the dioceses of Clermont, Lyons, and Le Puy. Of these, 261 sisters and 39 houses were in Lyons. The number of sisters in 1836 is not available, but by that time there were 105 houses in the Lyons diocese (ibid., 202, 210).

88. Félicité de Duras to Bishop Rosati, Chambery, June 10, 1835, copy and translation in ACSJC-SLP; original in AASL.

89. Records of the Lyons motherhouse show that the number of novices received from 1832 to 1836 was 354 (Byrne, "French Roots," 321).

Chapter Two

1. Memoirs of Sr. St. Protais Deboille, ACSJC-SLP. Sr. St. Protais was the only member of the original six who recorded her experiences and thoughts about the

journey and early days of the community. She handwrote this memoir (around 1890) in her somewhat "broken" English. She died in 1892 at the age of seventy-eight.

2. Mary Ewens, *The Role of the Nun in Nineteenth-Century America* (New York: Arno Press, 1978), 7. Her book and subsequent work provide some of the earliest scholarship on nineteenth-century American nuns. Canon law is the official body of laws that govern the Roman Catholic Church. Richard P. McBrien, ed., *The Encyclopedia of Catholicism* (San Francisco: HarperCollins, 1995), 219–20.

3. Catholic population data is difficult to assess, particularly prior to the Civil War. Gerald Shaughnessy, *Has the Immigrant Kept the Faith? A Study of Immigration and Catholic Growth in the United States, 1790–1920* (New York: Macmillan, 1925), 134, 145, estimates the Catholic population at 660,000 (1840), 1.6 million (1850), and 3.1 million (1860). For additional information including regional maps displaying concentrations of Catholic populations see Edwin Scott Gaustad, *Historical Atlas of Religion in America* (New York: Harper and Row, 1976), 103–12.

4. Cited in Ray Allen Billington, *The Protestant Crusade 1800–1860: A Study of the Origins of American Nativism* (New York: Rinehart, 1938; reprint, Chicago: Quadrangle Books, 1964), 53. Billington's book is still considered one of the best descriptions of the anti-Catholic mood prevalent in antebellum America. For more recent discussion on the anti-Catholic climate of the early nineteenth century see Jenny Franchot, *Roads to Rome: The Antebellum Protestant Encounter with Catholicism* (Berkeley: University of California Press, 1994). Franchot analyzes "the discourse through which antebellum writers of popular and elite fictional and historical texts indirectly voiced the tensions and limitations of mainstream Protestant culture." See also Jay Dolan, *The American Catholic Experience: A History from Colonial Times to the Present* (Garden City, N.Y.: Image Books, 1985), 201–3, 295.

5. Nikola Baumgarten, "Education and Democracy in Frontier St. Louis: The Society of the Sacred Heart," *History of Education Quarterly* 34, no. 2 (Summer 1994): 171–92. William B. Faherty, *Dream by the River: Two Centuries of Saint Louis Catholicism, 1766–1980*, rev. ed. (St. Louis: River City Pub., 1981), 44–48, 76; and "Nativism and Midwestern Education: The Experience of St. Louis University, 1832–1856," *History of Education Quarterly* 8 (Winter 1968): 447–58. See also an early history of the St. Louis diocese by John Rothensteiner, *History of the Archdiocese of St. Louis*, 2 vols. (St. Louis: Blackwell Wielandy Co., 1928). The violence against CSJs that took place in 1846 probably resulted from a combination of racism and anti-Catholic sentiments; it will be described later in this chapter.

6. Gaustad, *Historical Atlas*, 108. Although activities, membership, and length and region of influence varied, the beginning dates for these groups are as follows: American Protestant Association (1842), the Know-Nothing Party (1854), the Ku Klux Klan (1865; 1915), and the American Protective Association (1887).

7. Memoirs of Sr. St. Protais Deboille, 11. The CSJs continued to deal with anti-Catholic sentiment throughout the nineteenth century, and all the CSJ archives contain many examples, some of which will be integrated throughout this book. For more examples of anti-Catholic sentiments experienced by the CSJs and other religious orders of women see Mary Ewens, *Role of the Nun*, 70–73, 120, and "The Leadership of Nuns in Immigrant Catholicism," in *Women and Religion in America*, vol. 1, ed.

Rosemary Radford Ruether and Rosemary Skinner Keller (San Francisco: Harper and Row, 1981), 101–4; Karen J. Kennelly, "Ideals of American Catholic Womanhood," in *American Catholic Women: An Historical Exploration*, ed. Karen J. Kennelly (New York: Macmillan, 1989), 2; and Patricia Byrne, "Sisters of St. Joseph: The Americanization of a French Tradition," *U.S. Catholic Historian* (Summer/Fall 1986): 262.

8. For a description of this event see Jeanne Hamilton, "The Nunnery As Menace: The Burning of the Charlestown Convent, 1834," *U.S. Catholic Historian* 14, no. 1 (Winter 1996): 35–65. This was a shocking incident for many reasons. The sisters and student boarders barely escaped with their lives, and the mob spent hours defacing the structure, desecrating the cemetery, opening sisters' coffins, and pulling teeth from corpses. Local police and firefighters stood and watched while the convent was torched. Many of these "exposé" books were written by men; some were later recanted by the authors as fictitious. For example see Maria Monk, *Awful Disclosures of the Hotel Dieu Nunnery* (New York: D. M. Bennett, 1836), and Theodore Dwight, *Open Convents* (New York: Van Nostrand and Dwight, 1836). Rebecca Reed, the woman who has often been cited as inciting rancor for the burning of the Ursuline convent in Charlestown, Massachusetts, wrote *Six Months in a Convent* (Boston: Russell, Odiorne and Metcalf, 1835). This spate of "exposés" about convents continued into the late nineteenth and early twentieth centuries. See Edith O'Gorman, *Trials and Persecutions of Miss Edith O'Gorman* (Hartford: Connecticut Pub., 1881), and Fred Hendrickson, *The "Black Convent" Slave or Nunnery Life Unveiled* (Toledo: Protestant Missionary Publishing, 1914).

9. Ann Braude, "Women's History *Is* American Religious History," in *Retelling U.S. Religious History*, ed. Thomas A. Tweed (Berkeley: University of California Press, 1997), 105–6.

10. Mary Lucida Savage, *The Congregation of St. Joseph of Carondelet: A Brief Account of Its Origin and Its Work in the United States, 1650–1922* (St. Louis: Herder Book Co., 1923), 36–37. Rothensteiner, *History of the Archdiocese of St. Louis*, 1:300, 314, 447, 626, 634. St. Louis's population grew rapidly between 1830 and 1840 from 5,000 (whites) to over 14,000, and Bishop Rosati sought additional sisters to support the growing Catholic population. U.S. Bureau of Census, *Fifth Census of the United States* and *Sixth Census of the United States* (Washington, D.C., U.S. Census Bureau, 1830 and 1840).

11. Memoirs of Sr. St. Protais Deboille, 13–23. The following narrative information and all quoted material about arrivals at Cahokia and Carondelet are taken from Sr. Protais's memoirs. Although she was with the original three sent to Cahokia, she became ill and was sent to Carondelet to recover. This placed her in the position of being present in the earliest time periods at both missions. The material on the early foundations has been further researched and elaborated by Savage, *Congregation of St. Joseph*, 27–50, and Dolorita Maria Dougherty et al., eds., *Sisters of St. Joseph of Carondelet* (St. Louis: Herder Book Co., 1966), 51–64.

12. Cahokia, Illinois, was located on the "bottoms" of the eastern bank of the Mississippi River, and serious epidemics and floods continually plagued the village. In 1844, a major flood destroyed the sisters' convent and school and almost cost them their lives. They were rescued by boat from their second-story windows. Ill and discouraged, the CSJs did not return to Cahokia until 1848; they closed the school per-

manently in 1855 when once again floodwaters threatened their lives (1851) and after two cholera epidemics (1849, 1851) killed thousands, including three CSJs who were nursing the sick.

13. Although government payment for services was the exception rather than the rule, the CSJs and other religious communities did secure state monies for short periods of time. The CSJ school for the deaf in St. Louis received monies from the legislature between 1839 and 1847. Bishop Rosati's political connections helped secure state money since the CSJ school was the only school for the deaf in the state. Locally, the city paid the sisters temporarily to educate girls between six and eighteen years of age. Dougherty et al., *Sisters of St. Joseph*, 67. Later, the CSJs also received some government monies for schools on Indian reservations. These contracts and subsidy arrangements occurred more in the nineteenth century than the twentieth century because local, state, or federal officials desperately needed the sisters' services, particularly in isolated settings.

14. Ewens, *Role of the Nun*, 65–69. Although the CSJs did not use slave labor, Ewens states that many religious communities did, and no communities that used slaves failed to survive in the American milieu. The eight communities that used slaves were the Sisters of Charity, Carmelites, Sisters of Loretto, Visitandines, Nazareth Sisters of Charity, Dominicans, Religious of the Sacred Heart, and New Orleans's Ursulines.

15. Memoirs of Sr. St. Protais Deboille, 25; Savage, *Congregation of St. Joseph*, 46–47.

16. The term "Mother" is used instead of "Sister" when the individual serves as the superior or leader at a mission site or local community.

17. Memoirs of Sr. St. Protais Deboille, 26–28.

18. "Copy of a Letter from Mother St. John Fournier to the Superior General of the Sisters of St. Joseph in Lyons, 1873," cited in Maria Kostka Logue, *Sisters of St. Joseph of Philadelphia: A Century of Growth and Development, 1847–1947* (Westminster, Md.: Newman Press, 1950), 327–52. Mother St. John, who later became the superior of the Philadelphia community, described her voyage with Sr. Celestine Pommerel. Held in Havana because of the outbreak of yellow fever in New Orleans, the sisters did not arrive in St. Louis when expected. Bishop Rosati became concerned and feared they were lost at sea. When they arrived weeks late and in secular dress Rosati had them demonstrate their ability to communicate in sign language before he was convinced they were indeed his long-awaited nuns. Teasing them, the bishop "scolded" them by saying he had believed they had run away with the 400 soldiers who were also on the ship.

19. This was more than a clash of male egos. In Europe it was customary for communities to be assigned a specific cleric as "spiritual father" who advised the sisters. In the United States, the shortage of priests did not always make this possible, so the practice was often ignored or the local parish priest served in this capacity. Father Saulnier regarded the sisters as "his community" since they resided in his parish, and he felt Father Fontbonne was usurping his authority with the sisters (Dougherty et al., *Sisters of St. Joseph*, 68).

20. Letter from Fr. Edmund Saulnier to Bishop Rosati, October 5, 1837. Between October 1837 and December 1838, Saulnier wrote the bishop nine letters concerning

the CSJs and his concerns about Fontbonne (copies of Eng. trans. ACSJC-SLP; originals in AASL).

21. Letters from Fr. Saulnier to Bishop Rosati, November 24 and 27, 1837.

22. Letter from Fr. Fontbonne to Bishop Rosati, May 26, 1837 (copy of Eng. trans. ACSJC-SLP; original in AASL).

23. Bishop Rosati's appointment of Sr. Delphine to head the Carondelet group was surprising. At twenty-three, she was the second youngest member of the original six from Lyons. He may have done this out of respect for her aunt, Mother St. John Fontbonne, who allowed the group to come to St. Louis, or it is quite possible that he might have relied on Fr. Fontbonne, who came with the sisters, to make the decision. Based on Fontbonne's affection for his younger sister and his own desire for influence, Sr. Delphine certainly would have been his first choice.

24. Letter from Sr. Mary Joseph Dillon to Bishop Rosati, March 22, 1838, copy in ACSJC-SLP; original in AASL. Unfortunately, her physical problems continued; in 1842 she died of consumption.

25. Letter from Sr. St. John Fournier to Bishop Rosati, November 24, 1837, and (n.d.), 1838 (copy in ACSJC-SLP; original in AASL).

26. The importance of these actions cannot be overemphasized in regard to CSJ survival. The coalition of Srs. Celestine Pommerel, St. John Fournier, and Mary Joseph Dillon proved to be an important one. Highly respected, Pommerel became superior and led the CSJs for eighteen years. Fournier eventually founded the Philadelphia community, and Dillon remained the only American-born novice and native English-speaker until 1841 (CSJ Profession Book, ACSJC-G).

27. Not wanting to miss an opportunity to blast his nemesis, Fr. Fontbonne, Saulnier, after lambasting Mother Delphine, added, "She has the same character as her brother (rustic)." Letter from Fr. Saulnier to Bishop Rosati, February 9, 1838.

28. Although her early youthful struggles as superior were traumatic, Mother Delphine Fontbonne continued with the American CSJs and, after spending one year in the CSJ Philadelphia community, was missioned in 1851 as the first CSJ superior in their newly established mission in Toronto, Canada. She led this community until her death in 1856 at age forty-two. Her sister, Febronie Fontbonne, continued in poor health after her dramatic rescue in the woods and later in the 1844 flood at Cahokia. Subsequent illness forced her to return with Sr. Febronie Chapellon, another of the original six sisters, to France in 1844, where she lived and worked until her death in 1881 at the age of seventy-five.

29. CSJ Profession Book; Savage, *Congregation of St. Joseph*, 55–56.

30. This bill was adopted February 8, 1839; cited in Savage, *Congregation of St. Joseph*, 52. It was not repealed until 1847, when the legislature finally provided money for a state institute.

31. "Minutes of the Board of Trustees," April 23, 1839, cited in Savage, *Congregation of St. Joseph*, 53. See also, "Copy of a Letter from Mother St. John Fournier," 329. Fournier stated that although it was short on cash "the city paid us every year in land." The city hired a male teacher for the boys of the village.

32. The Mullanphy family were early donors to Catholic charities in St. Louis. Cotton merchant and realtor John Mullanphy contributed land for a hospital for the

poor, regardless of their "color, country or religion," and gave a house to the Sacred Heart Sisters for the first girls' school in St. Louis. In 1850, the Sisters of Charity opened a facility for elderly women and orphans in a building bequeathed by the Mullanphy family. See Mary J. Oates, *The Catholic Philanthropic Tradition in America* (Bloomington: Indiana University Press, 1995), 10, 30.

33. Memoirs of Eliza McKenney Brouillet, 1890–91, ACSJC-SLP. See also Savage, *Congregation of St. Joseph*, 56–60.

34. "Statistics of Carondelet School and St. Joseph's Academy," ACSJC-SLP.

35. Memoirs of Eliza McKenney Brouillet. Information about St. Joseph's Academy has been taken from Brouillet's memoirs unless noted otherwise.

36. Ewens, *Role of the Nun*, 67–69; Baumgarten, "Education and Democracy," 173; Maureen Fitzgerald, "Irish-Catholic Nuns and the Development of New York City's Welfare System, 1840–1900" (Ph.D. diss., University of Wisconsin, 1992), 234. Academies and parish schools will be discussed extensively in Chapters 5 and 6.

37. Ewens, *Role of the Nun*, 69.

38. Savage, *Congregation of St. Joseph*, 66.

39. CSJ Profession Book. This ledger includes demographic data on name, birthplace, residence before entrance, entrance date, province, reception date, profession date, and date of death for all sisters who took final vows in the community. This does not include data on any women who left the community during the postulant or novice stage.

40. Memoirs of Sr. St. Protais Deboille, 29; "Copy of a Letter from Mother St. John Fournier," 332–33. Mother St. John and Sr. Protais were both assigned to the school, so their memoirs were based on firsthand information. The CSJs were not the only group of nuns to battle with locals over education for blacks prior to the Civil War. See Baumgarten, "Education and Democracy," 176–77.

41. This undated and unsigned quote is from a longer essay recorded in the "Community Annals" and cited in Savage, *Congregation of St. Joseph*, 64.

42. "Copy of a Letter from Mother St. John Fournier," 333. "Extract from the Records of St. Louis Diocese," Book 1:221, copy ACSJC-SLP, original AASL. The CSJs had to take this threat very seriously and probably understood that not only racism but also anti-Catholic bigotry was involved. Only one year earlier, anti-Catholic sentiments had surfaced in St. Louis when the Jesuit St. Louis University Medical School had been harassed by a mob who threatened to burn the school to the ground. See Faherty, "Nativism and Midwestern Education," 447–58. In 1847 the state of Missouri passed a law prohibiting the education of slaves.

43. In St. Louis and later in Philadelphia, the CSJs took over the institution from the Sisters of Charity, who withdrew from the male orphanage upon their affiliation with the French Daughters of Charity, whose constitution banned working with male orphans. See Byrne, "Sisters of St. Joseph," 254. Byrne goes on to explain that the problem often was not with the women's communities but with European-born, male clerics who did not think it was proper for nuns to work with male children, particularly adolescent boys. For a discussion on the Sisters of Charity and their battle with Archbishop John Hughes on this issue see Fitzgerald, "Irish-Catholic Nuns," 250–53.

44. This was St. Joseph's Hospital in Philadelphia. Although the CSJs maintained

it for only ten years, it was an important step in furthering the CSJ mission in America. For a detailed description of the facility and its history see Logue, *Sisters of St. Joseph*, 49–56.

45. CSJ Profession Book. This number is approximate because although the profession book shows that 149 women had been professed by 1857, there had been a few deaths and any novices who left before profession would not be counted in this tally.

46. CSJ Constitution (1847), 9–11, ACSJC-SPP. The 1847 constitution was the first English translation of the French constitution that the sisters brought with them. The French version is thought to date back to the late seventeenth century. Joseph Rosati died in 1843, and Peter Richard Kenrick succeeded him. In 1847 St. Louis became an archdiocese and Bishop Kenrick then became Archbishop Kenrick.

47. Memoirs of Sr. Febronie Boyer, ACSJC-SLP. Like Sr. Protais's memoirs, these are handwritten notes, undated but probably written around 1890, when Sr. Monica Corrigan was attempting to acquire information for a community history.

48. Ibid.

49. Savage, *Congregation of St. Joseph*, 112–14. Savage's book, published in 1923, is both a primary and a secondary source. Sr. Lucida Savage entered the community in 1887 and knew Mother St. John Facemaz and many of the earliest sisters, and she was an eyewitness to many events in the late nineteenth century. With a Ph.D. in history, she was able to write an objective, well-documented history incorporating her first-hand experiences with the people and events that took place in the community.

50. Ibid., 113–14.

51. Byrne, "Sisters of St. Joseph," 255–57. Byrne states and we would agree that there seems to be little written documentation in either the archives in St. Louis or Lyons on how this "mutual agreement" was achieved. Savage (108) cites correspondence from Fr. S. Auguste Paris to Mother Celestine Pommerel dating from 1856 that indicates discussions had already begun between the American and French communities.

52. The section of the CSJ Constitution (1860), 24–25, did in fact give Archbishop Kenrick superior powers over CSJ houses in other dioceses. In 1863 Rome changed this clause, limiting Kenrick's power ("Observations of Cardinal Quaglia on the Constitutions," as cited in Byrne, "Sisters of St. Joseph," 257).

53. Margaret Susan Thompson, "To Serve the People of God: Nineteenth-Century Sisters and the Creation of a Religious Life," Working Paper Series, Cushwa Center, University of Notre Dame, ser. 18, no. 2, Spring 1987, 9. In studying nineteenth-century communities, Mary Ewens concurs with Thompson's assessment. "When given a free hand, bishops and other [male] directors . . . could work havoc in communities under their control" (*Role of the Nun*, 286).

54. For brief discussions of bishops' reactions to general government see the following histories of CSJ communities in Philadelphia, Wheeling, and Buffalo, where they became diocesan: Logue, *Sisters of St. Joseph*, 172–73; Rose Anita Kelly, *Song of the Hills: The Story of the Sisters of St. Joseph of Wheeling* (Wheeling, W.Va.: Mt. St. Joseph, 1962), 203–5; and M. Dunne, *The Congregation of St. Joseph of the Diocese of Buffalo, 1854–1933* (Buffalo: Holling Press, 1934), 87–88. These histories provide very little information on the difficult times before and after separation from St. Louis.

55. Letter from Mother St. John Facemaz to Cardinal Quaglia, 1869, ACSJC-SLP.

56. This quote is attributed to Mother de Chantal Keating, who came from the CSJ community in Flushing, N.Y., in 1864 to lead the fledgling community in Wheeling. Byrne, "Sisters of St. Joseph," 258; Kelly, *Song of the Hills*, 211–12.

57. According to all CSJ historians, Sr. St. John Fournier and Mother Celestine were very close. Fournier had been raised as a "foster child" in Celestine's home. Fournier continued to correspond with the Pommerel family and they with her for years after Celestine's death. One author wrote that Fournier's years "without her counselor and friend, loomed lonely and difficult." Logue, *Sisters of St. Joseph*, 83–84. Lists of Philadelphia CSJ institutions are found in ibid., 321–25.

58. Memoirs of Sr. Ignatius Loyola Cox, as cited in Genevieve Schillo, "Dynamics for Change: Papal Approval for General Government in the Sisters of St. Joseph of Carondelet, 1836–1877" (unpublished manuscript, ACSJC-SPP). Schillo has spent years attempting to unravel the complex interactions involved in the formation of CSJ general government. We are grateful for her continuing work on this topic and her recent paper, "Yes or No: General Government in Sisters of St. Joseph of Carondelet and Related Daughter/Mother Houses (1836–1877)," presented at the History of Women Religious Conference at Loyola University, June 1998. Mother Seraphine died soon after general government was created. Bishop Grace continued to struggle with general government and his loss of direct control over the CSJs. The 1860s continued to be a time of turmoil for the St. Paul community, but they remained under the new constitution and did not become diocesan.

59. Byrne, "Sisters of St. Joseph," 264–66.

60. Letter to Mother Agnes Gonzaga Ryan from Sr. M. Irene, St. Joseph's Convent, Toronto, March 13, 1913, ACSJC-SLP.

61. Examples of the struggles between American bishops and women religious fill the convent archives of every congregation. The battle for autonomy in a sexist and hierarchical setting took energy, perseverance, and constant effort on the part of the sisters. Margaret Susan Thompson's work on nineteenth-century American sisterhoods provides extensive examples. See her "To Serve the People" and "Women, Feminism, and the New Religious History: Catholic Sisters As a Case Study," in *Belief and Behavior: Essays in the New Religious History*, ed. Philip R. Vandermeer and Robert P. Swerienga (New Brunswick: Rutgers University Press, 1991), 136–63. For other examples from a variety of community archives see George C. Stewart, *Marvels of Charity: History of American Sisters and Nuns* (Huntington, Ind.: Our Sunday Visitor, Inc., 1994).

62. "Notes of Sr. Monica Corrigan from Sr. de Chantal Martin taken July 23, 1890, Nazareth Convent, St. Louis," ACSJC-SLP. Sr. de Chantal was a young nun who was one of Mother St. John Facemaz's companions during her first visit to Rome.

63. The "Decree of Commendation" is dated September 1863 and signed by Cardinal Quaglia (original Latin decree at ACSJC-SLP); English translation appears in Savage, *Congregation of St. Joseph*, 119–20. Letters in support of the CSJs' constitution and general government were sent to Rome between 1861 and 1877, when final approbation was given. These letters came from bishops in St. Paul; Albany; Alton, Ill.; Dubuque, Iowa; Nashville, Tenn.; Marquette, Mich.; Natchez, Miss.; St. Joseph,

Mo.; Tucson; and Chicago. Archbishop Kenrick of St. Louis wrote numerous letters to the Vatican in support of the CSJ constitution, and his support was invaluable to the sisters.

64. CSJ Profession Book; Savage, *Congregation of St. Joseph*, 160–61.

65. The CSJs received final approbation on May 16, 1877. For a brief history on formation of general government and events leading up to final approbation see Emily Joseph Daly, "History of the Generalate," in Dougherty et al., *Sisters of St. Joseph*, 363–84, and Schillo, "Dynamics for Change."

66. This story and quotes are cited in Savage, *Congregation of St. Joseph*, 130–31. The trip to Mississippi in 1855 had been by stage, and the sisters and the priest traveling with them were accosted by a male passenger who verbally harassed and spit tobacco juice on them. According to the sisters, when the coach stopped to change horses the priest threw the man out of the coach and he rode the rest of the way with the driver. Later in the trip, in Mississippi, the sisters boarded one evening with a Catholic judge who "expressed fear of being mobbed if he were known to harbor nuns" (Savage, *Congregation of St. Joseph*, 104–5).

67. Ibid., 133–35. Demographic information about Sr. Winifred Sullivan found in CSJ Profession Book.

68. Savage, *Congregation of St. Joseph*, 133.

69. Ewens, *Role of the Nun*, 208; Mary Denis Maher, *To Bind up the Wounds: Catholic Sister Nurses in the U.S. Civil War* (Westport, Conn.: Greenwood Press, 1989), 27–43. This book is extremely well documented and is probably the best source on Catholic sisters' nursing activities before and during the Civil War. See also Ursula Stepsis and Dolores Liptak, eds. *Pioneer Healers: The History of Women Religious in American Health Care* (New York: Crossroad, 1989). An older, less scholarly but interesting source is Ellen Ryan Jolly, *Nuns on the Battlefield*, 4th ed. (Providence, R.I.: Providence Visitor Press, 1930). Information on which orders provided nurses can be confusing because local newspaper reports and government documents typically listed all nursing nuns as Sisters of Charity or as Sisters of Mercy.

70. The CSJs in Philadelphia worked on hospital ships, and the CSJs in Wheeling had a military hospital. We will discuss the CSJs' contribution to nursing in Chapter 7. For discussions on Protestant attitudes and CSJs' interactions with soldiers and army doctors see Christopher J. Kauffman, *Ministry and Meaning: A Religious History of Catholic Health Care in the United States* (New York: Crossroad, 1995), 82–95; Carr Elizabeth Worland, "American Catholic Women and the Church to 1920" (Ph.D. diss., St. Louis University, 1982), 72–75; Maher, *To Bind up the Wounds*, 125–54; and Lori D. Ginzberg, *Women and the Work of Benevolence: Morality, Politics and Class in the Nineteenth-Century United States* (New Haven: Yale University Press, 1990), 143–48.

71. This information is taken from a speech given by Ambrose Kennedy (R.I.) in the House of Representatives, March 18, 1918, cited in Jolly, *Nuns on the Battlefield*, 172–73. For more information about Mother de Chantal Keating and the CSJ nursing sisters in Wheeling see Kelly, *Song of the Hills*, 213–22.

72. CSJ Profession Book; "General Chapter Report, 1869," ACSJC-G. Dolorita Maria Dougherty, "Chronological List of Establishments," in Dougherty et al., *Sisters of St. Joseph*, 427–28.

73. CSJ Profession Book; Savage, *Congregation of St. Joseph*, 154–59.

74. Savage, *Congregation of St. Joseph*, 157. Savage had an opportunity to live and work around Mother Agatha for seventeen years before her death, so it is quite likely that Savage heard these sayings and stories herself.

Chapter Three

1. CSJ Constitution (1860), 1, and (1884), 1, 12, ACSJC-SLP.

2. Most communities that came from Europe to the United States were active or apostolic. The term "apostolate" means "the saving mission of Christ in the world and the participation of Christian faithful in that mission." A smaller number of European religious orders that came to the United States were "contemplative" and followed a life of "solitude and prayer." Richard P. McBrien, ed., *The Encyclopedia of Catholicism* (San Francisco: HarperCollins, 1995), 76, 264. For contemplative orders to survive in America they had to provide "services" for the vast numbers of Catholic immigrants that flocked into the country in the nineteenth century. Contemplative orders such as the Carmelites and Benedictines had to begin or expand their teaching endeavor to survive financially and also to pacify American bishops who needed their services. See Mary Ewens, *The Role of the Nun in Nineteenth-Century America* (New York: Arno Press, 1978), 34. See also Charles Warren Currier, *Carmel in America: A Centennial History of the Discalced Carmelites in the United States* (Darien, Ill.: Carmelite Press, 1989), and Ephrem Hollerman, *The Reshaping of a Tradition: American Benedictine Women, 1852–1881* (St. Joseph, Minn.: Benedictine Press, 1994).

3. CSJ Profession Book, ACSJC-G.

4. Memoirs of Srs. Grace Aurelia Flanagan (entered 1916) and Mary Guadalupe Apodaca (entered 1917) in *Jubilarse*, ed. Margaret John Purcell (St. Louis: Sisters of St. Joseph of Carondelet, 1981), 147, 89.

5. Memoirs of Sr. Mary Charitina Flynn (entered 1900) in Purcell, *Jubilarse*, 1. According to the written memoirs and oral interviews available, this type of mystical or spiritual experience was not unusual for some sisters. These kinds of experiences, particularly for women, have been a part of most religious traditions across cultures. For examples of the multicultural experiences of American women see Rosemary Radford Ruether and Rosemary Skinner Keller, eds., *In Our Own Voices: Four Centuries of American Women's Religious Writing* (San Francisco: HarperCollins, 1995).

6. M. Anselm O'Brien (with Anna Marie Dickens), . . . *The Likes of Kitty O'Brien* (Florissant, Mo.: Huntington Press, 1977), 25. O'Brien entered the CSJs in 1915.

7. Maureen Fitzgerald, "Irish-Catholic Nuns and the Development of New York City's Welfare System, 1840–1900" (Ph.D. diss., University of Wisconsin, 1992), 226.

8. For examples from the Middle Ages to modern times see Gerda Lerner, *The Creation of Feminist Consciousness: From the Middle Ages to 1870* (New York: Oxford University Press, 1993), 46–115, and Jo Ann Kay McNamara, *Sisters in Arms: Catholic Nuns through Two Millennia* (Cambridge: Harvard University Press, 1996). For examples from a variety of religious traditions in the United States see Betty DeBerg, *UnGodly Women: Gender and the First Wave of American Fundamentalism* (Minneapolis: Fortress Press, 1990); Evelyn Brooks Higginbotham, *Righteous Discontent: The Women's Movement in the*

Black Baptist Church, 1880–1920 (Cambridge: Harvard University Press, 1993); Rosemary Ruether and Eleanor McLaughlin, eds., *Women of Spirit: Female Leadership in the Jewish and Christian Traditions* (New York: Simon and Schuster, 1979); and Rosemary Radford Ruether and Rosemary Skinner Keller, eds., *Women and Religion in America*, 3 vols. (San Francisco: Harper and Row, 1981, 1983, 1986), and *In Our Own Voices.*

9. Marta Danylewycz, *Taking the Veil: An Alternative to Marriage, Motherhood, and Spinsterhood in Quebec, 1840–1920* (Toronto: McClelland and Stewart, 1987), 96; Margaret Susan Thompson, "Discovering Foremothers: Sisters, Society, and the American Catholic Experience," in *The American Catholic Religious Life*, ed. Joseph M. White (New York: Garland Press, 1988), 275; Mary Ewens, "The Leadership of Nuns in Immigrant Catholicism," in Ruether and Keller, *Women and Religion*, 1:101–4; Jay P. Dolan, *The American Catholic Experience: A History from Colonial Times to the Present* (Garden City, N.Y.: Image Books, 1985), 290.

10. Ewens, "Leadership of Nuns," 107.

11. CSJ Constitution (1884), 33–35. These prerequisite qualities are listed in all versions of the CSJ Constitution (1847, ACSJC-SPP) and (1860, 1884). In the 1860 version, the superior general was allowed to assess a dowry amount.

12. Although entry after the age of forty was rare, sisters between thirty and thirty-nine years of age did enter the community in significant numbers, accounting for 19 percent of candidates between 1836 and 1920. The mean age of first marriage for American women was 22.0 (1890), 21.9 (1900), and 21.6 (1910) (*Historical Statistics of the United States: From Colonial Times to 1970* [Washington, D.C.: Bureau of Commerce, 1975], 19).

13. The dowry was a continuous stumbling block for European orders that were transplanted to the United States. Since the vast majority of the Catholic population in the nineteenth and early twentieth centuries were working-class, even American-born girls had difficulty in fulfilling dowry obligations. Most U.S. communities had to make exceptions on this issue even though most constitutions required between $100 and $500 for a dowry. See Fitzgerald, "Irish Catholic Nuns," 238–39, and Ewens, *Role of the Nun*, 135.

14. Letter from Mother St. John Facemaz to Bishop Peter Richard Kenrick, February 10, 1868, and letter from Kenrick to Facemaz, March 17, 1868, ACSJC-SLP and AASL.

15. Postulant and Novitiate Records can be found at all four CSJ provincial archives (ACSJC-SLP, ACSJC-SPP, ACSJC-LAP, ACSJC-AP). If dowry payment is used as a means to determine class diversity of the candidates, the records indicate a broad range of socioeconomic levels.

16. Although all CSJ Constitutions mandated separation of postulants, novices, and professed, this was not always possible in the nineteenth and early twentieth centuries. In the early days of the community, lack of space made separation impossible. Even when more living space became available, second-year novices were needed in the workforce, so they often lived and worked with professed sisters away from the novitiate.

17. "Postulant Outfit," CSJ Customs Book (1868), 145–46, ACSJC-SLP. Besides the clothes the candidates were to bring six yards of white bleached muslin, six yards

of blue calico or check, six yards of brown drilling, six yards of black cambric, twelve yards of Irish linen, and one table service.

18. This is an undated novice manual, probably used in the mid-nineteenth century. It was thought to be translated from a French manual the sisters brought with them (ACSJC-AP). The CSJs wrote their first American customs book in 1868, and it was revised and expanded in 1917. In 1900 a spiritual directory was added to the prescriptive literature. All printed constitutions contained specific requirements for behavior and religious practices as well as guidelines concerning interactions among sisters and with seculars.

19. Sr. Winifred (Kate) Hogan, "My Reminiscences," 1922, part 2, p. 14, ACSJC-SPP.

20. O'Brien, *Likes of Kitty O'Brien*, 49.

21. Interview of Sr. Aloysia Joseph McCarthy (entered 1901) by Susan Marie O'Connor, March 4, 1975, Latham, N.Y., ACSJC-AP.

22. Sr. Cecilia Marie Hurley (entered 1919), "Reflections," October 1, 1981, ACSJC-AP.

23. Victor Turner, *The Ritual Process: Structure and Anti-Structure* (Chicago: Aldine Publishing, 1969), 44–55, 94–111, 147–60. Arnold Van Gennep's work is taken from his *Rites of Passage* (London: Routledge and Kegan Paul, 1909).

24. Postulant and Novitiate Records, ACSJC-SLP. For examples from other orders see Fitzgerald, "Irish-Catholic Nuns," 230–31. For an interesting discussion on the Sisters of the Immaculate Heart of Mary formation see Mary Ann Hinsdale, "The Roughest Kind of Prose: IHM Socialization, 1860–1960," in *Building Sisterhood: A Feminist History of the Sisters, Servants of the Immaculate Heart of Mary* (Syracuse: Syracuse University Press, 1997), 119–50.

25. Kathryn Kish Sklar, *Florence Kelly and the Nation's Work: The Rise of Women's Political Culture, 1830–1900* (New Haven: Yale University Press, 1995), 186–92, and "Hull House in the 1890s: A Community of Women Reformers," *Signs* 10 (Summer 1985): 110; Nancy F. Cott, *The Bonds of Womanhood: "Woman's Sphere" in New England, 1780–1835* (New Haven: Yale University Press, 1977), 126–59; Carroll Smith-Rosenberg, *Disorderly Conduct: Visions of Gender in Victorian America* (New York: Oxford University Press, 1985), 254; Higginbotham, *Righteous Discontent*.

26. Sklar, "Hull House," 110.

27. Canon law required a minimum of one year in the novitiate. Depending on how soon the novices were needed in the workforce, the second year of the novitiate was usually less structured since they often were living and working with professed sisters outside the novitiate and away from the motherhouse.

28. Smith-Rosenberg, *Disorderly Conduct*, 65.

29. Memoirs of Sr. Rose Edward Dailey (entered 1916) in Purcell, *Jubilarse*, 45.

30. For examples in a variety of settings see Estelle Freedman, "Separatism as Strategy: Female Institution Building and American Feminism, 1870–1930," *Feminist Studies* 5 (Fall 1979): 512–29; Blanche Wieson Cook, "Female Support Networks and Political Activism," in *A Heritage of Her Own: Toward a New Social History of American Women*, ed. Nancy F. Cott and Elizabeth H. Pleck (New York: Simon and Schuster, 1979), 423–24; Sklar, "Hull House," 110–11; Janice G. Raymond, *A Passion for Friends:*

Toward a Philosophy of Female Affection (Boston: Beacon Press, 1986), 82; Carol K. Coburn, *Life at Four Corners: Religion, Gender, and Education in a German-Lutheran Community, 1868–1945* (Lawrence: University Press of Kansas, 1992), 94–95, 158; and Lynn Gordon, *Gender and Higher Education in the Progressive Era, 1890–1920* (New Haven: Yale University Press, 1990), 41.

31. Raymond, *Passion for Friends*, 90. This quote is taken from a chapter devoted to friendship in convents, titled "Varieties of Female Friendship: The Nun as Loose Woman," 73–112.

32. Carroll Smith-Rosenberg, "The Female World of Love and Ritual: Relations between Women in Nineteenth-Century America," *Signs* 1 (Autumn 1975): 1–29. Smith-Rosenberg's article redefined and expanded the discussion of women's love and friendship by placing it within the context of gender relationships in nineteenth-century America. See also Lillian Faderman, *Surpassing the Love of Men: Romantic Friendship and Love between Women from the Renaissance to the Present* (New York: William Morrow and Co., 1981).

33. Discussions of this issue are very brief in the CSJ prescriptive literature. Prohibitions against "particular friendships" were usually included in the section on the vow of chastity and placed amid warnings on intimacies with the opposite sex. CSJ Constitution (1860), 42, (1884), 17, and the CSJ Customs Book (1917), 54. See also Fitzgerald, "Irish-Catholic Nuns," 226–27, and Raymond, *Passion for Friends*, 91–98. For Catholic theological discussions on female friendship and relationships see Mary E. Hunt, *Fierce Tenderness: A Feminist Theology of Friendship* (New York: Crossroad, 1992), and Thomas C. Fox, *Sexuality and Catholicism* (New York: Geo. Braziller, Inc., 1994).

34. Letter from Mother Elizabeth Parrott to Sr. Cecelia O'Grady, September 22, 1907, ACSJC-LAP.

35. Lillian Faderman has argued that romantic friendships between women remained possible for the first two decades of the twentieth century, particularly for women born into "Victorian households." When Americans began reading the work of Sigmund Freud and Havelock Ellis, attitudes began to change and women in particular were seen as more sexual beings. A "companionate marriage," which advocated friendship *and* sex within heterosexual marriage became the only accepted norm, and consequently same-sex friendships came under suspicion. The same-sex bonding so typical of the nineteenth century was no longer seen as "natural" but as potentially pathological. See Faderman, *Surpassing the Love of Men*, 298, and Christina Simmons, "Companionate Marriage and the Lesbian Threat," in *Women and Power in American History: A Reader*, vol. 2, ed. Kathryn Kish Sklar and Thomas Dublin (Englewood Cliffs, N.J.: Prentice Hall, 1991), 183–94.

36. Correspondence between sisters, obituaries, necrologies, and community histories written in the early part of the twentieth century or earlier use the terms "dear companion" or "life-long friend or companion" to designate special friendships between sisters. The point here is not to try to define what these words meant but to point out that nineteenth- and early-twentieth-century writers felt comfortable noting these close friendships, unlike women born later in the twentieth century who had been socialized to view women's friendships with suspicion. For an interesting dis-

cussion on this issue within the IHM community see Joan Glisky, "The Official IHM Stance on Friendship, 1845–1960," 153–72, and Nancy Sylvester, "PFs: Persistent Friendships," 173–92, in *Building Sisterhood*.

37. Ewens, *Role of the Nun*, 108–15, and McNamara, *Sisters in Arms*, 627. This was less of a problem for the CSJs than other communities such as the Carmelites, Dominicans, School Sisters of Notre Dame, Religious of the Sacred Heart, and the Visitandines, but all communities of women religious struggled with the balancing act between religious activities and public work in the United States (Ewens, "Leadership of Nuns," 113–16). As the demands of professionalization and time commitments increased in the twentieth century, the dissonance between religious practices and the demands of public work increased for all communities of nuns.

38. Mary Ewens, "Women in the Convent," in *American Catholic Women: An Historical Exploration*, ed. Karen J. Kennelly (New York: Macmillan, 1989), 37.

39. The "Chapter of Faults" is described in the CSJ Constitution (1860), 70, (1884), 52–55. The French constitution and its English version (1847) as well as the later American versions stipulated the use of a "monitor" or, as it was later called, "admonitrix." The monitor's role was to "admonish the Superior of her faults, and to receive such complaints as may be made against her." CSJ Constitution (1847), 63–64.

40. See McDannell's discussion of "Catholic domesticity," in her book *The Christian Home in Victorian America, 1840–1900* (Bloomington: Indiana University Press, 1986), 52–76. See also Karen Kennelly, "Ideas of American Catholic Womanhood," in Kennelly, *American Catholic Women*, 1–16; James J. Kenneally, "Eve, Mary, and the Historians," in *Women in American Religion*, ed. Janet Wilson James (Philadelphia: University of Pennsylvania Press, 1980), 191–206; David G. Hackett, "Gender and Religion in American Culture, 1870–1930," *Religion and American Culture* 5, no. 2 (Summer 1995): 127–57; and Joseph G. Mannard, "Maternity . . . of the Spirit: Nuns and Domesticity in Antebellum America," *U.S. Catholic Historian* 5 (Summer 1986): 305–24.

41. For examples of Catholic prescriptive literature for girls and women during the late nineteenth century see George Deshon, *Guide for Catholic Young Women* (New York: The Catholic Publication House, 1871); Orestes A. Brownson, "The Woman Question," in *The Works of Orestes A. Brownson*, ed. Henry F. Brownson (Detroit: T. Nourse, 1882–85), 18:381–97; William Stang, *Socialism and Christianity* (New York: Benziger, 1905), 178–83; and Bernard O'Reilly, *Mirror of True Womanhood* (New York: P. J. Kenedy, 1892). For a gender comparison see O'Reilly's earlier book for men entitled *True Men As We Need Them* (New York: P. J. Kenedy, 1878).

42. "Maxims of Perfection," CSJ Constitution (1884), 129–46. There are ninety-eight Maxims of Perfection in this version of the constitution. More than twenty discuss the need for self-effacement and humility and nine deal with self-sacrifice. Humility is discussed so extensively in all the prescriptive documents that it is almost a de facto fourth vow.

43. Patricia Byrne, "Sisters of St. Joseph: The Americanization of a French Tradition," *U.S. Catholic Historian* (Summer/Fall 1986): 263.

44. Much of what we know about these events is gleaned from sisters' correspondence with the motherhouse. At times superiors did request sisters to keep a journal. Sr. Monica Corrigan was one of those asked to do so. Her journal documented the

journey she and her companions made to Tucson in 1870. Fortunately for us, Corrigan became interested in community history and began collecting memoirs in 1890 for a CSJ history. Although Corrigan never completed her CSJ history, Sr. Lucida Savage, a Ph.D. historian, utilized some of her collected materials and acquired more for her book *The Congregation of St. Joseph of Carondelet: A Brief Account of Its Origin and Its Work in the United States, 1650–1922* (St. Louis: Herder Book Co., 1923).

45. Although there are some recent exceptions that have been cited in this book, the vast majority of Catholic national, diocesan, or local parish histories have been written with great reverence for bishops and local priests with scant mention of the sisters. We are not attempting to devalue the contributions of these male clerics, but the invisibility and lack of recognition of the sisters' work are astounding, particularly since nuns were present in far larger numbers than either priests or orders of religious men.

46. "Maxims of Perfection," Nos. 23 and 25, CSJ Constitution (1884), 133.

47. What we are referring to is the ideology of "maternal feminism" as defined and described by some historians of women. This is the idea that women could utilize their power as mothers to actively take on abuses of patriarchy and at times of capitalism in defense of their concern for children, not necessarily their own self-interest. See Linda Gordon, "Putting Children First: Women, Maternalism, and Welfare in the Early Twentieth Century," in *U.S. History as Women's History: New Feminist Essays*, ed. Linda K. Kerber, Alice Kessler-Harris, and Kathryn Kish Sklar (Chapel Hill: University of North Carolina Press, 1995), 63–86; Theda Skocpol, *Protecting Soldiers and Mothers: The Political Origins of Social Policy in the United States* (Cambridge: Harvard University Press, 1992); and "Maternalism as a Paradigm," a symposium in the *Journal of Women's History* 5, no. 2 (Fall 1993): 95–131.

48. Caroline Walker Bynum, introduction to *Gender and Religion: On the Complexity of Symbols*, ed. Caroline Walker Bynum, Stevan Harrel, and Paula Richman (Boston: Beacon Press, 1986), 2, 13.

49. One of the earliest attempts to reinterpret gender within the Protestant tradition was Elizabeth Cady Stanton, *The Woman's Bible* (New York: European Publishing Co., 1898; reprint, Seattle: Seattle Coalition Task Force on Women and Religion, 1974). See also Margaret Lamberts Bendroth, *Fundamentalism and Gender, 1875 to the Present* (New Haven: Yale University Press, 1993); DeBerg, *Ungodly Women*; Higginbotham, *Righteous Discontent*, 122–36; and Ruether and Keller, *Women and Religion*, 1:ix–xii. The quote from St. Paul comes from Galatians 3:28 (King James Bible).

50. Madeleine Sophie Barat quote cited in McNamara, *Sisters in Arms*, 600.

51. The sisters viewed St. Joseph as Mary's "silent spouse," who was hardworking and faithful, an important, behind-the-scenes player who was seen as a "protector" of the CSJ community. The vast majority of institutions created by the CSJs were named for their patron. The feast of St. Joseph was always celebrated, and the postulants were routinely "received" into the community (novitiate) and given the habit on March 19, St. Joseph's Day. Nine of ninety-eight "Maxims of Perfection" encouraged the sisters to emulate Christ, particularly in "self-sacrifice." Although fewer in number, references are also made to the "heavenly father" and the Holy Spirit (CSJ Constitution [1884], 129–46). For a general discussion of nuns and the emulation of

Jesus see Mary Ewens, "Removing the Veil: The Liberated American Nun," in Ruether and McLaughlin, *Women of Spirit*, 257–59.

52. Fitzgerald, "Irish-Catholic Nuns," 225.

53. Speaking bluntly about male physical aggression historically directed at nuns, McNamara wrote, "Something in the very nature of [nuns'] inaccessibility, their integrity, and their devotion seems to raise testosterone levels" (*Sisters in Arms*, 571).

54. "She is a man" quoted in Mary Daly, *The Church and the Second Sex* (Boston: Beacon Press, 1985), 98. All other quotes come from Alison Weber, *Teresa of Avila and the Rhetoric of Feminism* (Princeton, N.J.: Princeton University Press, 1990), 17. For scholarly discussions of these women's lives in the convent see Emile Zum Brunn and Georgette Epiney-Burgard, *Women Mystics in Medieval Europe* (New York: Paragon Press, 1989); McNamara, *Sisters in Arms*; and Lerner, *Creation of Feminist Consciousness*. All five CSJ colleges are named for women: Avila College (formerly St. Teresa's College) in Kansas City, Mo., The College of St. Catherine in St. Paul, Minn., The College of St. Rose in Albany, N.Y., Fontbonne College in St. Louis, Mo., and Mt. St. Mary's College in Los Angeles, Calif.

55. All CSJ constitutions discuss these vows in specific detail: 1847, 38–47; 1860, 36–46; 1884, 13–21.

56. Nancy F. Cott, "Passionlessness: An Interpretation of Victorian Sexual Ideology, 1790–1850," in *a Heritage of Her Own: Toward a New Social History of American Women*, ed. Nancy F. Cott and Elizabeth H. Pleck (New York: Simon and Schuster, 1979), 162–81.

57. For discussions of the choir/lay sister controversy in other orders of religious women see McNamara, *Sisters in Arms*, 582–84; Ewens, *Role of the Nun*, 92–94, 279–80; Fitzgerald, "Irish-Catholic Nuns," 238–42; and Margaret Susan Thompson, "To Serve the People of God: Nineteenth-Century Sisters and the Creation of a Religious Life," Working Paper Series, Cushwa Center, University of Notre Dame, ser. 18, no. 2, Spring 1987, 15, and "Sisterhood and Power: Class, Culture, and Ethnicity in the American Convent," *Colby Library Quarterly* 25, no. 3 (September 1989): 151, 160. For examples of controversies in CSJ diocesan communities, particularly Wheeling and Philadelphia, see Byrne, "Sisters of St. Joseph," 266–70.

58. CSJ Constitution (1860), 22–23, and (1884), 5–6. Years in the community, not chronological age, determined rank, and once a term of office was completed the sister returned to her previous rank. Before 1908, choir sisters (professed and novices) ranked above lay sisters.

59. CSJ historian Patricia Byrne believes that it was Sr. Philomene Vilaine who came from France as a lay sister. Based on letters and records of Bishops Rosati and Kenrick, Sr. Philomene, on the advice of Rosati, may have worn a choir habit to avoid any taint of "anti-Americanism" in 1836. Her record of work is mixed, with both domestic and teaching duties, and no picture has survived to provide visual confirmation of her habit. See Byrne, "Sisters of St. Joseph," 249, 267.

60. Memoirs of Sr. Febronie Boyer, ACSJC-SLP.

61. CSJ Constitution (1860), 23.

62. "Deceased Membership Information Reports," ACSJC-SLP, list Sr. Febronie as

a teacher in the 1850s in Cahokia and as a chapter councillor and procurator in the 1870s in Troy, N.Y.

63. "Decrees of the General Chapter," 1908, and letter from Archbishop John Ireland to the General Chapter, 1908, ACSJC-G. Emily Joseph Daly, "The Generalate," in *The Sisters of St. Joseph of Carondelet*, ed. Dolorita Maria Dougherty et al. (St. Louis: Herder Book Co., 1966), 369.

64. "Autobiography of Sr. Assissium Shockley," April 24, 1912, ACSJC-SLP. At the end of her three-year term as provincial superior in 1869, Mother Assissium was recalled to St. Louis and replaced as provincial superior.

65. Thompson, "Sisterhood and Power," 157–75, and "To Serve the People," 19–22; McNamara, *Sisters in Arms*, 589–91; Fitzgerald, "Irish-Catholic Nuns," 220.

66. Thompson, "To Serve the People," 21. See also M. Georgia Costin, *Priceless Spirit: A History of the Sisters of the Holy Cross, 1841–1893* (Notre Dame, Ind.: University of Notre Dame Press, 1994).

67. CSJ Constitution (1860), 40, and (1884), 15.

68. CSJ Customs Book (1917), 80.

69. CSJ Profession Book. CSJ provincial records are inconsistent in regard to information on parents of candidates. Some records list the location of parental baptism, and others do not.

70. The Western province was the last of the four provinces to be formed between 1860 and 1920. From 1876 to 1890 the headquarters of the province and novitiate was located in Tucson, Arizona. Between 1890 and 1900 the novitiate for the Western province was in St. Louis. Since 1903 the Western novitiate and province headquarters have been in Los Angeles.

71. CSJ Profession Book.

72. For other examples of recruiting trips by religious orders see Suellen Hoy, "The Journey Out: The Recruitment and Emigration of Irish Religious Women to the United States, 1812–1914," *Journal of Women's History* 6/7 (Winter/Spring 1995): 64–98; Thompson, "To Serve the People," 20; and Fitzgerald, "Irish-Catholic Nuns," 240–41. CSJ Postulant Records (St. Louis province), 1898–99.

73. Interview of Sr. M. Ailbe O'Kelly (entered 1912) by Sr. Susan Marie O'Connor on January 23, 1981, in Syracuse, N.Y.

74. Hasia Diner, *Erin's Daughters in America: Irish Immigrant Women in the Nineteenth Century* (Baltimore: Johns Hopkins University Press, 1983), 28–29.

75. Ibid., 1–29. Diner lists the Sisters of Mercy, Presentation Sisters of the Blessed Virgin Mary, the Sisters of Loretto, the Dominicans, and the Ursulines as orders that were influential in Ireland before coming to the United States. For a wonderful description of two Irish women immigrating to the United States to join the Dominican order see Suellen Hoy and Margaret MacCurtain, *From Dublin to New Orleans: The Journey of Nora and Alice* (Dublin: Attic Press, 1994).

76. Savage, *Congregation of St. Joseph*, 199, 259; Thomas Marie McMahon, "The Sisters of St. Joseph of Carondelet: Arizona's Pioneer Religious Congregation, 1870–1890" (master's thesis, St. Louis University, 1952), 111. "List of Sisters of St. Joseph from Early Mexican Families," ACSJC-LAP.

77. Postulant Records of St. Louis Province (1892), ACSJC-SLP.

78. St. Claire Coyne, "The Los Angeles Province," in Dougherty et al., *Sisters of St. Joseph*, 298. One of six persons in the Los Angeles–Monterey diocese was Catholic, and this mixture included diverse ethnic groups from eastern, western, and southern Europe as well as a large Hispanic population. "Dates of Reception and Profession, Los Angeles Province," 1902–43, ACSJC-LAP.

79. Dolan, *American Catholic Experience*, 127–94; Thompson, "Sisterhood and Power," 164–67; Ewens, "Removing the Veil," 263–64.

80. Memoirs of Sr. Mary Eustace Huster in Purcell, *Jubilarse*, 3.

81. Dolan, *American Catholic Experience*, 143–44, 302. Quoting from a work on Polish Catholics by Anthony J. Kuzniewski, Dolan writes that the Irish continued to dominate the seats of power and "before long people began describing the church in the United States as One, Holy, Irish, and Apostolic" (302).

82. Irish surnames are prominent among provincial leaders in the Troy, N.Y., province. However, the most notable Irish connection occurred in the St. Paul province, where Seraphine Ireland served as CSJ provincial superior for almost four decades, teaming with her notable brother, Archbishop John Ireland, in the St. Paul diocese. Provincial leadership in the Los Angeles and St. Louis provinces appears far more ethnically diverse, with smaller "pockets" of Irish leadership in the geographically diverse local communities.

83. Cited in Byrne, "Sisters of St. Joseph," 264.

84. Helen Angela Hurley, *On Good Ground: The Story of the Sisters of St. Joseph in St. Paul* (Minneapolis: University of Minnesota Press, 1951), 138–40; Sisters of St. Joseph, *Sisters of St. Joseph of Cleveland* (Cleveland: Saint Joseph Convent, 1951), 43–45.

85. Mother Stanislaus Leary left with her two biological sisters for Arizona, but they ended up in Kansas, where they founded the Concordia community, which later expanded into a separate community in Wichita. In 1899, while in Chicago for her health, she accepted the invitation to found the LaGrange, Illinois, community, which later expanded into a separate community in Orange, California. A Sister of St. Joseph, *Sisters of St. Joseph of Rochester* (Rochester: Sisters of St. Joseph, 1950), 38–70; Evangeline Thomas, *Footprints on the Frontier: A History of the Sisters of St. Joseph, Concordia, Kansas* (Westminster, Md.: Newman Press, 1948), 125–98; Eileen Quinlan, *Planted on the Plains: A History of the Sisters of St. Joseph of Wichita, Kansas* (Wichita: Greg D. Jones, 1984), 72–83; Brad Geagley, *A Compassionate Presence* (Orange, Calif.: Sisters of St. Joseph of Orange, 1987), 3–4.

86. Sr. Mary Herman Lacy's case is extraordinary because it involves so many people and dioceses. Standard community histories, parish histories, and diocesan histories are often problematic because they tend to omit entirely or place a positive "spin" on conflict within a religious community or between a sister and a priest or bishop. Two recent historians have researched this case extensively and analyzed the surviving primary documents. The following information is taken from Wanda Swantek's "The Sisters of St. Joseph of Nazareth, Michigan, 1889–1900" (unpublished manuscript, November 11, 1972, copy in ACSJC-AP) and *Sisters of St. Joseph of Nazareth, 1889–1929* (Kalamazoo, Mich.: Borgess Hospital Printing, 1983) and Mary Alice Murphy's "Reflections on the Life of Sister Mary Herman Lacy" (unpublished manuscript, February 11, 1981, copy in ACSJC-AP). Murphy completed this research

"in hopes that others might be moved to continue to seek out the truth of this woman, who has touched so many in our Congregation."

87. Sr. Grace Aurelia, "Notes on the Life of Sister Mary Herman," as cited in Swantek, *Sisters of St. Joseph*, 5.

88. Sr. Winifred Maloney, "Story of Sister Herman," as cited in Swantek, *Sisters of St. Joseph*, 3–5.

89. Swantek, *Sisters of St. Joseph*, 5; Murphy, "Reflections," 2.

90. Srs. George Bradley and Mary Herman Lacy were both supporters and helpers in the founding of the Tipton community. See the *History of the Sisters of Saint Joseph, Tipton, Indiana* (Tipton, Ind.: Sisters of St. Joseph, 1986).

91. Lecture of Fr. Frank O'Brien to the Kalamazoo Sisters of St. Joseph, July 1890, as cited in Swantek, "The Sisters of St. Joseph," 61–62.

92. George C. Stewart, *Marvels of Charity: History of American Sisters and Nuns* (Huntington, Ind.: Our Sunday Visitor, Inc., 1994), 565. Stewart estimates that by 1920 there were 90,558 American sisters. The CSJs of Carondelet numbered over 2,300. If their former diocesan communities and daughter communities (most of whom were connected to the original motherhouse in St. Louis) were added to that number it would be over 4,000.

Chapter Four

1. In 1834 and 1835 Lyman Beecher, a well-known New England minister and father of educator Catharine Beecher, minister Henry Ward Beecher, and author Harriet Beecher Stowe, made speeches to acquire donations for Lane Seminary in Cincinnati. These were published in *A Plea for the West* (Cincinnati: n.p., 1835). For more discussion on Beecher and other anti-Catholic rhetoric concerning Western expansion see Ray Allen Billington, *The Protestant Crusade 1800–1860: A Study of the Origins of American Nativism* (New York: Rinehart, 1938; reprint, Chicago: Quadrangle Books, 1964), 68–76; Kathryn Kish Sklar, *Catharine Beecher: A Study in American Domesticity* (New York: W. W. Norton, 1976), 116–17 and 170–83; James Hennesey, *American Catholics: A History of the Roman Catholic Community in the United States* (New York: Oxford University Press, 1981), 116–27; and Bryan Le Beau, "'Saving the West from the Pope': Anti-Catholic Propaganda and the Settlement of the Mississippi River Valley," *American Studies* 32 (Spring 1991): 101–14.

2. Le Beau, "'Saving the West,'" 103. Two of the most prominent philanthropic societies were the Society for the Propagation of the Faith, organized in Lyons, France, in 1822 and the Leopold (or Leopoldine) Association, established in 1829 in Vienna. It was publications from the Society for the Propagation of the Faith that provided the incentive for Countess Félicité de la Rochejaquelin to fund the CSJ mission to America in 1836.

3. There are many excellent sources describing women in the West, but a good representative sample includes Susan Armitage and Elizabeth Jameson, eds., *The Women's West* (Norman: University of Oklahoma Press, 1987); Elizabeth Jameson and Susan Armitage, eds., *Writing the Range: Race, Class, and Culture in the Women's West* (Norman: University of Oklahoma Press, 1997); Lillian Schlissel, Vicki L. Ruiz, and Janice

Monk, eds., *Western Women: Their Land, Their Lives* (Albuquerque: University of New Mexico Press, 1988); Ruth B. Moynihan and Susan Armitage, eds., *So Much to Be Done: Women Settlers on the Mining and Ranching Frontier* (Lincoln: University of Nebraska Press, 1990); Peggy Pascoe, *Relations of Rescue: The Search for Female Moral Authority in the American West, 1874–1939* (New York: Oxford University Press, 1990); a special issue on women in the West, in *Frontiers: A Journal of Women's Studies* 15, no. 3 (1995); and Susan Armitage, Helen Bannan, Katherine G. Morrissey, and Vicki Ruiz, *Women in the West: A Guide to Manuscript Sources* (New York: Garland Pub., 1991).

4. Schlissel, Ruiz, and Monk, *Western Women*, 47.

5. John Rothensteiner, in *History of the Archdiocese of St. Louis*, 2 vols. (St. Louis: Blackwell Wielandy Co., 1928), states that in the St. Louis diocese (which at one time included much of the territory in the Louisiana Purchase and beyond) in the late 1830s, one priest was responsible for 2,000 Catholics who lived scattered across Missouri, Illinois, and Wisconsin territory (1:581–85, 730–35). For other discussions on the shortage of priests in the West see Hennesey, *American Catholics*, 128–42; Dolores Liptak, *Immigrants and Their Church* (New York: Macmillan, 1989), 13–32; Jay P. Dolan, *Catholic Revivalism: The American Experience, 1830–1900* (Notre Dame: University of Notre Dame Press, 1971), 1–24; and Richard C. Wade, *The Urban Frontier* (Chicago: University of Chicago Press, 1964), 263. For some general discussion on Catholics in the West see James P. Shannon, *Catholic Colonization on the Western Frontier* (New Haven: Yale University Press, 1957); Michael E. Engh, *Frontier Faiths: Church, Temple, and Synagogue in Los Angeles, 1846–1888* (Albuquerque: University of New Mexico Press, 1992); and numerous articles on frontier Catholicism in *U.S. Catholic Historian* (special issue) 12, no. 4 (Fall 1994).

6. Some sources that have attempted to integrate nuns in the history of the American West include Mary Ewens, "Catholic Sisterhoods in North Dakota," in *Day In, Day Out: Women's Lives in North Dakota*, ed. Elizabeth Hampsten (Grand Forks: University of North Dakota, 1988), and Susan Carol Peterson and Courtney Ann Vaughn-Roberson, *Women with Vision: The Presentation Sisters of South Dakota, 1880–1985* (Urbana: University of Illinois, 1991). See also Susan Carol Peterson, "Religious Communities of Women in the West: The Presentation Sisters' Adaptation to the Northern Plains Frontier," *Journal of the West* 21 (April 1992): 65–70, and Carol K. Coburn and Martha Smith, "'Pray for Your Wanderers': Women Religious on the Colorado Mining Frontier," *Frontiers: A Journal of Women's Studies* 15, no. 3 (1995): 27–52.

7. Mary Ewens, "The Leadership of Nuns in Immigrant Catholicism," in *Women and Religion in America*, vol. 1, ed. Rosemary Radford Ruether and Rosemary Skinner Keller (San Francisco: Harper and Row, 1981), 101. The list of female religious orders that established foundations and institutions in the trans-Mississippi West is voluminous, but representative examples include Religious of the Sacred Heart, Benedictines, Daughters of Charity, Dominicans, Sisters of Mercy, Presentation Sisters, Sisters of Loretto, and Sisters of Charity.

8. "Report to the Society for the Propagation of the Faith," Lyons, France, January 1851, as cited in Helen Angela Hurley, *On Good Ground: The Story of the Sisters of St. Joseph in St. Paul* (Minneapolis: University of Minnesota Press, 1951), 17–18.

9. Hurley, *On Good Ground*, 19. Hurley reports that the Visitation Sisters and "other

communities refused [Bishop Cretin's] appeals." The Sisters of Charity of the Blessed Virgin Mary (Dubuque, Iowa) reportedly refused because they had no French-speaking sisters. Of the original four CSJs sent to St. Paul, three of the four were native French-speaking sisters.

10. William E. Lass, "Minnesota," *The Encyclopedia of the American West* (New York: Macmillan, 1996), 3:995–99. See also James M. Reardon, *The Catholic Church in the Diocese of St. Paul* (St. Paul: North Central Pub. Co., 1952), 72–83.

11. Letter from Sr. Francis Joseph Ivory to Sr. Monica Corrigan, August 12, 1890, ACSJC-SLP. The early years in St. Paul are also described in three articles by Sr. Ignatius Loyola Cox in *Acta et Dicta* 3, no. 2 (July 1914): 270–89, and in Mary Lucida Savage, *The Congregation of St. Joseph of Carondelet: A Brief Account of Its Origin and Its Work in the United States, 1650–1922* (St. Louis: Herder Book Co., 1923), 80–93, and Hurley, *On Good Ground*, 1–109.

12. A chronological list of the sisters' institutions in St. Paul and Minneapolis can be found in Helen Angela Hurley, "The St. Paul Province," in *Sisters of St. Joseph of Carondelet*, ed. Dolorita Maria Dougherty et al. (St. Louis: Herder Book Co., 1966), 139–214, and Dougherty, "Chronological List of Establishments" and "Alphabetical List of Establishments," 432–34 and appendix V, 439, in ibid. In the 1860s and 1870s other female religious orders came to St. Paul, including the Dominicans, Sisters of the Good Shepherd, and the Sisters of the Visitation.

13. "Report of the General Chapter—St. Paul Province, 1920," ACSJC-G. This report lists the institutions in each city and how many adults and children were served throughout the entire Northern province.

14. Lawrence H. Larsen, "Kansas City, Missouri," in *Encyclopedia of the American West*, 2:803–4; A. Theodore Brown and Lyle W. Dorsett, *K.C.: A History of Kansas City, Missouri* (Boulder: Pruett Publishing Co., 1978), 9; Savage, *Congregation of St. Joseph*, 142–43.

15. Dorothy Brandt Marra, "The Story," in *This Far by Faith: A Popular History of the Catholic People of West and Northwest Missouri*, vol. 2, ed. Michael Coleman (Kansas City, Mo.: Diocese of Kansas City–St. Joseph, 1992), 21–58; Gilbert J. Gerraghan, *Catholic Beginnings in Kansas City: An Historical Sketch* (Chicago: Loyola Press, 1920); Savage, *Congregation of St. Joseph*, 142–43.

16. Letters from Sr. Francis Joseph Ivory to Sr. Monica Corrigan, August 12 and September 10, 1890, ACSJC-SLP. Ivory was indeed a pioneer sister of many new foundations. She participated in the earliest beginnings in St. Paul, Kansas City, Canadaigua, and Buffalo, N.Y., and probably more. Personnel records of CSJs from the St. Louis province who died before 1949 are incomplete, but other records indicate that Ivory also spent many years in the Troy province in Glens Falls and Binghamton, N.Y. For a brief history of her active life see Ann Thomasine Sampson, "Sister Francis Joseph Ivory," (unpublished manuscript, ACSJC-SPP). Other orders of women religious joined the CSJs in Kansas City before 1920, and some of these include Daughters of Charity, Little Sisters of the Poor, Dominicans, Benedictines, Sisters of the Blessed Virgin Mary, Sisters of St. Francis, Sisters of Mercy, Sisters of Charity, Sisters of Loretto, and School Sisters of Notre Dame.

17. Martha Smith, "Sisters of St. Joseph of Carondelet," in Coleman, *This Far by*

Faith, 2:607–13, and Michael Coleman, "Saint Joseph Health Center," 572–75; "St. Joseph Orphan Home for Girls," 575–77, and "St. Teresa's Academy," 582–86, in ibid. See also James L. Soward, *Hospital Hill: An Illustrated Account of Public Healthcare Institutions in Kansas City, Missouri* (Kansas City: Truman Medical Center Foundation, 1995), 14–15.

18. Although Kansas City was populated with fewer foreign-born than many cities, the 1910 census registered 10.2 percent of the population as foreign-born, 10 percent black, and for the first time a larger proportion of females to males (Brown and Dorsett, *K.C.*, 183–86).

19. "Report to the General Chapter—St. Louis Province, 1920," ACSJC-G. This report lists Kansas City and St. Joseph, Mo., statistics and institutions. For another list of Kansas City institutions see Dougherty, "Chronological List of Establishments," 427–31.

20. Marra, "Story," 55. American sisters almost always started schools for girls when they came into a new area. This was a continuation of their European traditions in most cases, but their efforts in the United States provided some of the earliest educational opportunities for girls and women, Protestant or Catholic. Records in St. Paul and Kansas City, as was the practice with most convent schools, listed the religious preference of each student. For additional examples see Mary J. Oates, "Catholic Female Academies on the Frontier," *U.S. Catholic Historian* 12, no. 4 (Fall 1994): 121–36. Academies will be discussed in detail in Chapter 6.

21. Although we have provided an extensive list of sources that document this interpretation in note 3, the following sources supplement that list and emphasize the particular importance of families and community building: John Mack Faragher, *Sugar Creek: Life on the Illinois Prairie* (New Haven: Yale University Press, 1986); Joseph V. Hickey, *Ghost Settlement on the Prairie: A Biography of Thurman, Kansas* (Lawrence: University Press of Kansas, 1995); Robert V. Hine, *Community on the American Frontier: Separate but Not Alone* (Norman: University of Oklahoma Press, 1980); Carol K. Coburn, *Life at Four Corners: Religion, Gender, and Education in a German-Lutheran Community, 1868–1945* (Lawrence: University Press of Kansas, 1992); William Loren Katz, *The Black West* (Seattle: Open Hand Publishing Co., 1987).

22. John Ireland served the Cathedral parish from 1867 to 1875, when he was appointed coadjutor bishop. He became the bishop of St. Paul in 1884 and archbishop in 1888. His two sisters and cousin were CSJs, and this was a family dynasty that served the CSJs well until 1918, the year of the archbishop's death. Ireland was seemingly loved or hated, but neither his power and influence nor that he proved to be an invaluable ally to the CSJs can be denied. See Hurley, *On Good Ground*, 197–227; Marvin O'Connell, *John Ireland and the American Catholic Church* (St. Paul: Minnesota Historical Society Press, 1988); and Ann Thomasine Sampson, "The Ireland Connection" (unpublished manuscript, ACSJC-SPP).

23. Although there are many stories of his obvious favoritism to the CSJs, CSJ historian Hurley, in her *On Good Ground*, relates the following scenario. In the 1890s the pastor at Bird Island, Minn., came to Ireland to discuss his plans for a new school that he had asked the Sisters of Notre Dame to staff. Ireland told him: "You will do much better to have the Srs. of St. Joseph." Not wanting to argue with the archbishop, he

went to the CSJs, and they agreed to staff the school (223–24). See also, Christopher J. Kauffman, *Ministry and Meaning: A Religious History of Catholic Health Care in the United States* (New York: Crossroad, 1995), 97–99. Kauffman describes Ireland's strategy in taking a Minneapolis hospital from the Sisters of Mercy and awarding it to the CSJs in 1887.

24. Fr. Donnelly was a true entrepreneur. In the 1850s he convinced civic planners that he could bring in crews to lower the bluffs along the Missouri River to allow the city to spread south. He sent ads to a Boston and New York newspaper requesting 150 Irish men from each area to come to Kansas City to complete the task. His only stipulation was that all the men from each group be from the same county in Ireland, "so that they could get along with each other." The men came, completed the work, began an Irish immigration to the city, and significantly increased the Catholic population. A few years later, to facilitate building in the city, Donnelly had the soil surveyed on the church grounds and founded a brickyard that made thousands of dollars of profit for the parish and other Catholic institutions in the city (Marra, "Story," 47–48).

25. Marra, "Story," 71–73; Smith, "Sisters of St. Joseph," 611; William J. Dalton, *Pioneer Priest: The Life of Father Bernard Donnelly* (Kansas City: Grimes-Joyce Printing Co., 1921), 139–43.

26. Sklar, *Catharine Beecher*, 122–25; Polly Welts Kaufman, *Women Teachers on the Frontier* (New Haven: Yale University Press, 1984), 1–49.

27. Pascoe, *Relations of Rescue*, 43–44, 58; Mary P. Ryan, *Cradle of the Middle Class: The Family in Oneida County, New York, 1790–1865* (New York: Cambridge University Press, 1981), 217–18. Both religion and ethnicity fueled competition between institutions in St. Paul. Six years after the CSJs opened an orphanage in 1859, the Protestant Orphanage was founded, and in 1877 the Benedictines opened a German-Catholic orphanage.

28. Letter from Fr. Zephyrin Engelhardt to Rev. Mother Agatha Guthrie, February 4, 1886, ACSJC-SLP. The Society for the Propagation of the Faith published *Annals*, which provided written descriptions about Catholic missionary work from priests and bishops in the United States.

29. This is not a complete list of CSJ institutions but one that highlights the larger urban settings in the trans-Mississippi West. A complete list can be found in Dougherty, "Chronological List of Establishments," 427–38. Independent CSJ diocesan communities established institutions in Wichita, Kansas; Lewiston, Idaho; and Pasco, Washington. The Idaho and Washington CSJs affiliated with the Carondelet group in 1925.

30. Peggy Pascoe, "Western Women at the Cultural Crossroads," in *Trails: Toward a New Western History*, ed. Patricia Nelson Limerick, Clyde A. Milner II, and Charles E. Rankin (Lawrence: University Press of Kansas, 1991), 46. See also Elizabeth Jameson, "Toward a Multicultural History of Women in the United States," *Signs* 13 (Summer 1988): 761–91, and two particularly good anthologies edited by Armitage and Jameson: *Women's West* and *Writing the Range*.

31. Although CSJs served in Hispanic parishes in the Southwest and other parts of the country, almost no primary documents provide particular insight into this inter-

cultural exchange. The Native American population was clearly a mixture of ethnicities and cultures as many Native American children had Spanish surnames. For good sources on the Hispanic population in the Southwest and the Catholic Church's interactions with them see Jay P. Dolan and Gilberto M. Hinojosa, eds., *Mexican Americans and the Catholic Church, 1900–1965* (Notre Dame, Ind.: University of Notre Dame Press, 1994); Jay P. Dolan and Allan Figueroa Deck, eds., *Hispanic Catholic Culture in the U.S.: Issues and Concerns* (Notre Dame, Ind.: University of Notre Dame Press, 1996); and Timothy Walch, "More Pluribus Than Unum: Hispanic Catholics and Their American Church," *Journal of American Ethnic History* 15, no. 4 (Summer 1996): 49–52. For good general sources see George Sanchez, *Becoming Mexican American: Ethnicity, Culture, and Identity in Chicano Los Angeles, 1900–1945* (New York: Oxford University Press, 1993), and Sarah Deutsch, *No Separate Refuge: Culture, Class, and Gender on an Anglo-Hispanic Frontier in the American Southwest, 1880–1940* (New York: Oxford University Press, 1987).

32. For example, the Sisters of Loretto and the Sisters of Charity worked in New Mexico and the Sisters of Notre Dame de Namur and the Daughters of Charity worked in California as early as the 1850s. For information on New Mexico and the early religious orders see Louis Avant, "History of Catholic Education in New Mexico since American Occupation" (master's thesis, University of New Mexico, 1940), 16–18, 56, 60, 73, 77–79. For information on the Sisters of Notre Dame de Namur in California see Martha Smith, "Sister Mary Catherine Cabareaux," in *Encyclopedia of the American West*, 1:217, and for a thorough discussion on the Daughters of Charity in Los Angeles see Engh, *Frontier Faiths*, 139–63.

33. Although we will be quoting from the original journal written in 1870, an edited and condensed version was published as *Trek of the Seven Sisters* (Tucson, Ariz.: Carondelet Health Services, 1991). Typed copies of the original journal are found in ACSJC-LAP, ACSJC-AP, and ACSJC-SLP. A *Playhouse 90* television adaptation of this story was broadcast April 25, 1957, with Helen Hayes playing the role of Sr. Monica Corrigan.

34. Oral history interview of Sr. Emmelia James by Sr. Dolorita Dougherty at Nazareth Convent, St. Louis, on June 21, 1979. See also oral history interviews of Sr. M. Anthony Byrne by Dougherty and handwritten memoirs of Sr. Guadalupe Saucedo, who traveled from Mexico with her sisters under Corrigan's care (ACSJC-LAP and ACSJC-SLP). Stories about Corrigan (many from eyewitnesses) are legendary. Sisters marveled at her business acumen, strong will, and forthrightness, if not daring. She was credited with being a premier fund-raiser and "an arbitrator of civil and domestic disputes . . . who had little regard for the unfavorable judgement of others and courageously undertook what many, who lacked her convictions, would have avoided" (unpublished essay by Sr. Alberta Cammack, ACSJC-LAP). See also the appendix in Monica Corrigan, *Trek of the Seven Sisters (Diary, 1870)* (Tucson: Carondelet Health Services, 1991).

35. Journal of Sr. Monica Corrigan, 1870, ACSJC-LAP. All further quoted material on the journey to Tucson will be from this source unless specified otherwise. Probably the most famous written documentation of a nun's life in the Southwest is Sr. Blandina Segale, *At the End of the Santa Fe Trail* (Milwaukee: Bruce Pub. Co., 1948).

36. This quotation completes the writings from Sr. Monica Corrigan's journal.

There would be two other harrowing journeys to Arizona, in 1873 and 1876, before the railroads made the ocean voyage and overland trek unnecessary. In the 1873 journey, the CSJs went by train as far as Kit Carson, Colo. (southeast of Denver), then they traveled by wagon and foot. Lost and fighting their way through a heavy snowstorm, they found a deserted cabin and barely avoided freezing to death. The next day they reached Trinidad, Colo., and lodged overnight with the Sisters of Charity and probably Sr. Blandina Segale (Anonymous Account of the 1873 journey, ACSJC-SLP). In 1876, the sisters repeated the route of the original band, but instead of arriving in San Diego they continued their ocean voyage around San Lucas (Baja) to the mouth of the Colorado River and took a riverboat to Yuma, avoiding the California desert. They walked the last 250 miles to Tucson (Sr. John Berchmans Hartrich, "Journal to Tucson," April 17 to June 8, 1876, ACSJC-SLP).

37. CSJs worked in four schools and one hospital in four locations. In Minnesota the CSJs staffed the Winnebago Indian Mission School, Long Prairie (1852–55), and St. Mary's Academy, Graceville (1885–98); in Michigan, St. Xavier's School (1866–1906) and L'Anse (Baraga); and in Wisconsin, St. Joseph's Industrial School (1883–?) and Menominee Hospital (1886–1912), Keshena.

38. Henry Warner Bowden, *American Indians and the Christian Missions: Studies in Cultural Conflict* (Chicago: University of Chicago Press, 1981), 192–97. Bowden writes that churches were invited to nominate men for the agency positions scattered throughout the country. As a result of this policy, thirteen denominations gained control over the seventy-three Indian agencies. Because of centuries of native contact, particularly in the Southwest, Catholics had expected to receive a large number of protectorates, but because of the Protestant bias of the board, they received only seven. Methodists received fourteen, the largest share (192). See also Francis Paul Prucha, *The Churches and the Indian Schools, 1888–1912* (Lincoln: University of Nebraska Press, 1979) and *American Indian Policy in Crisis: Christian Reformers and the Indians, 1865–1900* (Norman: University of Oklahoma Press, 1976); David Wallace Adams, *Education for Extinction: American Indians and the Boarding School Experience, 1875–1928* (Lawrence: University Press of Kansas, 1995); and Jorge Noriega, "American Indian Education in the United States: Indoctrination for Subordination to Colonization," in *The State of Native America: Genocide, Colonization, and Extinction*, ed. M. Annette Jaimes (Boston: South End Press, 1992), 371–402.

39. Mary J. Oates, *The Catholic Philanthropic Tradition in America* (Bloomington: Indiana University Press, 1995), 67. Oates states that when the government began offering contracts in 1877, many religious communities applied for them, and between 1886 and 1891 the BCIM was very successful in acquiring funds, much to the disgust of the anti-Catholic Office of the National League for Protection of American Institutions. A quote from one of their publications in 1890 stated that only Protestant schools should be funded because they "recognize allegiance to our Constitution and laws, and . . . are devoted to American principles and institutions."

40. For information on nuns' work with Native Americans see Susan Carol Peterson's three articles, "Challenges to the Stereotypes: The Adaptation of the Sisters of St. Francis to South Dakota Missions, 1885–1910," *Upper Midwest History* 84 (1984): 1–9; "Doing 'Women's' Work: The Grey Nuns of Fort Totten Indian Reser-

vation, 1874–1900," *North Dakota History* 52 (Spring 1985): 18–25; and "Holy Women and Housekeepers: Women Teachers on South Dakota Reservations, 1885–1910," *South Dakota History* 13 (Fall 1983): 245–60. See also S. Carol Berg, "The Economic Foundations of a Mission: The Benedictines at White Earth Reservation," *Midwest Review* 9 (Spring 1987): 22–29.

41. Savage, *Congregation of St. Joseph*, 272, and St. Claire Coyne, "The Los Angeles Province," in Dougherty et al., *Sisters of St. Joseph*, 334. The sisters were withdrawn in 1876 when the Papago and Pima agencies were merged and the school was closed. They returned in 1888 to teach both Papago and Pima children.

42. Some very useful secondary sources provide details on some of these CSJ missions. See Teresa Baksh McNeil's three articles: "Catholic Indian Schools of the Southwest Frontier: Curriculum and Management," *Southern California Quarterly* (Winter 1990): 321–38; "Sisters of St. Joseph under Fire: Pioneer Convent School on the Colorado River," *Journal of Arizona History* 29, no. 1 (1988): 35–50; and "St. Anthony's Indian School in San Diego, 1886–1907," *Journal of San Diego History* 34 (Summer 1988): 187–200. For works that include but are not limited to the CSJs' work with Native Americans see Barbara Alice Perkins, "Educational Work of the Sisters of St. Joseph, 1903–1963" (master's thesis, Mt. St. Mary's College–Los Angeles, 1965); Ann Cecilia Smith, "Educational Activities of the Sisters of St. Joseph of Carondelet in the Western Province from 1870–1903" (master's thesis, Catholic University, 1953); and George Dyke, "History of Catholic Education in Arizona" (Ph.D. diss., Catholic University, 1951).

43. Drexel, who was born in 1858, and her two sisters inherited a $14 million estate in 1885 after the death of their parents. After taking vows in 1891, Drexel spent the next forty years directing every aspect of her community's work in the South, urban North, and Indian territory, contributing millions of dollars of her personal fortune to work for Native Americans and blacks. She also founded Xavier College in New Orleans, the only Catholic college for blacks in the United States. See Nancy A. Hewitt, "Mother Mary Katharine Drexel," in *Notable American Women: The Modern Period*, ed. Barbara Sicherman and Carol Hurd Green (Cambridge: Harvard University Press, 1980), 206–8. See also Consuela Marie Duffy, *Katharine Drexel: A Biography* (Cornwell Heights, Pa.: Sisters of the Blessed Sacrament, 1972), and Anne M. Butler, "Mother Katharine Drexel," in *By Grit and Grace: Pioneer Women Who Shaped the West*, ed. Glenda Riley and Richard Etulain (Golden, Colo.: Fulcrum Publishing, 1997), 198–220.

44. Oates, *Catholic Philanthropic Tradition*, 68–69. Oates also states that Drexel refused to give money to older, financially solvent religious orders such as the Jesuits "because she believed that this order had the financial means to support" its own schools. Drexel helped support all CSJ Indian missions either through the BCIM or directly. Interestingly, Fr. J. A. Stephan, longtime director of the BCIM, received some of his strongest financial support from a group of prominent Catholic laywomen.

45. Letter from Sr. Julia Littenecker to Rev. Mother Agatha Guthrie from Ft. Yuma, Calif., May 3, 1886, ACSJC-SLP. Littenecker, who had done the preliminary negotiations with government officials to staff the school, accompanied the first group of sisters to the fort to help them get settled.

46. Memoirs of Sr. Bernadette Smith upon her arrival in 1888 at San Xavier del Bac, outside Tucson, ACSJC-LAP.

47. Ibid.

48. Memoirs of Sr. Magdalen Gaffney at Ft. Yuma, Calif., written in 1946, ACSJC-LAP. Sr. Magdalen came to Yuma in 1890.

49. Anonymous CSJ, "Arrival of the First Sisters to St. John's Indian Mission," AACSJC-LAP.

50. For general information on curriculum and practices in reservation and non-reservation boarding schools see Adams, *Education for Extinction*, 136–63; Robert A. Trennert Jr., *The Phoenix Indian School: Forced Assimilation in Arizona, 1891–1935* (Norman: University of Oklahoma Press, 1988); and Melissa A. Davis, "Indian Schools on the Reservation," in *Encyclopedia of the American West*, 2:733–35.

51. The December Quarterly Report for 1908 at St. Boniface Indian School in Banning, Calif., listed two priests, eight CSJs, and four laymen (a farmer, a carpenter, a gardener, and a disciplinarian). The *Indian Sentinel*, published by BCIM, featured one or more schools in each issue, providing information about the curriculum, discipline, and socialization. The schools were remarkably standardized in schedule, curriculum, military drill, and regimentation. Annual reports from all BCIM schools and copies of the *Indian Sentinel* can be found at BCIM-AMU.

52. Sources listed in notes 38 and 50 discuss the problematic, if not destructive, nature of education for Native American children. Catholic historian Jay Dolan also documents the small enrollments, financial limitations, resistance to Christianity, and the "destructive effect" of "forced civilization" (*The American Catholic Experience: A History from Colonial Times to the Present* [Garden City, N.Y.: Image Books, 1985], 285–87). For a perspective from Native Americans who attended some of these schools in the nineteenth and twentieth centuries see Patricia Riley, ed., *Growing Up Native American* (New York: Avon Books, 1993).

53. Memoirs of Sr. Marsina Power, ACSJC-LAP.

54. Memoirs of Sr. Bernadette Smith.

55. Anonymous CSJ, "Brief History of San Xavier del Bac," and Memoirs of Sr. Mary Thomas Lavin, ACSJC-LAP.

56. Jacqueline Peterson and Mary Druke, "American Indian Women and Religion," in Ruether and Keller, *Women and Religion in America*, 2:9. See also Peterson, "Women Dreaming: The Religiopsychology of Indian-White Marriages and the Rise of a Metis Culture," in Schlissel, Ruiz, and Monk, *Western Women*, 49–79, and Bowden, *American Indians*, 46–48.

57. Memoirs of Sr. Bernadette Smith.

58. Anonymous CSJ, "Arrival of the First Sisters."

59. Memoirs of Sr. Bernadette Smith.

60. Dolan, *American Catholic Experience*, 286; Bowden, *American Indians*, 191. CSJ statistics for fourteen years at Ft. Yuma demonstrate the small number of conversions. The final total shows 120–30 "Christians on Reservation" and 500–600 "Pagans on the Reservation" (from "Statistics on the Fort Yuma School," March 31, 1900, ACSJC-LAP). Conversion statistics tend to be exaggerated or misrepresented since

Native Americans allowed themselves to be baptized more than once or received baptism but continued with their traditional religious practices.

61. Pascoe, "Western Women," 55.

62. Letter from Mother Ambrosia O'Neill to Rev. Mother Agatha Guthrie, April 16, 1887, ACSJC-SLP.

63. Memoirs of Sr. Mary Aquinas Duffy and Memoirs of Sr. Mary Thomas Lavin, ACSJC-LAP.

64. For information about Protestant women missionaries and the hiring practices of various denominations see Barbara Welter, "She Hath Done What She Could: Protestant Women's Missionary Careers in Nineteenth-Century America," in *Women in American Religion*, ed. Janet Wilson James (Philadelphia: University of Pennsylvania Press, 1980), 111–25; Frances B. Cogan, *All-American Girl: The Ideal of Real Womanhood in Mid-Nineteenth-Century America* (Athens, Ga.: University of Georgia Press, 1989), 246–48; and Deutsch, *No Separate Refuge*, 63–86.

65. Letter from Fr. Zephyrin Engelhardt to Rev. Mother Agatha Guthrie, February 4, 1986, ACSJC-SLP.

66. The Yuma reservation ran along both sides of the Colorado River and encompassed 45,000 acres, mostly desert. The school had first been contracted with Presbyterians in 1884, but the missionaries left within two years. There were approximately 800–1,000 Yumans on the reservation. Correspondence from March 18 to May 13, 1886, between Sr. Julia Littenecker and the St. Louis motherhouse describes the CSJs' initial contact and negotiations with the government officials and the Yuma chief, Pascual. The letters describe the fort and people in detail (ACSJC-SLP).

67. Letter from Thomas J. Morgan to Mother Ambrosia O'Neill, October 29, 1891, ACSJC-SLP. Morgan sent O'Neill a notice to announce the upcoming superintendents' meeting in Washington. However, he immediately "exempted" her from coming since, he said, "you would be the only woman there, with the possible exception of one woman special agent."

68. Letter from Mother Ambrosia O'Neill to Rev. Mother Agatha Guthrie, June 8, 1886, ACSJC-SLP. Mother Ambrosia had no choice but to sign her name as Mary O'Neill. Women religious were required by law to sign their birth name on legal documents.

69. *San Francisco Argonaut*, November 15, 1886, ACSJC-LAP.

70. Letter from Mother Ambrosia O'Neill to Rev. Mother Agatha Guthrie, November 20, 1887, ACSJC-SLP. Stephan's behavior was typical for many whites at the time who viewed Indian males as either "savages" or "child-like." Stephan's behavior probably only aggravated the situation for the sisters. As director of the BCIM, Stephan was amazingly unaware and unprepared for the hostility. Mother Ambrosia wrote that Fr. Stephan came to the fort under the impression that all the Yumans were Christians. He "seemed quite surprised to find it otherwise."

71. *Los Angeles Herald*, July 15, 1893.

72. Savage, *Congregation of St. Joseph*, 286. Details on tribal politics can be found in Robert Bee, *Crosscurrents along the Colorado: The Impact of Government Policy on the Quechan Indians* (Tucson: University of Arizona Press, 1981), 24–43.

73. Letter from Sr. Aniceta Byrne to Mother Agatha Guthrie, March 7, 1890, ACSJC-SLP. Thomas Morgan, a Baptist minister and staunch Republican, became Indian Commissioner in 1889 and began pushing his agenda of off-reservation schools. From his first visit to Ft. Yuma, the CSJs expressed concerns about his "bigotry" against Catholics and they feared that he would close their reservation school. Morgan was indeed successful in creating off-reservation schools, but he resigned in 1893, expressing his unwillingness to work for Democratic president Grover Cleveland (Trennert, *Phoenix Indian School*, 9–40).

74. Letters from Mother Ambrosia O'Neill to Rev. Mother Agatha Guthrie, April 7 and 20, 1899, ACSJC-SLP.

75. Letters from Sr. Perpetua Seiler to Mother Julia Littenecker, April 1 and 15, 1877, ACSJC-SLP. For a more detailed analysis of the CSJs in Colorado see Coburn and Smith, "'Pray for Your Wanderers.'"

76. The CSJs also came to Denver in 1883 to begin teaching in parish schools: St. Patrick's in 1883, St. Ann's (later Annunciation) in 1888, St. Leo's in 1891, and St. Francis de Sales in 1906. Unlike those in St. Paul and Kansas City, CSJs in Denver worked in schools, never creating hospitals or orphanages.

77. Thomas J. Noel, *Colorado Catholicism and the Archdiocese of Denver, 1857–1989* (Boulder: University Press of Colorado, 1989), 22–27. Machebeuf brought the Sisters of Loretto to Denver in 1864 to establish an academy, the Sisters of Charity of Cincinnati to Trinidad in 1869 to open a school, and the Sisters of Charity of Leavenworth to Denver in 1872 to begin a hospital.

78. Nuns often obtained free railroad passes when traveling. Lottery prizes included religious relics, valuable gemstones, minerals, and altar items of silver or gold. If nuns did not have members of their own order with whom to stay, they often boarded at the convents of other religious orders or in the homes of local parishioners. Hotels and other boarding establishments were viewed as unsuitable because they were too worldly. However, boarding at the Loretto Academy later proved to be problematic when it was discovered that the Lorettines were secretly negotiating with the bishop for the Central City School, offering him cash and a higher price than the CSJs.

79. Biographical data is limited because all personnel records of sisters in the St. Louis province who died before 1949 have been lost. Other records have been used to piece together information on age, birthplace, and work locations.

80. Correspondence between Fr. Burion and Bishop Machebeuf document months of feuding on the financial status of the Central City parish and academy in Denver (AAD).

81. Between March 25 and May 31, 1877, Sr. Perpetua wrote sixteen letters to her superiors in St. Louis documenting her negotiating and fund-raising efforts for the Colorado missions (ACSJC-SLP). We would like to thank Elaine Coburn Watskey for her analysis of the real estate transactions.

82. Letters from Sr. Perpetua to St. Louis motherhouse, April 27 and May 1, 1877, ACSJC-SLP, describe these incidents. When the bishop made a demand, Sr. Perpetua would use her vow of obedience to refuse him or buy time to contact her superiors. This gave her time to write to the motherhouse in St. Louis, explaining the situation

and suggesting to her superiors how they should respond to the bishop's telegrams, allowing her to "officially" refuse him.

83. Letters from Sr. Perpetua Seiler to Mother Julia Littenecker, April 27 and May 2, 1877, ACSJC-SLP. Mother Julia must have agreed because she appointed Sr. Perpetua as the first superior of the Central City community, and three years later she became the first superior of the second CSJ institution in Georgetown, Colorado.

84. Letter from Sr. Perpetua Seiler to Mother Julia Littenecker, May 1, 1877, ACSJC-SLP.

85. Carroll Smith-Rosenberg, *Disorderly Conduct: Visions of Gender in Victorian America* (New York: Oxford University Press, 1985), 17.

86. Diary of Sr. Angelica Porter, June–July 1877, ACSJC-SLP.

87. Letter from Sr. Perpetua Seiler to Mother Julia Littenecker, May 24, 1877, ACSJC-SLP.

88. In diaries, correspondence, and other personal papers, secular women described nature, health concerns, adventure, and physical challenges. Sr. Angelica's diary and other CSJ diaries of travel and life in the West provide similar information. Both the older and younger nun write positively of their travels; their accounts are particularly similar to those by single women traveling west. Elizabeth Jameson, "Women as Workers, Women as Civilizers: True Womanhood in the American West," in Armitage and Jameson, *Women's West*, 149. For information on travel diaries and correspondence see Lillian Schlissel, *Women's Diaries of the Westward Journey* (New York: Schocken Books, 1982); Moynihan and Armitage, *So Much to Be Done*; and Vera Norwood "Women's Place: Continuity and Change in Response to Western Landscapes," in Schlissel, Ruiz, and Monk, *Western Women*, 155–81.

89. The prescriptive literature is quite clear as to the goal of a Sister of St. Joseph of Carondelet. The 1860 and 1884 CSJ Constitutions state in the first paragraph that sisters must "apply themselves to the attainment of Christian perfection, and devote themselves to the service of their neighbor." They are to "practice a profound humility" and "endeavor to act from the supernatural motives of faith, of hope, and of divine love" (ACSJC-SLP). We would argue that this philosophy and goal was representative of many religious orders of Catholic women.

90. From 1877 to 1917 the CSJs staffed seven separate institutions in three different locations in Colorado: Central City, Georgetown, and Denver. The total Catholic population grew dramatically during this period. In 1875 approximately 18,500 Catholics resided in the Colorado territory; by 1915 108,336 Catholics resided within the state of Colorado. This data is taken from the *Official Catholic Directory* (New York: P. J. Kenedy, 1875 and 1915). For a decade-by-decade analysis from 1870 to 1920 see Gerald Shaughnessy, *Has the Immigrant Kept the Faith? A Study of Immigration and Catholic Growth in the United States, 1790–1920* (New York: Macmillan, 1925), 155–83.

91. Margaret S. Woyski, "Women and Mining in the Old West," *Journal of the West* 20 (1981): 38–47. For a more detailed account of Central City and its influence in mining and commerce see Richard Hogan, *Class and Community in Frontier Colorado* (Lawrence: University Press of Kansas, 1990), 49–78; Duane A. Smith, *Rocky Mountain West: Colorado, Wyoming, and Montana, 1859–1915* (Albuquerque: University Press of New Mexico,

1992), 1–22, 112; and Carl Ubbelohde, Maxine Benson, and Duane A. Smith, *A Colorado History*, 6th ed. (Boulder, Colo.: Pruett Publishing Co., 1988), 69, 117–18. For more detail on the importance of early missionaries and churches throughout the state see Noel, *Colorado Catholicism,* and the research of Alice Cowan Cochran in *Miners, Merchants, and Missionaries: The Role of Missionaries and Pioneer Churches in the Colorado Gold Rush and Its Aftermath, 1858–1870* (Metuchen, N.J.: Scarecrow Press, 1980). Cochran compares and contrasts all Protestant and Catholic denominations who were present in Colorado.

92. Noel, *Colorado Catholicism,* 301–3. "Population—States and Territories," *Twelfth Census of the United States* (Washington, D.C.: U.S. Census Bureau, 1901), 83.

93. "Population and Statistics," *Tenth Census of the United States* (Washington, D.C.: U.S. Census Bureau, 1881), 113.

94. Smith, *Rocky Mountain West,* 82. See also Elliott West, *The Saloon on the Rocky Mountain Mining Frontier* (Lincoln: University of Nebraska Press, 1970), 133–41, and "Beyond Baby Doe: Childrearing on the Mining Frontier," in Armitage and Jameson, *Women's West,* 182, 186–87. For an older description of early Georgetown see Kathryn DePew, "William A. Hamill: Early Colorado Pioneer of Georgetown," *Colorado Magazine* 32 (October 1935): 266–79.

95. Noel, *Colorado Catholicism,* 384–85. "Annual Report of Our Lady of Lourdes Parish, 1885," ADD.

96. Woyski, "Women and Mining," 45.

97. The hospital is mentioned consistently in the *Georgetown Courier,* the local newspaper, from 1880 to even after the hospital's closing in 1914. Data in the ACSJC-SLP include files on the Georgetown hospital, two patient ledgers, and lists of sisters who were missioned there. The ledgers are a valuable resource that list each patient's name, birthplace, condition, and entrance and exit dates. Often males who had been "leaded" or "blasted" were brought in, but many patients had "La Grippe," pneumonia, or other illnesses. As was the tradition at other CSJ institutions, the hospital also housed orphan children of the community. Often these children were orphans of miners. Less than 3 percent of all patients were under twenty-one.

98. Letters from Sr. Perpetua Seiler to Mother Julia Littenecker, March 25 and 29, 1877, ACSJC-SLP.

99. This story is told in numerous written (unpublished) accounts concerning the CSJs' years in Central City (see ACSJC-SLP).

100. William D. Copeland, *One Man's Georgetown* (Polson, Mont.: W. D. Copeland, 1973), as quoted in Noel, *Colorado Catholicism,* 385.

101. Undated newspaper clipping thought to be from 1915–16, after the hospital had closed for lack of funds (ACSJC-SLP).

102. One miner was so grateful for the sisters' care that he left his mining claims to them upon his death ("Will and Testament of Jeremiah O'Brien, September 27, 1884," ACSJC-SLP).

103. To avoid conflict, many Catholic parishes were organized along ethnic lines. In Denver, some parishes were predominantly German or Irish, the predominant ethnic groups.

104. This data is compiled from the "Population and Statistics," *Tenth Census of the*

United States and *Twelfth Census of the United States* (Washington, D.C.: U.S. Census Bureau, 1881 and 1901), 492 and 739.

105. Patient Record Book—St. Joseph's Hospital, 1880–89 and 1890–1913, recorded birthplace for each patient (ACSJC-SLP).

106. This information is compiled from biographical and mission information for each sister in the CSJ community (ACSJC-SLP). The Central City data comes from the *Tenth Census* and the *Twelfth Census*, 499 and 739.

107. See Introduction, note 24, for a brief discussion of this issue.

108. West, "Beyond Baby Doe," 183–85. See Robert L. Griswold, "Anglo Women and Domestic Ideology in the American West in the Nineteenth and Early Twentieth Century," in Schlissel, Ruiz, and Monk, *Western Women*, 15–33.

109. "Customs Relating to Christian Politeness," CSJ Customs Book (1868), 18–20, ACSJC-SLP.

Chapter Five

1. Bishop John Hughes of New York is given credit for this advice, and many bishops and Catholic educators used his idea as a battle cry throughout the nineteenth century. Vincent P. Lannie, *Public Money and Parochial Education: Bishop Hughes, Governor Seward and the New York School Controversy* (Cleveland: Case Western Reserve Press, 1968), 255; Jay P. Dolan, *The American Catholic Experience: A History from Colonial Times to the Present* (Garden City, N.Y.: Image Books, 1985), 263; Timothy Walch, *Parish School: American Catholic Parochial Education from Colonial Times to the Present* (New York: Crossroad, 1996), 40–43.

2. American sisterhoods worked in education far more than in any other endeavor. Between 1829 and 1884 there were forty-four nondiocesan teaching orders (like the CSJs) of religious women. The number of diocesan teaching communities runs into the hundreds. By comparison there were eleven male orders teaching during this same time period. See Harold A. Buetow, *Of Singular Benefit: The Story of Catholic Education in the United States* (New York: Macmillan, 1970), 115–17.

3. Most early colonial schools taught the sons of white male elites who wanted their sons prepared for the law or the ministry. The local schools were taught by male clergy or young men earning money for college. By the mid-eighteenth century, a larger number of white middle-class boys began attending English grammar schools or district schools. Young white middle-class girls had few opportunities, but some attended "Dame Schools," which taught the three R's and some ornamental skills (embroidery, music, French). These schools were held in the homes of matrons in the town. When district or grammar schools did admit girls, it was only for Saturdays or summers. See David Tyack and Elisabeth Hansot, *Learning Together: A History of Coeducation in American Schools* (New Haven: Yale University Press, 1990).

4. For additional information on colonial and postcolonial attitudes on education and schools prior to the common school movement see Lawrence A. Cremin, *American Education: The Colonial Experience, 1607–1783* (New York: Harper and Row, 1970) and *American Education: The National Experience, 1783–1876* (New York: Harper and

Row, 1980), 1–147; Tyack and Hansot, *Learning Together*, 1–45; and Joel Spring, *The American School, 1642–1993*, 3rd ed. (New York: McGraw-Hill, 1994), 1–61.

5. For discussion on the common schools and for a variety of interpretations on their purposes and effectiveness see Lawrence A. Cremin, *The American Common School: An Historic Conception* (New York: Teachers College Press, 1951); Carl F. Kaestle, *Pillars of the Republic: Common Schools and American Society, 1780–1860* (New York: Hill and Wang, 1983); Michael B. Katz, *The Irony of Early School Reform* (Cambridge: Harvard University Press, 1968); and Spring, *American School*, 62–96.

6. Spring, *American School*, 63. Although larger national purposes were important to the creation of common schools, it is important to remember that the U.S. Constitution says nothing about education. All authority to create schools had been given to the states and the local communities. This is why (to the present day) there is so much variability in financing, curriculum, etc., from state to state and from one public school district to another.

7. "To the Honorable the Board of Aldermen of the City of New York" in *Catholic Education in America: A Documentary History*, ed. Neil McCluskey (New York: Teachers College Press, 1964), 72. The most widely read textbooks of the nineteenth century, the *McGuffey Readers*, were notorious in the early editions for their anti-Catholic text and caricatures of the pope. Between 1836 and 1920, 120 million textbooks were sold.

8. Dolan, *American Catholic Experience*, 269–70. For additional analysis of the public school versus Catholic school controversy and the evolution of the Catholic school system see James A. Burns, *The Catholic School System in the United States: Its Principles, Origin, and Establishment* (New York: Benziger Bros., 1908) and *The Growth and Development of the Catholic School System in the United States* (New York: Benziger Bros., 1912). For more current analyses that incorporate discussions on race, ethnicity, class, and, to a lesser extent, gender, see Michael F. Perko, ed., *Enlightening the Next Generation: Catholics and Their Schools, 1830–1980* (New York: Garland Press, 1988), and Walch, *Parish School*.

9. Peter Guilday, *A History of the Councils of Baltimore, 1791–1884* (New York: Arno Press, 1969), 237–39; Buetow, *Of Singular Benefit*, 148–50; Marvin Lazerson, "Understanding American Catholic Educational History," in Perko, *Enlightening the Next Generation*, 297–353.

10. Guilday, *History of the Councils*, 238–39; Spring, *American School*, 84–86; Dolan, *American Catholic Experience*, 271–77; Buetow, *Of Singular Benefit*, 146–54; Philip Gleason, "Baltimore III and Education," in Perko, *Enlightening the Next Generation*, 381–417. In 1875 American bishops received a strong message of support for Catholic schools from Rome. See "Instruction of the Congregation of Propaganda de Fide Concerning Catholic Children Attending American Public Schools, November 24, 1875," in *Documents of American Catholic History*, ed. John Tracy Ellis (Milwaukee: Bruce Publishing Co., 1956), 416–20.

11. Joel Perlman, *Ethnic Differences: Schooling and Social Structure among the Irish, Italians, Jews, and Blacks in an American City, 1880–1935* (Cambridge: Harvard University Press, 1988), 64, and Dolan, *American Catholic Experience*, 277. Mary Jo Weaver has called the parochial schools "one of the most amazing building and educational programs in the history of the world." See Weaver, *New Catholic Women: A Continuous Challenge to Tra-*

ditional Religious Authority (San Francisco: Harper and Row, 1985), 27. Leslie Woodcock Tentler has echoed these sentiments in "On the Margins: The State of American Catholic History," *American Quarterly* 45, no. 1 (March 1993): 107–9.

12. Dolan, *American Catholic Experience*, 271; Buetow, *Of Singular Benefit*, 159–61; Walch, *Parish School*, 69–71, 88–90. The "Poughkeepsie Plan" and others in the state of New York were officially terminated by the New York state legislature in 1898.

13. M. Aida Doyle, *History of the Sisters of St. Joseph of Carondelet in the Troy Province* (Albany: Argus Press, 1936), 167–70; Mary Ancilla Leary, *The History of Catholic Education in the Diocese of Albany* (Washington, D.C.: Catholic University Press, 1957), 61–64.

14. The Stillwater arrangement ended in 1892, and Faribault ended one year later. Ireland evoked strong sentiment from Protestants and some Catholics, particularly German Catholics who feared that the German language and culture would be lost if Catholics did not have separate schools. Many bishops disagreed strongly with Ireland's ideas on Americanization, and his speech to the National Education Association in 1890, in which he advocated state-supported church schools, had created a storm of controversy. See Dolan, *American Catholic Experience*, 274–76; James M. Reardon, *The Catholic Church in the Diocese of St. Paul* (St. Paul: North Central Pub., 1952), 290–303; La Vern J. Rippley, "Archbishop Ireland and the School Language Controversy," in Perko, *Enlightening the Next Generation*, 38–53; Thomas T. McAvoy, *A History of the Catholic Church in the United States* (Notre Dame: University of Notre Dame Press, 1969), 296–99; and Timothy H. Morrissey, "Archbishop John Ireland and the Faribault-Stillwater School Plan of the 1890s: A Reappraisal" (Ph.D. diss., University of Notre Dame, 1975).

15. Reardon, *Catholic Church*, 292–94. The quote is cited in Reardon, and he states it is taken from a letter from Ireland to Cardinal Gibbons, October 17, 1891.

16. Helen Angela Hurley, *On Good Ground: The Story of the Sisters of St. Joseph in St. Paul* (Minneapolis: University of Minnesota Press, 1951), 210–15.

17. Ibid., 215. Florence Deacon reports that in Wisconsin nuns taught in the public schools, particularly rural schools, without such difficulties. See her "Handmaids or Autonomous Women: The Charitable Activities, Institution Building and Communal Relationships of Catholic Sisters in Nineteenth-Century Wisconsin" (Ph.D. diss., University of Wisconsin, 1989), 153–87. However, many states enacted "anti-garb laws" to keep nuns out of public school classrooms, which effectively kept sisters from obtaining teacher certification in many states. For a legal analysis of the anti-garb issue in North Dakota and the School Sisters of Notre Dame see Linda Grathwohl, "The North Dakota Anti-Garb Law: Constitutional Conflict and Religious Strife," *Great Plains Quarterly* 13, no. 3 (Summer 1993): 187–202.

18. *Official Catholic Directory* (New York: P. J. Kenedy, 1920), 1011. As with all national Catholic statistics and directories, there are some inconsistencies, although most historians agree within a few percentage points on school and population data. The other difficulty with school data is that parish and private academies or select schools were often lumped together, changing the total number of schools. For additional discussion and demographic detail see Buetow, *Of Singular Benefit*, 179; Dolan, *American Catholic Experience*, 275–76; and Gerald Shaughnessy, *Has the Immigrant Kept*

the Faith? A Study of Immigration and Catholic Growth in the United States, 1790–1920 (New York: Macmillan, 1925).

19. George C. Stewart, *Marvels of Charity: History of American Sisters and Nuns* (Huntington, Ind.: Our Sunday Visitor, Inc., 1994), 322, 564.

20. "CSJ General Chapter Report, 1920," ACSJC-G.

21. Srs. Celestine Pommerel and St. John Fournier were chosen to be a part of the original group of sisters sent to the United States, but they spent a year in special training before coming to St. Louis in 1837. In the early nineteenth century the French were considered leaders in deaf education, so the two sisters probably received some of the best training available at the time. Dolorita Maria Dougherty et al., eds., *The Sisters of St. Joseph of Carondelet* (St. Louis: Herder Book Co., 1966), 120–22, 344–47. Although the large institute for the deaf in Buffalo became diocesan after the formation of general government, its earliest teachers came from St. Louis. Other CSJ communities that have worked with the deaf include those in Philadelphia, Boston, Rutland, Vt., and Brentwood, Brooklyn, and Queens, N.Y. See Sr. Rose Gertrude, "The Education of the Deaf in America by Sisters of St. Joseph" (unpublished manuscript, November 1958, ACSJC-SLP).

22. Letter from A. J. Meyer to Rev. Mother Agatha Guthrie, November 24, 1888, ACSJC-LAP. After 1920 and as parish elementary and high schools continued to increase, the CSJ academies that survived typically remained as private secondary schools for girls only—separate from the parish schools and funded by the CSJs and through tuition.

23. Letter from Sr. Flavia Waldron to Sr. Charles Brennan, October 6, 1898, ACSJC-AP. See also Doyle, *History of the Sisters*, 57–62, and Emily Joseph Daly, "The Albany Province," in Dougherty et al., *Sisters of St. Joseph*, 222–24. For information about working-class Catholic families in Cohoes and Troy, N.Y., see Daniel J. Walkowitz, "Working-Class Culture in the Gilded Age: The Iron Workers of Troy, New York, and the Cotton Workers of Cohoes, New York—1855–1884" (Ph.D. diss., University of Rochester, 1972).

24. Tyack and Hansot, *Learning Together*, 78–80. Tyack and Hansot argue that this was often a reflection of class bias. Middle-class and upper-class parents did not want their daughters mixing with working-class males.

25. Letter from Fr. A. J. Meyer to Rev. Mother Agatha Guthrie, November 24, 1888, ACSJC-LAP.

26. Ignatius Loyola Cox, "The Mission at St. Anthony Falls, or East Minneapolis," *Acta et Dicta* 3, no. 2 (July 1914): 289.

27. "Report to the General Chapter—Troy Province 1920" and John F. Glavin, "Diamond Jubilee History—Albany Diocese 1847–1922," ACSJC-AP. The high numbers in the first and second grade mirror attendance patterns in public schools.

28. Letter from Fr. J. J. Donnelly to Rev. Mother Agnes Gonzaga Ryan, January 12, 1906, ACSJC-SLP. There are other letters from Donnelly dating to 1916 expressing concern about the need for more teachers in the fast-growing parish. In a letter dated May 26, 1915, Donnelly stated that there were seventy children each in the first and second grade classes (ACSJC-SLP).

29. Letter from Fr. J. B. McNally to Rev. Mother Agatha Guthrie, July 28, 1885, ACSJC-SLP.

30. Although the manual was decades, if not a century old, the version of the manual that the original CSJs brought from France had been most recently published in 1832 in Lyons.

31. The *School Manual for the Use of the Sisters of St. Joseph of Carondelet* (St. Louis: Carreras Pub. Co., 1884), revised 1910, ACSJC-SLP. See Mary Lucida Savage, *The Congregation of St. Joseph of Carondelet: A Brief Account of Its Origin and Its Work in the United States, 1650–1922* (St. Louis: Herder Book Co., 1923), 94–96, and Dougherty et al., *Sisters of St. Joseph*, 218–19.

32. For discussions on the widespread use and high quality of the CSJ school manual see Buetow, *Of Singular Benefit*, 191–92, and Susan Carol Peterson and Courtney Ann Vaughn-Roberson, *Women with Vision: The Presentation Sisters of South Dakota, 1880–1985* (Urbana: University of Illinois Press, 1991), 78–79. Many of the larger teaching orders, female and male, that originated in Europe had teaching guides.

33. *CSJ School Manual* (1884), introduction.

34. Ibid., 13–16, and *CSJ School Manual* (1910), 16–19. We wish to thank Dr. Laura Sloan of the Education Department at Avila College for her helpful analysis and comments on the manuals.

35. *Catholic Child's Letter Writer* (St. Louis: Carreras Pub., 1886) incorporates geography and history to teach writing for grades 1–8; *Child's Geography and History of St. Louis City* (St. Louis: Carreras Pub., 1886) includes a teacher's edition for grades 3–4; and *Language Manual* incorporates language, letter writing, and arithmetic for grades 1–3 (St. Louis: Carreras Pub., 1890). All books are located in the ACSJC-SLP. Unfortunately we do not know the author(s) because in each case the books were "Compiled by the Sisters of St. Joseph." It would be impossible to discern whether they were indeed a group effort or whether humility and avoiding singularity kept the author from stating her name.

36. Timothy Walch, "Catholic School Books and American Values: The Nineteenth-Century Experience," in Perko, *Enlightening the Next Generation*, 267–76. Some of the most popular Catholic textbooks were published by the Christian Brothers, Sadlier, and Benziger Brothers.

37. Dolan, *American Catholic Experience*, 276. For a more extensive discussion on the importance and prevalence of ethnic parishes and the varieties of Catholic immigrant experiences see Walch, *Parish School*, 76–82; Jay P. Dolan, ed., *The American Catholic Parish: A History from 1850 to the Present*, 2 vols. (New York: Paulist Press, 1987), and *The Immigrant Church: New York's Irish and German Catholics, 1815–1865* (Baltimore: Johns Hopkins University Press, 1975; reprint, Notre Dame: University of Notre Dame Press, 1983); Jay P. Dolan and Gilberto M. Hinojosa, eds., *Mexican Americans and the Catholic Church, 1900–1965* (Notre Dame, Ind.: University of Notre Dame Press, 1994); Stephen Shaw, *The Catholic Parish as a Way Station of Ethnicity and Americanization* (New York: Carlsen Publishing Co., 1991); David O'Brien, *Public Catholicism* (New York: Macmillan, 1989), 34–61; and Michael Perko, "Catholics and Their Culturist Perspective," in Perko, *Enlightening the Next Generation*, 311–16. For additional information on the importance of ethnic, religious, and cultural networks that includes dis-

cussions on immigrant Catholics see Stanley Nadel, *Little Germany: Ethnicity, Religion, and Class in New York City, 1845–1880* (Urbana: University of Illinois Press, 1990); Robert A. Slayton, *Back of the Yards: The Making of a Local Democracy* (Chicago: University of Chicago Press, 1986); Virginia Yans-McLaughlin, *Family and Community: Italian Immigrants in Buffalo, 1880–1930* (Ithaca: Cornell University Press, 1978); and Kathleen Neils Conzen, *Immigrant Milwaukee, 1836–1860* (Cambridge: Harvard University Press, 1976).

38. German Lutherans, particularly those affiliated with the Lutheran Church–Missouri Synod believed that to achieve *reine Lehre* (pure doctrine) children had to be taught the Lutheran faith in the language of Martin Luther. In the nineteenth century, they established the largest parochial school system of all Protestant denominations. Two sources provide extensive information about these schools: Walter H. Beck, *Lutheran Elementary Schools in the United States* (St. Louis: Concordia Pub., 1939), and August C. Stellhorn, *Schools of the Lutheran Church–Missouri Synod* (St. Louis: Concordia Pub., 1963).

39. Hasia R. Diner, *Erin's Daughters in America: Irish Immigrant Women in the Nineteenth Century* (Baltimore: Johns Hopkins University Press, 1983), 96–99. School teaching was a popular occupational choice for young Irish women on the Eastern seaboard, and they filled the ranks of urban public schools. Diner states that "school teaching for the second generation was what domestic service had been for the first" (97).

40. Dolan, *American Catholic Experience*, 276–84.

41. Quoted in Mary J. Oates, *The Catholic Philanthropic Tradition in America* (Bloomington: Indiana University Press, 1995), 153. Oates also states that by the mid-1920s many of the 798 sisters teaching African American children came from Mother Katherine Drexel's order, the Sisters of the Blessed Sacrament. This order focused its work on Native Americans and African Americans. A CSJ diocesan order that came from Le Puy to Florida and eventually Georgia was also heavily invested in the education of African Americans. Called the "nigger sisters" by local whites, the Florida community remained diocesan, but the Georgia group eventually affiliated with the CSJs of Carondelet in 1922. For more information on African American Catholic experience see Cyprian Davis, *The History of Black Catholics in the United States* (New York: Crossroad, 1995) and "African-American Catholics and Their Church," *U.S. Catholic Historian* (special issue) 12, no. 1 (Winter 1994).

42. Dolan, *American Catholic Experience*, 282–83. Dolan states that in rural areas with fewer than 2,500 people, it took an average of fourteen years to build a school. In small towns of 2,500 to 10,000 people it took an average of eleven years for the parish to create a school. In cities with a population over 50,000 a school was built within five years of the founding of a new parish.

43. For specific CSJ demographic data see Chapter 3. By the late nineteenth century, the CSJs still had a number of sisters who were bilingual, speaking fluent French, Spanish, or German as well as English. Although they probably did not have enough German- and Spanish-speaking sisters to meet the needs of various ethnic groups, they continued to staff bilingual schools for French Canadian, German, and Hispanic populations.

44. Margaret Susan Thompson, "Sisterhood and Power: Class, Culture and Eth-

nicity in the American Convent," *Colby Library Quarterly* 25, no. 3 (September 1989): 149–75; Dolan, *American Catholic Experience*, 241–81. For additional reading on the significance of ethnic and linguistic differences among American Catholics see note 37, above, and Colman J. Barry, *The Catholic Church and German Americans* (Milwaukee: Bruce Pub., 1953); Diner, *Erin's Daughters in America*; Robert A. Orsi, *The Madonna of 115th Street: Faith and Community in Italian Harlem, 1880–1950* (New Haven: Yale University Press, 1985); and John J. Bukowczyk, *And My Children Did Not Know Me: A History of the Polish-Americans* (Bloomington: Indiana University Press, 1987).

45. Hurley, *On Good Ground*, 18–20, 149–50, 169–70; Annabelle Raiche and Ann Marie Biermaier, *They Came to Teach: The Story of Sisters Who Taught in Parochial Schools and Their Contribution to Elementary Education in Minnesota* (St. Cloud, Minn.: North Star Press, 1994), 73–74. The two German schools in St. Paul and Hastings were eventually staffed by two German orders, School Sisters of Notre Dame and Benedictines when the CSJs could not continue to supply enough German-speaking sisters.

46. Interview of Sr. Ailbe O'Kelly by Sr. Susan Marie O'Connor, Syracuse, N.Y., January 23, 1981, ACSJC-AP.

47. "Florence, Arizona, 1883–1889" and "List of Sisters of St. Joseph from Early Mexican Families," ACSJC-LAP. Six young women, Mexican-born or first-generation American-born, entered the Western province when it was located in Tucson in the late 1870s. Ann Cecilia Smith's interview with Sr. Serena McCarthy about her experiences at St. Augustine's in 1898 is cited in Ann Cecilia Smith, "Educational Activities of the Sisters of St. Joseph of Carondelet in the Western Province from 1870 to 1903" (master's thesis, Catholic University, 1953), 35–36.

48. "Notes on St. Mary's School—Oswego, N.Y.," ACSJC-AP; Doyle, *History of the Sisters*, 45–55.

49. Dougherty et al., *Sisters of St. Joseph*, 113, 177. Eventually, ethnic rivalries divided some of these groups into separate parishes in Hancock. The French and Germans stayed together and the Italians and Irish each had their own parish.

50. "History of the Sisters of St. Joseph of Carondelet in the Diocese of Mobile," ACSJC-SLP; Lucida Savage, *The Century's Harvest, 1836–1936* (St. Louis: Herder Book Co., 1936), 52.

51. "Notes on St. Patrick's Parish—Los Angeles," ACSJC-LAP.

52. Leary's *History of Catholic Education* examines each educational institution in the diocese of Albany (which originally included Syracuse and other parts of upstate New York), and in almost every case lay teachers had been the forerunners of sister-teachers in the parish schools. Even with the increase in teaching sisters, many schools hired lay teachers to serve in the larger schools because there were never enough sisters to fill all the needs of parish education, particularly since these New York parishes often offered secondary course work before parish schools in other parts of the country.

53. Mary J. Oates, "Organized Voluntarism: The Catholic Sisters in Massachusetts, 1870–1940," in *Women in American Religion*, ed. Janet Wilson James (Philadelphia: University of Pennsylvania Press, 1980), 154–59; Dolan, *American Catholic Experience*, 289; Raiche and Biermaier, *They Came to Teach*, 105.

54. Historians of education have extensively researched this transition from male to female teachers in the United States. For more discussion on this phenomenon see Tyack and Hansot, *Learning Together*; Spring, *American School*; Kaestle, *Pillars of the Republic*; Nancy Hoffman, *Woman's "True" Profession: Voices from the History of Teaching* (Old Westbury, N.Y.: Feminist Press, 1981); and Polly Welts Kaufman, *Women Teachers on the Frontier* (New Haven: Yale University Press, 1984).

55. Oates, "Organized Voluntarism," 154–56; Dolan, *American Catholic Experience*, 289. Oates has made a very careful study of sisters' salaries and compared them to those of female public school teachers and to the cost of living expenses of the late nineteenth and early twentieth centuries.

56. Burns, *Growth and Development*, 23, 100, 282.

57. "Silver Jubilee" program for St. Mary's Parish, St. Paul, Minn., ACSJC-SPP. The nuns may have earned even less since their salaries were recorded for 1898 and the Brothers' salaries were recorded from 1876.

58. "The Institute Journal," Amsterdam, N.Y., 1889–90, ACSJC-AP.

59. Financial Report (1914) from St. Vincent's Convent, Los Angeles, ACSJC-LAP.

60. Memoirs of Sr. Rose Edward Dailey in *Jubilarse*, ed. Margaret John Purcell (St. Louis: Sisters of St. Joseph of Carondelet, 1981), 45.

61. "Statement of Account—St. John's Parish, Kansas City, Mo.," June 1882–Dec. 1904, ACSJC-SLP. The CSJs came to the parish in 1887 to open the school and stayed until 1935.

62. Letter from Fr. J. B. McNally to Rev. Mother Agatha Guthrie, July 26, 1883, ACSJC-LAP.

63. Account statement and itemization of the St. Mary's Academy Convent, Hoosick Falls, N.Y., ACSJC-AP. The CSJ contribution included everything from carpet to window fixtures and the appliances for the laundry and the kitchen.

64. "Ascension [Parish] Builds a House [for Sister-Teachers]," n.d., ACSJC-SPP.

65. Interview of Sr. Liboria Wendling by Sr. St. Henry Palmer, July 1964, in Tucson, Arizona, ACSJC-LAP.

66. Mary Ewens, *The Role of the Nun in Nineteenth-Century America* (New York: Arno Press, 1978), 68, 98, 215.

67. Letter to the Rev. Andrew Duplang from the "Sisters of St. Joseph," June 2, 1911, ACSJC-AP. Although only the Duplang letter survives, it was sent to all "Reverend Pastors" in the Albany and Syracuse dioceses. The letter probably came from Mother Odilia Bogan, the provincial superior. The CSJs in the other three provinces did not close their academies, so when the Troy province closed these schools in 1883, the order probably came from the bishop. James Hennesey states that in 1883 in a preliminary meeting, American bishops created the agenda for the 1884 Baltimore Council that mandated parish schools. Therefore, the timing of the change is probably not coincidental since bishops certainly understood the upcoming need for more parish teachers. Closing the select academies freed up sisters to staff parish schools (*American Catholics*, 182).

68. Thomas J. Noel, *Colorado Catholicism and the Archdiocese of Denver, 1857–1989* (Boulder: University of Colorado Press, 1989), 362–64. A series of articles on the feud can be found in the *Denver Republican* beginning May 1909 and appearing for a

year, until the civil court case was completed. Carrigan had friends in the press and city hall, but Matz prevailed and reassigned him to Glenwood Springs in 1910. Fr. Carrigan was appointed to St. Patrick's by French-born bishop Machebeuf, but he was greatly disappointed when in 1889 French-born Matz was appointed at Machebeuf's death. Carrigan had hoped for an Irish bishop, and he proceeded to challenge Matz and criticize him in the diocese.

69. The letters and telegrams were sent from May to August 1909 (ACSJC-SLP). Matz communicated only with the motherhouse in St. Louis. He sent a representative to talk with the local sisters at St. Patrick's. Sr. Marguerite Murphy was superior of the Denver convent, and she wrote the motherhouse continuously about how the sisters were put in untenable situations. Coming close to blows on several occasions, Fr. Carrigan and the bishop's representative, Fr. Donovan, battled over who would hear the sisters' confessions, who would provide the "Blessed Sacrament," and who would have coffee and breakfast in the morning with the sisters. Carrigan labeled Sr. Marguerite "hysterical" in a June 4, 1909, telegram to St. Louis, and Matz sent a telegram on June 11, 1909, advising the Reverend Mother to tell her Denver sisters to "mind their own business and not waste their sympathies upon a suspended and excommunicated priest." If they do this, he continued, "they will have nothing to fear [from him]."

70. Letter from Rev. Mother Agnes Gonzaga Ryan to Bishop Matz, June 18, 1912, ACSJC-SLP.

71. Kathryn Kish Sklar and Thomas Dublin, introduction to *Women and Power in American History: A Reader*, vol. 2, ed. Sklar and Dublin (Englewood Cliffs, N.J.: Prentice Hall, 1991), 2.

72. Once again, the fact that the CSJs had papal approbation and were not a diocesan community ruled by the bishop gave them an additional buffer against his demands. This chronic problem of male interference may be the most common one experienced across all orders of women religious. For examples similar to the CSJ experience see M. Georgia Costin, *Priceless Spirit: A History of the Sisters of the Holy Cross, 1841–1893* (Notre Dame, Ind.: University of Notre Dame Press, 1994); Mary Roger Madden, *The Path Marked Out: History of the Sisters of Providence of St. Mary-of-the-Woods*, vol. 3 (Terre Haute, Ind.: Sisters of Providence, 1991); Stewart, *Marvels of Charity*; and Ewens, *Role of the Nun*. For an interesting cross-cultural comparison of gender politics in the church see Anne McLay, *Women out of Their Sphere: A History of the Sisters of Mercy in Western Australia* (Western Australia: Vanguard Press, 1992).

73. Hoffman, *Woman's "True" Profession*, 210–11. For additional analysis on the shift to a bureaucratic, business model for schools see Michael Katz, *Class, Bureaucracy, and Schools* (New York: Rhinehart and Winston, 1975), and David B. Tyack, *The One Best System: A History of American Urban Education* (Cambridge, Mass: Harvard University Press, 1974).

74. Guilday, *History of the Councils*, 239.

75. For a chronological analysis of this transition and the similarities of Catholic and public schools see Lazerson, "Understanding American Catholic Educational History," 340–50. Lazerson states that it took decades for the transition to reach all

Catholic parishes and that the larger cities were advantaged because they had many lay Catholics who were involved in the standardization of the public schools as well.

76. Hennesey, *American Catholics*, 210; Leary, *History of Catholic Education*, 315–17; Lazerson, "Understanding American Catholic History," 348–50; Buetow, *Of Singular Benefit*, 180–84; John F. Murphy, "Professional Preparation of Catholic Teachers in the Nineteen Hundreds," in Perko, *Enlightening the Next Generation*, 243–53.

77. R. G. T., "Fifty Years in Retrospect," in the *Souvenir Program of the Fiftieth-Anniversary Celebration, St. Mary's Institute, Amsterdam, N.Y.*, June 22–27, 1930. Leary, *History of Catholic Education*, 40–42. Leary indicates that the state instituted the exams in 1877 (139, 336).

78. Interview of Sr. Petronilla McGowan by Sr. Susan O'Connor, January 17, 1985, in Latham, N.Y., ACSJC-AP. Sr. Petronilla also told the story about Sr. Blanche Rooney.

79. For the vast majority of states we feel this to be true, although there are some notable exceptions. Mary Oates has documented the high quality of public school teachers compared to sister-teachers in Massachusetts. However, as she has stated, Massachusetts was always ahead of the national norm in education and therefore is the exception, not the rule. See Oates, "Organized Voluntarism," and Walch, *Parish School*, 134–55.

80. Hoffman, *Woman's "True" Profession*, xiv–xxi.

81. Ibid., 13, 212.

82. Katherine M. Cook, *State Laws and Regulations Governing Teacher's Certificates* (Washington, D.C.: U.S. Government Printing Office, 1921), 16, and P. P. Claxton, foreword to *Annual Report of the State Commissioner of Education for 1912—New York* (Washington, D.C.: Government Printing Office, 1913), xviii.

83. For examples from other religious orders see Oates, "Organized Voluntarism," 166, and Mary J. Oates, "'The Good Sisters': The Work and Position of Catholic Churchwomen in Boston, 1870–1940," in *The American Catholic Religious Life*, ed. Joseph M. White (New York: Garland Press, 1988), 181; Deacon, "Handmaids or Autonomous Women," 198–204; Weaver, *New Catholic Women*, 80; and Peterson and Vaughn-Roberson, *Women with Vision*, 67–77.

84. Memoirs of Sr. Mary Eustace Huster in Purcell, *Jubilarse*, 3–4.

85. Raiche and Biermaier, *They Came to Teach*, 37. The orders of teaching sisters in Minnesota include CSJs, Sisters of St. Benedict, Franciscan Sisters, School Sisters of Notre Dame, and Sisters of St. Francis.

86. Bertrande Meyer, *The Education of Sisters* (New York: Sheed and Ward, 1941), 6–7; Deacon, "Handmaids or Autonomous Women," 187–98; Raiche and Biermaier, *They Came to Teach*, 63–64; Stewart, *Marvels of Charity*, 323–24; Madden, *Path Marked Out*, 558–59.

87. Raiche and Biermaier, *They Came to Teach*, 37–41; Sr. Winifred (Kate) Hogan, "My Reminiscences," 1922, ACSJC-SPP.

88. Savage, *Congregation of St. Joseph*, 176.

89. A. C. Mason, *1,000 Ways of 1,000 Teachers: Being a Compilation of Methods of Instruction and Discipline Practiced by Prominent Public School Teachers of the Country* (Chicago: S. R. Winchell, 1882).

90. Meyer, *Education of Sisters*. This work uses a variety of archival sources from female teaching orders to elaborate on all three components of teacher preparation used in the nineteenth and twentieth centuries.

91. For one of the best primary sources on the early years of the Sisters' College summer institute and degree programs see the *Catholic Educational Review* (1911–20). Thomas E. Shields of Catholic University began the journal in January 1911, and as an avid proponent of Sisters' College he provided extensive coverage of its early years. A good overview of the college after eight years can be found in Shields, "The Need of the Catholic Sisters' College and the Scope of Its Work," *Catholic Educational Review* 17 (September 1919): 420–29. See also Murphy, "Professional Preparation," 248–53, and Philip Gleason, *Contending with Modernity: Catholic Higher Education in the Twentieth Century* (New York: Oxford University Press, 1995), 88–89.

92. Since all-male Catholic colleges would not admit women, even women religious, sisters typically attended the closest state institution that had an education program. According to Meyer, *Education of Sisters*, the Paulist Fathers inaugurated a Sisters' Institute in New York City in 1895 and Catholic University began an Institute of Pedagogy in New York in 1902. Eventually other colleges, such as the University of Chicago, St. Louis University, and Marquette University, established a Saturday, 4–6 P.M., session and a full summer session, designed to take advantage of times when few male students were on campus (16–17).

93. Interview of Sr. Letitia Lirette by Sr. Patricia Kelly, March 7, 1985, at Carondelet Convent in St. Louis, ACSJC-SLP.

94. Raiche and Biermaier, *They Came to Teach*, 62.

95. Letter to the Rev. Andrew Duplang from "Sisters of St. Joseph," June 2, 1911.

96. Thomas J. Shahan, "The Summer School," and Patrick J. McCormick, "The Summer School and Report of the Secretary," *Catholic Educational Review* 2, no. 2 (September 1911): 593–604 and 658–61. The thirty-one Sisters of St. Joseph included the Carondelet group and other CSJ communities. The Sisters of Mercy had the largest number with fifty-two and the Benedictines were second with thirty-six. Twenty-nine lay women teachers also attended.

97. An Ursuline of St. Ursula Convent, "The First Session the Summer School of the Catholic University," *Catholic Educational Review* 2, no. 2 (September 1911): 654–57, and A Sister of Holy Names, "What the First Summer School at the Catholic University of America Was to Students," *Catholic Educational Review* 2, no. 3 (October 1911): 673–81. The sisters wrote the essays anonymously to avoid "singularity." Their identity is still not known.

98. J. A. Burns, "A Constructive Policy for Catholic Higher Education," *Catholic Educational Review* 17 (1919): 458.

99. Raiche and Biermaier, *They Came to Teach*, 62–63.

100. Deacon, "Handmaids or Autonomous Women," 197–98. This was particularly ironic in Wisconsin, where local districts were allowed to hire nuns (in habit) for public schools.

101. "University Degrees Conferred on Sisters," *Catholic Educational Review* 5 (June 1913): 47–50.

102. Thomas E. Shields, "The Sisters College," *Catholic Educational Review* 3, no. 1

(January 1912): 1–12, and "The Summer Session," *Catholic Educational Review* 9, no. 1 (January 1915): 36–42.

Chapter Six

1. Although some female institutions were called academies and others seminaries, in reality there was very little difference between them. Both included moral and religious training, as did almost every school in the nineteenth century. Although some institutions were not affiliated with a particular Protestant denomination, they were rarely secular and espoused a "pan-Protestant" moral and religious perspective. We will use the terms "academy" and "seminary" interchangeably in this chapter.

2. Thomas Woody, *A History of Women's Education in the United States*, vol. 1 (New York: Science Press, 1929; reprint, New York: Octagon Books, 1980), 329–30. Woody states that the curriculum was very rudimentary and it is difficult to know if course work went beyond the three R's, industrial training, and religion. His two-volume work provides abundant detail on all aspects of women's education in the United States. For more information about these early academies see H. C. Semple, ed., *The Ursulines in New Orleans, 1725–1925* (New York: P. J. Kenedy, 1925); Lyman P. Powell, *History of Education in Delaware* (Washington, D.C.: Government Printing Office, 1893); and W. C. Reichel, *History of Bethlehem Female Seminary* (Philadelphia: J. P. Lippincott, 1858).

3. Gerda Lerner, *The Creation of Feminist Consciousness from the Middle Ages to 1870* (New York: Oxford University Press, 1993), 209–15; Linda Kerber, *Women of the Republic: Intellect and Ideology in Revolutionary America* (New York: W. W. Norton, 1988), chs. 7 and 8, and "The Republican Mother: Women and the Enlightenment—An American Perspective," *American Quarterly* 28 (Summer 1976): 187–205; Mary Beth Norton, *Liberty's Daughters: The Revolutionary Experience of American Women, 1750–1800* (Boston: Little, Brown, 1980), 243–55.

4. Kathryn Kish Sklar, *Catharine Beecher: A Study in American Domesticity* (New York: W. W. Norton, 1976); Barbara Miller Solomon, *In the Company of Educated Women* (New Haven: Yale University Press, 1985), 14–42; Polly Welts Kaufman, *Women Teachers on the Frontier* (New Haven: Yale University Press, 1984); Nancy Hoffman, *Woman's "True" Profession: Voices from the History of Teaching* (Old Westbury, N.Y.: The Feminist Press, 1981), 1–63.

5. For an extensive chronological list with descriptions of some academies see Woody, *History of Women's Education*, 1:329–96. The importance of these academies probably cannot be overstated in their ability to encourage women to expand their influence and expectations beyond the home. Some scholars have argued, quite convincingly, that the academy/seminary experience created a generation of women with the skills and confidence to participate in nineteenth-century social activism in moral reform societies and abolitionist, temperance, and women's rights movements. For example see Solomon, *In the Company of Educated Women*, 15–42; Nancy F. Cott, *The Bonds of Womanhood: "Woman's Sphere" in New England, 1780–1835* (New Haven: Yale University Press, 1977), 101–25; Catherine Clinton, *The Other Civil War: American Women in the Nineteenth Century* (New York: Hill and Wang, 1984), 40–71; and Sara

Evans, *Born for Liberty: A History of Women in America* (New York: The Free Press, 1989), 70–81, 93–118.

6. For a discussion of the importance of European convent schools see Lerner, *Creation of Feminist Consciousness*, 26–28, 198–200, and Bonnie S. Anderson and Judith P. Zinsser, *A History of Their Own: Women in Europe from Prehistory to the Present*, vol. 1 (New York: Harper and Row, 1988), 184–93. Besides the Ursulines, other communities that opened academies in the United States include Visitandines, Sisters of Charity, Dominicans, and Religious of the Sacred Heart. See Barbara Misner, *Highly Respectable and Accomplished Ladies: Catholic Women Religious in America, 1790–1850* (New York: Garland Press, 1988).

7. For information on these antebellum academies see Sr. M. Benedict Murphy, "Pioneer Roman Catholic Girls' Academies: Their Growth, Character, and Contribution to American Education: A Study of Roman Catholic Education for Girls from Colonial Times to the First Plenary Council of 1852" (Ph.D. diss., Columbia University, 1958). For information on the state school systems and Catholic sisters' schools see Maria Alma, *Standard Bearers: The Place of Catholic Sisterhoods in the Early History of Education . . . until 1850* (New York: P. J. Kenedy and Sons, 1928); see also Misner, *Highly Respectable Ladies*; Mary Ewens, *The Role of the Nun in Nineteenth-Century America* (New York: Arno Press, 1978), 35–68; Eileen Mary Brewer, *Nuns and the Education of American Catholic Women, 1860–1920* (Chicago: Loyola University Press, 1987); and Mary J. Oates, "Catholic Female Academies on the Frontier," *U.S. Catholic Historian* 12, no. 4 (1994): 121–36.

8. For reasons discussed in Chapter 5, the Eastern province (Troy, N.Y.) closed its secondary academies in 1883 and allowed them to be absorbed into the parish system in upstate New York (Albany and later Syracuse dioceses). Many of these schools retained their academy names but functioned as parish high schools, receiving a charter under the New York Regents System. Although CSJs in the other three provinces taught in parish and diocesan high schools, they retained their private academies.

9. Whether analyzing Catholic or non-Catholic academies or public schools, studies show that girls attended in larger numbers at the secondary level. For a comparison of male and female Catholic secondary education in Antebellum America see Edmund J. Goebel, *A Study of Catholic Secondary Education during the Colonial Period up to the First Plenary Council of Baltimore, 1852* (New York: Benziger Brothers, 1937). Catholic directories (1840–1920), as well as research done by Catholic University, verify this phenomenon. See "The Condition of Catholic Secondary Education," *Catholic Educational Review* 10 (1915): 204–10. This "Report of the Advisory Board" surveyed Catholic schools and reported 557 secondary schools for girls educating 39,740 students, compared to 438 secondary schools for boys educating 34,798 students. According to historian Thomas Woody, girls attended in larger numbers in private secondary schools, both Catholic and non-Catholic, and public high schools showed the same disparity. By 1920 over one million girls were in public high schools compared to 800,000 boys. For more analysis and data on public school attendance see Woody, *History of Women's Education*, 1:545–46.

10. This organization sponsored hundreds of graduates from these eastern acade-

mies, and between 1848 and 1854 seminary graduates from New York and New England received teaching assignments in seventeen states, from western Pennsylvania to as far west as Oregon. For discussion on the NBPE see Kaufman, *Women Teachers*, 5–39, and Sklar, *Catharine Beecher*, 183, 217.

11. Letter from Harriet Bishop in *New York Evangelist*, October 13, 1853, cited in Annabelle Raiche and Ann Marie Biermaier, *They Came to Teach: The Story of Sisters Who Taught in Parochial Schools and Their Contribution to Elementary Education in Minnesota* (St. Cloud, Minn.: North Star Press, 1994), 6.

12. The quote is attributed to Fredrika Bremer, who met Catharine in Milwaukee in 1851, and is cited in Sklar, *Catharine Beecher*, 220.

13. Ibid., 170–72. Some of these quoted phrases and a list of convent academies in the West can be found in Catharine Beecher, *An Address to the Protestant Clergy of the United States* (New York: Harper and Bros., 1846) and *Evils Suffered by American Women and American Children: The Causes and the Remedy* (New York: Harper and Bros., 1846).

14. Solomon, *In the Company of Educated Women*, 17–22; Woody, *History of Women's Education*, 1:349–62; Oates, "Catholic Female Academies," 123–24; Murphy, "Pioneer Roman Catholic Girls' Academies," 111.

15. Woody, *History of Women's Education*, 1:379; Nikola Baumgarten, "Education and Democracy in Frontier St. Louis: The Society of the Sacred Heart," *History of Education Quarterly* 34 (Summer 1994): 171–92.

16. Baumgarten, "Education and Democracy," 182–83. See also Woody, *History of Women's Education*, 1:409–22; Solomon, *In the Company of Educated Women*, 23; Oates, "Catholic Female Academies," 124–26; and Anne Firor Scott, "The Ever Widening Circle: The Diffusion of Feminist Values from the Troy Female Seminary, 1822–1872," *History of Education Quarterly* 19 (Spring 1979): 3–25.

17. Memoirs of Eliza McKenney Brouillet, ACSJC-SLP. These are comprised of a series of letters written in the 1890s to Sr. Monica Corrigan to provide information for a community history.

18. Sr. Mary Rose Marsteller was born in Virginia and educated in Baltimore; she entered the CSJ community in 1841 at the age of thirty-one. The CSJs were extremely fortunate that she came to St. Louis and began teaching in the academy during the illness and eventual death of their first American-born and only English-speaking sister, Sr. Mary Joseph Dillon. It is probable that Marsteller entered the community after she had already begun to teach at the academy. In Brouillet's memoirs (ACSJC-SLP), she is referred to as "Miss Marsteller of Baltimore," implying that Marsteller was teaching before she became a postulant—a postulancy that was reduced to three months after Dillon's death. Mary Lucida Savage, *The Congregation of St. Joseph of Carondelet: A Brief Account of Its Origins and Its Work in the United States, 1650–1922* (St. Louis: Herder Book Co., 1923), 62, 94–96, and Catharine Frances Redmond, "The Convent School of French Origin in the United States, 1727–1843" (Ph.D. diss., University of Pennsylvania, 1936), 117. This dissertation also provides a good overview of curriculum and structure of the early French-based convent academies.

19. The academies all existed for different periods of time, and some states had as many as seven different academies within their borders. The secondary academies were located in Missouri, New York, California, Arizona, Alabama, Illinois, Wis-

consin, Oklahoma, Michigan, Minnesota, and North Dakota. Academies in Mississippi, Colorado, and Tennessee existed for only a short time and never developed much beyond the elementary grades. Georgia is not included in this list because the formerly diocesan Georgia community did not merge with the CSJs of Carondelet until the 1920s, after the time period of this study.

20. *Palladium Times*, September 6, 1858, Oswego, N.Y.

21. Baumgarten, "Education and Democracy," 182–83; Oates, "Catholic Female Academies," 123–25; Kim Tolley, "Science for Ladies, Classics for Gentlemen: A Comparative Analysis of Scientific Subjects in the Curricula of Boys' and Girls' Secondary Schools in the United States," *History of Education Quarterly* 36, no. 2 (Summer 1996): 129–53. Tolley presents a strong argument on this issue and blames this "misinterpretation" of the importance of "ornamentals" on the unquestioned acceptance of Woody's 1929 classic, *History of Women's Education*, 1:415.

22. For comparisons of a variety of Catholic orders regarding curriculum and costs see Ewens, *Role of the Nun*, 98–104; Brewer, *Nuns and the Education*; Baumgarten, "Education and Democracy"; and Oates, "Catholic Female Academies."

23. Surviving catalogs and documents are from the three provinces that maintained secondary academies through 1920. Examples include "Prospectus of St. Joseph's Academy, St. Louis," 1861, *Academy of the Sisters of St. Joseph of Carondelet*, 1893 and 1913, ACSJC-SLP; H. W. Wells, "Academy of Our Lady," in *The Schools and the Teachers of Early Peoria* (Peoria, Ill.: Jacquin and Co., 1900), 127–31, and *St. Teresa's Junior College and Academy Yearbook*, Kansas City, 1919–20, ACSJC-SLP; "St. Joseph's Academy for Young Ladies, St. Paul, 1861," *Annual Catalogue of St. Joseph's Academy, St. Paul*, 1875 and 1907, *Annual Catalogue of St. Margaret's Academy*, Minneapolis, 1907, and *Annual Catalogue of St. John's Academy*, Jamestown, N.D., 1909, ACSJC-SPP; and *Annual Catalogue of St. Mary's Academy*, Los Angeles, 1904–5, and *Annual Catalogue of St. Joseph's Academy*, Prescott, Ariz., 1909, ACSJC-LAP.

24. Tolley, "Science for Ladies," 129–53. Tolley confirms that boys' academies and colleges had increased their science offerings significantly by the late nineteenth century. For an expanded analysis of Tolley's work see her "Science Education of American Girls, 1794–1932" (Ph.D. diss., University of California–Berkeley, 1997), and Deborah Jean Warner, "Science Education for Women in Antebellum America," *Isis* 69 (March 1978): 58–67. See also Woody, *History of Women's Education*, 1:563–65. His analysis of 162 academy catalogs published between 1742 and 1871 confirms that natural philosophy (physics), astronomy, chemistry, and botany were among the ten subjects most frequently listed in the standard curriculum.

25. Savage, *Congregation of St. Joseph*, 95–96; "St. Joseph's Academy," St. Paul, 1861, ACSJC-SPP; "Prospectus of St. Joseph's Academy," Cohoes, N.Y., 1861, ACSJC-AP.

26. Woody, *History of Women's Education*, 2:52–97; David Tyack and Elisabeth Hansot, *Learning Together: A History of Coeducation in American Schools* (New Haven: Yale University Press, 1990), 165–242. Tyack and Hansot describe the "differentiating by sex" of the American public high school. Although girls outnumbered boys in coeducational high schools, gender-segregated courses produced a detrimental effect on girls' enrollment in math and science courses. Girls actually lost ground between 1890 and 1930, when boys were tracked into math and science and girls "counseled out"

of these subjects in favor of a practical education (i.e., home economics and commercial courses). The curricular trends also impacted racial and ethnic minorities who were consistently channeled into vocational tracks in high schools. See also William J. Reese, *The Origins of the American High School* (New Haven: Yale University Press, 1995), 220–30. For discussion on how gender-segregated curricula affected women's higher education see Solomon, *In the Company of Educated Women*, 82–87, 149–56.

27. *Academy of the Sisters of St. Joseph of Carondelet*, St. Louis, 1913; Wells, "Academy of Our Lady," and "St. Joseph's Academy," Green Bay, Wisc., ACSJC-SLP; *St. Teresa's Junior College and Academy*, Kansas City, Mo., 1919–20, Avila College Records, Kansas City, Mo.; *Annual Catalogue of St. Joseph's Academy*, Prescott, Ariz., 1910, and *Annual Catalogue of St. Mary's Academy*, Los Angeles, 1904–5, ACSJC-LAP; *Annual Catalogue of St. Joseph's Academy*, St. Paul, 1907–8, *Annual Catalogue of St. John's Academy*, Jamestown, N.D., 1909, *Annual Catalogue of St. Margaret's Academy*, Minneapolis, 1907, and "Derham Hall—Program of Study, 1918–1919," St. Paul, ACSJC-SPP.

28. For sources on and examples of convent academy life in a variety of communities see Brewer, *Nuns and the Education*, 45–77, and Murphy, "Pioneer Roman Catholic Girls' Academies," 44–45. For examples of sources published for popular audiences in the late nineteenth and early twentieth centuries see Mary Elliott, "School Days at the Sacred Heart," *Putnam's Magazine*, March 1870, 275–86; Agnes Repplier, *In Our Convent Days* (Boston: Houghton Mifflin Co., 1905); and George Sand, *My Convent Life*, trans. Maria Ellery McKay (Boston: Roberts, 1893; reprint, Chicago: Academy Press, 1978).

29. Savage, *Congregation of St. Joseph*, 60.

30. Memoirs of Eliza McKenney Brouillet, ACSJC-SLP. These memoirs provide rich descriptions of the early years (1840s) of St. Joseph's Academy in St. Louis.

31. Ibid.

32. Sr. Winifred (Kate) Hogan, "My Reminiscences," 1922, ACSJC-SPP.

33. Woody, *History of Women's Education*, 434–56; Brewer, *Nuns and the Education*, 45–77. This comparison is probably based on a difference of degree of student supervision and regulation, which certainly varied depending upon the time period. Early Protestant seminaries were extremely restrictive with student behavior codes, but toward the end of the nineteenth century and definitely by the early twentieth century, Catholic convent academies retained more conservative student regulations than many private academies and certainly far more than public high schools.

34. Hogan, "My Reminiscences."

35. Brouillet's and Hogan's memoirs describe many student pranks. See also Evelyn O'Neill, "St. Teresa's Academy," Kansas City (unpublished manuscript, May 1925, ACSJC-SLP and STAA).

36. Hogan, "My Reminiscences."

37. *St. Teresa's Academy Catalogue*, 1919, 5, ACSJC-SLP; *St. Joseph's Academy Catalogue*, 1910, 5, ACSJC-LAP; *Tucson City Directory (1881)*, 5, ACSJC-LAP; Wells, *Schools*, 129.

38. Protestant attendance at convent academies is well documented. Some communities kept specific records on religious affiliation and actually had a Protestant majority in the early days of the academies. For information and discussion on this issue see Baumgarten, "Education and Democracy," 174–75, 182, 186–88; Brewer,

Nuns and the Education, 87–91; Murphy, "Pioneer Roman Catholic Girls' Academies," 143–49; Ewens, *Role of the Nun*, 66–67; Oates, "Catholic Female Academies," 127–28; and Joseph G. Mannard, "Maternity . . . of the Spirit: Nuns and Domesticity in Antebellum America," *U.S. Catholic Historian* 5 (Summer 1986): 311–16.

39. This quote and others are cited in Mannard, "Maternity . . . of the Spirit," 310–11. See *The American Ladies Magazine*, September 1834, and *The Mother's Magazine*, May 1835. Editors of these magazines, Sarah Hale and Abigail G. Whittelsey, often used the writings and speeches of Catharine Beecher to promote these ideas.

40. Baumgarten, "Education and Democracy," 186; Mary Ewens, "The Leadership of Nuns in Immigrant Catholicism," in *Women and Religion in America*, vol. 1, ed. Rosemary Radford Ruether and Rosemary Skinner Keller (San Francisco: Harper and Row, 1981), 102; Mary Ewens "Removing the Veil: The Liberated American Nun," in *Women of Spirit: Female Leadership in the Jewish and Christian Traditions*, ed. Rosemary Ruether and Eleanor McLaughlin (New York: Simon and Schuster, 1979), 269.

41. Hogan, "My Reminiscences."

42. These four became leaders in the community, but there certainly were others of lesser status; unfortunately, biographic information is sketchy or absent on nineteenth-century CSJs. For a discussion on the "social appeal" of Catholic religious life see Joseph Mannard, "Converts in Convents: Protestant Women and the Social Appeal of Catholic Religious Life in Antebellum America," *Records of the American Catholic Historical Society of Philadelphia* 104 (Spring/Winter 1993): 79–90.

43. "Annals of the Sisters of St. Joseph at Chillicothe, Mo.," ACSJC-SLP. Mother Herman Lacy was one of the "mavericks" discussed in Chapter 3. Chillicothe appears to be where she was reassigned after her clash with a bishop while at the Cathedral School in New York. It is rare that a nun's loss of temper would be recorded by another sister, so Lacy's frustration over having been banished from the relative comforts of an Eastern academy to "primitive" northwestern Missouri must have been intense.

44. Diary of Sr. Justine LeMay, Hancock, Mich., ACSJC-SLP.

45. Sr. Dolorosa Mannix, "St. Joseph's Academy, Tucson"; Reminiscences of Sr. St. Barbara Reilly, ACSJC-LAP.

46. Ledger Book 3, 1873–83, St. Teresa's Academy, Kansas City, Mo., STAA.

47. "Brief Items Connected with the Establishment of the Home of Our Lady of Peace, San Diego, Calif.," ACSJC-LAP.

48. In the first eighteen years of the conservatory 4,421 pupils were registered in art or music classes ("St. Agatha's Conservatory—Number of Pupils, 1884–1902," ACSJC-SPP).

49. Although the provincial archives (ACSJC-SPP) contain many materials about St. Agatha's, the most accessible and interesting information can be found in Ann Thomasine Sampson, "St. Agatha's Conservatory and the Pursuit of Excellence," *Ramsey County History* 24, no. 1 (1989): 3–19. The conservatory closed in 1962.

50. Memoirs of Sr. Francis Joseph Ivory, ACSJC-SLP.

51. See Chapter 4 for descriptions of CSJ fund-raising activities in the Rocky Mountains and Southwest.

52. Depending upon the location of the academies, boarders came from sur-

rounding states. In St. Paul, academies had high representations from Minnesota, Wisconsin, and North Dakota. In a central location like St. Louis or Kansas City as many as ten states might be represented at the academy.

53. Letter from Bishop Nicholas Matz to Rev. Mother Agnes Gonzaga Ryan, August 31, 1911, ACSJC-SLP. The sisters' behavior was not unusual for nineteenth-century nuns on recruiting trips, so this clash probably had more to do with the power struggles between the nun and bishop. Matz and Ryan had not been on the best of terms ever since Ryan had withdrawn CSJs from St. Patrick's School (Denver) during Matz's legal dispute with Fr. Michael Carrigan two years earlier. As of this date she had refused to send sisters back to St. Patrick's.

54. By the mid-nineteenth century CSJs and other sisterhoods filed for incorporation status to alleviate ownership disputes over their institutions. Examples of the struggles between male clerics and nuns fill the convent archives of every congregation. For examples from a variety of religious communities see Margaret Susan Thompson, "To Serve the People of God: Nineteenth-Century Sisters and the Creation of a Religious Life," Working Paper Series, Cushwa Center, University of Notre Dame, ser. 18, no. 2, Spring 1987, and "Women, Feminism, and the New Religious History: Catholic Sisters As a Case Study," in *Belief and Behavior: Essays in the New Religious History*, ed. Philip R. Vandermeer and Robert P. Swerienga (New Brunswick: Rutgers University Press, 1991), 136–63; Ewens, *Role of the Nun*; George C. Stewart, *Marvels of Charity: History of American Sisters and Nuns* (Huntington, Ind.: Our Sunday Visitor, Inc., 1994); and Florence Deacon, "Handmaids or Autonomous Women: The Charitable Activities, Institution Building and Communal Relationships of Catholic Sisters in Nineteenth-Century Wisconsin" (Ph.D. diss., University of Wisconsin, 1989), 340–85.

55. O'Neill, "St. Teresa's Academy," 39–47.

56. Ibid., 47. Fifty-one years later the CSJs in Kansas City "lost" in another property negotiation. The St. Joseph's Orphan Home for Girls was owned outright by the CSJs. They had never received remuneration for their seventy-seven years of service to the Catholic community in Kansas City, having assumed renovation costs and other expenses during that time. After the sisters refused Bishop John Cody's request to make it coeducational in 1957, he pressured them to sell it to him for $100,000. Less than one year later he placed the property on the market for over four times that amount. See Michael Coleman, ed., *This Far by Faith*, vol. 2 (Kansas City, Mo.: Diocese of Kansas City–St. Joseph, 1992), 575–77.

57. Solomon, *In the Company of Educated Women*, 50; Stewart, *Marvels of Charity*, 549–56; Mary J. Oates, introduction to *Higher Education for Catholic Women: An Historical Anthology*, ed. Mary J. Oates (New York: Garland Press, 1987), and "The Development of Catholic Colleges for Women, 1895–1960," *U.S. Catholic Historian* 7 (Fall 1988): 413–26; Edward J. Powers, *A History of Catholic Higher Education in the United States* (Milwaukee: Bruce Pub. Co., 1958), 184; Philip Gleason, *Contending with Modernity: Catholic Higher Education in the Twentieth Century* (New York: Oxford University Press, 1995), 89.

58. See note 9 for documentation; however, it is important to note that many male colleges, Catholic or Protestant, included preparatory programs; therefore, some males were receiving secondary course work but under the auspices of a "college."

59. Mabel Newcomer, *A Century of Higher Education for American Women* (New York: Harper, 1959), 46. In 1870 this figure included only .7 percent of women between eighteen and twenty-one, and in 1920 it included 7.6 percent of this age group.

60. Edward H. Clarke, *Sex in Education; Or, a Fair Chance for the Girls* (Boston: Osgood, 1873), 18, 23, 63, 69, 116, 122–29. This book was widely read and went through seventeen printings. In 1874 Clarke wrote a sequel, *The Building of a Brain* (Boston: Osgood, 1874). For further discussion of Clarke's impact on the debate on women's higher education see Rosalind Rosenberg, *Beyond Separate Spheres: The Intellectual Roots of Modern Feminism* (New Haven: Yale University Press, 1982), 1–27.

61. Charles Darwin, *The Descent of Man and Selection in Relation to Sex* (London: John Murray, 1871), 1:278–79.

62. G. Stanley Hall, *Adolescence: Its Psychology and Its Relations to Physiology, Anthropology, Sociology, Sex, Crime, Religion and Education* (New York: Appleton, 1904), 2:602. These arguments are fully detailed in Henry Maudsley's *Sex in Mind and Education* (Boston: Osgood, 1884). Both Edward Clarke and Maudsley quote extensively from the writings of S. Weir Mitchell, a noted neurologist who recommended a "rest cure" for such "high-strung" women. One of his most notable patients was Charlotte Perkins Gilman, who later wrote "The Yellow Wallpaper," fictionalizing her real-life experiences with Dr. Mitchell and the "rest cure."

63. Rosenberg, *Beyond Separate Spheres*, 30–31, and "The Academic Prism: The New View of American Women," in *Women of America: A History*, ed. Carol Ruth Berkin and Mary Beth Norton (Boston: Houghton Mifflin Co., 1979), 318–41. The nineteenth-century American West has often been portrayed as egalitarian in its early acceptance of coeducational colleges. In reality, the small struggling universities throughout the Midwest and West had no choice but to allow and encourage women to attend if they were to remain open. See John S. Brubacher and Willis Rudy, *Higher Education in Transition: A History of American Colleges and Universities, 1636–1976* (New York: Harper and Row, 1976), 66–69, and Lester F. Goodchild and Harold S. Wechsler, eds., *The History of Higher Education*, 2nd ed. (New York: Simon and Schuster, 1997).

64. Rosenberg, "Academic Prism," 320–23; Solomon, *In the Company of Educated Women*, 58. Solomon states that by 1900 more than twice as many women were enrolled in coeducational institutions than in women-only colleges. See Newcomer, *Century of Higher Education*, 37, 46, and Woody, *History of Women's Education*, 2:256–57, 281.

65. Opponents and proponents of women's higher education used cultural arguments to predict contradictory outcomes on how women's education would impact sex roles, marriage, and childbirth. For examples see Mary Ashton Livermore, *What Shall We Do With Our Daughters?* (Boston: Lee and Shepard, 1883), 43–45; Ely Van deWarker, *Women's Unfitness for Higher Education* (New York: Grafton Press, 1903), 8; John Bascom, "Coeducation," *Educational Review* 36 (1908): 444; and Willystine Goodsell, *The Education of Women: Its Social Background and Its Problems* (New York: Macmillan, 1923). For a discussion on the concept of "race suicide" and how college-educated women were blamed for the lower white birthrate see Linda Gordon, *Woman's Body, Woman's Right* (New York: Penguin Press, 1976), 131–58.

66. Thomas J. Shahan, "The Summer School," *Catholic Educational Review* 2, no. 2 (September 1911): 593–604.

67. Woody, *History of Women's Education*, 2:280–81.

68. For an excellent anthology of primary documents that illuminate the debates on Catholic women's higher education see Oates, *Higher Education*. Two of the more outspoken bishops who were proponents of higher education for women were John Ireland (St. Paul) and John Lancaster Spalding (Peoria, Ill.). For a related discussion of clerical and lay attitudes toward women's place, suffrage, and higher education for Catholic women see Karen J. Kennelly, "Ideals of American Catholic Womanhood," in *American Catholic Women: An Historical Exploration*, ed. Karen Kennelly (New York: Macmillan, 1989), 1–16; James J. Kenneally, *The History of American Catholic Women* (New York: Crossroad, 1990); and Colleen McDannell, "Catholic Domesticity, 1860–1960," in Kennelly, *American Catholic Women*, 48–80.

69. Educators at Catholic University in 1911 did inaugurate Sisters' College, which is described in more detail in Chapter 5, adjacent to the university. Mary J. Oates, "The Development of Catholic Colleges," 413–14, and introduction to Oates, *Higher Education*; Powers, *A History of Catholic Higher Education*, 182–84; Gleason, *Contending with Modernity*, 87–89.

70. Oates, "Development of Catholic Colleges," 415; A Sister of Notre Dame (Mary Patricia Butler), *An Historical Sketch of Trinity College, Washington, D.C., 1897–1925* (Washington, D.C.: Trinity College, 1925), 72–73. See also Oates, *Higher Education*.

71. Gleason, *Contending with Modernity*, 89–95. The CSJs' College of St. Catherine in St. Paul was on this list of accredited institutions. By 1918 there was concern about Catholic women's colleges proliferating too quickly without enough concern for trained faculty and high-quality curriculum. See Mary Molloy, "Catholic Colleges for Women," and Grace Dammann, "The American Catholic College for Women," in Oates, *Higher Education*, 342–49 and 149–70.

72. For an overview of St. Catherine's see Carol K. Coburn, "The College of St. Catherine," in *Historical Dictionary of Women's Education*, ed. Linda Eisenmann (Westport, Conn.: Greenwood Press, 1998), 86–88.

73. Karen Kennelly, "The Dynamic Sister Antonia and the College of St. Catherine," *Ramsey County History* 14, no. 1 (Fall/Winter 1978): 7. Ann Thomasine Sampson, "The Ireland Connection" (unpublished manuscript, ACSJC-SPP).

74. "Sermon on the Occasion of the Fiftieth Anniversary of the Sisters of St. Joseph in St. Paul, Minnesota," published in a modified version under the title "A Catholic Sisterhood in the Northwest," in John Ireland, *The Church and Modern Society*, vol. 2 (Chicago: D. H. McBride, 1896), 279–301.

75. The Ireland family came to the United States in 1850. Ellen Ireland became Sr. Seraphine and governed the CSJ St. Paul province for thirty-nine years. Eliza became Sr. St. John and taught in many CSJ academies in St. Paul and Minneapolis. Ellen Howard, a first cousin, became Sr. Celestine and was the creator of St. Agatha's Conservatory, which provided decades of financial support for the province, and John Ireland was the bishop of St. Paul from 1884 until his death in 1918. This Irish immigrant family had a powerful affect on Minnesota Catholicism for decades.

76. *Northwest Chronicle*, April 10, 1891.

77. Ibid.

78. Woody, *History of Women's Education*, 2:179, 258–59. Many early women's colleges existed because of individual benefactors. For example, Woody states that Henry Sage's endowment opened the doors to women at Cornell and that Matthew Vassar generously endowed Vassar College. The women of Michigan raised $100,000 for women to be allowed into the state university, and large donations helped women enter Johns Hopkins University. Susan B. Anthony worked for many years to open the University of Rochester to women.

79. Helen Angela Hurley, *On Good Ground: The Story of the Sisters of St. Joseph in St. Paul* (Minneapolis: University of Minnesota Press, 1951), 228–37; Kennelly, "Dynamic Sister Antonia," 7; Rosalie Ryan and John Christine Wolkerstorfer, *More Than a Dream: Eighty-Five Years at the College of St. Catherine* (St. Paul: College of St. Catherine, 1992), 2–3.

80. Diary of Sr. Hyacinth Werden, 1903, CSCA. This is a fascinating document that details their many stops in Germany, France, and Belgium. Werden was German-born and fluent in the German language. Her notes are in excellent English, but they are supplemented with German script at times. She was fascinated with the aesthetic surroundings of these places and supplemented her diary with "lessons" on European history. See also Savage, *Congregation of St. Joseph*, 242–45.

81. Ryan and Wolkerstorfer, *More Than a Dream*, 6.

82. Oral interview of Margaret Shelly, n.d., CSCA.

83. Kennelly, "Dynamic Sister Antonia," 10–11. Attending classes from 1905 to 1909, when she completed her master's thesis, McHugh was exposed to esteemed women faculty and an undergraduate population that included a majority of women. Her contacts included University of Chicago president William Rainey Harper, who had received a letter of introduction about her from Bishop John Ireland.

84. For a discussion of the energized atmosphere at the University of Chicago in the early 1900s, see Rosenberg, *Beyond Separate Spheres*. A debate over gender-separate curriculum ensued once Chicago had "too many women." For details about the curriculum at St. Catherine's and McHugh's changes see Kennelly, "Dynamic Sister Antonia," 12–13; Helen Margaret Peck, "Academic History of the College of St. Catherine, 1905–1920" (unpublished manuscript, 1982); and *College of St. Catherine Catalog*, 1907–8, 1910–11, 1915–16, 1919–20, CSCA.

85. "Faculty Lists with Master's Degrees," 1919–20, CSCA. See Helen Margaret Peck, "The Growth and Expansion of the College of St. Catherine to the End of the Presidency of Sr. Antonia McHugh, 1905–1937" (unpublished manuscript, 1984, 46–47, CSCA).

86. Kennelly, "Dynamic Sister Antonia," 12–13; Peck, "Growth and Expansion," 19–20; Ryan and Wolkerstorfer, *More Than a Dream*, 7. McHugh's ingenuity and connections helped her obtain North Central Accreditation. Up to that point the only problem with accreditation had been that the college did not have an endowment and therefore could not qualify. With the help of friends in the educational establishment she convinced North Central that the sisters' lack of salary compensation more than represented the equivalent of a cash endowment for the institution. The agency agreed, awarding accreditation in 1916.

87. "The College of St. Catherine," brochure, 1916, CSCA.

88. Letter from Bishop Edmund Gibbons to Clergy, August 15, 1920, cited by Mary Ancilla Leary, *The History of Catholic Education in the Diocese of Albany* (Washington, D.C.: Catholic University Press, 1957), 212.

89. All five CSJ institutions continue to the present day. All have become coeducational except the College of St. Catherine. St. Teresa's Junior College in Kansas City became a four-year institution in 1940 and in 1963 changed its name to Avila College.

90. Hurley, *On Good Ground*, 233–34; Kennelly, "Dynamic Sister Antonia," 14.

91. Letter from Rev. Mother Agnes Gonzaga Ryan to Sr. Evelyn O'Neill, March 25, 1913, ACSJC-SLP.

Chapter Seven

1. Many religious communities specialized in one particular area such as health care or education. For a detailed listing of work done by communities of sisters see Elinor Tong Dehey, *Religious Communities of Women in the United States* (Hammond, Ind.: W. B. Conkey, 1930). Although the work of schools and orphanages began immediately, the CSJs opened their first hospital in Philadelphia in 1849 at about the same time that St. Louis CSJs began treating cholera victims.

2. For a variety of sources on the history of nursing see Ann Doyle, "Nursing by Religious Orders in the United States," *American Journal of Nursing* 29 (July–Dec. 1929): 775–86, 959–69, 1085–95, 1197–1207, 1331–43, 1466–86. The classic history of nursing is Mary Adelaide Nutting and Lavinia Dock, *A History of Nursing*, 2 vols. (New York: G. P. Putnam's Sons, 1907, 1912). See also Josephine A. Dolan, *Nursing in Society: A Historical Perspective* (Philadelphia: W. B. Saunders, 1978); Philip Kalish and Beatrice Kalish, *The Advancement of American Nursing* (Boston: Little, Brown, 1978); Susan Reverby, *Ordered to Care: The Dilemma of American Nursing, 1850–1945* (New York: Cambridge University Press, 1987); and Joan I. Roberts and Thetis M. Group, *Feminism and Nursing: An Historical Perspective on Power, Status, and Political Activism in the Nursing Profession* (Westport, Conn.: Greenwood Press, 1995). For a general history of American medicine see Paul Starr, *The Social Transformation of American Medicine* (New York: Basic Books, 1982).

3. CSJ Constitution (1847), ACSJC-SLP. With the earliest constitution the sisters were mandated to "consecrate themselves to the service of their neighbor" and "undertake in general all the duties of charity and works of mercy; they serve the poor in hospitals" (21). For an older but useful work on sister-nurses' training and attitudes see Doyle, "Nursing by Religious Orders." Another useful source is John O'Grady, *Catholic Charities in the United States* (Washington, D.C., 1930; reprint, New York: Arno Press, 1971), 183–212. For recent information on sister-nurses see Ursula Stepsis and Dolores Liptak, eds., *Pioneer Healers: The History of Women Religious in American Health Care* (New York: Crossroad, 1989), and Mary J. Oates, *The Catholic Philanthropic Tradition in America* (Bloomington: Indiana University Press, 1995).

4. Mary Denis Maher, *To Bind up the Wounds: Catholic Sister Nurses in the U.S. Civil War* (Westport, Conn.: Greenwood Press, 1989), 27–33; Carlan Kraman, "Women Religious in Health Care: The Early Years," in Stepsis and Liptak, *Pioneer Healers*, 26; Cecil

Woodham-Smith, *Florence Nightingale* (New York: McGraw-Hill, 1951), 34–38; Martha Vicinus, *Independent Women: Work and Community for Single Women, 1850–1920* (Chicago: University of Chicago Press, 1985), 88–89; Starr, *Social Transformation*, 154–57. For a list of activities of Catholic and non-Catholic sisterhoods see Evangeline Thomas, ed., *Women Religious History Sources: A Guide to Repositories in the United States* (New York: R. R. Bowker Co., 1983).

5. This nursing was done at a great human cost to the small and struggling community, which lost three of its members to the disease. It was a particularly devastating loss because the three sisters were all American-born (therefore English-speaking) sisters between the ages of eighteen and thirty-two. CSJ Profession Book, ACSJC-G; Mary Lucida Savage, *The Congregation of St. Joseph of Carondelet: A Brief Account of Its Origin and Its Work in the United States, 1650–1922* (St. Louis: Herder Book Co., 1923), 100–101; Christopher J. Kauffman, *Ministry and Meaning: A Religious History of Catholic Health Care in the United States* (New York: Crossroad, 1995), 52, 60–61. Kauffman states that because cholera strikes the poor in much higher numbers, "nearly eighty percent of those who died of cholera in St. Louis were Catholic." For a detailed analysis of the cholera epidemic and the social, religious, and medical responses to the disease see Charles E. Rosenberg, *The Cholera Years: The United States in 1832, 1849, and 1866* (Chicago: University of Chicago Press, 1962).

6. Savage, *Congregation of St. Joseph*, 68–74; Maria Kostka Logue, *Sisters of St. Joseph of Philadelphia: A Century of Growth and Development, 1847–1947* (Westminster, Md.: Newman Press, 1950), 49–56; Rose Anita Kelly, *Song of the Hills: The Story of the Sisters of St. Joseph of Wheeling* (Wheeling, W.Va.: Mt. St. Joseph, 1962), 179–90. For information about the Canadian CSJs and their activities see Mary Agnes Murphy, *The Congregation of the Sisters of St. Joseph: Le Puy–Lyons–St. Louis–Toronto* (Toronto: University of Toronto Press, 1951). Mother Delphine Fontbonne, one of the six original CSJs who came to the United States, died in 1856 while nursing epidemic victims in Toronto. Although the Canadian foundation separated from Carondelet after general government took effect, in the 1890s they founded St. Michael's Hospital, the first Catholic hospital in Toronto and the first Catholic school of nursing in Canada. See Irene McDonald, *For the Least of My Brethren* (Toronto: Dundern Press, 1992).

7. Helen Angela Hurley, *On Good Ground: The Story of the Sisters of St. Joseph in St. Paul* (Minneapolis: University of Minnesota Press, 1951), 75–79; Kauffman, *Ministry and Meaning*, 60. See also O'Grady, *Catholic Charities*, 187–88. Other orders provided emergency or temporary care, but O'Grady writes that the CSJs were the third group of women religious to organize a Catholic hospital in the United States, with Sisters of Charity and Sisters of Mercy first and second, respectively.

8. Nutting and Dock, *History of Nursing*, 2:366; Kraman, "Women Religious in Health Care," 21–38, and Ursula Stepsis, "Statistics," 287, in Stepsis and Liptak, *Pioneer Healers*; Kauffman, *Ministry and Meaning*, 50–81; Maher, *To Bind up the Wounds*, 38–40.

9. Maher, *To Bind up the Wounds*, 69–70. This is an excellent source on sister-nurses during the Civil War. Maher states that of the 600 or more sisters, over 200 were estimated to be Daughters of Charity, whose headquarters was in Emmitsburg, Md. The Holy Cross sisters were second, with Sisters of Mercy and Sisters of Charity also

highly represented. When the CSJs established general government and received papal approbation in 1867, the Philadelphia and Wheeling sisters became diocesan and were no longer a formal part of the CSJs of Carondelet. We included them in this discussion, however, because the communities, their nursing activities, and many of the individual sisters involved were from the Carondelet group and still technically part of the community until 1867. See Chapter 2 concerning papal approbation and separate diocesan communities.

10. Cited in Ellen Ryan Jolly, *Nuns on the Battlefield*, 4th ed. (Providence, R.I.: Providence Visitor Press, 1930), 45. Convent archives are strangely silent on the experiences of these sisters. Unfortunately, secular newspapers tended to call all nursing sisters "Sisters of Charity" or "Sisters of Mercy."

11. "Copy of a Letter from Mother St. John Fournier to the Superior General of the Sisters of St. Joseph of Lyons, 1873," in Logue, *Sisters of St. Joseph*, 128, 132–33, 335–36, 351–52. See also Jolly, *Nuns on the Battlefield*, 158–69.

12. Kelly, *Song of the Hills*, 213–22. This information is taken from Keating's war journal located in the CSJ archives in Wheeling. See also Jolly, *Nuns on the Battlefield*, 170–80.

13. See note 12. Mother de Chantal Keating received the Grand Army of the Republic bronze medal for her service, and she wore it on her habit each memorial day until her death.

14. Maher, *To Bind up the Wounds*, 148–49; Carr Elizabeth Worland, "American Catholic Women and the Church to 1920" (Ph.D. diss., St. Louis University, 1982), 72–75; Mary Ewens, *The Role of the Nun in Nineteenth-Century America* (New York: Arno Press, 1978), 240–45. Ewens's book analyzes nineteenth-century perceptions of American nuns as described in literature.

15. Kate Cumming, *Kate: The Journal of a Confederate Nurse*, quoted in Mary Ewens, "Removing the Veil: The Liberated American Nun," in *Women of Spirit: Female Leadership in the Jewish and Christian Traditions*, ed. Rosemary Ruether and Eleanor McLaughlin (New York: Simon and Schuster, 1979), 271.

16. Judith Metz, "In Times of War," in Stepsis and Liptak, *Pioneer Healers*, 39–68; Kauffman, *Ministry and Meaning*, 82–95; Maher, *To Bind up the Wounds*, 148–49; Oates, *Catholic Philanthropic Tradition*, 47–48; Ewens, *Role of the Nun*, 240–45.

17. James L. Soward, *Hospital Hill: An Illustrated Account of Public Healthcare Institutions in Kansas City, Missouri* (Kansas City: Truman Medical Center Foundation, 1995), 15–16.

18. "Accounts of the Yellow Fever in Memphis," ACSJC-SLP; Sr. Giles Phillips, "St. Joseph Hospital School of Nursing," SJHA-KC. See also Leo Kalmer, *Stronger Than Death: Heroic Sacrifices of Catholic Priests and Religious during the Yellow Fever Epidemics at Memphis in 1873, 1878, 1879* (Memphis: n.p., 1929). For an account of the yellow fever epidemic in Charleston, N.C., and the response of the Sisters of Mercy see Mary Ewens, "The Leadership of Nuns in Immigrant Catholicism," in *Women and Religion in America*, vol. 1, ed. Rosemary Radford Ruether and Rosemary Skinner Keller (San Francisco: Harper and Row, 1981), 137–38.

19. Although some of the sister-run hospitals did not survive, women's congregations established almost 500 hospitals between 1860 and 1920. In 1872 approximately

178 hospitals existed in the United States, 75 of which were under Catholic auspices. By 1910 there were over 4,000 American hospitals, and approximately 400 were Catholic, most under the direction of women religious. For a compilation of data on this subject see George C. Stewart, *Marvels of Charity: History of American Sisters and Nuns* (Huntington, Ind.: Our Sunday Visitor, Inc., 1994), 330; Kauffman, *Ministry and Meaning*, 130; Ewens, *Role of the Nun*, 252; Starr, *Social Transformation*, 73; Stepsis, "Statistics," 287; and *Historical Statistics of the U.S.: Colonial America to the Present* (Washington, D.C.: Bureau of the Census, 1975), 79.

20. St. Mary's Hospital in Tucson became highly successful, but with the loss of the railroad money and after eight unsuccessful years, St. Joseph's Hospital in Prescott closed and the building was converted into an academy. The Georgetown hospital prospered until the mining boom collapsed; the CSJs closed the hospital in 1914. For additional information on Georgetown see Chapter 4. Other communities of nuns staffed "frontier" hospitals that served mostly male populations in the American West. See Edna Marie Leroux, "In Times of Socioeconomic Crisis," in Stepsis and Liptak, *Pioneer Healers*, 118–26, and Kauffman, *Ministry and Meaning*, 96–128.

21. CSJ Constitution (1884), pt. 4, pp. 96–97, and CSJ Manual of Customs (1917), 117–18, ACSJC-SLP. Apparently this policy of tolerance did not extend to race. Mary Oates states that as late as 1922, of the 540 Catholic hospitals in the United States, not one was for or admitted African Americans (*Catholic Philanthropic Tradition*, 64–65).

22. Advertising booklet for "St. Joseph's Hospital, St. Paul, Minn." (1908), p. 5, ACSJC-SPP.

23. St. Joseph Hospital–Patient Ledger Books, Georgetown, Colo., 1880–89 and 1890–1913, ACSJC-SLP. This diversity was also evident in other hospitals in the trans-Mississippi West, such as St. Joseph's Hospital in Kansas City, Mo. (see Patient Ledger Books, 1875–94, SJHA-KC); Ann Thomasine Sampson, *Care with Prayer: A History of St. Mary's Hospital and Rehabilitation Center* (Minneapolis: St. Mary's Hospital, 1987), 5; and Alberta Cammack and Leo G. Byrne, *Heritage: The Story of St. Mary's Hospital* (Tucson: St. Mary's Hospital, 1981), 17.

24. Kauffman, *Ministry and Meaning*, 129–67; Mary Carol Conroy, "The Transition Years," in Stepsis and Liptak, *Pioneer Healers*, 86–117; Starr, *Social Transformation*, 145–62; Oates, *Catholic Philanthropic Tradition*, 39–45, 63–65.

25. Caring for special groups usually in separate facilities or separate wings of the building, these Kansas City hospitals divided patients by religion, race, class, ethnicity, gender, age, and specific infirmities. This eclectic mix of hospitals also included the "city pest-house boat" for smallpox patients, emergency hospitals, psychiatric hospitals, an eye and ear infirmary, and a tuberculosis hospital. Soward, *Hospital Hill*, 20–21, 34–35, 52–53, 68. Two other CSJ hospitals also specialized in type of patient care—a maternity and infant hospital in Troy, N.Y., and a large tuberculosis clinic at St. Mary's in Tucson.

26. All quoted material comes from a series of twenty-three letters written to the St. Louis motherhouse between October 5, 1898, and April 22, 1899. Except where indicated, the letters were written by the group's superior, Liguori McNamara (ACSJC-SLP).

27. Letter from Sr. Bonaventure Nealon (Nolan) at Camp Hamilton, Kentucky, to Rev. Mother Agatha Guthrie, October 1898, ACSJC-SLP.

28. Ibid.

29. Letter from Sr. Liguori McNamara to Sr. Lucida Savage, November 1, 1918, ACSJC-SLP.

30. Metz, "In Times of War," 65–66. Metz writes that the Daughters of Charity were sent to the Italian front in 1918. Other orders of nuns were not commissioned overseas but helped to staff "emergency" hospitals at training camps (in the United States) to nurse the large numbers of soldiers during the flu epidemic.

31. "General Statistics—Congregation of the Sisters of St. Joseph," May 1920, ACSJC-G.

32. Savage, *Congregation of St. Joseph*, 327; Dolorita Dougherty et al., eds., *The Sisters of St. Joseph of Carondelet* (St. Louis: Herder Book Co., 1966), appendix 5. George Stewart's recent analysis of the years 1866 to 1917 placed the Sisters of St. Joseph (which include the Carondelet CSJs and other affiliated groups) as fourth in hospital founding behind the Sisters of Mercy (79 hospitals), Daughters of Charity (58), and Franciscans (57) (*Marvels of Charity*, 329).

33. Protestant nurse Jane Woolsey expressed the sentiments of some Protestant women when she stated, "[We] might have had an order of Protestant women better than the Romish sisterhoods, by so much as heart and intelligence are better than machinery." *Hospital Days* (New York, 1868), 44, as quoted in Maher, *To Bind up the Wounds*, 132.

34. "Copy of a Letter from Mother St. John Fournier," 335–36.

35. Letter from Sr. Liguori McNamara to Sr. Lucida Savage, November 1, 1918, ACSJC-SLP.

36. Memoirs of Sr. Mary Thomas Lavin, ACSJC-LAP.

37. Letter from Sr. Liguori McNamara to Rev. Mother Agatha Guthrie, October 13 and 22, 1898, ACSJC-SLP.

38. The number of nursing schools in the United States had increased to 432 by 1900 and 1,129 by 1910. Starr, *Social Transformation*, 155–56, and Jo Ann Ashley, *Hospitals, Paternalism, and the Role of the Nurse* (New York: Teacher College Press, 1976), 20. By 1915 there were 220 Catholic nursing schools run by thirty different orders of nuns (Kauffman, *Ministry and Meaning*, 154–67).

39. Kauffman, *Ministry and Meaning*, 158. Kauffman also states that in secular nursing schools, the "convent metaphor" was used to foster the idealism of heroic, religious self-sacrifice (156–57).

40. "Application for Admission to Training School for Nurses—Hulda Olivia Larson" and "Circular Containing Terms of Admission," n.d. (probably around 1915), ACSJC-SPP. Other CSJ nursing brochures have similar requirements and regulations. See also "St. John's Hospital Nursing School—Fargo, N.D.," ACSJC-SPP; "St. Joseph's Hospital—St. Paul, 1908," ACSJC-SPP; Sampson, *Care with Prayer*, 10–14; Phillips, "St. Joseph Hospital School of Nursing"; and Cammack and Byrne, *Story of St. Mary's*, 24–26. St. Mary's Hospital School of Nursing in Amsterdam, New York, opened in 1920. Although few records are available, since the early sisters

received their training at the CSJ hospital in Kansas City, their training school probably looked very similar.

41. St. Mary's Hospital in Minneapolis began its program in 1900, and St. Joseph's Hospital in Kansas City began in 1901. Laywomen were admitted to these schools from their inception. For additional information on the history of these three early programs see John M. Culligan and Harold J. Prendergast, "St. Joseph's Hospital in St. Paul," *Acta et Dicta* 6, no. 2 (October 1934): 1–16; Sampson, *Prayer with Care*, 10–12; and Phillips, "St. Joseph Hospital School of Nursing."

42. Sampson, *Prayer with Care*, 17.

43. This information on Sr. Giles Phillips is taken from a letter written by Sr. Anne Catherine McDonald to "My Dear Friends," soon after the death of Sister Giles (letter dated November 27, 1962, SJHA-KC). Phillips was also the first sister-nurse on the State Board of Nursing of Missouri and an officeholder in the Kansas City district of the American Nurses Association and the National League of Nursing.

44. The smaller hospitals located in North Dakota, Tucson, and Amsterdam, N.Y., began their nursing schools later and had the benefit of expertise from the St. Louis and St. Paul provinces. The "Standard Curriculum for Schools of Nursing" was introduced in 1917 by the National League of Nursing Education (Kauffman, *Ministry and Meaning*, 161).

45. "St. Mary's Hospital—Amsterdam, N.Y.," ACSJC-AP. Although Fr. William Browne purchased the original property and equipment in 1902, the CSJs paid $7,000 to acquire the property and added $10,000 in improvements. Some sisters were sent to Kansas City for nurses' training. The hospital was incorporated in 1909. It was not unusual for some early hospitals to have a garden and chickens on the premises to supplement food for the hospital.

46. Letter from Dr. J. D. Griffith to Rev. Mother Agnes Gonzaga Ryan, February 27, 1914, SJHA-KC. There are two other surviving documents on this issue, one unsigned and formatted more like a petition, and another from a physician, Dr. J. N. Scott. The CSJs did build a new hospital three years later (see SJHA-KC).

47. Sr. Evangelista Weyand was a founder of the Arizona State Nurses Association and campaigned to establish a statewide certification board. She became a charter member of the State Board of Nursing Examiners. Sr. Giles Phillips was the first sister-member and later president of the State Board of Nursing of Missouri. The National League of Nursing Education included many CSJs and other sisters. Approximately 10 percent of its membership collaborated to form a Sisters' Committee within the league. Sr. Esperance Finn was elected and served as a founding member and second vice president for the Catholic Hospital Association.

48. Kauffman, *Ministry and Meaning*, 171.

49. Ibid., 171–92, 230–32.

50. Letter from Apostolic Delegate D. Falconio to Rev. Mother Agnes Gonzaga Ryan, November 10, 1909, copy in ACSJC-AP; letter from St. Paul province (probably Mother Seraphine Ireland) to Falconio, December 12, 1909, ACSJC-SPP.

51. For data on specific Catholic sisterhoods and their social service activity see Dehey, *Religious Communities of Women*.

52. Kathryn Kish Sklar, "Two Political Cultures in the Progressive Era: The National Consumer's League," in *U.S. History as Women's History: New Feminist Essays*, ed. Linda K. Kerber, Alice Kessler-Harris, and Kathryn Kish Sklar (Chapel Hill: University of North Carolina Press, 1995), 37. There is a plethora of sources discussing American women's organizations and benevolent activity. For excellent examples see chapters by Linda Gordon and Estelle Freedman in Kerber et al., *U.S. History as Women's History*. See also Mary P. Ryan, *The Cradle of the Middle Class: The Family in Oneida County, New York, 1790–1865* (New York: Cambridge University Press, 1981); Nancy A. Hewitt, *Women's Activism and Social Change, Rochester, New York, 1822–1872* (Ithaca: Cornell University Press, 1984); Lori D. Ginzberg, *Women and the Work of Benevolence: Morality, Politics and Class in the Nineteenth-Century United States* (New Haven: Yale University Press, 1990); Kathleen D. McCarthy, ed., *Lady Bountiful Revisited: Women, Philanthropy, and Power* (New Brunswick: Rutgers University Press, 1990); Anne Firor Scott, *Natural Allies: Women's Associations in American History* (Urbana: University of Illinois Press, 1992); and Kathryn Kish Sklar, *Florence Kelly and the Nations's Work: The Rise of Women's Political Culture, 1830–1900* (New Haven: Yale University Press, 1995).

53. Scott, *Natural Allies*, 2.

54. For sources that discuss women's organizations but also examine the important religious motivations for women's activities see Scott, *Natural Allies*; Ryan, *Cradle of the Middle Class*; Ruth Bordin, *Women and Temperance: The Quest for Power and Liberty, 1873–1900*, 2nd ed. (New Brunswick: Rutgers University Press, 1990); Peggy Pascoe, *Relations of Rescue: The Search for Female Moral Authority in the American West, 1874–1939* (New York: Oxford University Press, 1990); and Evelyn Brooks Higginbotham, *Righteous Discontent: The Women's Movement in the Black Baptist Church, 1880–1920* (Cambridge: Harvard University Press, 1993).

55. Scott, *Natural Allies*, 14–15. Scott writes that the "deserving poor" were the "working poor" who were considered "respectable" but had fallen on hard times. The "undeserving poor" were those who seemed "unembarrassed by their poverty" or who drank and seemed "unworthy." She adds that foreigners were often viewed with suspicion. For a discussion of seventeenth- and eighteenth-century French ideas and policies on this issue and how they affected nuns see Chapter 1. For a discussion of the perceptions of the European poor over centuries and the Catholic Church's responses see Jo Ann Kay McNamara, *Sisters in Arms: Catholic Nuns through Two Millennia* (Cambridge: Harvard University Press, 1996).

56. Hewitt, *Women's Activism*, 237; Ginzberg, *Women and Benevolence*, 8.

57. Carroll Smith-Rosenberg, *Disorderly Conduct: Visions of Gender in Victorian America* (New York: Oxford University Press, 1985), 16. For a discussion of Protestant attitudes toward Catholic immigrant children see Priscilla Ferguson Clement, "The City and the Child, 1860–1885," and Ronald D. Cohen, "Child Saving and Progressivism, 1885–1915," in *American Childhood: A Research Guide and Historical Handbook*, ed. Joseph M. Hawes and N. Ray Hiner (Westport, Conn.: Greenwood Press, 1985), 235–72 and 273–310. Protestant cleric Charles Loring Brace created the Children's Aid Society, which took children from orphanages and sent them on trains to be adopted in the West. For a description of the "Orphan Trains" that took urban (and

many Catholic) children to Midwestern and Western states for adoption by "farm families" see Marilyn Holt, *The Orphan Trains: Placing out in America* (Lincoln: University of Nebraska Press, 1992). Since the prior religious training of the children was ignored, many Catholic children were "lost to the faith" through this type of adoption.

58. Maureen Fitzgerald, "Irish-Catholic Nuns and the Development of New York City's Welfare System, 1840–1900" (Ph.D. diss., University of Wisconsin, 1992), 395.

59. Oates, *Catholic Philanthropic Tradition*, 7–8, 21.

60. Fitzgerald, "Irish-Catholic Nuns," 29–33. Cities that had large Catholic populations and powerful political machines often provided nuns with more autonomy and influence in conducting their welfare activities.

61. "General Chapter Summary—Sisters of St. Joseph," 1893 and 1920, ACSJC-G. Besides the five listed states, the CSJs had an orphanage in Marquette, Michigan, but it closed in 1902. In the 1920 report seven of the nine institutions are listed as orphanages in the summary, but two, a "Home for the Friendless" and an "Infant Home," provided for large numbers of orphaned children also. The term "half-orphan" was used to designate a child who had one living parent who, because of poverty or illness, could not care for the child. There were over 300 Catholic orphanages by 1900, caring for over 80,000 children. By 1920 institutional care had peaked and a steady decline began in favor of foster care (Stewart, *Marvels of Charity*, 334).

62. Papers from the St. Joseph Orphan Home for Boys, St. Louis, ACSJC-SLP.

63. "Thousands of Children Have Been Cared for in Orphanage," *The Tucson Citizen*, May 23, 1920. All surviving record books document the variety of ways that children came to the CSJ orphanages. These include the Record Book of St. Joseph's Orphan Home for Girls—Kansas City, 1890–1917; Papers from the St. Joseph Orphan Home for Boys, St. Louis; Record Book for the St. Bridget's Half-Orphanage —St. Louis, 1862–1885; and *First Annual of St. Joseph's Home for the Friendless*—Chicago, 1912, ACSJC-SLP.

64. Record Book for St. Bridget's Half-Orphanage.

65. Letter from J. A. Charlebois to Archbishop J. E. Quigley, Chicago, Ill., March 14, 1911, ACSJC-SLP.

66. Record Book of St. Joseph's Orphan Home for Girls, January 31, 1910.

67. *First Annual of St. Joseph's Home for the Friendless*—Chicago, 1912.

68. Record Book of St. Joseph's Orphan Home for Girls, 1880–1917.

69. Ibid., August 4, 1892.

70. Claire Lynch, *St. Joseph Home for Children, 1877–1960* (St. Paul: North Central Pub. Co., 1982), 21. Although this institution and the author of the book are Benedictine, there is some discussion of the CSJs' orphanage, and the state regulations are included in her description.

71. Aida Doyle, *The History of the Sisters of St. Joseph of Carondelet* (Troy, N.Y.: Srs. of St. Joseph, 1936), 203–4; Emily Joseph Daly, "The Albany Province," in Dougherty et al., *Sisters of St. Joseph*, 277–78.

72. "Sr. M. Incarnation McDonough's account of the Chicago Fire," ACSJC-SLP. The children and sisters walked for three hours until they reached the outskirts of town, where, out of sheer exhaustion, they rested. They were found five hours later

by Jesuits from Loyola University who took the nuns and the children back to the college and temporarily housed them in classrooms.

73. Some constitutions of Catholic sisterhoods barred them from teaching or caring for males of any age. Although the CSJs had traditionally worked with females in France, their constitution did not expressly forbid working with males, so they taught and cared for American boys, but in most cases only until the boys became adolescents.

74. "Chapter Summary Data, 1920" for the Troy and Los Angeles provinces, ACSJC-G.

75. "Chapter Summary Data, 1887, 1893, 1908, 1920" for the Troy, Los Angeles, St. Louis, and St. Paul provinces, ACSJC-G. In New York orphanages there was one CSJ per eleven children, and in Arizona the adult-to-child ratio was approximately one sister to thirteen children. Missouri and Illinois orphanages averaged one sister per eleven children, with two orphanages having as few as seven children per sister. Minnesota orphanages averaged one sister per eight or nine children.

76. Nurith Zmora, *Orphanages Reconsidered: Child Care Institutions in Progressive Era Baltimore* (Philadelphia: Temple University Press, 1994). Zmora concludes that orphanages were not isolating agencies of social control but provided for the multiple needs of nineteenth-century children.

77. Papers from the St. Joseph Orphan Home for Boys.

78. Record Book of St. Joseph's Home for Girls—Kansas City, June 5, 1883. Although this was a home for girls, the thirteen-year-old brother was allowed to work at the orphanage. He stayed with his three younger sisters for seven years. The CSJ orphan records, where available, provide interesting anecdotal information on the follow-up status of children who stayed for any length of time.

79. "Copy of a Letter from Mother St. John Fournier," 345.

80. Lelia Hardin Bugg, "Catholic Life in St. Louis," *Catholic World* 68, no. 403 (1898): 14–30. See also Hasia Diner, *Erin's Daughters in America: Irish Immigrant Women in the Nineteenth Century* (Baltimore: John Hopkins University Press, 1983), 132. CSJ archives have no surviving documents from this institution, which Bugg reported served over 1,500 girls and women each year.

81. *First Annual of St. Joseph's Home for the Friendless*—Chicago, 1912, and *Third Annual Report—St. Joseph's Home for the Friendless—Chicago*, 1916, ACSJC-SLP.

82. "Masterson Day Nursery," *Diamond Jubilee History* (n.d.), 104–5, ACSJC-AP. See also Daly, "Albany Province," 281–83.

83. Fitzgerald, "Irish-Catholic Nuns," 301–81. Fitzgerald provides extensive detail on the work of Irish orders and their support of single women in spite of clerical disinterest. See also Diner, *Erin's Daughters*, 130–38.

84. Diner, *Erin's Daughters*, 132. For a discussion of CSJ demographics, ethnicity, and the Irish influence see Chapter 3.

85. Oates, *Catholic Philanthropic Tradition*, 75–76, 87–89.

86. Jessie Benton Fremont quote cited in Florence B. Yount, "Hospitals in Prescott," *Arizona Medicine*, August 1976, 837–42. Jessie Fremont, wife of the military governor John C. Fremont, met the CSJs in St. Louis during the Civil War.

87. *Arizona Miner*, September 2, 1881.

88. Sr. Magdalen Gaffney, "History of St. Joseph's Home," ACSJC-LAP; Thomas Marie McMahon, "The Sisters of St. Joseph of Carondelet: Arizona's Pioneer Religious Congregation, 1870–1890" (master's thesis, St. Louis University, 1952), 115–16. Gaffney wrote that on one trip the conductor either did not believe that Sr. Angelica had permission to ride in the caboose for free or was hostile to nuns, but he stopped the train, making her and her orphan girl walk three miles through the desert to Tucson.

89. Yount, "Hospitals in Prescott," 838; Carol K. Coburn and Martha Smith, "'Pray for Your Wanderers': Women Religious on the Colorado Mining Frontier, 1870–1917," *Frontiers: A Journal of Women's Studies* 15, no. 3 (1995): 36.

90. *St. Paul Dispatch*, December 29, 1876.

91. "St. Michael's Hospital—Grand Forks, N.D.," ACSJC-SPP, and "Sisters' Hospital—Georgetown, Col.," ACSJC-SLP. Both towns helped acquire property and begin the hospitals, but the nuns were expected to administer them, financially and practically.

92. "St. Mary's Hospital—Amsterdam, N.Y."

93. "St. Mary's Hospital—A Few Highlights," ACSJC-AP.

94. "The Sisters' Hospital and . . . a New Asylum for Homeless Children," *Tucson Daily Star*, December 25, 1889.

95. "St. Mary's Hospital—Amsterdam, N.Y."

96. Although it was typical for sister-nurses to work in orphan homes, sisters working in orphanages in Minneapolis, St. Paul, Kansas City, Tucson, and Troy were particularly fortunate because they had CSJ hospitals close by or available in the same city. Sisters who worked in orphanages in cities that did not have CSJ hospitals had to depend on the generosity of doctors who donated their time to see the children.

97. "St. Mary's Home—Binghamton, N.Y." and the "History of St. Mary's Home—Binghamton, N.Y.," ACSJC-AP. By the time Kennedy died in 1911, she had nearly repaid the entire debt.

98. Marian Devoy, "The Catholic Boys' Home: History of the Minneapolis Catholic Orphan Asylum" (master's thesis, University of Minnesota, 1944), 81.

99. "History of St. Joseph's Home for Boys—St. Louis, Mo." and "St. Joseph's Orphan Home for Girls—Kansas City," ACSJC-SLP. Donnelly had purchased the property for the cemetery. After he died in 1880, Sr. Alicia McCusker solicited food and clothing for the next six years. It was not until Sr. Alicia's death in 1886 that Hogan honored Donnelly's request and gave the asylum $100 a month. "A few years later this amount was reduced to fifty dollars per month," and the July picnic was the only other source of income until 1913, when a new bishop, Thomas Lillis, "relieved the sisters from soliciting funds" by providing diocesan funds.

100. "History of St. Mary's Home—Binghamton, N.Y." The Binghamton orphanage was not unusual. Every history of CSJ orphanages includes mention of door-to-door soliciting and begging for food, clothing, and money. One or two sisters would be assigned to this job, and some nuns spent years performing this task.

101. *Third Annual Report—St. Joseph's Home for the Friendless—Chicago* and *Annual Reports, Home for the Friendless, 1912–17.* The list of benefactors and lay groups is impressive and includes the St. Vincent de Paul Society, the Ladies Aid Society, St. Cathe-

rine's Conference, Knights of Columbus, Ladies of Isabella, and the St. Thomas Aquinas Council.

102. O'Grady, *Catholic Charities*, 318–42; Oates, *Catholic Philanthropic Tradition*, 3, 13, 21–23, 87.

103. Devoy, "Catholic Boys' Home," 63.

104. Phillips, "St. Joseph Hospital School of Nursing." Phillips writes that St. Anthony's Maternity Hospital was really just a large residence and a hospital in name only.

105. Devoy, "Catholic Boys' Home," 37–84. The author obtained all information from official meeting minutes from February 18, 1878, and August 10, 1894.

106. Oates, *Catholic Philanthropic Tradition*, 26–28, 71–97.

107. Ibid., 81–84. For a discussion on "scientific charity" and the loss of autonomy for laywomen and nuns see Fitzgerald, "Irish-Catholic Nuns," 477–95, 567–69; Debra Campbell, "Reformers and Activists," in *American Catholic Women: An Historical Exploration*, ed. Karen Kennelly (New York: Macmillan, 1989), 152–81; James Kenneally, *The History of American Catholic Women* (New York: Crossroad, 1990), 89–112; and a special edition on social activism in *U.S. Catholic Historian* 13, no. 3 (Summer 1995).

108. Oates, *Catholic Philanthropic Tradition*, 92. Oates writes, "Hospitals, more than other institutions, resisted oversight by central charitable bureaus."

Epilogue

1. George Stewart, "Sister-Population Statistics, 1830–1990," in George C. Stewart, *Marvels of Charity: History of American Sisters and Nuns* (Huntington, Ind.: Our Sunday Visitor, Inc., 1994), 565.

2. The Second Vatican Council (October 1962 to December 1965) "is regarded by many as the most significant religious event since the 16th Century Reformation and certainly the most important of the twentieth century" (Richard P. McBrien, ed., *Encyclopedia of Catholicism*, [San Francisco: HarperCollins, 1995], 1299–1306). Attended by 3,000 people (mostly bishops) from all over the world, the council's goal was "to promote peace and the unity of all humankind." The end result was dramatic changes in all aspects of Catholic life. Although only ten nuns were allowed to be present, the changes enacted by the council had significant effects on life for women religious, who were encouraged to reexamine all aspects of their constitutions and practices in light of contemporary needs and issues.

3. Mary Ewens, "Women in the Convent," in *American Catholic Women: An Historical Exploration*, ed. Karen Kennelly (New York: Macmillan, 1989), 33, and "Removing the Veil: The Liberated American Nun," in *Women of Spirit: Female Leadership in the Jewish and Christian Traditions*, ed. Rosemary Ruether and Eleanor McLaughlin (New York: Simon and Schuster, 1979), 273; Jo Ann Kay McNamara, *Sisters in Arms: Catholic Nuns through Two Millennia* (Cambridge: Harvard University Press, 1996), 613–14; Susan Carol Peterson and Courtney Vaughn-Roberson, *Women with Vision: The Presentation Sisters of South Dakota, 1880–1985* (Urbana: University of Illinois Press, 1988), 224–26.

4. Mary Jo Weaver, *New Catholic Women: A Continuous Challenge to Traditional Religious Authority* (San Francisco: Harper and Row, 1985), 35–36.

5. Ewens, "Removing the Veil," 273.

6. Ibid., 272–74; Ewens, "Women in the Convent," 33–37; Peterson and Vaughn-Roberson, *Women with Vision*, 226–27; McNamara, *Sisters in Arms*, 616.

7. Jay P. Dolan, *The American Catholic Experience: A History from Colonial Times to the Present* (Garden City, N.Y.: Image Books, 1985), 192. See also Leslie Woodcock Tentler, "On the Margins: The State of American Catholic History," *American Quarterly* 45, no. 1 (March 1993): 112–13.

8. McNamara, *Sisters in Arms*, 616–17. For information concerning Protestant women's status in the church see Ann Braude, "Women's History *Is* American Religious History," in *Retelling U.S. Religious History*, ed. Thomas A. Tweed (Berkeley: University of California Press, 1997), 91.

9. Braude, "Women's History," 102; Barbara Welter, "She Hath Done What She Could: Protestant Women's Missionary Careers in Nineteenth-Century America," in *Women in American Religion*, ed. Janet Wilson James (Philadelphia: University of Pennsylvania Press, 1980), 111–26. For examples of secular women's organizations that lost autonomy when combining with men's organizations see two essays: Estelle Freedman, "Separatism Revisited: Women's Institutions, Social Reform, and the Career of Miriam Van Waters," 171, and Linda Gordon, "Putting Children First: Women, Maternalism and Welfare in the Early Twentieth Century," in *U.S. History as Women's History: New Feminist Essays*, ed. Linda K. Kerber, Alice Kessler-Harris, and Kathryn Kish Sklar (Chapel Hill: University of North Carolina Press, 1995), 63.

10. Ewens, "Removing the Veil," 272; McNamara, *Sisters in Arms*, 613.

Selected Bibliography

Primary Sources

Manuscript and Archival Collections

Denver, Colorado
  Archdiocese of Denver Archives
Kansas City, Missouri
  Diocese of Kansas City – St. Joseph Archives
  Saint Joseph Health Center Archives
  Saint Teresa's Academy Archives
Latham, New York
  Sisters of St. Joseph of Carondelet, Albany Province, Archives
Los Angeles, California
  Sisters of St. Joseph of Carondelet, Los Angeles Province, Archives
Milwaukee, Wisconsin
  Bureau of Catholic Indian Mission Collection, Marquette University Archives
St. Louis, Missouri
  Archdiocese of St. Louis Archives
  Sisters of St. Joseph of Carondelet, Generalate, Archives
  Sisters of St. Joseph of Carondelet, St. Louis Province, Archives
St. Paul, Minnesota
  College of St. Catherine Archives
  Sisters of St. Joseph of Carondelet, St. Paul Province, Archives
Tucson, Arizona
  Saint Mary's Hospital Archives

Selected Primary Documents

The following sources were utilized throughout our research and have been obtained from the five CSJ archives in St. Louis, Missouri; Latham, New York; Los Angeles, California; and St. Paul, Minnesota. Although actual documents differ from one archive to another, each CSJ archive has similar types of materials.

Correspondence of individual sisters and superiors, 1836–1920.
Correspondence of Félicité de Duras Rochejaquelin to Bishop Joseph Rosati, St.
  Louis, 1835–36.

CSJ Constitutions, 1847 (trans. from French), 1860, and 1884.

CSJ Customs Books, 1868 and 1917.

CSJ Demographic information and mission records, 1836–1920.

CSJ Novitiate Manual, circa 1850.

CSJ Profession Book, 1836–1920.

CSJ School/Teachers' Manuals, 1832 (French), 1884, and 1910.

CSJ Spiritual Directory, 1900.

General Chapter Recommendations and Reports, 1869, 1875, 1881, 1887, 1893, 1899, 1908, 1914, 1920.

Institution records and annals for schools, academies, hospitals, orphanages, conservatories, and miscellaneous institutions.

Memorabilia collections, scrapbooks, photographs.

Oral history interviews, diaries, journals, reminiscences.

Postulant/Novitiate Records, 1837–1920.

Selected Published (Primary and Secondary) Sources and Theses/Dissertations on the Sisters of St. Joseph of Carondelet

French Background

Byrne, Patricia. "French Roots of a Women's Movement: The Sisters of St. Joseph, 1650–1836." Ph.D. diss., Boston College, 1985.

Médaille, Jean-Pierre. *Constitutions for the Little Congregation of the Sisters of St. Joseph.* Translated by Research Team of the U.S.A. Federation of the Sisters of St. Joseph. Erie, Pa.: Sisters of St. Joseph, 1969.

———. *Documents of the Little Design, St. Flour: The Règlements, the Eucharistic Letter.* Translated by Research Team of the U.S.A. Federation of the Sisters of St. Joseph. Erie, Pa.: Sisters of St. Joseph, 1973.

———. *Maxims of the Little Institute.* Translated by Research Team of the U.S.A. Federation of the Sisters of St. Joseph. Erie, Pa.: Sisters of St. Joseph, 1975.

Vacher, Marguerite. *Des "régulières" dans le siècle: Les soeurs de Saint-Joseph du Père Médaille aux XXVII et XXVIII siècles.* Clermont-Ferrand: Editions Adosa, 1991.

American Experience (1836–1920)

Ames, Aloysia. *The St. Mary's I Knew.* Tucson, Ariz.: St. Mary's Hospital, 1970.

Byrne, Patricia. "Sisters of St. Joseph: The Americanization of a French Tradition." *U.S. Catholic Historian* 5 (Summer/Fall 1986): 241–72.

Cammack, Alberta, and Leo G. Byrne. *Heritage: The Story of St. Mary's Hospital.* Tucson: St. Mary's Hospital, 1981.

Cantwell, Laurent. *A Design for Living: A History of the Sisters of St. Joseph of Carondelet in the Northwest.* St. Paul: North Central Pub. Co., 1973.

Coburn, Carol K. "The College of St. Catherine." In *Historical Dictionary of Women's Education,* edited by Linda Eisenmann. Westport, Conn.: Greenwood Press, 1998.

———. "Sister Monica Corrigan." In *Encyclopedia of the American West.* Vol. 1, edited by Charles Phillips and Alan Axelrod. New York: Macmillan, 1996.

Coburn, Carol K., and Martha Smith. "Creating Community and Identity: Exploring Religious and Gender Ideology in the Lives of American Women Religious, 1836–1920." *U.S. Catholic Historian* 14, no. 1 (Winter 1996): 91–108.

———. "'Pray for Your Wanderers': Women Religious on the Colorado Mining Frontier, 1877–1917." *Frontiers: A Journal of Women's Studies* 15, no. 3 (1995): 27–52.

Corrigan, Monica. *Trek of the Seven Sisters (Diary, 1870)*. Tucson: Carondelet Health Services, 1991.

Cox, Ignatius Loyola. "The Mission in Long Prairie." *Acta et Dicta* 3 (July 1914): 276–82.

———. "The Mission in St. Anthony Falls, or East Minneapolis." *Acta et Dicta* 3 (July 1914): 283–89.

———. "Notes on the Misson of the Sisters of St. Joseph in St. Paul." *Acta et Dicta* 3 (July 1914): 270–75.

Culligan, John M., and Harold J. Prendergast. "St. Joseph's Hospital in St. Paul." *Acta et Dicta* 6, no. 2 (October 1934): 1–16.

Devoy, Marian. "The Catholic Boy's Home: History of the Minneapolis Catholic Orphan Asylum." Master's thesis, University of Minnesota, 1944.

Dougherty, Dolorita Maria, et al., eds. *Sisters of St. Joseph of Carondelet*. St. Louis: Herder Book Co., 1966. (Separate chapters by Emily Joseph Daly, "Genesis of a Congregation: The European Story," "The Albany Province," and "Generalate"; Dougherty, "St. Louis Province"; Helen Angela Hurley, "The St. Paul Province"; and St. Claire Coyne, "The Los Angeles Province.")

Doyle, M. Aida. *History of the Sisters of St. Joseph of Carondelet in the Troy Province*. Albany: Argus Press, 1936.

Hurley, Helen Angela. *On Good Ground: The Story of the Sisters of St. Joseph in St. Paul*. Minneapolis: University of Minnesota Press, 1951.

———. "The Sisters of St. Joseph and the Minnesota Frontier." *Minnesota History* 30, no. 1 (March 1949): 1–13.

Johnson, Patricia C. "Reflected Glory: The Story of Ellen Ireland." *Minnesota History* 48 (Spring 1982): 12–23.

Kennelly, Karen. "The Dynamic Sister Antonia and the College of St. Catherine." *Ramsey County History* 14, no. 1 (1978): 3–18.

McMahon, Thomas Marie. "The Sisters of St. Joseph of Carondelet: Arizona's Pioneer Religious Congregation, 1870–1890." Master's thesis, St. Louis University, 1952.

McNeil, Teresa Baksh. "Catholic Indian Schools of the Southwest Frontier: Curriculum and Management." *Southern California Quarterly* (Winter 1990): 321–38.

———. "Sisters of St. Joseph under Fire: Pioneer Convent School on the Colorado River." *Journal of Arizona History* 29, no. 1 (1988): 35–50.

———. "St. Anthony's Indian School in San Diego, 1886–1907." *Journal of San Diego History* 34 (Summer 1988): 187–200.

Martens, Elizabeth Marie. *Academy for a Century*. St. Paul: North Central Pub. Co., 1951.

O'Brien, M. Anselm. . . . *The Likes of Kitty O'Brien*. Florissant, Mo.: Huntington Press, 1977.

Perkins, Barbara Alice. "Educational Work of the Sisters of St. Joseph, 1903–1963." Master's thesis, Mt. St. Mary's College–Los Angeles, 1965.

Purcell, Margaret John, ed. *Jubilarse*. St. Louis: Sisters of St. Joseph of Carondelet, 1981.

Ryan, Rosalie, and John Christine Wolkerstorfer. *More Than a Dream: Eighty-Five Years at the College of St. Catherine*. St. Paul: College of St. Catherine, 1992.

Sampson, Ann Thomasine. *Care with Prayer: A History of St. Mary's Hospital and Rehabilitation Center*. Minneapolis: St. Mary's Hospital, 1987.

———. "St. Agatha's Conservatory and the Pursuit of Excellence." *Ramsey County History* 24, no. 1 (1989): 3–19.

Savage, Mary Lucida. *The Century's Harvest, 1836–1936*. St. Louis: Herder Book Co., 1936.

———. *The Congregation of St. Joseph of Carondelet: A Brief Account of Its Origins and Its Work in the United States, 1650–1922*. St. Louis: Herder Book Co., 1923.

Smith, Ann Cecilia. "Educational Activities of the Sisters of St. Joseph of Carondelet in the Western Province from 1870–1903." Master's thesis, Catholic University, 1953.

Soulier, Catherine Francis, "A History of the College of St. Rose–Albany, NY." Master's thesis, College of St. Rose, 1951.

Selected Secondary Sources

The following sources were chosen because they were cited in two or more chapters and/or reflect the interdisciplinary nature of our research in women's history, religious history, history of women religious, educational history, and Catholic history.

Baumgarten, Nikola. "Education and Democracy in Frontier St. Louis: The Society of the Sacred Heart." *History of Education Quarterly* 34, no. 2 (Summer 1994): 171–92.

Braude, Ann. "Women's History *Is* American Religious History." In *Retelling U.S. Religious History*, edited by Thomas A. Tweed. Berkeley: University of California Press, 1997.

Brewer, Eileen Mary. *Nuns and the Education of American Catholic Women, 1860–1920*. Chicago: Loyola University, 1987.

Buetow, Harold A. *Of Singular Benefit: The Story of Catholic Education in the United States*. New York: Macmillan, 1970.

Burns, James A. *The Catholic School System in the United States: Its Principles, Origin, and Establishment*. New York: Benziger Bros., 1908.

———. *The Growth and Development of the Catholic School System in the United States*. New York: Benziger Bros., 1912.

Cott, Nancy F. *The Bonds of Womanhood: "Women's Sphere" in New England, 1780–1835*. New Haven: Yale University Press, 1977.

Danylewycz, Marta. *Taking the Veil: An Alternative to Marriage, Motherhood, and Spinsterhood in Quebec, 1840–1920*. Toronto: McClelland and Stewart, 1987.

Davis, Cyprian. *The History of Black Catholics in the United States*. New York: Crossroad Publishing Co., 1995.

Deacon, Florence Jean. "Handmaids or Autonomous Women: The Charitable Activities, Institution Building and Communal Relationships of Catholic Sisters in Nineteenth-Century Wisconsin." Ph.D. diss., University of Wisconsin, 1989.

Deutsch, Sarah. *No Separate Refuge: Culture, Class, and Gender on an Anglo-Hispanic Frontier in the American Southwest, 1880–1940.* New York: Oxford University Press, 1987.

Diner, Hasia. *Erin's Daughters in America: Irish Immigrant Women in the Nineteenth Century.* Baltimore: Johns Hopkins University Press, 1983.

Dolan, Jay. *The American Catholic Experience: A History from Colonial Times to the Present.* Garden City, N.Y.: Image Books, 1985.

———, ed. *The American Catholic Parish: A History from 1850 to the Present.* 2 vols. New York: Paulist Press, 1987.

Dolan, Jay P., and Gilberto M. Hinojosa, eds. *Mexican Americans and the Catholic Church, 1900–1965.* Notre Dame, Ind.: University of Notre Dame Press, 1994.

DuBois, Ellen Carol, and Vicki L. Ruiz, eds. *Unequal Sisters: A Multicultural Reader in U.S. Women's History.* New York: Routledge, 1990.

Ellis, John Tracy, ed. *Documents of American Catholic History.* Milwaukee, Wisc.: Bruce Pub. Co., 1956.

Engh, Michael E. *Frontier Faiths: Church, Temple, and Synagogue in Los Angeles, 1846–1888.* Albuquerque: University of New Mexico Press, 1992.

Ewens, Mary. "The Leadership of Nuns in Immigrant Catholicism." In *Women in American Religion.* Vol. 1, edited by Rosemary Radford Ruether and Rosemary Skinner Keller. New York: Harper and Row, 1981.

———. "Removing the Veil: The Liberated American Nun." In *Women of Spirit: Female Leadership in the Jewish and Christian Traditions,* edited by Rosemary Ruether and Eleanor McLaughlin. New York: Simon and Schuster, 1979.

———. *The Role of the Nun in Nineteenth-Century America.* New York: Arno Press, 1978.

———. "Women in the Convent." In *American Catholic Women: A Historical Exploration,* edited by Karen J. Kennelly. New York: Macmillan, 1989.

Fitzgerald, Maureen. "Irish-Catholic Nuns and the Development of New York City's Welfare System, 1840–1900." Ph.D. diss., University of Wisconsin, 1992.

Getz, Lorine M. "Women Struggle for an American Catholic Identity." In *Women and Religion in America,* edited by Janet Wilson James. Philadelphia: University of Pennsylvania Press, 1980.

Ginsberg, Lori D. *Women and the Work of Benevolence: Morality, Politics, and Class in the Nineteenth-Century United States.* New Haven: Yale University Press, 1990.

Hackett, David G. "Gender and Religion in American Culture, 1870–1930." *Religion and American Culture* 5, no. 2 (Summer 1995): 127–57.

Hennesey, James. *American Catholics: A History of the Roman Catholic Community in the United States.* New York: Oxford University Press, 1981.

Hewitt, Nancy A. *Women's Activism and Social Change: Rochester, New York, 1822–1872.* Ithaca: Cornell University Press, 1984.

Higginbotham, Evelyn Brooks. *Righteous Discontent: The Women's Movement in the Black Baptist Church, 1880–1920.* Cambridge: Harvard University Press, 1993.

Hoffman, Nancy. *Woman's "True" Profession: Voices from the History of Teaching.* Old Westbury, N.Y.: Feminist Press, 1981.

Hoy, Suellen. "The Journey Out: The Recruitment and Emigration of Irish Religious Women to the United States, 1812–1914." *Journal of Women's History* 6/7 (Winter/Spring 1995): 64–98.

Hufton, Olwen. *The Poor of Eighteenth-Century France, 1750–1789.* London: Oxford University Press, 1974.

———. "Women and the Family Economy in Eighteenth-Century France." *French Historical Studies* 9 (1975): 3–22.

Hufton, Olwen, and F. Tallett. "Communities of Women, the Religious Life and Public Service in Seventeenth-Century France." In *Connecting Spheres: Women in the Western World, 1500 to the Present,* edited by Marilyn J. Boxer and Jean H. Quataert. New York: Oxford University Press, 1987.

James, Janet Wilson, ed. *Women in American Religion.* Philadelphia: University of Pennsylvania Press, 1980.

Jutte, Robert. *Poverty and Deviance in Early Modern Europe.* Cambridge: Cambridge University Press, 1994.

Kauffman, Christopher J. *Ministry and Meaning: A Religious History of Catholic Health Care in the United States.* New York: Crossroad Publishing Co., 1995.

Kaufman, Polly Welts. *Women Teachers on the Frontier.* New Haven: Yale University Press, 1984.

Kenneally, James J. *The History of American Catholic Women.* New York: Crossroad Publishing Co., 1990.

Kennelly, Karen J., ed. *American Catholic Women: An Historical Exploration.* New York: Macmillian, 1989.

Kerber, Linda, Alice Kessler-Harris, and Kathryn Kish Sklar, eds. *U.S. History as Women's History: New Feminist Essays.* Chapel Hill: University of North Carolina Press, 1995.

Kolmer, Elizabeth. "Catholic Women Religious and Women's History: A Survey of the Literature." In *Women in American Religion,* edited by Janet Wilson James. Philadelplhia: University of Pennsylvania Press, 1980.

Leary, Mary Ancilla. *The History of Catholic Education in the Diocese of Albany.* Washington, D.C.: Catholic University Press, 1957.

Lerner, Gerda. *The Creation of Feminist Consciousness: From the Middle Ages to 1870.* New York: Oxford University Press, 1993.

Liptak, Dolores. *Immigrants and Their Church.* New York: Macmillan, 1989.

Logue, Marie Kostka. *Sisters of St. Joseph of Philadelphia: A Century of Growth and Development, 1847–1947.* Westminster, Md.: Newman Press, 1950.

McDannell, Colleen. *The Christian Home in Victorian America, 1840–1900.* Bloomington: Indiana University Press, 1986.

McNamara, Jo Ann Kay. *Sisters in Arms: Catholic Nuns through Two Millennia.* Cambridge: Harvard University Press, 1996.

Maher, Mary Denis. *To Bind up the Wounds: Catholic Sister Nurses in the U.S. Civil War.* Westport, Conn.: Greenwood Press, 1989.

Mannard, Joseph G. "Maternity . . . of the Spirit: Nuns and Domesticity in Antebellum America." *U.S. Catholic Historian* 5 (Summer 1986): 305–24.

Meyer, Bertrande. *The Education of Sisters.* New York: Sheed and Ward, 1941.

Misner, Barbara. *Highly Respectable and Accomplished Ladies: Catholic Women Religious in America, 1790–1850.* New York: Garland Press, 1988.

Oates, Mary J. *The Catholic Philanthropic Tradition in America.* Bloomington: Indiana University Press, 1995.

———. "'The Good Sisters': The Work and Position of Catholic Churchwomen in Boston, 1870–1940." In *The American Catholic Religious Life,* edited by Joseph P. White. New York: Garland Press, 1988.

———. "Organized Voluntarism: The Catholic Sisters in Massachusetts, 1870–1940." In *Women in American Religion,* edited by Janet Wilson James. Philadelphia: University of Pennsylvania Press, 1980.

———, ed. *Higher Education for Catholic Women: An Historical Anthology.* New York: Garland Press, 1987.

O'Brien, David. *Public Catholicism.* New York: Macmillan, 1989.

Pascoe, Peggy. *Relations of Rescue: The Search for Female Moral Authority in the American West, 1874–1939.* New York: Oxford University Press, 1990.

Perko, Michael F., ed. *Enlightening the Next Generation: Catholics and Their Schools, 1830–1980.* New York: Garland Press, 1988.

Peterson, Susan Carol. "A Widening Horizon: Catholic Sisterhoods on the Northern Plains, 1874–1910." *Great Plains Quarterly* 5 (Spring 1985): 125–32.

Peterson, Susan Carol, and Courtney Ann Vaughn-Roberson. *Women with Vision: The Presentation Sisters of South Dakota.* Urbana: University of Illinois, 1991.

Raiche, Annabelle, and Ann Marie Biermaier. *They Came to Teach: The Story of Sisters Who Taught in Parochial Schools and Their Contribution to Elementary Education in Minnesota.* St. Cloud, Minn.: North Star Press, 1994.

Ranft, Patricia. *Women and the Religious Life in Premodern Europe.* New York: St. Martin's Press, 1996.

Rapley, Elizabeth. *The Dévotes: Women and Church in Seventeenth-Century France.* Montreal: McGill-Queen's University Press, 1990.

Raymond, Janice. *A Passion for Friends: Toward a Philosophy of Female Affection.* Boston: Beacon Press, 1986.

Ruether, Rosemary Radford, and Rosemary Skinner Keller, eds. *In Our Own Voices: Four Centuries of Women's Religious Writings.* San Francisco: HarperCollins, 1995.

———. *Women and Religion in America.* 3 vols. New York: Harper and Row, 1981, 1983, 1986.

Ruether, Rosemary, and Eleanor McLaughlin. *Women of Spirit: Female Leadership in the Jewish and Christian Traditions.* New York: Simon and Schuster, 1979.

Ryan, Mary P. *Cradle of the Middle Class: The Family in Oneida County, New York, 1790–1865.* Cambridge: Cambridge University Press, 1981.

Schlissel, Lillian, Vicki L. Ruiz, and Janice Monk, eds. *Western Women: Their Land, Their Lives.* Albuquerque: University of New Mexico Press, 1988.

Scott, Anne Firor. *Natural Allies: Women's Associations in American History.* Urbana: University of Illinois Press, 1992.

Shaughnessy, Gerald. *Has the Immigrant Kept the Faith?: A Study of Immigration and Catholic Growth in the United States.* New York: Macmillan, 1925.

Sisters, Servants of the Immaculate Heart of Mary. *Building Sisterhood: A Feminist His-*

tory of the Sisters, Servants of the Immaculate Heart of Mary. Syracuse: Syracuse University Press, 1997.

Sklar, Kathryn Kish. *Catharine Beecher: A Study in American Domesticity.* New York: W. W. Norton, 1976.

———. *Florence Kelly and the Nation's Work: The Rise of Women's Political Culture, 1830–1900.* New Haven: Yale University Press, 1995.

Sklar, Kathryn Kish, and Thomas Dublin, eds. *Women and Power in American History.* 2 vols. Englewood Cliffs, N.J.: Prentice-Hall, 1991.

Smith-Rosenberg, Carroll. *Disorderly Conduct: Visions of Gender in Victorian America.* New York: Oxford University Press, 1985.

Solomon, Barbara Miller. *In the Company of Educated Women.* New Haven: Yale University Press, 1985.

Spring, Joel. *The American School, 1642–1993.* 3rd ed. New York: McGraw-Hill, 1994.

Stepsis, Ursula, and Dolores Liptak, eds. *Pioneer Healers: The History of Women Religious in American Health Care.* New York: Crossroad Publishing Co., 1989.

Stewart, George C. *Marvels of Charity: History of American Sisters and Nuns.* Huntington, Ind.: Our Sunday Visitor, Inc., 1994.

Taylor, Judith Combes. "From Proselytizing to Social Reform: Three Generations of French Female Teaching Congregations, 1600–1720." Ph.D. diss., Arizona State University, 1980.

Tentler, Leslie Woodcock. "On the Margins: The State of American Catholic History." *American Quarterly* 45 (March 1993): 104–27.

Thomas, Evangeline. *Women Religious History Sources: A Guide to Repositories in the United States.* New York: R. R. Bowker Co., 1983.

Thompson, Margaret Susan. "Discovering Foremothers: Sisters, Society, and the American Catholic Experience." In *The American Catholic Religious Life,* edited by Joseph P. White. New York: Garland Press, 1988.

———. "Sisterhood and Power: Class, Culture, and Ethnicity in the American Convent." *Colby Library Quarterly* 25, no. 3 (September 1989): 149–75.

———. "To Serve the People of God: Nineteenth-Century Sisters and the Creation of an American Religious Life." Working Paper Series, Cushwa Center, University of Notre Dame, Series 18, no. 2, Spring 1987.

Tyack, David, and Elisabeth Hansot. *Learning Together: A History of Coeducation in the American Schools.* New Haven: Yale University Press, 1990.

U.S. Catholic Historian (Special Issue). "Women in the Catholic Community." 5 (Summer/Fall 1986).

U.S. Catholic Historian (Special Issue). "Conference on the History of Women Religious." 9 (Winter 1991).

U.S. Catholic Historian (Special Issue). "Frontier Catholicism." 12 (Fall 1994).

U.S. Catholic Historian (Special Issue). "African-American Catholics and Their Church." 12 (Winter 1994).

U.S. Catholic Historian (Special Issue). "Schools, Colleges and Universities." 13 (Fall 1995).

U.S. Catholic Historian (Special Issue). "Beyond the Walls: Women Religious in American Life." 14 (Winter 1996).

Walch, Timothy. *Parish School: American Catholic Parochial Education from Colonial Times to the Present.* New York: Crossroad Publishing Co., 1996.

Weaver, Mary Jo. *New Catholic Women: A Contemporary Challenge to Traditional Religious Authority.* San Francisco: Harper and Row, 1985.

White, Joseph, ed. *The American Catholic Religious Life.* New York: Garland Press, 1988.

Woody, Thomas. *A History of Women's Education in the United States.* 2 vols. New York: Science Press, 1929. Reprint, Octagon Books, 1980.

Index

Academies: Catholic-Protestant rivalry, 162–63, 281 (n. 10); curriculum offered, 165–67, 280 (n. 1); in nineteenth century, 160–62, 280 (n. 1); nuns as role models, 171, 172; sources of additional income for teaching orders, 50–52, 147, 276 (n. 67); viewed as offering French culture, 50–51, 164, 282 (n. 18). *See also* Boarding schools

"Academy," use of term, 135, 272 (n. 22)

Acarie, Madame, 17-18

Accommodations: for nuns attending summer courses at higher institutions, 155, 157; for parochial school nuns, 45, 100, 111–12, 145–47, 276 (n. 63); provided by clergy for academies, 173

Accreditation: of Catholic schools, 151; of early Catholic women's colleges, 180, 184–85, 288 (n. 71); proliferation of secular and Catholic boards, 225

Advertisements, newspaper, to recruit girls for Catholic schools, 170, 175, 183

African Americans: antebellum teaching of free and slave children, 53–54, 243 (nn. 40, 42); Catholic schools for, 141, 274 (n. 41); philanthropic works of Mother Katherine Drexel, 111, 263 (n. 43); recruitment for Catholic

religious orders, 90; as slave labor for some religious orders, 241 (n. 14); use of term "sister" or "mother" among churchwomen, 77

Americanization, 60; Bishop Ireland's views on, 133; in Catholic religious orders, 8, 41–42, 85; of CSJ teaching manual, 138–39, 273 (n. 30)

Anthony, Susan B., 289 (n. 78)

Anti-Catholicism: in Colorado, 123–24, 124–25; directed at women's religious orders, 1–2, 42–43, 86, 228 (n. 2), 231 (n. 21), 243 (n. 42); and nuns as Civil War nurses, 62–63, 193

Antiforeign bigotry, 140

"Anti-garb" laws, 134, 156, 271 (n. 17)

Apodaca, Sister Guadalupe, 68

"Apostolic" communities, 68, 247 (n. 2)

Apprenticeships, for novices, 77–78

Aquinas, Thomas, 14

Arizona Miner (newspaper), 213

Avila College (formerly St. Teresa's, Kansas City, Mo.), 185, 290 (n. 89)

Baltimore Council (1884), mandate for Catholic school systems, 150, 276 (n. 67)

Barat, Mother Madeleine Sophie, 82

Baumgarten, Nikola, 164

Beecher, Catharine, 161–62, 164

Beecher, Lyman, 98, 256 (n. 1)

Begging, by nuns, to raise funds, 120–21, 174–75, 182, 193, 212, 215

Beguines, in religious communities, 14, 233 (n. 6)

Behavior codes, student, 169–70, 284 (n. 33)

Biermaier, Sister Ann Marie, 153

Bilingualism, and demand for teachers in ethnic parishes, 141–42, 274 (n. 43)

Bishop, Harriet, 162

Bishops: attitudes toward CSJ general government proposal, 57–58, 60–62, 244 (n. 52), 245 (nn. 58, 61); authority of, and religious communities, 84; embroilment in local clerical feuds, 148–49, 276 (n. 68), 277 (n. 69); on establishing Catholic schools, 129, 131–32, 182, 276 (n. 67); ethnic backgrounds, 91, 255 (n. 81). See also Ireland, John

Blacks. See African Americans

Boarding schools, 77, 167; CSJ Academy in Carondelet for girls, 50–52; destruction of Ursuline school in Charlestown, Mass., 1, 43, 228 (n. 2), 240 (n. 8); for French girls of higher social status, 26, 33, 37. See also Academies

Boards of directors, male, for institutions staffed and operated by nuns, 215, 217–18

Bogan, Mother Odilia, 155–56, 276 (n. 67)

Bohan, Sister Bridget, 289 (n. 80)

Bonnefoy, Sister Emerentia, 108

Bon Pasteur (Good Shepherd), as establishment for confined prostitutes, 33–34

Bouté, Sister Marguerite-Félicité, 39

Boyer, Sister Febronie, 55–56, 84–85

Boys: attendance at secondary institutions, compared to girls, 162, 178, 281 (n. 9), 283 (n. 26); caring for in orphanages, 209; classical curriculum in antebellum academies, 165–66, 283 (nn. 21, 24); education of by CSJs, 54, 243 (n. 43)

Brace, Charles Loring, 296 (n. 57)

Bracken, Sister Aurelia, 91

Braude, Ann, 5–6, 43

"Bride of Christ," nun as, 82–83

Brouillet, Eliza McKenney, 50–52

Browne, Rev. William, 214

Burdier, Sister Jeanne, 27–28

Bureau of Catholic Indian Missions (BCIM), 110, 111, 262 (n. 39), 263 (n. 44)

Burion, Rev. Honoratus, 118–19, 266 (n. 78)

Bynum, Carolyn Walker, 81

Byrne, Patricia, 80, 229 (n. 9), 253 (n. 59)

Byrne, Sister Angelica, 213

Cahokia, Ill., as early CSJ convent site, 41, 43–45, 240 (nn. 11, 12)

Canon law: definitions of nun's role in nineteenth century, 42; restrictions on nuns in early 1900s, 223–24

Caregivers: women as, 103, 190. See also Nursing; Orphanages

Carmelite order, 18

Carondelet, Mo.: destruction of convent by fire in 1850s, 56–57; as initial CSJ convent site, 43, 44, 240 (n. 11)

Carrigan, Rev. Joseph, 148–49, 277 (n. 68), 277 (n. 69)

Casey, Julia, 216

Catherine of Siena, 14

Catholic Boy's Home (Minneapolis, Minn.), 217

Catholic Church: espousal of single-sex institutions, 179; during French Revolution, 35–37; Second Vatican Council and changes in roles within, 223, 225, 300 (n. 2); as target for Protestant movements in nineteenth-century America, 42–43, 239 (nn. 4, 6); Vatican's imposition of restrictions on American nuns, 203, 223–24. See also Anti-Catholicism

Catholic Education Association, 150, 180

Catholic Hospital Association (CHA), 202, 212

Catholic Philanthropic Tradition in America, The (Oates), 111

Catholics: as minority in nineteenth-century America, 42, 239 (n. 3). *See also* Anti-Catholicism; Ethnic identity

Catholic University (Washington, D.C.). *See* Sisters' College

Central City, Colo., CSJ forty-year ministry in, 118, 122–23

Chapellon, Sister Febronie, 39, 242 (n. 28)

"Chapter of Faults," as public confession, 79–80, 251 (n. 39)

Charlestown, Mass., destruction of Ursuline boarding school, 1, 43, 228 (n. 2), 240 (n. 8)

Chastity, vow of, 9–10, 83–84

Chicago Fire (1871), 208–9, 297 (n. 72)

Children: conditions for in seventeenth-century France, 16–17; education of the deaf, 39, 48, 49–50, 134, 272 (n. 21); "saving" from Catholicism by Protestant organizations, 205, 296 (n. 57). *See also* Education; Orphanages

Children's Aid Society, and "Orphan Trains," 296 (n. 57)

Choir sisters, as class distinction in early CSJ convents, 8, 84, 186, 231 (n. 20), 253 (nn. 58, 59), 107 (ill.)

Cholera epidemics, 44, 101, 191, 194, 240 (n. 12), 291 (n. 5)

Church and Modern Society, The (Ireland), 182–83

Civil War, CSJs as military nurses in, 62–64, 192–94, 291 (n. 9)

Clarke, Edward, 178

Class distinctions: attitudes of upper-class women in European convents, 24, 28–29, 84; choir and lay sister distinctions, 8, 84, 186, 231 (n. 20), 253 (nn. 58, 59); diversity of Catholic women in American religious communities, 8, 52–53

Class sizes, in Catholic schools, 137, 272 (n. 28)

Clerics/clergy: concern over nuns' service as nurses, 202–3; demand for bilingual parish priests, 141; disputes with CSJs over ownership of property, 176–77, 286 (nn. 54, 56); emphasis on in parish histories, 223, 252 (n. 45); feuds between, and positions of local nuns, 148–49, 276 (n. 68), 277 (n. 69); influence of in areas served, 104; as itinerant priests in the West, 98–99, 257 (n. 5); power struggles over control of nuns' activities, 9, 46–48, 92–94; role of parish priest in local school, 148; salaries of brothers as teachers, 144, 276 (n. 57); views on higher education for nuns, 186. *See also* Bishops

Cloister: enforcement under Council of Trent, 13–14, 232 (n. 3); partial cloister imposed in early 1900s, 223

Clothing
—religious garb: differences between lay and choir sisters, 84, 107 (ill.), 231 (n. 20); inappropriateness for desert clime, 108; in public schools, 133, 134, 156, 271 (n. 17)
—secular: worn by nuns in antebellum America, 2, 41, 43, 228 (n. 2), 241 (n. 18); worn by postulants, 71, 248 (n. 17)

Cody, John (bishop of Kansas City, Mo.), 286 (n. 56)

Coeducation, Catholic, 136–37, 272 (n. 24)

Coercion of women into convents, as Protestant view, 2, 42, 68, 228 (n. 2)

College of Notre Dame of Maryland, 180

College of St. Catherine (St. Paul, Minn.), 155, 159, 180–81, 182–85, 187

College of St. Rose (Albany, N.Y.),
185–86
College prep courses, as later academy
track, 166–67
Colleges: founded by religious orders of
nuns, 180–81 (*see also individual
schools*); views on attendance by
women, 178–79, 287 (n. 62)
Colorado, mining frontier missions in,
118–27
Commercial courses, as later academy
track, 166–67
Common school movement, in
nineteenth-century America, 130–31,
270 (nn. 6, 7)
Communities, religious, unique characteristics of, 7–11
Confession, public, "Chapter of Faults"
in convents, 79–80, 251 (n. 39)
Constitution, CSJ ("The Rule"), 9, 39,
236 (n. 43)
—approval of American version, 57, 63
—French version, 28; emphasis on hospital and orphanage works, 30; powers of bishops, 55, 244 (nn. 46, 52);
translation into English, 52
—"Living Rule" as the highest compli-
ment paid to a nun, 75
—*Maxims of the Little Institute*, 23
—on prohibiting nuns as rectory
housekeepers, 9
—provisions for entry into the community, 70–71
—as written by Médaille for original
CSJ foundation, 236 (n. 43)
"Contemplative" communities, changing role in America, 247 (n. 2)
Convent life: as experience of boarding
students, 167–68; purported descriptions in anti-Catholic literature, 43
Convent schools. *See* Academies;
Boarding schools
Conversions, among Native Americans,
264 (n. 60)
Corrigan, Sister Monica (Anna

Taggert), 90, 106, 108–9, 121, 172,
244 (n. 47), 251 (n. 44), 261 (n. 34);
on begging trips for hospital and
orphanage funds, 174–75, 212–13
Coughlin, Mother Seraphine, 55, 60,
245 (n. 58)
Creoles, CSJ school for in Mobile, Ala.,
143
Cretin, Joseph (bishop of St. Paul,
Minn.), 100, 162, 257 (n. 9)
CSJ Profession Book, 230 (n. 12)
CSJs (Sisters of St. Joseph of
Carondelet), 13–14
—in America: antebellum activities,
41–55, 191; Colorado mining frontier outposts, 118–27; embroilment
in local clerical feuds, 148–49, 277
(n. 68), 277 (n. 69); ethnic diversity,
86–91; frontier activities in the
Southwest, 105–18; service in frontier cities, 99–105; struggle to create
a general government structure,
55–62. *See also* Education; Nursing;
Orphanages
—in France, 39, 238 (n. 87), 89; foundation and activities before the Revolution, 20–35, 235 (n. 34); during the
Revolution, 35–36, 238 (n. 85)
Curriculum: classical studies in boys'
antebellum academies, 165–66, 283
(nn. 21, 24); CSJ flexible teaching
manual, 137–38, 273 (n. 30); gender
ideology in secondary education, 163,
283 (n. 26); of Indian mission
schools, 112–13; "male" oriented
subjects taught at St. Catherine's, 184;
of nineteenth-century common
schools, 130–31, 270 (n. 7); in
nineteenth-century women's academies, 165–66, 280 (n. 1); standardization of in Catholic school systems,
150–51, 277 (n. 75)

Dailey, Sister Rose Edward, 78, 145
Darwin, Charles, 178

Episcopal Church: women as nurses and in sisterhoods, 191

Erin's Daughters in America (Diner), 88

Ethnic identity: in Catholic women religious communities, 8, 86–91, 231 (n. 19); in parishes and schools, 140–43; rivalries among American Catholics in Colorado, 123, 125, 268 (n. 103)

Eucharistic Letter (Médaille), 236 (n. 43)

Euphrasia, Sister, 109

Ewens, Mary, 42, 70, 230 (n. 11), 231 (n. 21), 239 (n. 2); on contributions of nuns in frontier areas, 99; on religious exercises for nuns, 79, 251 (n. 37)

Eyraud, Françoise, as a founder of the CSJs, 21, 22, 25, 26

Facemaz, Mother St. John, 55–59, 64, 71

Faribault-Stillwater (Minn.) plan, use of public funds for Catholic schools, 133, 271 (n. 14)

Feminist attitudes, of contemporary American nuns, 225

"Feminization" of Catholic Church, as seen by American Protestants, 43

Financial obligations, 52; control of parochial schools by diocese, 143–48; for CSJ institutions, 173–76; Faribault-Stillwater plan for public funding, 133, 271 (n. 14); Missouri state support of CSJ school for the deaf, 49–50, 242 (n. 30); orphanages' ways of meeting, 212–19; problems in antebellum convents, 44, 241 (n. 13). *See also* Begging; Fund-raising programs

Fine arts: founding of St. Agatha's Conservatory, 174, 285 (n. 48); as separate school fee courses, 165, 283 (nn. 21, 24). *See also* Music lessons

Finn, Sister Esperance, 295 (n. 47)

Fitzgerald, Maureen, 205–6, 297 (n. 60)

Flanagan, Sister Grace Aurelia, 68

Flynn, Sister Charitina, 68, 247 (n. 5)

Fontbonne, Mother St. John, 38–39, 48, 52

Fontbonne, Rev. Jacques, 46–48, 241 (nn. 19, 20)

Fontbonne, Sister/Mother Delphine, 39, 45, 48–49, 242 (n. 23), 291 (n. 6)

Fontbonne, Sister/Mother Febronie, 39, 45, 47, 48

Fontbonne College (St. Louis, Mo.), 186

Food donations: to orphanages, 215; for parochial school nuns, 147

Fort Yuma Government School (Yuma, Calif.), 110, 116–18, 265 (n. 66)

Fournier, Sister/Mother St. John (Julie), 39, 46, 49, 53–54, 59, 199, 245 (n. 57), 272 (n. 21)

France: seventeenth-century life in, 15–18. *See also* CSJs—in France

Frappa, Catherine, as a founder of the CSJs, 22

Fremont, Jessie Benton, 212–13, 298 (n. 86)

French-born members, of the CSJs, 87

French Canadians: as CSJ members, 87; parishes for, 140

French regime, in early American CSJ convents, 48

Friendships, among nuns, 78–79, 250 (nn. 32–36)

Fund-raising programs, 173; to found College of St. Catherine, 182–83; in frontier West, 118–19, 120–21, 124, 266 (n. 78); hospital "insurance" policies, 213

Gaffney, Sister Magdalen, 299 (n. 88)

Garb, religious. *See* Clothing—religious garb

Gender, 222

—conforming to nineteenth-century ideals of women, 80–84

—curriculum biases in secondary education, 163, 283 (n. 26)

Ireland, John (archbishop of St. Paul, Minn.), 85, 104, 133, 259 (nn. 22, 23), 271 (n. 14), 288 (n. 75); founding of CSJ-staffed boys' orphanage, 217–18; as proponent of higher education for women, 181–82, 288 (n. 68)

Ireland, Sister St. John (Eliza), 181, 288 (n. 75)

Ireland, Sister Seraphine (Ellen), 181, 288 (n. 75)

Irish Americans: aid for girls and women by nuns, 211; as clerical and religious superiors, 255 (nn. 81, 82); as teachers in public school systems, 140–41, 274 (n. 39)

Irish-born women, entering American convents, 53, 87–90, 243 (n. 39)

Italian Americans, Catholic schools for, 141

Ivory, Sister Francis Joseph, 100, 101–2, 174, 258 (n. 16)

Jesus, androgynous qualities of used by Protestant women, 82

Jewish girls, as students in Catholic institutions, 170–71

Joseph, Saint, as CSJ patron and male role model, 82, 252 (n. 51)

Julian of Norwich, 24

Kansas City, Mo.: arrival of the CSJs, 101–2, 259 (n. 18); segregated hospitals in, 195–96, 293 (n. 25)

Kauffmann, Christopher, 202

Keating, Mother de Chantal, 63, 193, 292 (n. 13)

Kennedy, Mother Mary Joseph, 208–9

Kenrick, Peter Richard (archbishop of St. Louis, Mo.), 71; role in creating CSJ general government structure, 55–59, 61, 244 (nn. 46, 52)

Know-Nothing Party, 42, 86, 239 (n. 6)

Labas, Mother Saint Agnes, 33, 34

Lacy, Sister Mary Herman (a.k.a

Margaret Mary), disputes with the male hierarchy, 92–94, 173, 255 (n. 86), 256 (n. 90), 285 (n. 43)

Ladies of Mercy (France), 34

Laity: role in supporting nun-operated institutions, 215–19; as teachers in nineteenth-century Catholic schools, 143–44, 275 (n. 52)

Languages: insistence on use of German in schools, 140, 141–42, 271 (n. 14), 274 (n. 38), 275 (n. 45); nuns learn Indian tongues, 113; use of English in America, 43, 48, 53

Larson, Hulda Olivia, 200

Lavin, Sister Mary Thomas, 113, 199

Lay sisters, and class distinctions in early CSJ convents, 8, 84, 107 (ill.) 186, 231 (n. 20), 253 (nn. 58, 59)

Leary, Sister Stanislaus, 92, 255 (n. 85)

LeMay, Sister Justine, 173

Le Puy, France, as historical foundation for the CSJs, 20–21

Lillis, Thomas (bishop of Kansas City, Mo.), 299 (n. 99)

Littenecker, Sister Julia, 62, 90, 116, 118, 263 (n. 45)

Littenecker sisters, vocations for, 68

Los Angeles province, creation of, 90, 255 (n. 78)

Louis XIV (king of France), 237 (n. 59)

Louis XV (king of France), 29

Lovejoy, Eli P., 42

Luther, Martin, 17

Lutheran Church: German language seen as vehicle of doctrine, 140, 274 (n. 38); women as nurses and in sisterhoods, 191

Lynch, Sister Cyril, 74–75

Lynch, Sister Mary Louis, 62–63

McCarthy, Sister Serena, 142, 275 (n. 47)

McCusker, Sister Alicia, 299 (n. 99)

McDannell, Colleen, 80

Names, of religious, use of male saints or martyrs as, 82

Natchez (ship), 1, 39, 227 (n. 1)

National Board of Popular Education (NBPE), 162, 281 (n. 10)

National Conference of Catholic Charities, 211–12

National League for Protection of American Institutions, 262 (n. 39)

National League of Nursing Education (NLNE), 202, 295 (n. 47)

Native Americans (Indians): CSJ missionary work among in the Southwest and California, 109–18; recruitment for Catholic religious orders, 90

Neenan, Sister Mary Pius, 157

Nightingale, Florence, 191

Novices: leaving convent life, 76; period of training and expectations of, 72–74, 249 (n. 27); rites of passage for, 76

Nuns: attitudes of upper-class women in French convents, 24, 28–29; conforming to Victorian ideal, 80–84; embroilment in local clerical feuds, 148–49, 277 (n. 68), 277 (n. 69); foreign-born entering American orders, 53, 71, 78, 87–90, 243 (n. 39), 255; numbers in religious orders, 2, 4, 39, 95, 221, 228 (n. 4), 230 (n. 11), 238 (n. 87), 256 (n. 92); peasants accepted into new active French orders, 19–20; property rights during seventeenth-century, 15; recruitment of Americans as postulants, 52; role in religious organizations, 3–4; as surrogate priests in isolated areas, 99, 114, 222; unattached sisters sought by bishops, 91–92. *See also* Nursing; Teaching

Nursing: as a career for nineteenth-century Protestant women, 190, 193; CSJ Civil War record, 62–64, 192–94, 291 (n. 9); CSJ secular grad-

uates' service in World War I, 198; the CSJs in Spanish-American War, 195–96, 200, 229 (n. 9); as a major ministry for the CSJs, 54, 123, 190–203; training programs for, 199–201, 294 (n. 38), 39; treatment of sick orphans by sister-nurses, 200 (n. 96), 214

Oates, Mary J., 205, 206, 218, 274 (n. 41), 278 (n. 79), 300 (n. 108)

Obedience, vow of: regulations in the 1900s prior to Second Vatican Council, 224; used to circumvent local demands by bishops and clergy, 9, 119–20, 149, 266 (n. 82)

O'Brien, Rev. Frank, 93–94

O'Brien, Sister Anselm, 69, 74–75

O'Gorman sisters, vocations for, 68

O'Kelly, Sister Ailbe, 88, 142

O'Neill, Mother Ambrosia, 115, 116, 265 (nn. 67, 68)

O'Neill, Sister Evelyn, 176–77, 185, 187

"Ornamental" courses, offered by academies, 165, 283 (n. 21)

Orosco, Sister Agnes, 142

Orphanages, 101, 104, 203–12, 297 (n. 61); acquisition of boys' home in Philadelphia, 54, 243 (n. 43); in Colorado, 268 (n. 97); in France, 25–27; half-orphanages for children with surviving parents, 207

"Orphan Trains," 296 (n. 57)

Oswego Palladium Times (newspaper), 164–65

Our Lady of Lourdes parish school (Georgetown, Colo.), 123

Papal approbation, for religious communities, 61–62, 84, 223, 277 (n. 72), 291 (n. 9)

Parrott, Mother Elizabeth, 79, 147

Pascoe, Peggy, 105, 115

Pascual (Yuma chief), 117, 265 (n. 66)

"Passionlessness," ideology of, utilized

by Protestant women in public sphere, 84

Patriotism, as theme in nineteenth-century textbooks, 139–40

Paul, Saint (New Testament), on women's role, 14

Peasants, French: schools for rural girls, 32; women accepted into new active religious orders, 19–20

Pedagogy, nineteenth-century, flexibility of CSJ teaching manual, 138–39, 273 (n. 30)

Penitents, repentant prostitutes seen as in France, 33–34, 238 (n. 79)

Peters, Sister Martha, 108, 109

Peterson, Jacqueline, 113

Philadelphia, Pa.: CSJ acquisition of boys' orphanage in, 54, 243 (n. 43); first CSJ hospital in, 191; loss of CSJ house in, 59–60

Philadelphia Bible Riots, 131

Philanthropy, Catholic, 215–17

Phillips, Sister Giles, 172, 201, 295 (n. 47)

Piccolomini, Rev. Francis, SJ, 21

Plea for the West, A (Beecher), 98

Polish immigrants, parishes for, 140

Pommerel, Sister/Mother Celestine, 39, 46, 48, 55, 168, 241 (n. 18), 272 (n. 21)

Poor, as deserving or undeserving, 205, 212, 296 (n. 55)

Porter, Sister Angelica, 119, 120–22

Postulants: age of, 70–71; dowries brought by, 24, 26, 71–72, 237 (n. 58), 248 (nn. 11, 13); entering Lyons motherhouse, 238 (n. 89); leaving convent life, 76

"Poughkeepsie Plan," use of Catholic schools, 132

Poverty: of reservation Indians, 112; in seventeenth-century France, 16

Poverty, vow of, 9, 83, 232 (n. 24); as a way to empathize with the needy, 126

Power: perceived loss by bishops in proposed CSJ general government, 58, 244 (n. 52), 245 (n. 61); struggles over control of nuns' activities, 9, 46–48, 92–94

Power, Sister Marsina, 113

Priests, surrogate, nuns as in isolated areas, 99, 114, 222

Proff, Sister Radegunda, 141–42

Property rights: of religious orders, 176–77, 286 (nn. 54, 56); of women in French orders, 15, 18–19, 232 (n. 3)

Prostitutes, confinement in French convents, 32–34

Protestant, The (newspaper), 42

Protestants

—American: and common school curriculum, 130–31, 270 (n. 7); effect of men entering previously all-female organizations, 225; establishment of female academies, 160–61, 280 (n. 5); treatment of in CSJ hospitals, 194–95. *See also* Anti-Catholicism; Protestants—women

—European: criticisms of and Council of Trent, 232 (n. 3); schools for converts to Catholicism, 26, 31, 237 (nn. 59, 73)

—women: as converts and nuns, 172; girls as students in Catholic institutions, 161, 170–72, 284 (n. 38); in nineteenth-century public charitable work, 204–5; public voice on social issues, 222; religious activities of, compared to Catholic nuns, 9, 10, 84, 105, 191, 232 (n. 24); religious activities of in a male dominated society, 6–7; restrictions on doing missionary work, 115–16; suitability of nursing as career, 190, 193; use of Jesus' androgynous qualities, 82; use of terms "sister" and "mother," 77; perceived competition with nuns on frontier, 103–4, 126–27

Provinces, regional, of the CSJs, 87

South, Catholic parish schools in, 141, 274 (n. 41)

Southwestern frontier missions, as CSJ activities in Arizona, 105–18

Spanish-American War, CSJ nurses in, 195–96, 200, 229 (n. 9)

Spaulding, John Lancaster (bishop of Peoria, Ill.), 181, 288 (n. 68)

Steinmetz, Sister Honorata, 142

Stephan, Rev. J. A. (director of Bureau of Catholic Indian Missions), 117, 263 (n. 44), 265 (n. 70)

Subservience, as perceived virtue of female teachers, 150

Sullivan, Sister Winifred, 63

Superior general, CSJ, creation of post of as controversial, 57–62

Support system, convent, mentors for fledgling teachers as, 78, 153, 155

Svenson, Sister Kathla, 172, 201

Taylor, Judith, 20, 24

Teachers: antebellum academies as sources for, 161; apprenticeships for novices, 77–78; comparison of nuns and public school teachers, 151–52, 278 (n. 79); Irish Americans in public schools, 141; nuns as bilingual teachers, 141–42, 274 (n. 43)

Teaching: establishment of Catholic schools for girls, 103, 259 (n. 20); as major area of CSJ activity, 54; nuns used in public schools, 132–34, 271 (nn. 14, 17); original French concepts, 30. *See also* Academies; Education

Tentler, Leslie Woodcock, 6

Teresa of Avila, 17, 83

Terror, Reign of (1793–94), execution of CSJ nuns in, 36–37, 238 (n. 85)

Tertiaries, in religious organizations, 14, 233 (n. 6)

Textbooks, use in nineteenth-century grammar schools, 139–40, 270 (n. 7)

Thompson, Margaret Susan, 58, 86

1,000 Ways of 1,000 Teachers. . . (book), 154–55

Tolley, Kim, 165–66, 283 (nn. 21, 24)

Trades: taught to American orphans, 209; taught to French orphan girls, 25, 39; vocational courses for Native American students, 113

Travel: opportunities for nuns, compared to secular women, 221–22; restrictions imposed during the early 1900s, 223–24; via railroads, 183, 213, 266 (n. 78), 299 (n. 88)

Trent, Council of: as attempt to enforce cloistered living of women religious, 13–14, 232 (nn. 1, 3); on doctrine of good works, 17; on instruction of the faithful, 30

Trinity College (Sisters of Notre Dame de Namur), 180

Tucson, Ariz. Terr., CSJ activities in, 105–18

Tucson Daily Star (newspaper), 214

Tuition: college costs for summer courses, 155, 157; for pre-Revolutionary French religious schools, 32; waived for poor American Catholics, 50

Turner, Victor, 76

Universities, state, nuns taking summer courses at, 155, 279 (n. 92)

University of Chicago (Chicago, Ill.), degrees for women from, 184, 289 (n. 83)

University of Missouri (Columbia), nuns attending summer school at, 155

Upper class, attitudes of in French convents, 24, 28–29

Ursulines, 18, 160; destruction of school of in Charlestown, Mass., 1–2, 43, 228 (n. 2), 240 (n. 8)

Van Gennep, Arnold, 76

Victorian era, concepts of work suitable for women in, 80, 190

Vilaine, Sister Philomene, 39, 168, 253 (n. 59)

Visitandines (Visitation order), 18–19

Vocational courses: for French girls, 25, 39; for Native American boys, 113; as later academy track, 166–67; for orphans, 209

Vocations, religious, 68–70, 247 (n. 5); decrease in twentieth century, 225

Vows, perpetual: effect on women's property rights, 232 (n. 3); taken by nuns, 9–10

Waldron, Sister Flavia, 135

Walsh, Mother Bernard, 215

Walsh, Sister Irene, 142

Walsh, Sister Mary, 199

Ward, Mary, 236 (n. 39)

Wendling, Sister Liboria, 147

Werden, Sister Hyacinth, 183, 289 (n. 80)

West Troy Union Free School (Watervliet, N.Y.), leasing of St. Brigid's School as, 132–33

Weyand, Sister Evangelista, 295 (n. 47)

Wheeling, W.Va., staffing of first CSJ hospital in, 191, 192–93

Widows, CSJ homes for, 210–11

Willard, Emma, 161, 162, 164

Winnebago Indian Mission, 101

Wisconsin, normal school regulations in, 156–57, 279 (n. 100)

Women, 163; aid given to homeless or destitute, 211; nineteenth-century academies for, 160–62, 280 (nn. 1, 2, 5); role of Catholic laywomen, 215–17; roles in religious organizations, 3–4; "scientific" view of brain's capacity, 178, 182; St. Paul's views on role of, 14; use of term "sister" or "mother," 77; Victorian era concept of suitability of work, 80, 190; working-class, provisions for temporary care of children of, 207. *See also* Nuns; Nursing; Protestants—women; Teachers

Woody, Thomas, 280 (nn. 2, 5)

Work experiences, of nuns, compared to secular women, 221–22

World War I, CSJ-trained secular nurses serving in, 198, 294 (n. 30)

Yellow fever epidemics, 194, 199